GIGABIT ETHERNET
Migrating to High-Bandwidth LANs

**Prentice Hall Series in
Computer Networking and Distributed Systems**
Radia Perlman, editor

GIGABIT ETHERNET
Migrating to High-Bandwidth LANs

JAYANT KADAMBI
MOHAN KALKUNTE
IAN CRAYFORD

To join a Prentice Hall Internet mailing list,
point to http://www.phptr.com/mail_lists.

Prentice Hall PTR
Upper Saddle River, New Jersey 07458

© 1998 Prentice Hall PTR
Prentice-Hall, Inc.
A Simon & Shuster Company
Upper Saddle River, New Jersey 07458

Editorial/production supervision: *Joe Czerwinski*
Acquisitions editor: *Mary Franz*
Editorial assistant: *Noreen Regina*
Marketing manager: *Miles Williams*
Manufacturing manager: *Alexis Heydt*
Cover design director: *Jerry Votta*
Cover Illustration: *Tom Post*

Prentice Hall books are widely used by corporations and government agencies for training, marketing, and resale.

The publisher offers discounts on this book when ordered in bulk quantities.
For more information contact: Corporate Sales Department, Phone: 800-382-3419;
Fax: 201-236-7141; E-mail:corpsales@prenhall.com.
Or write: Prentice Hall PTR, Corp. Sales Dept., One Lake Street, Upper Saddle River, NJ 07458

Figures 2-1, 2-11, 2-12 reprinted or modified with permission from 8802-3:1996 (ISO/IEC) [ANSI/IEEE Std. 802.3,1996 Editorial information technology—Telecommunications and information exchange between systems—Local and metropolitan area networks—Specification requirements—Part 3: Carrier sense multiple access with collision detection (CSMA/CD) access method and physical layer specifications, ©1996, IEEE. All rights reserved.

Figures 3-1, 3-33-4, 3-5, 3-6, 3-12, 3-14, 3-24, 3-25, 3--26, Tables 3-1, 3-2, 3-3, 3-4, 3-5, 3-6 reprinted or modified with permission from 802.3u-1995 IEEE Standards for Local and Metropolitan Area Networks: Supplement to Carrier Sense Multiple Access with Collision Detection (CSMA/CD) Access Method and Physical Layer Specifications: Media Access Control (MAC) Parameters, Physical Layer, Medium Attachment Units, and Repeater for 100 Mb/s Operation, Type 100 Base-T (Clauses 21–30). ©1995, IEEE. All rights reserved.

Figures 3-16, 3-17, 3-35, 3-36 reprinted or modified with permission from 802.3x&y-1997 Supplements to ISO/IEC 8802-3:1996: Specification for 802.3 Full Duplex Operation and Physical Layer Specification for 100 Mb/s Operation on Two Pairs of Category 3 or Better Balanced Twisted Pair Cable (100BASE-T2): Parts 1 and 2. ©1997, IEEE. All rights reserved.

Figures 4-2, 4-8, 4-9, 4-10, 4-11, 4-12, 4-13, 4-14, 4-31, 4-34, 4-35, 4-36, 4-57, Tables 4-1, 4-2, 4-3, 4-4, 4-5, 4-7, 4-9, 4-10, 4-11, 4-13, 4-14, 4-15, 4-16, 4-17, 4-18, 4-20, 4-21, 4-22, 4-23, reprinted or modified with permission from P802.3z: Supplement to 802.3—Physical Layers, Repeater and Management Parameters for 1,000 Mb/s Operation. ©1997, IEEE. All rights reserved.

Figure 3-39 reprinted from P802.3ac/D2.2. ©1998, IEEE. All rights reserved.

Table 3-12 reprinted from P802.1Q/D10. ©1998, IEEE. All rights reserved.

Printed in the United States of America

10 9 8 7 6 5 4 3

ISBN 0-13-913286-4

Prentice-Hall International (UK) Limited, *London*
Prentice-Hall of Australia Pty. Limited, *Sydney*
Prentice-Hall Canada Inc., *Toronto*
Prentice-Hall Hispanoamericana, S.A., *Mexico*
Prentice-Hall of India Private Limited, *New Delhi*
Prentice-Hall of Japan, Inc., *Tokyo*
Simon & Schuster Asia Pte. Ltd., *Singapore*
Editora Prentice-Hall do Brasil, Ltda., *Rio de Janeiro*

Contents

CHAPTER 3   **The Second Generation:**
            100 Mb/s and Switched Ethernet   81

CHAPTER 4   **The Third Generation:**
            1000 Mb/s (Gigabit)   161

Appendix B   331

Appendix C   335

Glossary   337

Index   361

Preface

Gigabit Ethernet is the latest in a series of networks based upon Ethernet, simply the most successful LAN networking technology in history. Ethernet began as a 3 Mb/s network that operated over coaxial cable. It was then standardized by the IEEE in 1982 as a predominantly 10 Mb/s network. Ethernet then evolved to support thin coaxial cable, fiber optic cable, and unshielded twisted-pair. The standardization of Ethernet over ordinary unshielded twisted-pair cable led to a growth in Ethernet that few people at the time imagined. Millions upon millions of Ethernet adapters, repeaters, and other networking equipment required to connect Ethernets together were sold. But this wasn't enough. The rapid increase in computing power, computing resources, and the requirement to interconnect these computing environments led to a requirement for faster networks. These requirements, along with general improvements in technology, silicon processes, and the resulting ability to cost-effectively transmit and receive data over ordinary telephone cable at 100 Mb/s led to the development and standardization of a 100 Mb/s version of Ethernet, Fast Ethernet. Fast Ethernet networks ran the Ethernet protocol, only ten times faster. Therefore, Fast Ethernet provided a simple method to migrate overloaded 10 Mb/s networks. It too was, (and still is) hugely successful.

The rise in the dominance of the Ethernet protocol was accompanied by a subtle shift in the manner in which networks were installed and configured. Originally, Ethernet was operated as a shared-media network in which all attached stations would share the available bandwidth. As the number of users and demand on the network increased, shared networks gave way to switched networks which allowed each user to be granted the entire network bandwidth. This shift in deployment away from shared-media Ethernet toward switched Ethernet, coupled with the continuous advances in technology and the rise of Internet and multimedia applications set the stage for the next generation in Ethernet networks, Gigabit Ethernet. Gigabit Ethernet provides all the familiarity of Ethernet, at 1,000,000 bits per second. Gigabit Ethernet builds on the same principles that made Fast Ethernet such a success; it borrowed a well known, tested, physical layer technology and did not modify the Ethernet frame formats. It also supports the original Ethernet's shared media option and will be the last Ethernet network that does so.

This book provides a reference guide for people who want to understand the operation and implementation of Ethernet networks running at 1 Gb/s (or 1,000 Mb/s). Chapter 1 reviews the origins and development of the Ethernet, from a shared media only network operating at 10 Mb/s to both shared repeater-based topologies and fully switched half/full-duplex networks able to run at 100 Mb/s. Chapters 2 and 3 discuss the evolution of 10 Mb/s Ethernet and the detailed specifications for the various components, as well as how these specifications map to real implementations of 10 Mb/s Ethernet networks.

Chapter 3 examines the 100 Mb/s Ethernet derivatives, which moved to widespread adoption shortly after the 1995 completion of the IEEE 100BASE-T standard. Chapter 3 also explains the continued progression of equipment used to segment ever larger networks, in order to group users related by geographical location, bandwidth need, data access requirements, job function, security authorization, and other reasons. Those already familiar with or not specifically interested in these extremely popular preceding versions of Ethernet may want to skip over these chapters.

Chapter 4 provides a review of the IEEE 802.3z standards document, and the Gigabit Ethernet technology and is generally meant to provides a tutorial companion to the IEEE 802.3z document. A complete examination of all of the IEEE Clauses, jargon and an some insight into the decisions behind the standards document is provided. Chapter 5 examines some of the applications that benefit from Gigabit Ethernet, how Gigabit Ethernet can be deployed to assist these applications, and how other technologies such as ATM and FDDI compare to the solution provided by Gigabit Ethernet. Various switching technologies are discussed, such as IP switching and tag switching. Finally, Chapter 6 looks at the emerging trends for high-speed networking. How will Gigabit Ethernet compare and compete with other technologies of similar data rate? Is there yet another generation of Ethernet in the cards?

Throughout this book a chronological perspective has been maintained, aligning with the predominant themes in the industry. Hence, as the reader progresses through the book, the technology migrates from the initial 10 Mb/s media options, to the 100 Mb/s Fast Ethernet derivative and switched Ethernet topologies, and finally to Gigabit Ethernet.

Computer books and standards documents are full of jargon, and this book is no exception. A complete glossary of all the terms and acronyms used in this book along with an explanation of each is provided. In addition, a description of the Ethernet standards themselves is included.

We have done our best to provide an accurate assessment of the IEEE standard but would like to remind the reader that the definitive reference and documentation for Gigabit Ethernet is the IEEE 802.3z standards document which can be ordered from the IEEE standards office.

This book was mainly the result of the persistence of our editor at Prentice Hall, Mary Franz, who kept us motivated to write and throughout the process. We gratefully acknowledge Joe Czerwinski for his work on the book's production. We thank Bob Grow, Rich Taborek, Geoff Thompson, Larry Miller, G.Y. Hanna, and Shashank Merchant for providing use valuable feedback on drafts of this book. We also thank Dale Edwards for giving us the initial push to write the book and Judy, Padma, and Sujata for enduring while we spent many long days and nights in front of the keyboard. Lastly, we thank the hard work of the hundreds of individuals who created the IEEE 802.3z standard in record time.

Introduction

1.1 Overview of This Book

This book provides a reference guide for people who want to understand the operation and implementation of Ethernet networks running at 1 Gb/s (or 1000 Mb/s). Gigabit Ethernet is the natural progression in speed from the 10 Mb/s and 100 Mb/s versions of Ethernet.

The remainder of Chapter 1 reviews the origins and development of the Ethernet from a shared-media-only network operating at 10 Mb/s to both shared-repeater-based topologies and fully switched half-/full-duplex networks able to run at 100 Mb/s.

Chapters 2 and 3 discuss the evolution of Ethernet and the detailed specifications for the various components, as well as looking at how these standards map to real implementations in Ethernet networks. Chapter 2 focuses predominantly on the numerous 10 Mb/s versions of Ethernet, which developed gradually over a period of about ten years starting in the early 1980s, first with 10BASE5 ("Thick Net"), then with 10BASE2 (or "Cheapernet") initiating the high-volume ramp after completion in 1985, culminating in the completion of the IEEE 10BASE-T Standard in 1990, and leading to the explosive growth in the deployment of 10BASE-T networking equipment during the 1990s. During this period, the networking business and technology as a whole became a mainstream corporate business tool. Chapter 2 also discusses some of the early approaches to divide large networks into groups of smaller interconnected networks, driven by both the rapid growth in the number of network-connected devices and the use of network-intensive applications, which stressed the bandwidth capabilities available at the time.

Chapter 3 examines the 100 Mb/s Ethernet derivatives, which started to appear in prestandard form in around 1993 and moved to widespread adoption shortly after the 1995 completion of the IEEE 100BASE-T Standard. Fast Ethernet introduced the concept of providing a 10/100 Mb/s capable Ethernet device, employing an Auto-Negotiation protocol to determine the optimal common speed shared by two devices on a link. This was a very important factor in the early deployment of Fast Ethernet-capable equipment, initially operating at the original 10 Mb/s in legacy installation. Chapter 3 also explains the continued progression of equipment used to segment ever larger networks, in order to group users related either by geographical location, bandwidth need, data access requirements, job function, security authorization, and other reasons. Those already familiar with or not specifically interested in these extremely popular preceding versions of Ethernet may want to skip over these chapters.

Chapter 4 provides a review of the IEEE 802.3z[1] Standard document and the Gigabit Ethernet technology. The 802.3z document, published as a standard by the IEEE, is the definitive technical specification for Gigabit Ethernet. Documents of this type are drafted, critiqued, and edited by a volunteer force of individuals from companies interested in defining the detailed specifications and operation of a particular technology, in this case Gigabit Ethernet. However, little tutorial information remains in the final format. For those not involved in the standards development process and faced with implementing or deploying the technology after completion of the standard, it is often difficult to understand why particular technical decisions were made, or what subtleties lie within the rigid definitions. Chapter 4, therefore, provides a tutorial companion to the IEEE 802.3z document. However, it does not duplicate the enormous technical detail contained in 802.3z. Implementers should still consult the IEEE 802.3z document as the definitive reference. Gigabit Ethernet technology is explained in relation to 10 Mb/s and 100 Mb/s operation. In addition, performance of shared and switched Gigabit Ethernet and associated flow control issues are discussed.

Chapter 5 examines some of the applications that benefit from Gigabit Ethernet, how Gigabit Ethernet can be deployed to assist these applications, and how other technologies compare to the solution provided by Gigabit Ethernet. In addition, Chapter 5 compares emerging technologies and protocols that will be used to design Gigabit Ethernet products. Various switching technologies are discussed, such as IP switching and Tag switching. In addition, the capabilities of Asynchronous Transfer Mode (ATM) technology are reviewed and contrasted to Gigabit Ethernet.

---

[1] IEEE 802.3z—Media Access Control (MAC) Parameters, Physical Layer, Repeater and Management Parameters for 1000 Mb/s Operation.

Finally, Chapter 6 looks at the emerging trends for high-speed networking. How will Gigabit Ethernet compare and compete with other technologies of similar data rate, such as ATM and "Firewire" (IEEE P1396) in the businesses and homes of the future? Is there yet another generation of Ethernet? What applications are driving the deployment of these extremely high-bandwidth networks?

Throughout this book a chronological perspective has been maintained, aligning with the predominant themes in the industry. Hence as the reader progresses through the book, the technology migrates from the initial 10 Mb/s media options to the 100 Mb/s Fast Ethernet derivative and switched Ethernet topologies, and finally to Gigabit Ethernet.

1.2 Ethernet Origins

1.2.1 Historical Perspective

The Ethernet Local Area Network (LAN) has been in existence for some 25 years. The invention of Ethernet is credited to Bob Metcalfe and David Boggs, then at Xerox PARC (Palo Alto Research Center), in 1973.[2] Bob Metcalfe went on to found 3Com¨ Corporation and evangelize the use of Ethernet as a multivendor standard and also propose it as an IEEE Standard for Local Area Networks (LANs).[3] The first implementation developed was for a 3 Mb/s data rate in the Xerox research environment. During this period, which ran from the first controllers for a DG Nova 800 in 1973 until sometime after the 10 Mb/s specification was established in 1980, there were on the order of 5000 machines built with 3 Mb/s controllers. These were widely deployed within Xerox, as well as to a few select sites in industry (Boeing), government (the White House), and academia. Many hundreds of those built and deployed within Xerox Research and the rest of the Xerox Corporation were attached to a large corporate intranet, developed to connect them all, which was in turn connected to the ARPA Net, the precursor to the Internet. This large experience base was key to the industry sign-up for 10 Mb/s when it was being developed.

The initial Ethernet standard was developed by the Digital Equipment Corporation (DEC), Intel, and Xerox (DIX) consortium, formed in 1979, with the first Ethernet "Blue Book" being published in 1980.[4] The Ethernet standard was submitted to a

---

[2] Metcalfe, R. M., and Boggs, D. R.. Ethernet: Distributed Packet Switching for Local Computer Networks, *Communications of the ACM*, Volume 19 No. 7 (July 1976). (Also re-printed in *The Ethernet Local Network: Three Reports,* Xerox Palo Alto Research Center Technical Report CSL-80-2, Feb 1980.)

[3] Metcalfe, R., Let the Ethernet Chips Fall Where They May, *Network Computing*, Volume 2 Issue 11, PP 124-126 (November 1991).

newly formed IEEE group (later to be defined as IEEE Project 802). Initially, Project 802 was divided into three groups. The High Level Interface (HILI) group concentrated on high level internetwork protocols and management (and became 802.1); the Logical Link Control (LLC) group focussed on end-to-end link connectivity and the interface between the higher layers above and the medium-access-dependent layers below (and became 802.2), while the Data Link and Medium Access Control (DLMAC) group was responsible for the medium access protocol itself.

In 1982, after much wrangling, the DLMAC group split into three committees: 802.3 for CSMA/CD (Ethernet), 802.4 for Token Bus, and 802.5 for Token Ring. 802.3 was driven primarily by DEC, Intel, and Xerox, plus several others. 802.4 was initially sponsored by Burroughs, Concord Data Systems, Honeywell, and Western Digital, although later the primary advocates became Boeing and General Motors. 802.5 was almost exclusively the domain of IBM.

Late in 1982 the DIX and IEEE versions merged (with only minor changes from the original Ethernet), and became the first version of the 802.3 (Ethernet) standard.

The 802.3 standard has been adopted by numerous national and international standards bodies, including the National Institute of Standards and Technology (NIST), the European Computer Manufacturers Association (ECMA), the American National Standards Institute (ANSI), and in February 1990 by the International Standardization Organization (ISO), under which it is known as ISO/IEC 8802-3.

The IEEE 802.3 committee developed a series of specifications for 10 Mb/s Ethernet to support different kinds of media. Initially the original Ethernet was only supported over thick coaxial cable. Next came thin coaxial cable (Cheapernet), then Unshielded Twisted Pair (UTP), and fiber optic cable. There was even a broadband coaxial version (to work over cable TV systems) specified early in the development of 10 Mb/s Ethernet, although it is in very limited use compared with the others mentioned. Subsequently, the focus moved to accelerating the overall performance, first with the 100 Mb/s version, known as Fast Ethernet, and most recently with the development of the Gigabit Ethernet standard.

During the early development of Ethernet, observing and controlling network performance was limited, for two reasons. Firstly, networks were relatively small and network traffic was not pushing the bandwidth limits, making sophisticated monitoring unnecessary. Secondly, it was technically difficult, since early implementations were already relatively complex in terms of the technology available at the time, so adding significant complexity and cost by incorporating the capabilities to provide metering and control was not practical. However, as networks and traffic grew and

---

[4] Digital Equipment Corporation/Intel Corporation/Xerox Corporation, *The Ethernet, A Local Area Network, Data Link Layer and Physical Layer Specifications*, Version 1.0, DEC/Intel/Xerox, September 30,1980.

technology advanced, the need and capability to incorporate heterogeneous network management advanced. This also did not pass unnoticed by the many vendors that comprise the standards-making bodies, resulting in a small number of documents being developed within the IEEE 802.3, but many more within other standards organizations (defined in more detail later). A concise reference list of the various 802.3 standards is compiled in Appendix A.

However, it is not the multiplicity of enhancements to the original standard that have made Ethernet the dominant LAN technology in use. Ethernet is simple—and it works! In particular, unlike many other networks, Ethernet works without network management. Management is an addition to improve and monitor the operation of your network, not something you have to cope with to bring it up in the first place. In addition, and also of great importance, was the fact that Ethernet was first (the Blue Book was well ahead of similar Token-Ring publications), and from the outset it really was an open standard (the Blue Book was already multivendor, while IBM restricted other implementors of Token Ring). Further, CSMA/CD patents were inexpensive and easy to license, which led to the early availability of off-the-shelf Ethernet silicon from companies such as Intel and Advanced Micro Devices (AMD). The first off-the-shelf Token-Ring chip set from Texas Instruments (TI) was late by comparison. As a result, literally hundreds of companies manufacture Ethernet devices, and within those companies, dozens of engineers understand how to implement, innovate, and differentiate products based on the Ethernet protocol.

This has led to stiff competition and aggressive pricing, which is turn has helped make the technology widely accessible and has fueled high demand and widespread deployment. High volume had allowed the use of high-technology silicon and systems development and manufacturing processes, increasing performance and reducing costs, and so on.

1.2.2 Technology Perspective

In the early 1980s, when Ethernet first started to became commonly available, desktop computing was in its relative infancy. The centralized mainframe computer was the rule, and terminals connected via low-speed serial asynchronous links provided user access to compute resources. Few people could envisage how to use the seemingly massive bandwidth capabilities offered by 10 Mb/s Ethernet.

In fact, the 10 Mb/s bandwidth capability of the original Ethernet was sufficient for virtually all desktop connectivity needs until the early 1990s. Backbone connectivity however, where large numbers of desktop connections were aggregated, was recognized as requiring additional bandwidth at an early stage. As far back as 1982, proposals were made within the 802 committee to work on a 100 Mb/s interconnect standard. However, the 802 membership was preoccupied with its existing LAN standards developments at lower data rates. A home was found in the American National Standards Institute (ANSI) for this 100 Mb/s work to take place. A somewhat arbitrary split occurred between these standards bodies, with IEEE 802 restricting its initial focus to LANs in the 1 to 20 Mb/s range, and ANSI championing the work at 100 Mb/s, which ultimately developed into the Fiber Distributed Data Interface (FDDI) suite of standards.

FDDI was well accepted as a technology, but its relatively high cost structure, due to implicit features such as redundancy and sophisticated mandatory management, largely restricted its deployment to backbone applications. Ethernet continued to be the predominant LAN technology for desktop connectivity, with FDDI frequently used to connect geographically dispersed Ethernet LANs.

The adoption of the standard for 10 Mb/s Ethernet over UTP in 1990, defined as IEEE 10BASE-T, caused a massive surge in the installation of Ethernet. Now Ethernet could be run over inexpensive twisted-pair cable, allowing buildings to be wired for LAN connectivity in a similar manner to the telephone service. In addition, 10BASE-T provided technical benefits which allowed silicon and systems vendors to significantly reduce the implementation cost. The availability of simple and inexpensive Ethernet connectivity coincided with the accelerating trend to distribute high-performance computing power to the desktop, as the client-server model replaced that of the centralized mainframe. The results were larger networks, more network-aware application programs, and massively increasing bandwidth needs.

This rapid increase in bandwidth demands and lower silicon implementation costs for complex systems, led to two key trends during the early 1990s. The first was a move away from the shared Ethernet topology, which had been in existence since the original definition of Ethernet, to a switched topology. Shared Ethernet essentially meant that all stations shared the 10 Mb/s communication channel. As networks increase in the number of users and the quantity of traffic, sharing becomes a bottleneck. Switched Ethernet allowed each station to potentially be granted an entire 10 Mb/s bandwidth allocation, with no sharing. The second trend was the development and deployment of Ethernet devices capable of operating at 100 Mb/s, ten times the original data rate. Fast Ethernet, or IEEE 100BASE-T, was completed as a standard in 1995, with products quickly deployed. Fast Ethernet and Switched Ethernet were extremely complementary, since multiple 10 Mb/s networks could be aggregated onto a single 100 Mb/s connection. In addition, since both the 10 and 100 Mb/s versions used the same Ethernet frame format (whereas FDDI uses a different frame format than Ethernet), additional cost and performance efficiencies could be realized in internetworking devices. Fast Ethernet also encompassed the capability to allow a device to operate at either 10 or 100 Mb/s and defined an Auto-Negotiation mechanism to detect and select the appropriate speed detection. This capability proved extremely important, in that it allowed a large volume of 100 Mb/s capable network adapters to be deployed and used within the huge existing 10 Mb/s installed base. Effectively, this primed the need for 100 Mb/s capable infrastructure equipment, leading to the large-scale deployment of Fast Ethernet repeaters and switches.

The deployment of 10 Mb/s switched and 100 Mb/s Ethernet networks led again to increasing network traffic and bandwidth requirements, particularly in the backbone, or at any aggregation point where multiple 10 Mb/s and/or 100 Mb/s networks were interconnected. Coupled with the continuous advances in the power of desktop computers and workstations, new applications such as the World Wide Web, with rich content requirements for high-definition color images, have continued the need for increased bandwidth.

Hence we have the latest evolution of Ethernet, at gigabit speed. A data rate of 1,000,000,000 bits per second, one hundred times the original (and still hugely popular) 10 Mb/s version.

1.2.3 Standards Perspective

No review of a networking technology would be complete without the obligatory reproduction of the OSI (Open Systems Interconnection) 7-layer model (Figure 1-1). However, despite the layered model's overuse, it does serve as a good baseline to understand exactly where the "Ethernet" portion fits, and what is essentially outside the purview of the 802.3 standards (but nevertheless required to implement a real network product).

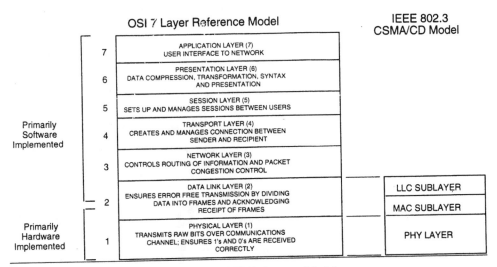

Figure 1-1 OSI Reference Model

The 802.3/Ethernet standard(s) reside within Layer 1 (Physical) and Layer 2 (Data Link) of the ISO/OSI 7-layer reference model.[5] The 802.3 standard is just one of the Layer 1 and 2 standards that are administered by the IEEE 802 standards body (see Figure 1-2). Others include 802.4 (Token Bus),[6] 802.5 (Token Ring),[7] 802.6 (Metropolitan Area Network),[8] 802.11 (Wireless Networks),[9] and 802.12 (Demand Priority).[10]

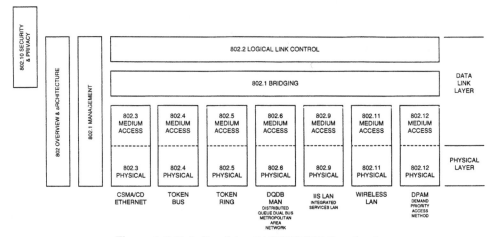

Figure 1-2 Relationship of ANSI/IEEE Standards

The whole standards process has humble beginnings, as illustrated in Figure 1-3. Initially, a single person or a group of persons request a parent working group to consider a new work area. Generally, this is achieved by like minded individuals collabo-

[5] Zemrowski, M. Z., Open Systems Interconnections (OSI), *The Handbook of International Connectivity Standards*, pp. 111-137, Van Nostrand Reinhold, New York, NY, 1992.

[6] American National Standards Institute/Institute of Electrical and Electronics Engineers, *Information Technology—Local and Metropolitan Area Networks—Part 4: Token-passing bus access method and physical layer specifications*, ISO/IEC 8802-4 :1990 (E) ANSI/IEEE Std 802.4-1990, IEEE, New York, NY, August 17, 1990.

[7] American National Standards Institute/Institute of Electrical and Electronics Engineers, *Information Technology—Local and Metropolitan Area Networks—Part 5: Token ring access method and physical layer specifications*, ISO/IEC 8802-5:1992 (E) IEEE Std 802.5-1995, IEEE, New York, NY, December 29, 1995.

[8] American National Standards Institute/Institute of Electrical and Electronics Engineers, *Local and Metropolitan Area Networks—Part 6: Distributed Queue Dual Bus (DQDB) Access Method and Physical Layer Specifications*, ISO/IEC 8802.6-1994 (E) ANSI/IEEE Std 802.6-1994, IEEE, New York, NY, March 7, 1994

[9] Institute of Electrical and Electronics Engineers, Local and Metropolitan Area Networks - Wireless LAN Medium Access Control (MAC) and Physical Layer (PHY) Specifications ; IEEE Std. 802.11-1997, IEEE, New York, NY, November 18, 1997..

[10] Institute of Electrical and Electronics Engineers, Local and Metropolitan Area Networks - Demand Priority Access Method, Physical Layer and Repeater Specification for 100 Mb/s ; IEEE Std. 802.12-1995, IEEE, New York, NY, November 2, 1995.

rating to define a problem and some potential solutions and to present these suggestions to the working group membership for consideration. Once a case is made that significant interest exists within the working group for members to contribute to investigate the topic in more detail, a study group is chartered by the working group (although this may not ultimately be the working group where the actual standards development work is performed). Study groups are formed with a defined time limit, normally the time between two IEEE plenary meetings (approximately eight months). To continue longer, a study group must request that its life be extended.

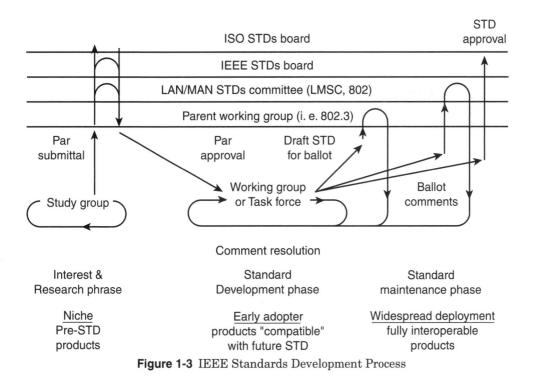

Figure 1-3 IEEE Standards Development Process

If successful in identifying a problem and possible technical solution(s), as well as sufficient member interest in proceeding, the output of the study group is a Project Authorization Request (PAR), and "Five Criteria." These are presented to the sponsoring working group, and if accepted, are moved up the chain of standards authority to the 802 Executive Committee and ultimately the IEEE Standards Board. The Five Criteria are the key requirements by which the work of the study group is measured, in order to justify that a future project is technically and economically sound. These are:

1. Broad market potential (has widespread industry interest)

2. Compatibility with existing standards (does not break an existing standard)

3. Distinct identity (is not duplicated by existing standards or work already in progress)

4. Technical feasibility (can be implemented with available technology)

5. Economic feasibility (can be implemented in a cost effective manner)

If the PAR is accepted, a new work request is approved, and the study group is effectively disbanded and a new working group or task force within an existing working group is formed. This is the place where the real standards-development work is performed. Normally, the actual writing of the draft document takes place over a period of months or even years. During this time, proposals and counterproposals are made, experiments performed, and different solutions considered and analyzed by the task force members. Participants are usually individuals from interested system vendors, silicon vendors, and users. In addition, liaison activities are often performed with other national and international standards bodies with interest in the subject.

Eventually, if the task force is successful, the output is a draft document that is ready to move to the balloting process. Again, this is a multilevel process. The document is balloted first within the task force, then within the working group (i.e., at the 802.3 level), then at the LSMC Sponsor Ballot level. At each stage, comments received from the voting members of each group must be resolved to ensure that the technical accuracy of the resulting standard. Note that this is the way 802.3 operates, some working groups operate slightly differently.

Finally, the (often considerably modified) draft document goes for IEEE Standards Board approval, and after success at this stage, becomes an official IEEE standard. Normally, documents are then forwarded for ISO approval, to be recognized and published by the International Standards Organization (ISO). If the working group has done a good job in resolving technical issues beforehand and has reached consensus with multiple vendors and international participation, these last two steps rarely result in any significant technical modifications to the documents.

The First Generation:
10 Mb/s Ethernet

2.1 Overview

Figure 2-1 shows the relationship between the ISO reference model and the actual implementation within an Ethernet node. An Ethernet node is commonly referred to as an Ethernet station (or end station), although the 802.3 Standard consistently refers to this as the DTE (Data Terminal Equipment). Regardless of terminology, it is the portion of the Ethernet system hardware that resides in any networked computer equipment, such as a desktop personal computer (PC), file server, mainframe computer, or printer.

Ethernet is a packet-based Local Area Network (LAN), built on the Carrier Sense Multiple Access with Collision Detect (CSMA/CD) access protocol. This access protocol is the means by which any Ethernet node determines it is permitted to transmit over the shared medium (regardless of medium type). The Media Access Control (MAC) layer is responsible for the enforcement of the CSMA/CD protocol.

In this architecture, devices are connected to a shared medium and have equal-priority access to it. The scheme is basically analogous to human conversation, which works very well while a single person speaks, allowing many others to simultaneously listen. However, if two or more people speak simultaneously, then the conversation becomes unintelligible. In the same manner, all Ethernet nodes are permitted to "listen" (receive), but only one device at any time is permitted to "talk" (transmit). Any

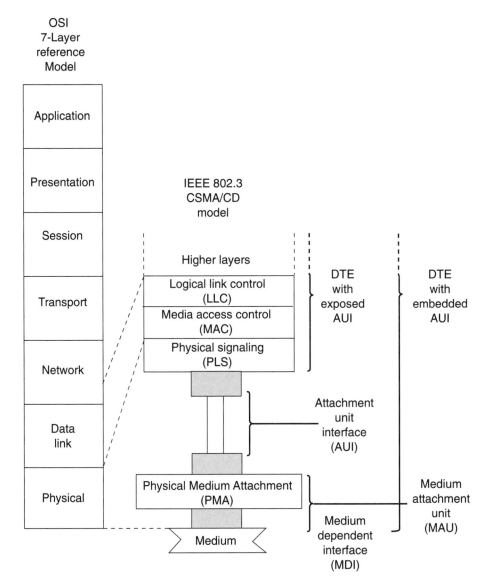

Figure 2-1 Relationship of OSI and IEEE Reference Models

device wishing to transmit must first sense whether the medium is currently active. This is effectively the "Carrier Sense" part of the algorithm. If the medium is already active, the node must wait until the activity stops and a predetermined period of silence passes. If the node detects that the channel is free, it may initiate a transmission attempt. If, after starting its transmission, its data collides with that of another station attempting to transmit at the same time, the transmitting station(s) will continue to transmit for a short additional period to ensure that the collision propagates throughout the network and then "backoff" for a random period of time before attempting the transmission again. This access protocol will be discussed in more detail in subsequent sections.

The Physical Signaling (PLS) and Attachment Unit Interface (AUI) subsystems support the signaling scheme between the MAC layer and the Medium Attachment Unit (MAU). The MAU is responsible for the actual physical and electrical interface to/from the particular type of medium. Note that, although considered part of the Physical (PHY) layer, the PLS function is normally implemented locally to the MAC function, shown in Figure 2-2a and 2-2b. The AUI provides a defined interface to allow a special cable and connector assembly to be used to connect the PLS function to the MAU. This allows the MAC/PLS to be located remotely from the MAU, and hence the network medium.

Due to the maturity of Ethernet technology, the functionality has been integrated into VLSI circuitry, which has permitted the continued reduction in size, cost, power consumption, and complexity of interfacing to an 802.3/Ethernet network.

The Media Access Control (MAC) sublayer and the Physical (PHY) layer are primarily supported directly in silicon, with implementations available from multiple semiconductor companies. The Logical Link Control (LLC) sublayer, which with the MAC forms the Data Link Layer (DLL), is normally implemented in software, as are the layers above. Early silicon solutions were typically partitioned into three functional integrated circuits (ICs), as shown in Figure 2-2a. As technology progressed, implementations integrated the system interface, MAC, and PLS components into a single chip, providing the AUI to connect the appropriate MAU, as shown in Figure 2-2b. Advanced silicon implementations are now being produced which integrate all of the functionality of the MAC and PHY, with hardware support for the LLC functions. In many of these solutions no provision is made for an exposed AUI connection, as originally defined by the 802.3 Standard model of Figure 2-1. Instead, the AUI exists only in a virtual sense, and the complete Ethernet node hardware can be integrated into a single integrated-circuit package. These issues will be discussed in more detail later.

From a practical implementation point of view, the 802.3 standard suite does not define the host bus interface or FIFO (first-in first-out) memories, integrated within a typical LAN controller, as shown in Figure 2-2a. Protocol and performance choice aspects of the bus interface are generally driven by market requirements. FIFO sizing is generally driven by a compromise between the amount of memory that can be implemented on the chip, versus the cost of this in silicon real estate

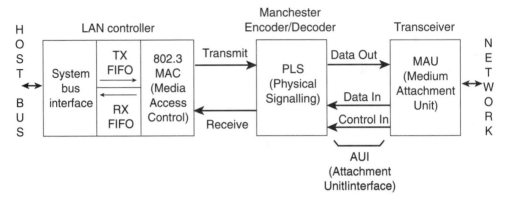

Figure 2-2a Typical Node Hardware

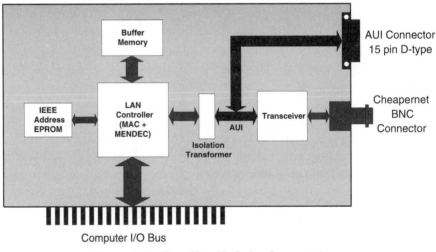

Computer I/O Bus

Figure 2-2b Two Chip Node Implementation

terms. Note that, in the case of the interface between the MAC and PLS functions, the standard defined a "service interface" (an abstract interface protocol). The lack of a defined electrical interface was later realized to be a significant oversight, since it resulted in several "almost compatible" implementations from major silicon vendors. Although these vendors ended up with nearly identical definition with seven digital (and functionally identical) signal lines, the timing and polarity-inversion differences between implementations made direct mixing of controller and Manchester encoder/decoder chips from different vendors impossible without (annoyingly) simple interface logic. The basics of the 7-wire interface between the MAC and PLS are shown in Fig 2-3.

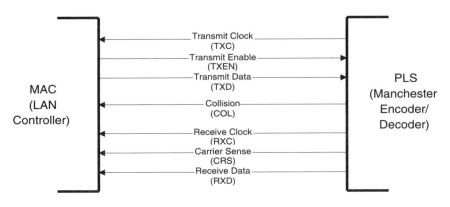

Figure 2-3 Typical MAC to PLS 7-Wire Interface

2.2 Media Access Control Frame Format

The Ethernet nodes on a network exchange data in a serial format (one data bit at a time). Ethernet originally supported only a 10 Mb/s data rate, hence a "bit time" (time taken to transfer a single bit of information) was 100 ns. Although the original 802.3 charter encompassed data rates between 1 and 20 Mb/s (in fact, a 1 Mb/s version of 802.3 was specified), there was no widespread use of anything but 10 Mb/s 802.3/Ethernet until the development and deployment of 100 Mb/s products starting around 1995, based on the IEEE 802.3u 100BASE-T Specification. 100 Mb/s operation is discussed in detail in Chapter 3.

The MAC functions of the Ethernet stations pass data frames between each other, which consist of data bits grouped in the specified MAC frame format. Figures 2-4a and 2-4b show the format for the 802.3 and Ethernet packets, respectively.

PREAMBLE 1010....1010	SFD 10101011	DA	SA	LENGTH	LLC DATA	LLC PAD	FCS
56 BITS	8 BITS	6 BYTES	6 BYTES	2 BYTES	46-1500 BYTES		4 BYTES

Figure 2-4a 802.3 Packet Format

PREAMBLE 1010....1010	SYNCH 11	DA	SA	TYPE	DATA	FCS
62 BITS	2 BITS	6 BYTES	6 BYTES	2 BYTES	46-1500 BYTES	4 BYTES

Figure 2-4b Ethernet Packet Format

A minor terminology difference within the 802.3 and Ethernet standards is the use of "octet" to refer to a byte (eight bits) of information. Throughout this text the term "byte" will be used, due to its widespread use in the computer and communications industries.

2.2.1 Preamble

The packet commences with a preamble sequence, which is an alternating "1, 0" pattern. The preamble provides a single frequency on the network (5 MHz) at the start of each packet, which allows the receiver to "lock" to the incoming bit stream. This is analogous to a training sequence in modem technology, allowing the receiving device to acquire the clock of the incoming waveform. The MAC function is idle between packets, although the network medium itself may not be completely inactive due to signaling mechanisms employed at the PHY layer (these are explained in more detail in the "Media and Topology Issues" section).

The preamble is used only by the Manchester encoder/decoder (the clock/data recovery circuit within the PLS function) to "lock on" to the incoming receive bit stream and allow data decoding. Preamble received on the network is not passed through the MAC to the host system. However, the MAC function is responsible for the generation of preamble for transmitted packets.

The preamble sequence is followed by a "start-of-frame" marker, which indicates that the data portion of the message will follow. Either the "Start Frame Delimiter" (802.3) or "Synch" sequence (Ethernet) is used (see later for additional details on the specific differences).

2.2.2 Destination Address (DA)

The Destination Address (DA) is a 48-bit value which is transmitted least significant bit (LSB) first (Figure 2-5). The DA is used by the receiving MAC, to determine if the incoming packet is addressed to this particular node. If the receiving node detects a match between its own unique node address and the address within the DA field, it will attempt to receive the packet. Other nodes, which do not detect a match, will ignore the remainder of the packet. Three types of destination addressing are supported:

1. Individual (Physical)—The DA field contains an individual and unique address assigned to one node on the network.

2. Multicast (Logical)—If the first bit (LSB) of the DA field is set, this denotes that a Group Address is being used. The "group" of nodes that will be addressed is determined by a higher layer function, but in general the intent is to transmit a message to a logically similar subset of the nodes on the network—for instance, to all printing devices.

3. Broadcast—The broadcast is a special form of multicast address, where the DA field is set to all 1s. The all 1s address is expressly reserved for the broadcast function, and all MAC devices on the network must be capable of receiving a broadcast message. Note however that upper-layer protocols may not support the broadcast function.

Note that 48-bit MAC addresses are written in a defined canonical format, to ensure that addresses are at least written in the same format, even if different LAN technologies use different bit-ordering conventions to exchange information. The canonical format as well as the OUI and vendor-assigned portions of the address are described in more detail in Appendix B.

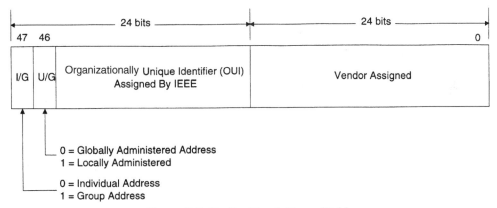

Figure 2-5 Destination Address Fields

Administration of network (node) addresses can be managed either locally or globally. If the second bit in the DA field is set, the address is locally administered. Hence address assignments will typically be managed by the local network manager. If the second bit in the DA field is clear, the address is globally administered by a registration authority such as the ISO or IEEE. Commercially available LAN adapters are shipped with globally administered addresses, which the hardware supplier programs during the manufacturing process. Global administration minimizes any potential conflicts as networks grow in size and are interconnected to other previously isolated LANs. Details of how to obtain globally administered addresses should be directed to the appropriate authority.[1]

---

[1] American National Standards Institute/Institute of Electrical and Electronics Engineers, Information Technology—Local and Metropolitan Area Networks—Part 3: Carrier sense multiple access with collision detection (CSMA/CD) access method and physical layer specifications, ISO/IEC 8802-3:1996 (E) ANSI/IEEE Std 802.3, 1996 Edition, IEEE, New York, NY, July 29, 1996. Section 3.2.3.1.

2.2.3 Source Address (SA)

The Source Address (SA) is a 48-bit value that is transmitted least significant bit (LSB) first. The SA field is supplied by the transmitting MAC, which inserts its own unique address into this field as the frame is transmitted, indicating it was the originating station. A receiving MAC is not required to take action based on the SA field. Note that the broadcast and multicast address formats are illegal within the SA field (i.e., the LSB is never set).

2.2.4 Length/Type

The 2-byte Length or Type field follows the SA field. The choice of Length or Type is dependent on whether the frame is 802.3 or Ethernet compatible respectively (see below for additional details on the specific differences). The high-order byte of the Length/Type field is transmitted first, with the LSB of each byte transmitted first.

2.2.5 Data

This field contains the actual frame data that is being transferred and is 46 to 1500 bytes in length. The LLC function is responsible for fragmenting data into block sizes suitable for transmission over the network. Data bytes are transmitted sequentially, with the LSB of each byte transmitted first.

2.2.6 Frame Check Sequence (FCS)

The Frame Check Sequence (FCS) is a 4-byte field that contains the Cyclic Redundancy Check (CRC) for the entire frame. The CRC is computed by the transmitting station on the Destination Address, Source Address, Length/Type, and Data fields and appended as the last 4 bytes of the frame. The same CRC algorithm is used by the receiving station to compute the CRC value for the frame as it is received. The value computed at the receiver is compared with that appended by the transmit station, providing an error-detection mechanism in case of corrupted data. The CRC bits within the FCS are transmitted in the order MSB to LSB.

Note that in 802.3 there is a technical difference between the terms "packet" and "frame." A packet is used to describe the entire transmitted serial bit sequence, as viewed on the physical medium, from the first bit of the preamble sequence to the last bit of the FCS field. However, a frame is defined as the portion of the 802.3 serial bit stream immediately following the preamble sequence and SFD pattern, which includes the Destination Address, Source Address, Length, LLC Data/Pad, and FCS fields. Hence, from the preceding definitions, legal frame sizes vary from a minimum of 64 bytes to a maximum of 1518 bytes.

2.2.7 802.3 and Ethernet Frame Format Exceptions

While the preceding frame format definitions remain true for all 802.3/Ethernet derivatives, there are some noteworthy exceptions.

First, there were some minor differences between the 802.3 and Ethernet packets—namely:

1. The "Start Frame Delimiter" (SFD) of 802.3 is defined as a byte with the "1, 0, 1, 0, 1, 0, 1, 1" pattern, whereas the "Synch" bits of Ethernet are a "1, 1" sequence. However, in both cases, the preamble plus start-of-frame indication is 64 bits long and of an identical pattern, hence an identical MAC function can deal with both packet formats.

2. 802.3 and Ethernet both specify that a frame must be in the range of 64 to 1518 bytes. However, the actual data field in 802.3 is permitted to be smaller than the 46-byte value that is necessary to ensure the minimum-size frame. 802.3 handles this by requiring the Media Access Control (MAC) layer to append "pad" characters to the LLC Data field before sending the data over the network. Ethernet assumes that the upper layer(s) ensure that the minimum data field is 46 bytes before passing the data to the MAC, and the existence of pad characters (although they may have effectively been inserted by the upper-layer software) is unknown to the MAC.

3. 802.3 uses a "Length" field which indicates the number of data bytes (excluding pad characters) that are in the data field only (excluding the FCS field). Ethernet, on the other hand, uses a "Type" field in the same 2 bytes to identify the message protocol type. Since the Length/Type field is passed transparently by the MAC function to/from higher-layer functions (neither inserted nor modified by the MAC), an identical MAC function can deal with both Ethernet and 802.3 packet formats. In addition, since valid Ethernet Type fields are always assigned to be above the maximum 802.3 packet size, Ethernet and 802.3 packets can coexist on the same network.

For additional details on these definitions, consult the current 802.3[2] and/or Ethernet[3] specifications.

From an implementation point of view, the Ethernet frame format is in much wider use than the true 802.3 format. However, 802.3 continued to acknowledge only the 802.3 packet format in all its documentation. This situation continued with Xerox administering the type field (commonly referred to as the "EtherType" field). In 1997, however, during the development of the 802.3x Full Duplex Standard, 802.3 finally acknowledged that it would be much simpler to have the EtherType values administered by IEEE. The rationale for this is discussed in the "Full Duplex/Flow Control" section in Chapter 3.

One additional modification to the 802.3/Ethernet frame format has been specified recently. Prior to this modification the frame length had always remained within the 64-byte minimum and 1518-byte maximum restrictions. This latest modification allows frames to be extended by an additional 4-byte "Virtual LAN Tag" (VLAN Tag) field. The VLAN Tag conveys information to allow network topology optimization. The VLAN Tag also means that legal 802.3/Ethernet frame lengths were extended to a maximum of 1522 bytes. The definition and use of VLAN tagging is described in the "VLAN Tagging" section in Chapter 3.

2.3 Functional Overview of the 802.3 Model

Referring to Figure 2-1, the DTE (Data Terminal Equipment) is the primary interface within each of the networked computers and/or resources. The following section will examine the functionality incorporated into each of the principal layers (or sublayers) that are defined within the 802.3 model of the DTE. In addition, this section will include a brief functional description of an 802.3 repeater (specified within the 802.3 standards suite) and an 802.3 bridge (bridge functionality is actually defined in 802.1),[4] which are implemented in typical real-world network installations.

---

[2] American National Standards Institute/Institute of Electrical and Electronics Engineers, Information Technology—Local and Metropolitan Area Networks—Part 3: Carrier sense multiple access with collision detection (CSMA/CD) access method and physical layer specifications, ISO/IEC 8802-3:1996 (E) ANSI/IEEE Std 802.3, 1996 Edition, IEEE, New York, NY, July 29, 1996. Section 3.2.

[3] Digital Equipment Corporation/Intel Corporation/Xerox Corporation, *The Ethernet, A Local Area Network, Data Link Layer and Physical Layer Specifications*, Version 1.0, DEC/Intel/Xerox, September 30, 1980. Section 6.2.

[4] American National Standards Institute/Institute of Electrical and Electronics Engineers, Information Technology—Telecommunications and information exchange between systems—Local area networks - Media access control (MAC) bridges, ISO/IEC 10038:1993 (E) ANSI/IEEE Std 802.1D, 1993 Edition, IEEE, New York, NY, July 8, 1993.

2.3.1 Media Access Control (MAC) Sublayer

The MAC sublayer is responsible for the enforcement of the CSMA/CD protocol. The primary requirements of the MAC are:

1. Transmit and receive message data encapsulation.

    a. Framing (frame boundary delimitation, frame synchronization).

    b. Addressing (source and destination address handling).

    c. Error detection (physical-medium transmission errors).

2. Media access management.

    a. Medium allocation (collision avoidance).

    b. Contention resolution (collision handling).

Transmit and Receive Message Data Encapsulation

The MAC layer is responsible for the formatting of the transmit frames. This requires that the relevant fields of the frame are transmitted in the correct order (as defined in the "Media Access Control Frame Format" section), starting with the correct preamble/SFD sequence, followed by the actual frame contents (including DA, SA, Length/Type, and Data), and finally by the calculated CRC, appended as the FCS field. The MAC effectively converts the byte-oriented data passed to it from the host (computer) side and serializes this into a bit stream that can be transmitted over the network medium.

When receiving, the MAC must deserialize the incoming bit stream to reassemble the frame into bytes. When a receive packet commences, the MAC receive function will inspect the incoming bit stream for the occurrence of the start-of-frame. Preamble bits and the start-of-frame are discarded by the receive MAC. Once the SFD is detected, the MAC must delineate the DA field from the receive frame and compare this with the appropriate stored address (dependent on the type of destination addressing being used). If no match exists, the MAC discards the receive frame and waits for the medium to become inactive. If a match exists, the MAC will receive the incoming frame, compute its own independent CRC, and compare this with the CRC obtained from the FCS field (the last four bytes) of the received frame.

If the CRC values computed at the transmitter and receiver do not match, the MAC must report an error. If the frame contained an exact number of bytes, a "CRC Error" is reported. If a partial byte is received, the MAC must report an "Alignment Error" instead of the CRC Error. Since the CRC at the receiver is computed on the number of complete bytes received, the Alignment Error is intended to show that some bits may have been lost (or added) due to an error in decoding the received data.

Note that a phenomenon referred to as "dribbling bits" may cause some additional bits to be detected at the receiver. This occurs in normal network operation and is due to the tolerances allowed in the various transmitters and receivers in the signal path. The MAC will discard from one to seven dribbling bits at the end of the packet with no effect. However, if eight or more bits are added, a full additional byte will be detected, causing the CRC to fail (since the last byte will consist of dribbling bits, not a true FCS byte). Normally configured or operating networks will not add eight dribbling bits.

The MAC is responsible for counting key transmit and receive operating characteristics and reporting the various medium-induced errors that are detected at the receiver for use by upper layers and/or a management entity. For additional information regarding the management aspects of the MAC, see the "Station Management" section later in this chapter.

Other errors can be monitored and/or reported by the MAC, although these are more physical-connection related and are therefore discussed within the PLS/AUI and PHY subsystem definitions.

Medium Access Management

All devices on an Ethernet network must time-share the common communications medium. All nodes on the network have equal-priority access to the medium. Multiple nodes may simultaneously receive data from the medium, but only one node at any time is permitted to transmit. A station wishing to transmit must first sense whether the medium is currently active. The PLS function detects and passes the state of "Carrier Sense" to the MAC. If the network is currently busy, carrier sense will be active, and the station will defer its transmission until the activity ceases and a predetermined period of silence passes. This period of inactivity is known as the Inter-Packet Gap (IPG) interval. The IPG delineates each packet (with a 9.6-μs interval), and allows all stations to detect carrier sense as inactive.

Once the IPG has expired, a station is permitted access to the medium and may start to transmit. If two (or more) stations have been waiting for medium access then they may start to transmit at essentially the same time. Since the medium is shared, their transmissions will interfere and become garbled, causing a "collision." All stations must have a "Collision-Detect" capability. The stations which are transmitting will detect the collision and commence a "jam" sequence, which means they will continue to transmit for a predetermined time after the collision has been detected. If the collision is detected during preamble, the preamble/SFD sequence will be completed (all 64 bits) prior to appending a 32-bit jam sequence, as shown in Figure 2-6a. This defines the minimum-size legal transmitted collision "fragment" as 96 bit times in duration. If the preamble was completed prior to the detection of collision, the station will jam for an additional 32 bit times, as shown in Figure 2-6b. Both these conditions are generally referred to as "in-window" collisions.

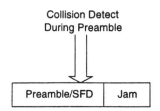

Figure 2-6a In-Window Collision—Within Preamble

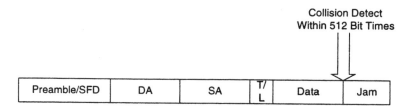

Figure 2-6b In-Window Collision—After Preamble

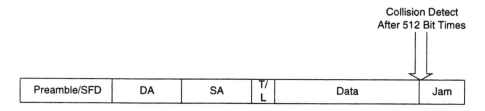

Figure 2-6c Out-of-Window Collision or Late Collision

The jam sequence is permitted to be any fixed or arbitrary pattern, provided it is not the CRC of the partially generated frame (typically the alternating "1, 0" pattern is used). The jam period guarantees that stations at the extremes of the network are able to detect the collision condition. As each station completes the jam sequence it will cease transmission, hence the network will become inactive again once the last station ceases. The stations which were transmitting will perform a "backoff" algorithm, which causes them to reschedule their transmissions at a later point. The backoff period is computed individually in each station using a pseudo-random sequence generator. This is intended to cause the colliding stations to reschedule their next transmission attempt at different intervals, to avoid a subsequent collision.

The time taken to guarantee that a station can detect a collision is determined by the round trip delay of the network. Assume that a station starts to transmit a message, and the message propagates through the network to another remote station, which starts to transmit just at the point that the first stations message begins to arrive. The remote station will detect a collision almost immediately (dependent on the actual implementation). However, the originating station will not be aware of the collision until the event propagates back through the network. So the round-trip delay, called the "slot time," determines how long it takes to detect a collision. The slot time imposes a maximum network length, in order to ensure that collisions are detected within a predetermined period of time. The slot time is 51.2 μs (512 bit times) for 802.3/Ethernet.

A transmission experiencing a collision within the slot time (an in-window collision) will be automatically retried by the sending node. A collision after the slot time (512 bits or 51.2 μs) on the other hand, will result in a "late collision" (or out-of-window collision), as in Fig 2-6c, and the node will abandon the transmission immediately.

In very busy networks, with high traffic rates, collisions are experienced as a normal part of the medium access protocol. Up to 15 retries (16 attempts total) are permitted before the node aborts the transmission of the particular packet (or frame). The Ethernet LAN controller (implemented in silicon) is responsible for the handling of retransmissions. The controller will compute the interval before the retransmission is allowed based on a "truncated binary exponential backoff" (TBEB) algorithm, which provides a controlled pseudo-random mechanism to enforce the collision backoff interval, before retransmission is attempted.

From ANSI / IEEE Std 8802.3, 1996 Edition, 4.2.3.2.5[5]

At the end of enforcing a collision (jamming), the CSMA/CD sublayer delays before attempting to re-transmit the frame. The delay is an integer multiple of slotTime. The number of slot times to delay before the nth re-transmission attempt is chosen as a uniformly distributed random integer r in the range:

$$0 \leq r < 2^k$$

where

$$k = \min (n, 10).$$

Notice that, according to this algorithm, as the number of retransmission attempts increase (as *n* gets larger), the number of choices for the retry interval (*r*, the randomly chosen integer) becomes larger. Hence the randomness allows the dispersion of retries when the network is heavily utilized and several stations are involved in the collision, in an attempt to alleviate congestion.

---

[5] American National Standards Institute/Institute of Electrical and Electronics Engineers, Information Technology—Local and Metropolitan Area Networks—Part 3: Carrier sense multiple access with collision detection (CSMA/CD) access method and physical layer specifications, ISO/IEC 8802-3:1996 (E) ANSI/IEEE Std 802.3, 1996 Edition, IEEE, New York, NY, July 29, 1996. ISBN 1-55937-555-8. Section 4.2.3.2.5. ©1996, IEEE. All rights reserved.

If the transmission is unsuccessful after all 16 attempts, the MAC will abandon the frame transmission and inform upper-layer software and/or a management entity, which is responsible for taking appropriate action.

A detailed review of the operation of the Ethernet MAC, as well as performance analysis and optimizations, is contained in the "Gigabit MAC Operation" section, in Chapter 4.

2.3.2 Physical Signaling (PLS) Specification

Although part of the Physical (PHY) Layer, the PLS function resides in the DTE and is responsible for four principal functions. These allow transmit Data Output, receive Data Input, Carrier Sense, and Error Sense. A fifth optional function is provided for in the 10 Mb/s 802.3 Standard (Monitor Mode), but this is so seldom implemented in practice that is not discussed here.[6]

The PLS provides the interface between the MAC layer and the AUI. The MAC transmits serial data which is output in "Non-Return-to-Zero" (NRZ) format. The MAC typically operates at standard logic levels (i.e., 5.0 V CMOS or 3.3/5.0 V TTL compatible). The data is "Manchester encoded" by the PLS and transmitted over the AUI to the MAU, using a differential signaling technique. Manchester encoding allows both clock and data information to be combined into a single "bit-symbol." Each bit-symbol consists of two halves, with the first half being the logical inverse of the data bit to be encoded, and the second half of the symbol always being the logical value of the data bit itself (or the inverse of the first half). This guarantees that there is always a signal transition in the center of each bit-symbol (or Bit Cell Center, BCC). Figure 2-7a shows the relationship of clock, NRZ, and Manchester encoded data. Note that a sequence where each successive data bit differs from the previous bit (such as preamble) exhibits a 5-MHz frequency, whereas a sequence containing identical data (all 0s or all 1s) exhibits a 10-MHz frequency. Figure 2-7b shows the transmit signal path, from the MAC, across the 7-wire interface to the PLS, through the Manchester encoder, and output to the DO pair of the AUI. An analogous process occurs for the receive path from the AUI DI pair, via a Manchester decoder (not shown), to the receive signals of the 7-wire interface.

---

[6] American National Standards Institute/Institute of Electrical and Electronics Engineers, Information Technology—Local and Metropolitan Area Networks—Part 3: Carrier sense multiple access with collision detection (CSMA/CD) access method and physical layer specifications, ISO/IEC 8802-3:1996 (E) ANSI/IEEE Std 802.3, 1996 Edition, IEEE, New York, NY, July 29, 1996. ISBN 1-55937-555-8. Sections 7.2.1.1.4 and 7.2.4.2.

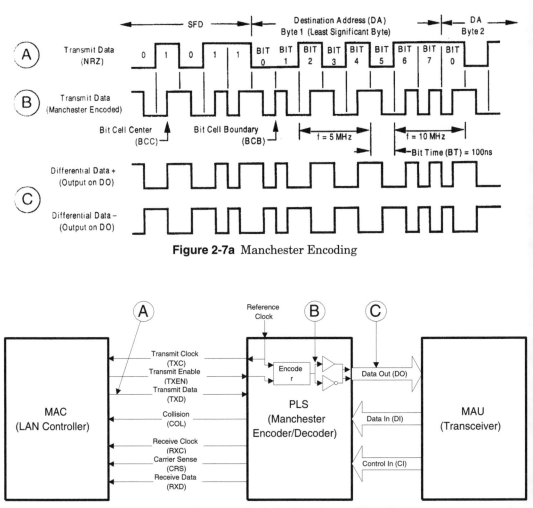

Figure 2-7a Manchester Encoding

Figure 2-7b Transmit Path for Manchester Encoding

The 10 Mb/s signaling rate is required to be maintained over the life of the device to 0.01% accuracy, which requires the incorporation of a high-stability crystal-based oscillator circuit at each DTE, shown as the Reference Clock input to the PLS in Figure 2-7b.

The conversion from single-ended logic levels from the MAC to the 2-wire differential signaling required by the AUI specification allows the AUI signals to pass through the transformer isolation barrier in the AUI path. This is designed to provide DC isolation between the DTE (host computer) and the network medium in the event of a network fault condition.

Manchester encoding has both good and bad properties in terms of data transmission. On the plus side, it allows both clock and data to be encoded into a single serial stream, so a separate clock line is not required. On the negative side, the encoded stream is two times the frequency that would be required to convey the same information in NRZ format (i.e., for an alternating "1, 0, 1, 0, ..." pattern and a 100 ns bit cell, NRZ requires a 5-MHz maximum frequency, whereas the Manchester encoded version requires 10 MHz).

Three input functions are provided by the PLS to the MAC, which allow the MAC to perform the CSMA/CD protocol.

The Data Input function takes the Manchester encoded bit stream received from the MAU, via the AUI, and decodes it to provide the receive data function for the MAC. The receive decoder uses the fact that the preamble sequence of the frame will exhibit a 5 MHz frequency. This allows a device such as a phase-locked loop to lock to the incoming waveform, effectively providing a clock reference to allow decoding of the remainder of the frame.

The Carrier Sense function allows the MAC to determine if there is network activity. The PLS will return the state of Carrier Sense as active when there is transmit activity from the node, or receive or collision activity is detected on the network.

The Error Sense function allows the node to detect if the MAU and the associated AUI are operational and connected. After each transmit packet from the MAC, the MAU is required to send back a signal to indicate that its collision logic has been tested and is operational. This signal is referred to as the "Signal Quality Error Test" or "SQE Test" function within the 802.3 standards and is also colloquially referred to as the "heartbeat" function. If the SQE Test indication is not passed back, the MAC will report that the MAU is either malfunctioning or not correctly connected. Note that no network medium activity results from the SQE Test; the signal is generated by the MAU and detected by the MAC using the PLS/AUI. SQE Test is described in more detail in the "MAU Specification" section.

In addition, the PLS and MAC can also use the fact that if no Carrier Sense is detected during an actual transmission, then the MAU or the AUI is malfunctioning.

2.3.3 Attachment Unit Interface (AUI) Specification

The AUI provides the signaling path between the PLS function of the DTE (or a repeater) and the MAU. The AUI cable typically consists of three differential signal pairs (although an optional fourth pair is allowed, it is virtually never implemented in practice), plus power and ground connections. Each of the signal pairs is individually screened. The maximum length of the AUI cable is limited to 50 m, which can consist of a number of cables joined together. The "Physical Signaling and Attachment Unit Interface Specification" of the IEEE 802.3 Standard specifies that the DTE should have a female connector and the MAU should have a male connector,[7] hence the AUI cable requires opposite mating connectors to complete the connection. All the connectors are the familiar 15-pin D-type found in many computer interconnect applications.

Initially, a "slide-latch" assembly was defined to retain the connectors in place, due to the concern that the AUI cable was fairly stiff, so it could dislodge the connector by its own weight or by someone's inadvertently knocking it. This slide latch proved to be a major problem, both to specify and manufacture. It was soon abandoned in practical implementations.

The three signal pairs are defined as Data Out (DO), Data In (DI) and Control In (CI, frequently although incorrectly referred to as "collision in"). The signals are defined in terms of the DTE (or repeater), hence DO is the transmit data path. Note that from the perspective of the MAU the signals appear reversed, so although DO is an output from the DTE, it is an input to the MAU. Differential signaling is employed on each of the interface signals to allow the signals to pass through a transformer isolation barrier, which provides the DTE (typically an expensive computer system) protection from severe network medium faults.

Data is output from the DTE on the DO pair (in Manchester encoded form) during transmission and is also returned (looped back) by the MAU to the DTE using the DI pair. In this way, the MAC/PLS functions are able to observe the complete operational status of the AUI and MAU.

During reception, Manchester encoded receive data passes to the DTE via the DI pair.

If a collision is detected, a 10-MHz pulse train is sent by the MAU over the CI pair to inform the DTE. In addition, for a short period after each frame transmission has completed, the MAU generates an SQE Test signal (a short-duration 10-MHz burst) which is returned to the DTE using the CI pair. The SQE Test burst must commence within a window of 0.6–1.6 µs, and should last 5–15 bit times. The SQE Test signal occurs only over the AUI and does not result in any observable network activity.

2.3.4 Medium Attachment Unit (MAU) Specification

The MAU provides the functional, electrical and mechanical interface between the DTE and the particular network medium in use. It is important to note that for 10 Mb/s Ethernet, the MAC, PLS and AUI functions are preserved regardless of medium, only the MAU is required to change.

---

[7] American National Standards Institute/Institute of Electrical and Electronics Engineers, Information Technology—Local and Metropolitan Area Networks - Part 3: Carrier sense multiple access with collision detection (CSMA/CD) access method and physical layer specifications, ISO/IEC 8802-3 :1996 (E) ANSI/IEEE Std 802.3 1996 Edition, IEEE, New York, NY, July 29, 1996. Section 7.6.1.

The MAU has six primary functions to perform. These are Transmit Data, Receive Data, Loopback, Collision Detection, SQE Test, and Jabber Protection. In addition, in some MAUs a seventh function of Link Integrity is performed.

Transmit Data

The DTE will present Manchester encoded data for transmission over the network on the DO pair of the AUI. The MAU is responsible for receiving the data on DO and forwarding this over the network. The MAU provides the necessary drive capability to transmit the data over the network and does not modify the content of the data in any way.

Receive Data

The MAU is responsible for ensuring that the valid Manchester data received from the network is passed to the DTE using the DI circuit of the AUI. The MAU performs signal-amplitude and pulse-width detection on the received signal to ensure its quality, before forwarding the unmodified data to the DTE.

Loopback

Manchester data output from the DTE to the MAU on the DO pair must be returned to the DTE using the DI pair. This loopback mechanism is used by the MAC to indicate that valid network transmission and reception paths exist.

Collision Detection

The MAU is responsible for the detection of collisions on the network. If the MAU detects a collision, it reports this back to the DTE by sending a 10 MHz waveform on the CI pair of the AUI. The actual mechanism of collision detection is dependent on the particular medium and will be discussed under the headings "Mixed Topologies" and "Technology Advantages of 10BASE-T."

During the collision condition, the MAU continues to return data to the DTE using the DI pair. When the node is no longer involved in the collision (ceases transmission), but the network is still active, the MAU returns data from the network over the DI pair. If the node is the last device to continue to transmit after the collision condition has ceased, the MAU returns the data received on the DO pair (from the DTE) to the DI pair.

SQE Test

After the transmission from the DTE completes, the MAU is responsible for sending a Signal Quality Error (SQE) Test message over the CI pair of the AUI. This requires the MAU to attempt to test as much of its collision detection logic as possible, and, if functional, indicate this by transmitting a short 10 MHz burst on the CI pair. The SQE

Test burst must commence within 0.6–1.6 μs of the transmission ending, and should last 5–15 bit times. Note that if the transmission attempt resulted in a collision and the CI pair was activated, the test is considered to have been performed and does not have to be repeated at the end of the transmission.

The SQE Test function is normally provided with an enable/disable feature. The function should be enabled when the MAU is connected to a DTE. The DTE provides a "blinding period," during which it looks for the SQE Test burst after each transmission and does not interpret this as a collision indication. The SQE Test feature must be disabled if the MAU is connected to a repeater, since the repeater does not provide any blinding period and will detect the SQE Test burst as a collision (the repeater function is described in more detail in the "Repeater Definition" section).

Jabber Function

The Jabber mechanism is provided to prevent a single node that continues to transmit for excessively long periods from completely utilizing the network. If a DTE transmits on DO for an abnormally long period (20–150 ms), the MAU will interrupt the transmission of data onto the network, disable the loopback path to DI, and indicate a collision using the CI pair. The MAU remains in this state until the data output from the DTE ceases (DO becomes silent) and an "unjab" time expires (0.5 s ± 0.25 s).

Link Integrity

Some MAUs provide a mechanism which detects whether a valid communications path exists over the network. This mechanism is primarily used in MAUs that use separate transmit and receive signaling paths, such as twisted pair and fiber. This facility is important in ensuring correct network operation in these systems, since a break in the receive signal path will render the Carrier Sense facility inoperable. This is discussed more fully in the section on "Technology Advantages of 10BASE-T."

2.4 Operation of an Ethernet Node

The following figures (Figures 2-8 through 2-10) explain in simple overview terms the functional capabilities of each part of an Ethernet node, the data flow for packets transmitted by the host over the network, and the reception of packets from the network and passed to the host. The example shown is for a 10BASE2 (Cheapernet) co-axial implementation,[8] although the functionality is equally valid for other media.

---

[8] American National Standards Institute/Institute of Electrical and Electronics Engineers, Information Technology—Local and Metropolitan Area Networks—Part 3: Carrier sense multiple access with collision detection (CSMA/CD) access method and physical layer specifications, ISO/IEC 8802-3:1996 (E) ANSI/IEEE Std 802.3, 1996 Edition, IEEE, New York, NY, July 29, 1996. Section 10.

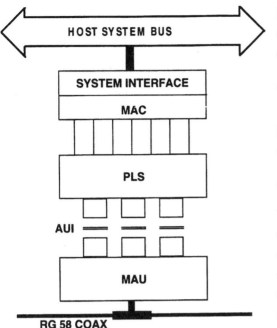

LAN Controller

- Provides interface to/from host bus.

- Performs all 802.3 protocol processing.

- Performs all parallel-to-serial and serial-to-parallel conversions.

Manchester Encoder/Decoder

- Converts single-ended logic to differential signaling.

- Manchester encoding/decoding.

Transceiver

- Transmit drive.

- Receive signal recognition.

- Collision detection.

- DO to DI loopback and SQE Test.

- Optional Link Integrity Test.

Figure 2-8 Ethernet Node—Hardware Functional Overview

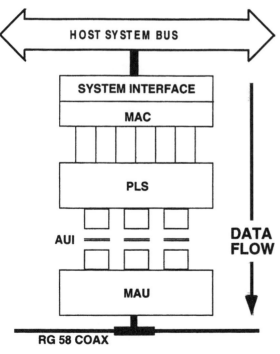

Transmit Operation

1. Data moved from host memory to temporary controller store (FIFO).

2. Wait for Carrier Sense inactive and IPG time to elapse.

3. Parallel-to-serial conversion. Send Preamble/SFD, DA, SA, Length, and Data; compute/send CRC.

4. If Collision Detect, then "backoff" and retry after random interval.

5. Manchester encode transmit bit stream and transmit on DO.

6. Receive on DO, transmit onto medium, loopback DO to DI.

7. Watch for transmit Jabber (faulty controller).

8. Perform SQE Test at end of transmission.

Figure 2-9 Ethernet Node—Transmit Data Flow

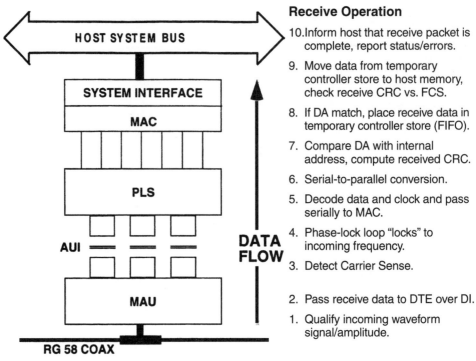

Receive Operation

10. Inform host that receive packet is complete, report status/errors.

9. Move data from temporary controller store to host memory, check receive CRC vs. FCS.

8. If DA match, place receive data in temporary controller store (FIFO).

7. Compare DA with internal address, compute received CRC.

6. Serial-to-parallel conversion.

5. Decode data and clock and pass serially to MAC.

4. Phase-lock loop "locks" to incoming frequency.

3. Detect Carrier Sense.

2. Pass receive data to DTE over DI.

1. Qualify incoming waveform signal/amplitude.

Figure 2-10 Ethernet Node—Receive Data Flow

2.5 Repeater Definition

A repeater is a device that allows extension of the physical network topology beyond the normal restrictions imposed using a single cable segment in terms of distance and node count. Figure 2-11 shows the relationship of the repeater in terms of both the OSI and IEEE 802.3 layered architectures. The repeater exists as a physical layer device. Note that the repeater example shown in Figure 2-11 uses unshielded twisted pair as the underlying PHY layer. However, the repeater behavior is identical for all 10 Mb/s implementations and independent of PHY technology.

Specific terminology is related to the exact definition of a repeater under the 802.3 standards, and a number of generalized industry terms also are used and occasionally cause conflict and confusion.

A "repeater unit" is defined within the 10 Mb/s 802.3 Standard to be the basic repeater function, which obeys the detailed requirements for restoration and repeating of data between segments.

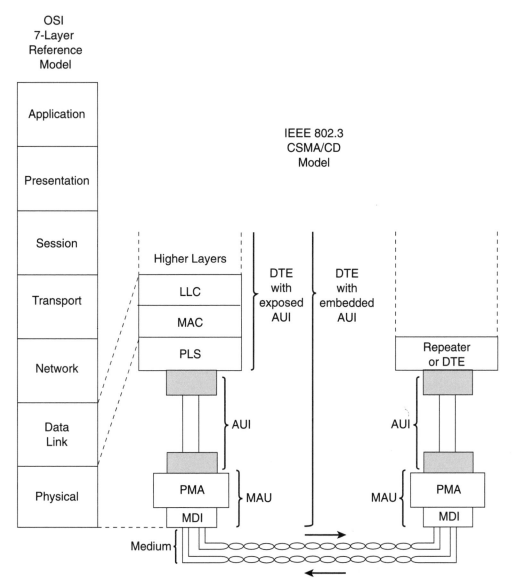

Figure 2-11 Repeater Relationship in OSI and IEEE Reference Models
(From IEEE Std. 8802-3:1996, ©1996, IEEE. All rights reserved.)

A "repeater set' is defined within the 10 Mb/s 802.3 Standard to include the "repeater unit" function plus the associated MAUs and AUIs (if explicitly provided). The difference is more readily apparent in Figure 2-12. Since a repeater set may have the MAUs physically embedded, there is no requirement for an external AUI to be present. In many practical implementations the realization of the AUI circuits is not even present internal to the design, although an equivalent "logical AUI" or "virtual AUI" normally exists.

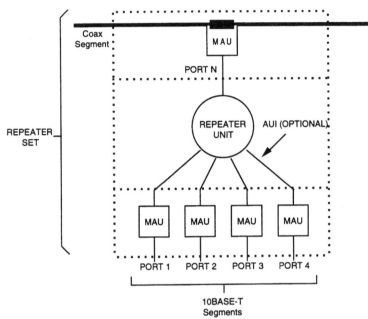

Figure 2-12 Generalized Repeater Definition
(From IEEE Std. 8802-3:1996, ©1996, IEEE. All rights reserved.)

The generic term "hub" is frequently used in industry to describe an interconnectivity device normally based on a star topology. The term "repeater" is more technically correct in the case of Ethernet/802.3 networks. Frequently, the terms "smart hub", "intelligent hub" and/or "enterprise hub" have been used (amongst others) to describe a class of inter-networking device which has the following general properties:

1. Multiple network protocols supported (i.e., 802.3/Ethernet, 802.5/Token Ring,[9] ANSI X3T9.5/Fiber Distributed Data Interface [FDDI]).[10]

---

[9] American National Standards Institute/ Institute of Electrical and Electronics Engineers, Information Technology—Local and Metropolitan Area Networks—Part 5—Token Ring Access Method and Physical Layer Specifications, ISO/IEC 8802-5:1995(E) IEEE Std. 802.5-1995, IEEE, New York, NY, December 29, 1995.

[10] American National Standards Institute for Information Systems—Fiber-Distributed Data Interface (FDDI) Token Ring Media Access Control (MAC), ANSI X3.139-1987, American National Standards Institute, Inc., November 1986.

2. Multiple media types supported (i.e., fiber optic, coaxial and twisted pair cables).

3. Manageable from a remote network management entity, which may routinely interrogate and/or receive notifications from the intelligent hub.

Items 1 and 3 are features that an 802.3 repeater may provide, but in terms of item 1, it can only interconnect 802.3 segments, not connect 802.3 to another LAN protocol. Furthermore, an Ethernet repeater can only interconnect Ethernet segments of identical speed. To connect dissimilar-speed Ethernet networks, a bridge, switch, or router is required.

Throughout this overview, the term repeater will be used consistently to refer to an 802.3/Ethernet defined repeater. However, be aware that in the network industry in general this strict terminology is not adhered to, and the term "hub" or "concentrator" may often be generally applied to any multiport network device, including 802.3 repeaters, multiport bridges (described later in the "Bridge Definition" section), and routers, including devices which incorporate technologies other than Ethernet.

In its most generic form the repeater is an n port device, as shown in Figure 2-12. Data received on one port is repeated to all ports except the active receiver, with signal amplitude and timing restored on the re-transmitted (repeated) waveforms. If the repeater detects receive activity from two (or more) ports, this constitutes a collision, and the repeater will send a jam pattern on all ports, including the active receive ports. In this way, a transmitting node connected to a repeater port will observe two or more devices actively transmitting (itself and the repeater), detect a collision, and backoff.

The reception and retransmission of the signals, and the associated delays through the repeater, are closely specified in the section "Repeater Unit for 10 Mb/s Baseband Networks" of the IEEE 802.3 Standard.[11] The external behavior of the repeater unit is specified assuming that the external ports are implemented as physical AUIs. However, simple calculations allow for the effect of integrated MAUs to be factored in, to derive the behavior of a repeater set. Since the repeater has at least two ports, it is also capable of connecting dissimilar media. For instance, it can allow a coax network segment to be connected to one or more UTP network segments, as the example in Figure 2-12 depicts. The result is a single homogeneous CSMA/CD network.

---

[11] American National Standards Institute/Institute of Electrical and Electronics Engineers, Information Technology—Local and Metropolitan Area Networks—Part 3: Carrier sense multiple access with collision detection (CSMA/CD) access method and physical layer specifications, ISO/IEC 8802-3:1996 (E) ANSI/IEEE Std 802.3, 1996 Edition, IEEE, New York, NY, July 29, 1996. Section 9.9, pp. 137-149.

2.5.1 Standards-Defined Repeater Functions

Signal Restoration

The intent of the repeater is to restore the signal and remove the effects of amplitude distortion (caused by signal attenuation) and timing distortion (caused by jitter, defined as the amount that transitions of the bit-symbol vary from the ideal) which the signal experiences as it propagates through each network segment.

Because of the active regeneration in the repeater, all ports are isolated from each other and do not rely on the operation of neighboring ports, or port-attached devices, for their own operation. Cumulative jitter effects cannot occur, and the performance of each individual port can be monitored.

Preamble Restoration

As a packet is received at a repeater port (or at any port, including end stations), some of the preamble bits are lost, due to sampling, asynchronous timing, and clock recovery effects. In the case of an end station this is unimportant, since there is ample preamble, and the remaining preamble is stripped by the MAC. However, in a repeater, these lost preamble bits need to be restored., since there may be several interconnected repeaters, and successive loss may leave insufficient preamble for a remote station to be able to successfully decode the receive packet.

The repeater restores preamble in order to combat this. This means that the repeater must include a FIFO, since it has to store the incoming frame, which has been shortened by preamble loss, to its original length. The amount by which preamble is allowed to be restored is carefully specified, so that preamble growth does not occur.

Collision Detection

Transmit and Receive Collision Detection

When a repeater is repeating a packet received on one port to all other ports (those not disabled or partitioned), and one of the ports being transmuted to (i.e., not the currently active receive port) detects a collision, this is defined as a transmit collision. In the case of a transmit collision, the repeater transmits the jam signal to all ports, for a minimum of 96 bit times. Transmission to all ports ensures that the start of collision is signaled to all devices on the network, including the original port being received from.

If a repeater detects a collision from the port it is currently receiving from, this is defined as a receive collision. In the receive collision case, the repeater transmits the jam sequence to all ports except the original active receive port, for a minimum of 96 bit times. There is no need to propagate the start of collision to the port that has already just detected a collision, the requirement is to propagate the collision to the rest of the network.

If an active receive port becomes inactive prior to 96 bits being received, this is also classified as a receive collision by the repeater. Packet fragments smaller than 96 bit times can only be the result of a collision condition. These fragments are extended to 96 bit times to ensure they are observed by all end stations, which will reject them as an illegally short message (defined as a runt packet).

One Port Left

The one-port-left state of a repeater is to avoid a network of interconnected repeaters from locking up, in the case of a transmit collision condition. Consider the simple two-repeater scenario in Figure 2-13. Assume that an end station on each repeater starts to transmit at essentially the same time. Both repeaters will detect the receive port as active and will retransmit the packet to their other ports, including the inter-repeater link port. As the packets simultaneously travel across the inter-repeater link, they are detected at both repeaters, causing a transmit collision to be detected. Transit collision sends jam to all ports, for a minimum of 96 bit times, and continues until either all ports go idle or there is only one port left. Without the one-port-left state, the repeaters would continue to jam to all ports and hence continue to detect activity from each other on the inter-repeater port, extending the transmit collision condition indefinitely. One port left requires that once the repeater has issued jam for 96 bit times and only one port remains in collision, it moves to sending jam to all ports except the port in collision.

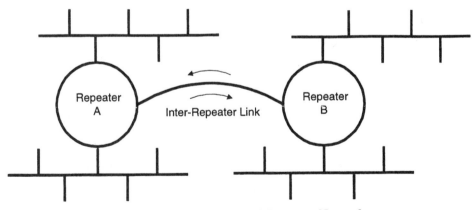

Figure 2-13 Interconnected Repeater Network

Assume repeater A reaches the one-port-left condition. Repeater A will cease transmission to the inter-repeater link port, continue to listen to the inter-repeater port, and jam to the rest of their local ports while there is receive activity in the inter-repeater link, indicating that the other repeater has not yet completed its 96-bit-time jam sequence. This ensures that repeater B, as the last repeater to resolve to the one-port-left condition, continues to propagate its jam activity to the rest of the network. Once repeater B resolves its local collision condition, it will also cease to transmit to the inter-repeater link, and the entire network becomes idle.

Note that for a CSMA/CD repeater network to operate, there must never be two active links interconnecting any two repeaters, and there must be no loop or ring topologies.

MAU Jabber Lockup Protection (MJLP)

MAU Jabber Lockup Protection (MJLP) is essentially a fix to allow the 802.3 10 Mb/s repeater to use an identical MAU as a DTE. This allows the repeater to be specified at the AUI port, and allows the use of any of the 10 Mb/s MAUs, making the repeater media independent. The initial focus for the MAU was for end stations when the initial coax-based versions of Ethernet were developed.

Each MAU has a jabber timer which prevents an end station from transmitting for an excessive duration (20–150 ms), causing the MAU to interrupt the transmit data process, disable the loopback path to DI, and indicate a collision using the CI pair. However, when connected to a repeater, these effects are undesirable.

To prevent the MAU entering the jabber state, the repeater implements a lower-value MJLP timer, which ensures the MAU's own jabber timer value will never be reached. The MJLP timer is 4–7.5 ms (40,000–75,000 bit times). If a repeater detects receive activity for a duration in excess of the MJLP timer, it interrupts the transmit data process to all ports. After 0.6–11.6 s (96–116 bit times), in the range of a normal IPG, the repeater resumes the transmit data process. The effect observed at the output ports of a repeater exhibiting MJLP is packet fragments of 40,000–75,000 bit times, interspersed by an IPG time.

MAU Considerations

There are two special provisions for MAUs that are connected to repeaters.

The first applies to some early coax MAUs, which were permitted to implement either "transmit mode collision detection" or "receive mode collision detection." Transmit mode collision detection only guarantees the MAU will detect a collision when it is actually transmitting (when the DO circuit is active), or when more than two nodes are involved in a collision if the node is not transmitting (when the DO circuit is idle). When only two nodes are participating in a collision and the MAU itself is not transmitting, it may or may not detect the collision. Receive mode collision detection, on the other hand, guarantees collision detection whenever two or more nodes are involved, regardless of the transmitting state of the sensing MAU. Since the repeater must detect and propagate collisions to the other interconnected segments, a MAU connected to a repeater must implement receive mode collision detection. Coax

MAUs which implement transmit mode collision detection will only be found in very early legacy equipment. All commercial products implemented receive mode collision detection from around the late 1980s.

The second requirement for MAUs connected to repeaters is that the SQE Test function must be disabled. A repeater does not provide any "blinding time" after packet transmission, as a DTE does. The SQE Test burst, issued by the MAU on the CI pair after each packet transmission (as a self-test of the collision logic and the AUI cable), will be detected as a collision by the repeater. All CI activity detected on the AUI port of a repeater will be detected as a collision, so the SQE Test function will cause extreme network degradation due to collision activity after each transmit packet. Refer to the section "Medium Attachment Unit (MAU) Specification" for more details.

Port Partitioning

A repeater may optionally isolate a port which is detected as experiencing either an excessive duration of collision or an excessive number of consecutive collisions. In this way, the repeater can be used to isolate faulty segments from the remainder of the network automatically, referred to as "partitioning" the port.

When a port is in the partitioned state, the repeater continues to transmit to the port, while reception from the port is monitored but not repeated by the repeater (including collisions) to the rest of the network. The repeater can "unpartition" the port if it transmits to the port in the normal course of retransmission and detects no collision indication for a specified time period. It may also unpartition the port if a successful reception with no collision is detected from the port.

Partition is often used in the network industry to merely indicate that a port on a repeater or hub has been disabled. Although this function was optional for 10 Mb/s repeater ports connected to mixing media (i.e., coax), it was made mandatory for 10BASE-T and 10BASE-F repeater ports. Commercial products in the market universally implement this feature for all ports, although some very old legacy repeaters that do not may still be in service.

Delay and Inter-Packet Gap (IPG) Shrinkage

While repeaters are extremely valuable devices which allow the network span to be increased and different choices of media to be interconnected, they do introduce some other effects which must be accounted for when building large networks. Two primary effects must be considered. The first is that the repeater introduces delay into the network signal as it propagates from one port to another. This delay must be factored into the overall round-trip delay (or slot time, as defined in the "Media Access Control (MAC) Sublayer" section) of the network. The second effect is referred to as "interpacket gap shrinkage" (IPG shrinkage). The main cause of IPG shrinkage is the variability of the delay path through the repeater for back-to-back packets.

In order to understand the effect of IPG shrinkage, consider the example shown in Figure 2-14, where two packets are issued from a transmitting station with minimum IPG (9.6 μs or 96 bit times). When the first packet reaches the MAU attached to a repeater, the MAU will take a finite time to recognize the signal, and pass it to the repeater unit over the AUI (or its logical equivalent). The repeater unit will also introduce a finite start-up delay before it commences retransmission to the MAU(s) connected to its other port(s), and similarly the MAU(s) will introduce some start-up delay before the packet is retransmitted onto the other connected network(s). Assume that the cumulative delay on the first packet accounts for some 15 bit times. So, 15 bit times after the receiving port observes the last bit of the first packet, the output port(s) will cease retransmission. After the 96-bit-time IPG interval, the first bit of the second packet arrives at the MAU on the receiving port. However, in this case the packet experiences only a 10-bit-time delay before it is repeated on the output ports. Although the IPG time is 9.6 μs on the receiving port, the retransmitted IPG is shortened by the difference in delay experienced on the two packets. Hence in this case the repeated IPG will be only 91 bit times. If the retransmitted packets subsequently suffer a similar effect at another repeater in the end-to-end signal path, the effect could be cumulative and reduce the IPG further.

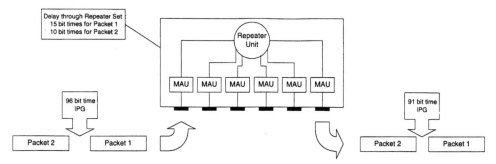

Figure 2-14 IPG Shrinkage Example

The period of silence provided by the IPG interval allows the clock recovery circuits within the DTEs and repeaters to "recover" and effectively re-lock to the known good local frequency. If the IPG becomes too small, DTEs and repeaters may not be able to re-acquire lock to the incoming packet and may decode some of the packet data incorrectly.

The basic outcome of both the repeater delay and IPG shrinkage issues is that the number of repeaters permitted in the end-to-end path of the network must be restricted. The rules for sizing the network appropriately are covered in more detail in the section "Mixed Topologies."

Management

Since the repeater is centrally located, and all traffic received from any segment connected to it is repeated to all other segments, the repeater is an excellent place to monitor traffic conditions and locate network management tasks. Topologies that rely on repeaters for connectivity, such as 10BASE-T and 10BASE-F, are ideal candidates for centralized network management and administration.

By specifying the type and accuracy of key statistics to be monitored in the repeater and providing a method of reading and/or setting these statistics, as well as generating alert messages from the repeater, a remote network management process can gather and react to performance information accumulated in the repeater(s).

The specification for the statistics to be monitored were first published in the IEEE 802.3k supplement,[12] which is covered in more detail in the "Repeater Management" section.

A key differentiating feature of Ethernet is that all management features are optional. Most other network technologies, such as Token Ring, need some rudimentary management capabilities to make setup and operation easier. FDDI in fact mandates substantial network management capabilities (called Station Management), which substantially complicates the complexity and cost of the implementation. The approach in Ethernet is to allow no management, but, where management is provided, to specify it such that it is consistent and interoperable across multiple vendors' equipment.

The gathering of these statistics, and the communication between a remote management process and the management "agent" (the intelligent process in the repeater which gathers statistics and responds to network manager generated commands or requests), are performed by either "in-band" or "out-of-band" communications. In-band communications is generally much more popular in medium-to-large network installations. The network itself is used to carry the information between the agent and the manager in the form of normal Ethernet packets. Out-of-band communications uses any other form of non-Ethernet related communications method, such as a serial port connection. In either case, a management protocol is employed and overlaid on top of the actual physical communications method to allow management data to be exchanged. By far the most popular management protocol in use today is the Simple Network Management Protocol (SNMP), defined in RFC 1157[13]. This is discussed in very broad terms in the "Network Management Overview" section in Chapter 4. and in detail in the references cited therein.

---

[12] Institute of Electrical and Electronic Engineers, Local and Metropolitan Area Networks—Layer Management for 10 Mb/s Repeaters (Section 19), IEEE Std. 802.3k (Supplement to ISO/IEC 8802.3:1992 [ANSI/IEEE Std. 802.3:1992 Edition]), IEEE, New York, NY November 2, 1992

[13] RFC 1157 Simple Network Management Protocol (SNMP).

2.5.2 Vendor-Differentiated Repeater Functions

Repeater Implementations

Actual implementations of repeater products have broken into different classes, dependent primarily on features and form factor. There are three main categories of products: non-modular, modular, and "stackable." Examples of each are shown in Figure 2-15a, b, and c, respectively.

Figure 2-15a Non-Modular Repeater

Figure 2-15b Modular Repeater

Figure 2-15c "Stackable" Repeaters

Non-Modular

These repeaters are fixed-port-count boxes, with port densities generally in the 6-to-24 range. They normally have only one type of media supported, such as 10BASE-T (by far the most common), although they typically provide an AUI or coax port in addition (as shown in Figure 2-12, for instance). Management may not be provided, other than simple status and/or fault indicators for each port and for the unit as a whole. They are not expandable, other than that a port of one box can be connected to a port of another box. Simply cascading repeaters using this type of daisy-chain topology has some disadvantages. The total number of repeaters allowed in the end-to-end path of the network is governed by specific rules in the 802.3 standards to ensure network operation (this is covered in the "Mixed Topologies" section). By daisy-chaining repeaters, this number may be quickly exceeded in a larger network. However, these types of repeaters are very popular for small business and/or home networks, since they are inexpensive and simple to configure and operate (in general they are "plug-and-play"). They are also popular as "port expanders," used to provide several connections in a location where only a single connection was initially provisioned.

Modular

Modular repeaters generally consist of a multislot chassis unit which can be populated by a series of different personality cards, dependent on the network needs. Typically these personality cards consist not only of Ethernet modules, but also other LAN technologies such as Token Ring, FDDI, etc. The different modules are interconnected by a series of backplane signals in the chassis, allowing the various cards to interact with each other (the seamlessness of this integration is has become another vendor-differentiation feature). In order to allow interconnection between these technologies, other internetworking features are typically provided, such as bridge and/or router modules, as well as advanced management capabilities. See the "Bridge Definition" and "Router Definition" sections for an overview of these capabilities. Other sophisticated fault-tolerance features are frequently provided, such as redundant power supplies.

These devices clearly are more than just Ethernet repeaters, but typically Ethernet is provided as either one or more collision domains in the chassis to support large port densities, typically in the 48- to 200-port range. These high-featured units are generally used in large network installations, where port density, in-band management, and high-availability features are paramount.

Stackable

Stackable repeaters essentially combine the most attractive features of the modular and non-modular products. The form factor is of fixed-port-count stand-alone boxes, but these can be "stacked" in order to increase port density, so the network can grow gradually, allowing the network administrator to adopt a "pay-as-you-grow" approach. The separate boxes are usually interconnected using a special cable. This, in the better examples of these implementations, allows multiple boxes to be interconnected but ensures that the entire stack appears (in terms of signal delay) as a single repeater. This is a significant advantage over the typical non-modular implementation, and it means that modular and stackable repeaters essentially compete for the same customer base.

Stackable repeaters typically only permit one technology to be implemented in the stack, so in mixed LAN environments they may have some disadvantages by comparison with a modular chassis. However, virtually all management and fault-tolerant features can be provided in stackables (albeit usually as options over the base configuration), and they offer a simple migration path which is usually cheaper up-front. This is simply because the network administrator does not have to purchase a large chassis to provide future expansion, initially populating it with only a few modules.

Additional Management

While the IEEE 802.3k Supplement defined the management requirements for 10 Mb/s repeaters (subsequently amended, as 100 Mb/s and Gb/s Ethernet Standards were developed), most vendors offer additional management features in their managed repeaters. Note, however, that there is still a large market for extremely low cost repeaters that have no standards-based management capabilities.

Most of these enhancements are standardized by the IETF and are published as RFCs. Each management-related RFC identifies the Management Information Base (MIB) that a particular type of management device should provide. In fact, the 802.3k Supplement was also adopted as the base document for the Repeater MIB, first published as RFC 1516. Other notable RFCs related to repeaters are the MAU MIB (RFC 1515) and the RMON MIB (Remote Network Management MIB, RFC 1757).

In addition to RFC-based MIBs, many vendors have added vendor-specific extensions to their repeaters, such as the ability to learn the topology of the network and devices connected to it. A network management station can read this data from each repeater and then build a complete graphical representation of the network. However, it should be noted that advanced features such as these often do not work between different vendors' equipment, so all repeaters may have to be from the same vendor in order to provide the complete range of advanced management facilities.

Security

Network security is a much larger topic in itself than is intended to be covered in this overview. However, with specific regard to repeaters, several vendors offer features which we will generically refer to as "repeater security."

With a multiport repeater, packets received at an input port are repeated to all output ports. This repeating operation is performed to essentially mimic the performance of a shared cable system, where every device can observe the transmission of all other devices. However, in reality, most traffic is destined only for a single device (in the case of unicast traffic).

Two main types of security are offered in repeaters; often both are implemented.

"Eavesdrop protection" makes use of the fact that unicast traffic is single source to single destination. The repeater learns the addresses of the stations attached to each of its ports by copying the source addresses from packets received on the port.[14] Each 48-bit source address detected on a port is conversely the destination address for packets addressed to that station. Utilizing knowledge of which stations are connected to which ports, when a packet is received at a port, the repeater "looks up" the destination address to see if it is known in the table of learned addresses for its ports. If it is known on a particular port, the packet is repeated to that port only, while an alternative data packet is transmitted to all the other ports. So a repeater implementing eavesdrop protection does nothing to increase bandwidth: even though no valid packet data is presented on the unauthorized ports, packet activity must be present. The reason that a different packet is transmitted to all other ports is to ensure that the stations attached to those ports observe network activity, so the carrier sense part of the CSMA/CD access protocol still operates correctly. If no activity were presented to the other ports, a station attached to one of those ports might believe the network was inactive and start its own packet transmission. Now the repeater would be faced with the fact that it has two receive ports active, which we have already discussed as a collision condition.

So eavesdrop protection uses the simple port/destination address association of packets to repeat a normal copy of the packet to one port, while sending a modified packet to the other ports. The way it actually operates is a little more complex in practice. As a packet is received (starting with preamble), the repeating process commences to all ports in order to meet the delay specifications required of the repeater. As the next fields are received (SFD and DA), these too are repeated normally. Once the entire DA field is received, the repeater can commence the lookup operation to see if the DA is known to a particular port. Once the lookup has been performed, and assuming the DA was known on a specific port, the other ports have the data stream to them essentially corrupted, whereas the port to which the packet is destined has the packet repeated normally. The bit time delay from the receive port to the retransmitted ports is normally sufficient that, with a fast look-up process, the repeater can commence corruption to the required ports prior to the complete transmission of the SA field.

---

[14] Address Tracking Over Repeater Based Networks, US Patent 5,414,694, Issued May 9, 1995, Ian S. Crayford, William Lo, Nader Vijeh.

Hence anyone trying to listen to information on the network by connecting to a secure repeater port will only see packets that are addressed to stations attached to that port, while observing corrupted data for packets not addressed to a station on that port. This is very useful in topologies like 10BASE-T, where only a single end station is connected to a repeater port.

However, eavesdrop protection is not perfect, due primarily to practical complexity and cost considerations. For one thing, there may be literally hundreds of stations connected to some ports. This occurs not only in the case of ports which have multidrop coax segments attached, but also where two repeaters are connected together. In this case, the inter-repeater ports would need to learn all of the addresses that were attached to the other repeater. This is generally impractical due to lookup table size restrictions. Typically, the inter-repeater link ports have the disrupt capability disabled, so all packets travel this path uncorrupted. While this potentially compromises security for that link, it is normally a reasonable assumption that if security were important, this single link could be protected by physical security. For instance, it could be located inside a locked wiring closet, accessible only to authorized personnel.

Another potential problem is the fact that, as described, the eavesdrop-protection approach works only for unicast traffic. Broadcast traffic by definition must be repeated throughout the entire Ethernet collision domain, so it must be retransmitted normally to all ports of the repeater. Multicast traffic is also typically repeated to all ports, although more sophisticated lookup algorithms can associate the multicast address with only the ports that require it. This multiport address association is more complex to implement and often requires management intervention to manually assign the port map association.[15]

Finally, with respect to eavesdrop protection, we have not discussed any of the aspects of controlling the secure repeater's address-learning process. With no restrictions, any address could be learned, and therefore an unauthorized user (often referred to as a "malicious user") could potentially break into the secured network by simply transmitting packets using the address of a known user, or a whole series of addresses as random guesses of user addresses.

"Intrusion control" is the second type of repeater security method, which can be used to overcome malicious users. It can also be used to keep track of network topology changes. The intrusion-control mechanism relies on the fact that a station's address should only appear on one port of the repeater. Again, this is especially useful in the case of 10BASE-T, where in general a single end station will be connected to a repeater port.

---

[15] Programmable Disrupt of Multicast Packets for Secure Networks, US Patent: 5,539,737, Issued: July 23, 1996, William Lo, Ian Crayford.

Typically the repeater learns addresses for a specified period of time and then disables learning. It may alternatively use a defined table of authorized addresses to preload its lookup table and not perform the learning process (this is generally difficult to maintain in a real network, where there may be frequent moves, additions, and changes). In either case, the repeater has a list of the permissible station addresses and the associations of those addresses with its ports. If a new and previously unknown address appears, this can be easily detected. What action is taken after the detection will vary, dependent on the implementation and/or the degree of security required.

In some cases, a simple alert message may be generated from the repeater, saying that a new address has appeared on a particular port. In more security-sensitive installations the repeater port may be physically disabled, preventing all packet reception and transmission until the new address is authorized. Alternatively, this may be a known and authorized address, but it has moved from one port to another on the repeater. Again, this may be permissible, resulting in a message to allow a network administrator to simply update records, or it may be unauthorized, in which case the port(s) involved can be disabled.

These eavesdrop-protection and intrusion-control capabilities, in order to be useful, require the use of network management. For example, specific ports should have the eavesdrop-protection or intrusion-control capability enabled or disabled, and the address-learning process needs to be administered to allow new addresses to be authorized.

In summary, secure repeaters are useful, but they do place a significant burden on the network administrator to monitor and administer the addition of new addresses. In addition, they provide only a single level of security for all LAN traffic based on the unique 48-bit address of the station. In contrast, a large corporate network may require several levels of security, with some LAN traffic transmitted "in the clear." To provide more comprehensive and flexible security, methods such as password protection, encryption, etc. should be used either instead of or in conjunction with secure repeaters.

Topology Extension

The number of repeater "hops" that are permitted in the end-to-end path of a packet is governed by a series of topology rules. These are discussed in more detail in the "Mixed Topologies" section later in this chapter. The basic premise is that for collision detection to work correctly, the maximum path delay of the network must be constrained. Repeaters are one of the sources of delay in the network, due to the delay from receipt of a packet on one port to its retransmission on the other port(s). Hence the maximum number of repeaters in the path must also be constrained. A review of the overall delays is too detailed for this section.

When the repeater was first specified in 802.3, implementations were assumed to be based primarily on discrete components, so the allocation of delays for 10 Mb/s repeaters was made accordingly. Subsequent advances in silicon integration and speed capabilities have enabled vendors to implement repeaters with substantially reduced delays. This in turn means that, in some cases, the total number of repeaters in the maximum delay path of the network can be increased. Alternatively, the delay budget saved by the faster repeaters may be apportioned to another delay contributor in the network path, such as the cable delay (i.e., allowing a longer cable run).

2.6 Bridge Definition

Bridges are devices that operate at the MAC sublayer level, above the PHY layer at which the repeater operates. Bridge operation is defined by the IEEE 802.1D Standard.[16] The bridge may connect together identical MAC technologies (such as Ethernet to Ethernet) or dissimilar ones (such as Ethernet to Token Ring). A bridge uses the destination-address and source-address information contained in frames to attempt to make a more intelligent forwarding decision, rather than just duplicate each receive frame to all other ports (called "flooding" in bridge terminology).

The simplest bridge is a two-port device. In the case of an Ethernet-to-Ethernet bridge, the device not only allows extension of the physical network topology, it also isolates the "subnetworks" on each port into separate "collision domains". This means that a collision that occurs on one side of the bridge is not transferred to the other. Only valid MAC frames that appear on one subnetwork and are addressed to a node on the other subnetwork, are propagated through the bridge.

2.6.1 Local and Remote Bridges

If the device is a "local bridge," both the MAC functions will typically reside in the same physical enclosure and be internally connected by a high-speed bus/processor subsystem. Packets received on one port of the bridge will have the destination address field inspected, normally by a processor, compared against an internal set of stored addresses (the "filtering database"), and forwarded to one, several, all, or none of the other ports, dependent on the result of this comparison.

---

[16] American National Standards Institute/Institute of Electrical and Electronics Engineers, Information Technology—Telecommunications and information exchange between systems—Local area networks—Media access control (MAC) bridges, ISO/IEC 10038:1993 (E) ANSI/IEEE Std 802.1D, 1993 Edition, IEEE, New York, NY, July 8, 1993.

A "remote bridge" effectively converts the MAC protocol to another type of communications protocol, allowing two remote bridge devices to be connected together using a long-distance communications system, capable of achieving far greater distances than those possible with conventional LAN technology. A simple example is shown in Figure 2-16. The remote bridges are typically connected by a telephone or leased-line link. In this case, since the communications link will almost certainly be much slower than the LAN (e.g., 64 kb/s), the true benefit of transferring only those packets which are destined for a device on the remote subnetwork are readily observed. However, other issues, such as "chatty" protocols (protocols which make extensive use of multicast and/or broadcast traffic), still mean there may be substantial "overhead" traffic over the slow-speed (and often tariffed) link, making a "remote router" a preferable product. This is discussed in the section on "Layer 3 Switch Definition" in Chapter 3.

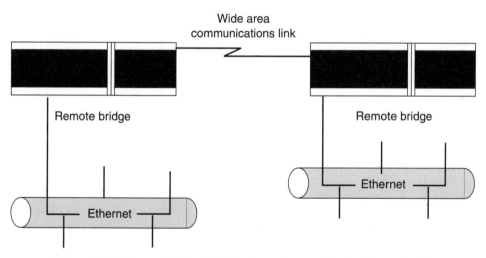

Figure 2-16 Remote Bridge Linking Two Geographically Distant LANs

2.6.2 Bridge Functions

The detailed mechanisms by which packets are known to be addressed to a remote subnetwork are outside the scope of this overview. However, an overview is appropriate. Although the preceding discussion focused on two-port bridges, multiport bridges are far more common. For additional details on the full operation and definition of bridges, refer to the 802.1D Standard.[17] In addition, the operation of fast (primarily hardware-optimized) multiport bridges is discussed in the "Layer 2 Switch Definition" section in Chapter 3.

Filtering, Learning, and Forwarding

The key function of the bridge is to isolate local traffic within a particular subnetwork. The bridge attempts to forward frames received on one port to the other bridge port(s) only if the destination MAC address contained in the frame does not exist on the received port.

The filtering process is responsible for comparing the destination and source address of received frames with the filtering database. The filtering database contains the 48-bit address entries, the port associations of the stations known to be connected to its ports, and the status of those ports. Some of the database entries are static, such as specially reserved addresses used for configuration and management frames that the bridge is required to respond to. Other address entries in the filtering database are dynamic and are actually learned by the bridge and instantiated into the tables.

The learning process is the mechanism by which new addresses are identified and the filtering database is updated. When a packet is received on a bridge port, the bridge's filtering process is responsible for determining whether the DA contained in the packet matches a station address known in the filtering database. If the address is known and identified as present on a port other than the original receive port, it will be forwarded to the port(s) that are identified by the filtering database and are in a state that permits forwarding. Note that several conditions may cause a bridge not to forward a packet to a port, even though the station address may be allocated to that port in the filtering database.

Learning is actually achieved by monitoring the SA of received frames. Since the received-frame SA contains the MAC address of a station, this information allows both the port association and the 48-bit MAC station address to be entered into the filtering database. A packet received on a bridge port, having an SA field that does not match any of the entries in the filtering database, results in an "unknown SA" classification and will be learned, given the restrictions of the physical size of the filtering database.

A packet received on a bridge port, having a DA field that does not match any of the entries in the filtering database, results in an "unknown DA" classification. Since a frame with an unknown DA will not yield a port identity for forwarding, the frame is forwarded to all ports that are in a suitable state. This is referred to as "flooding." Until a specific SA and port association can be detected and learned from a re-

---

[17] American National Standards Institute/Institute of Electrical and Electronics Engineers, Information Technology—Telecommunications and information exchange between systems—Local area networks—Media access control (MAC) bridges, ISO/IEC 10038:1993 (E) ANSI/IEEE Std 802.1D, 1993 Edition, IEEE, New York, NY, July 8, 1993.

ceive packet, the filtering database will be unable to resolve any packet addressed to that station (MAC) address. This will result in flooding to all (available) ports until the address is learned by the filtering database.

An address-aging process is also applied to the filtering database. Since any filtering database will be constrained in the number of address/port entries due to physical memory and cost constraints, entries are flushed from the table if there has been no activity from that address for a specific time. This allows newly learned addresses to be instantiated in the database.

Filtering, learning, and forwarding are all key performance parameters that bridge vendors use to differentiate their products.

The 802.1D Standard specifies the operation of "store-and-forward" bridges. In this type of bridge, the entire frame must be received before the filtering and forwarding processes are commenced. This allows the frame to be discarded at the receive port if it fails CRC integrity, avoiding unnecessary filtering and/or forwarding.

A specific type of bridge that is often implemented but not covered by the 802.1D Standard is a "cut-through" bridge. In this device, as a frame is received on one subnetwork port, filtering and forwarding to the destination port(s) is commenced prior to reception of the entire received frame. To achieve this, the address comparison must be performed as soon as possible during the frame reception, and the retransmission is commenced immediately, before the receive frame completes. The immediate-retransmission aspect assumes that the destination medium is available, requiring the transmitting port(s) to be idle, and that the IPG interval has expired. The advantage of this approach is that the delay through the bridge is minimized, important in some large installations where several bridges may be included in the end-to-end signal path. The disadvantage is that some frames are unnecessarily forwarded, resulting in increased bandwidth utilization at the destination subnetwork. For instance, a frame with a CRC error, or a packet which experiences a normal collision (within the slot time), may be forwarded to the destination sub-network on the basis of the address comparison, even though it is of no value. The 802.1D Standard requires that a receive frame is completed and verified prior to any retransmission.

Spanning Tree Algorithm

Spanning Tree is specified within the IEEE 802.1D Standard. Additionally, excellent tutorial references are available on its origins and operation.[18]

---

[18] Interconnection—Bridges and Routers, Radia Perlman. Addison-Wesley Professional Computing Series. ISBN 0-200-56332-0, Chapter 3.

The Spanning Tree algorithm is a packet-based protocol that permits bridges to dynamically discover a bridged topology and configure the network to ensure connectivity without loops (a "tree" structure). Avoidance of loops is very important in bridged networks for several reasons. Two key reasons are:

- A bridge will flood a frame to many ports if it is unknown or (generally) if it is a broadcast frame. This flooding may be replicated to another bridge, which may also replicate it. If these bridges have more than one interconnection (a loop), this may perpetuate or even replicate to eventually consume all the available bandwidth of the LANs (in the case of a broadcast, this is often referred to as a "broadcast storm").

- Bridge networks (unlike router protocols) do not contain any "hop-count" information. This goes hand-in-hand with the previous item. Routers keep track of the hop count, incrementing it each time it passes through a router, and deleting the frame once it exceeds a specified maximum.

Basically, Spanning Tree requires all bridges to pass specific configuration information, which is used to determine a "root" bridge and the distance or cost of the path(s) to this root bridge. If there are multiple paths between any other bridge and the root bridge, the Spanning Tree protocol chooses the lowest-cost path and blocks the duplicate(s) to ensure that there is only one physically active path to the root bridge.

Although this sounds complicated, Spanning Tree is based on simple concepts. If Spanning Tree has any deficiencies, these are largely due to the inherent performance of the bridged networks it is designed to optimize, rather than an implicit limitation of the algorithm itself.

Bridges use normal frames (with special content), to exchange Spanning Tree configuration information. These frame are defined to as Bridge Protocol Data Units (BPDUs). The BPDUs are exchanged between bridges and contain information to allow the root bridge and path cost to the root bridge to be calculated. The root bridge is defined as having the lowest 48-bit MAC address, which it advertises in the BPDU, compared with any other bridge. The distance/cost to the root bridge is also chosen to minimize the configuration parameters that are exchanged in the BPDUs.

This minimization—to seek the root bridge and select the designated path to the root bridge, based on the contents of the BPDU frame—allows the Spanning Tree protocol to reconfigure the network in the event that a bridge or a primary link to the root bridge fails. BPDUs are constantly exchanged to minimize the time that the network takes to reconfigure in the event of a failure. In addition, time-out values are invoked for receipt of BPDUs in order to ensure that, in the event the root bridge fails, the network will reconfigure. However, practical limitations mean that relatively long time-outs are required (compared with typical PHY and MAC parameters) in order to avoid a single packet loss causing the entire network to reconfigure, only to attempt to resume the original configuration once the next BPDU is transferred correctly.

2.7 Router Definition

Routers are devices that operate at the Network layer level (Layer 3), above the PHY and MAC sublayers at which both repeaters and bridges operate. Router operation is outside the scope of the IEEE 802 standards body, but is briefly discussed here for completeness. A router is generally capable of connecting disparate LAN technologies (iEthernet, Token Ring, AppleTalk®, etc.) as well as different protocol types (IP, IPX, DECnet, AppleTalk®, etc.). However, routers obviously may be optimized to support a minimal number of LAN technologies and/or protocols Routers use the network protocol type as well as the network layer address information contained in frames to attempt to make a more intelligent forwarding decision, eliminating issues such as broadcast storms in bridged networks.

Routers use complex protocols, normally executed in software on a processor, to perform the routing (forwarding) decision between ports as well as maintain current the state of the routing tables which determine the optimal paths for packets to be routed.

Routers are better able to deal with redundant links and to isolate specific protocols to specific ports, which bridges are unable to perform at the MAC sublayer level.

Since early implementations of routers were software and processor intensive, their performance was generally limited, so they were unable to forward frames at the maximum line rate. This was exemplified by the fact that multiple protocols were in common use and that many networks vendors wanted to continue to promulgate proprietary protocols. This meant that the LAN industry as a whole was unable to coalesce around a small number of strategic protocols.

As LAN and processor technology developed, a different approach was required. Industry trends eventually forced rationalization of the disparate protocol war, driven primarily by the World Wide Web phenomenon. These developments are discussed in more detail in the "Layer 3 Switching Definition" section in Chapter 4.

2.8 Media and Topology Options

Each topology detailed within the 802.3 specifications is defined using a specific nomenclature. For instance, Ethernet (thick coaxial cable) is defined as 10BASE5 (pronounced "ten-base-five"). This actually defines some of the key aspects of the network. The "10" is the network data rate (10 Mb/s). The "BASE" refers to the fact that baseband signaling is employed. The "5" is the maximum segment length in 100 m units and rounded off (500 m for thick Ethernet). So Cheapernet, which is defined as 10BASE2 (thin coaxial cable), is 10 Mb/s, baseband, 200 m (the distance is actually limited to 185 m, but is rounded up).

Additions to the 802.3 suite of standards from a media and topology-extension point of view have allowed the use of Unshielded Twisted Pair (UTP) and fiber optic media. Both of these break the previous nomenclature rules and cause some confusion.

The UTP standard is defined as 10BASE-T,[19] and is 10 Mb/s, baseband, using twisted-pair cable. The target cable length defined by the 10BASE-T standard is 100 m, although distances that exceed this are permitted if the cable is of higher quality than specified. The 10BASE-T specification received official approval as an 802.3 Standard in September 1990 and was first published as the 802.3i Supplement.[20] Although several proprietary "Twisted-Pair Ethernet" solutions appeared during the late 1980s, virtually all UTP solutions quickly migrated to the standard version.

Specifications for the use of a fiber optic medium are somewhat complicated by the fact that four categories are defined. These are FOIRL (Fiber Optic Inter Repeater Link),[21] 10BASE-FL (Fiber Link), 10BASE-FB (Fiber Backbone), and 10BASE-FP (Fiber Passive).[22] Since there are various lengths for these, they will be discussed in more detail within this section under the headings "Fiber Optic" and "Mixed Topologies." The FOIRL specification was approved as an 802.3 Standard in 1987. The 10BASE-FB/FL/FP specifications were the latest media additions to the 802.3 suite and were approved as formal 802.3 standards in 1993.

[19] American National Standards Institute/Institute of Electrical and Electronics Engineers, Information Technology—Local and Metropolitan Area Networks—Part 3: Carrier sense multiple access with collision detection (CSMA/CD) access method and physical layer specifications, ISO/IEC 8802-3:1996 (E) ANSI/IEEE Std 802.3, 1996 Edition, IEEE, New York, NY, July 29, 1996. Section 14.

[20] Institute of Electrical and Electronics Engineers, Local and Metropolitan Area Networks—System Considerations for Multisegment 10 Mb/s Baseband Networks and Twisted-Pair Medium Attachment Unit (MAU) and Baseband Medium, Type 10BASE-T (Sections 13 and 14), IEEE Std. 802.3i-1990 (Supplement to ISO/IEC 8802-3: 1990) (ANSI/IEEE Std 802.3, 1990 Edition), IEEE, New York, NY, December 31, 1990.

[21] American National Standards Institute/Institute of Electrical and Electronics Engineers, Information Technology - Local and Metropolitan Area Networks—Part 3: Carrier sense multiple access with collision detection (CSMA/CD) access method and physical layer specifications, ISO/IEC 8802-3:1996 (E) ANSI/IEEE Std 802.3, 1996 Edition, IEEE, New York, NY, July 29, 1996. Section 9.9.

[22] Institute of Electrical and Electronics Engineers, *Local and Metropolitan Area Networks—Fiber Optic Active and Passive Star-Based Segments, Type 10BASE-F (Sections 15-18)*, IEEE Std. 802.3j-1993 (Supplement to ISO/IEC 8802-3: 1993) (ANSI/IEEE Std 802.3, 1993 Edition), IEEE, New York, NY, October 12, 1993.

Other standards of note are StarLAN (1BASE5)[23] and broadband (10BROAD36).[24] StarLAN provides a 1 Mb/s data rate and employs UTP cable. However, due to the relatively high cost of connecting this into existing 10 Mb/s Ethernet networks (requiring a "store-and-forward" device such as a bridge or router), this particular implementation gained minimal popularity. The advent of 10BASE-T (discussed later in detail), providing the full 10 Mb/s Ethernet data rate over UTP cable, essentially stalled any significant deployment of StarLAN. 10BROAD36 (10 Mb/s, broadband, 3.6 km) allows the use of CATV (Community Antenna Television) or cable-TV type interconnection components to provide an 802.3 compatible network. Due to their very small comparative market share, neither of these derivatives of 802.3 will be discussed further.

2.8.1 Coaxial

Traditional Ethernet (802.3, 10BASE5) and Cheapernet (802.3, 10BASE2) are coaxial-wired systems (Figure 2-17). The coaxial cable provides the linear bus to which all nodes are connected. Signaling is accomplished by means of a current sink technique, using the center conductor for signal and the shield as a ground reference.

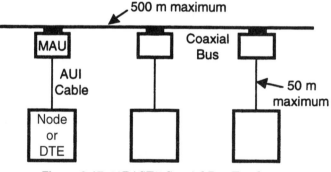

Figure 2-17 10BASE5 Coaxial Bus Topology

---

[23] American National Standards Institute/Institute of Electrical and Electronics Engineers, Information Technology—Local and Metropolitan Area Networks—Part 3: Carrier sense multiple access with collision detection (CSMA/CD) access method and physical layer specifications, ISO/IEC 8802-3:1996 (E) ANSI/IEEE Std 802.3, 1996 Edition, IEEE, New York, NY, July 29, 1996. Section 12.

[24] American National Standards Institute/Institute of Electrical and Electronics Engineers, Information Technology—Local and Metropolitan Area Networks—Part 3: Carrier sense multiple access with collision detection (CSMA/CD) access method and physical layer specifications, ISO/IEC 8802-3:1996 (E) ANSI/IEEE Std 802.3, 1996 Edition, IEEE, New York, NY, July 29, 1996. Section 11.

10BASE5 ("Thick" Ethernet)

10BASE5 was the original architecture defined by the DEC/Intel/Xerox (DIX) consortium and adopted by the IEEE 802.3 committee. The topology is far from friendly from a cost, installation, and maintenance point of view. The cable is thick (approximately 10 mm or 3/8 in.) and does not easily bend. It is generally installed in the above-ceiling or below-floor space, with the actual connection to the node (DTE) taking place via an Attachment Unit Interface (AUI) cable. This is a multipair cable that provides the required signal and power connections between the network node (DTE) and the Medium Attachment Unit (MAU), which is located on the coaxial cable (Figure 2-17). The AUI cable can be a maximum of 50 m long and is connected at each end with 15-pin "D-type" connectors, familiar in most computer applications. The MAU converts the digital signals from the DTE to the current drive required to signal over the coaxial bus. The 10BASE5 MAU is typically clamped to the coax cable, and integral probes pierce the cable to make connection to the inner center conductor and surrounding (but insulated) shield. This mechanism is often referred to as an extrusive or "vampire" tap connector (see Figure 2-25). An alternate intrusive tap mechanism requires the coaxial bus to be cut and connectorized; then two coaxial connectors provided on the intrusive MAU are used to rejoin the cable and connect into it.

10BASE5 specifies a maximum cable length of 500 m, a maximum number of nodes of 100, and a minimum separation distance between MAUs on the coax of 2.5 m. The length and node count can be increased by the use of repeaters (explained in more detail later), which allow multiple cable segments to be connected together.

In today's modern office environment this topology is difficult to work with. Even simple changes may require access to the coaxial cable, movement of the MAU, and rerouting of the AUI cable. The AUI cable is itself almost as thick as the coaxial cable. With an intrusive tap, the entire network will have to be broken and reconnected—clearly not a preferable situation. The vampire tap is a complex connector mechanism and is therefore relatively difficult to install and requires trained installation staff. New installations virtually never used this topology after the advent of 10BASE-T. However, despite its limitations, a significant installed base of 10BASE5 was built during the early years of Ethernet deployment, so this topology can still be found. These are primarily in older backbone applications, where the 500-m distance is an advantage and relatively few devices are directly connected.

10BASE2 (Cheapernet)

In order to alleviate many of the cost and installation difficulties associated with thick coax, the 10BASE2 Standard was defined to allow the use of thin coax, frequently referred to as "Cheapernet" or "Thin-net."

In 10BASE2, the fundamental difference is that the cable is brought to the DTE, and the MAU is (typically) integrated into the network node, eliminating the need for the AUI connectors and cables (Figure 2-18). The thin coax cable is much more flexible, due to its smaller diameter (approximately 5 mm), and can therefore be brought directly to the desktop system—either dropped down from the ceiling or picked up from the floor. The MAU connection to the coaxial bus is also simpler, requiring the use of a simple "T" or "BNC" (Bayonet-Neill-Concelman) connector (see Figure 2-26).

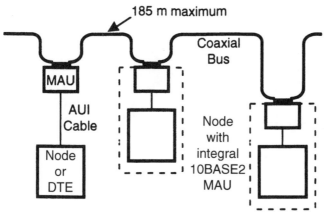

Figure 2-18 10BASE2 Coaxial Bus Topology

However, use of the cheaper cable has some drawbacks, since some of the key electrical properties are degraded over those exhibited by thick coax. As a direct result, the 10BASE2 Standard specifies a maximum cable length of 185 m, a maximum number of nodes of 30, and a minimum separation distance between MAUs of 0.5 m. Similarly to 10BASE5, the length and node count can be increased by the use of repeaters.

The distance limitation was still adequate for most office-size installations and initially led to the widespread deployment of Cheapernet-based networks, especially in the desktop Personal Computer (PC) connectivity arena. This was largely due to the fact that the connectors (BNC type), cable (RG58 A/U or RG58 C/U), and PC-compatible Ethernet adapter cards are all widely available and fairly simple to install with minimal training. While Cheapernet remains a popular choice for small networks (small business and even home offices), the advent of 10BASE-T soon meant that 10BASE2 shipments were eclipsed by those of 10BASE-T in the early 1990s.

A special cautionary note is worth adding in the case of 10BASE2, in that the specification requires that no more than 30 mating pairs be present. This may permit 30 nodes to be connected if no other breaks (requiring additional connectors) have been made in the cable. Each BNC "T" connector must be located at the MAU; it is not permitted to place the "T" in the Cheapernet coax and run a coax stub or drop cable to the MAU. Figure 2-26 shows a typical 10BASE2 stand-alone MAU application.

Although the AUI is not externally needed, many 10BASE2 products are offered with the option to bypass the integrated 10BASE2 MAU, and they provide an AUI connector to allow access to a remotely located MAU (such as a 10BASE5 or 10BASE-T version) via a standard AUI cable/connector.

2.8.2 Twisted Pair (10BASE-T)

Twisted Pair Ethernet (802.3 10BASE-T) is able to use standard voice-grade telephone cable (22–26 gauge), employing separate transmit and receive pairs (four wires).[25] The system uses a star topology with a "repeater" at the center of the star (Figure 2-19). The repeater (or hub) performs signal-amplitude and timing restoration (the repeater is described more exactly in the "Repeater Definition" section). It takes the incoming bit stream and repeats it to all other ports connected to it (but not back to the originating port). In this sense, the repeater acts as "logical coax," so that any node connected to the network will see another node's transmission. Differential signaling is employed, with one pair acting as the transmit path and the other as receive. Further introductory material on the 10BASE-T Standard and its primary differences from the earlier 10BASE2 and 10BASE5 coaxial topologies is available in various publications.[26,27]

Notice that the two-pair cable requires a crossover connector, which swaps the pairs such that the transmit pair at one end of the cable is connected to the receive pair at the other end. This allows the MDI connector at either end to retain the same signal/pin configuration. However, many repeaters (and other internetworking devices) incorporate the crossover function internal to the MDI, in which case this is defined as an MDI-X connector (and should be labeled as such on the equipment). This removes the need for a separate crossover in the cable plant. Only one crossover is re-

[25] American National Standards Institute/Institute of Electrical and Electronics Engineers, Information Technology—Local and Metropolitan Area Networks—Part 3: Carrier sense multiple access with collision detection (CSMA/CD) access method and physical layer specifications, ISO/IEC 8802-3:1996 (E) ANSI/IEEE Std 802.3, 1996 Edition, IEEE, New York, NY, July 29, 1996. Section 14.

[26] I. Crayford, 10BASE-T In The Office, Wescon, Nov 19–21, 1990, San Francisco, *Wescon Conference Record*, pp. 232–237, Western Periodicals Company, Ventura, CA.

[27] R. Anderson and K. Woods, 10BASE-T Ethernet: The Second Wave, *Data Communications*, Vol. 19, No. 15, pp. 49–64 (November 21, 1990).

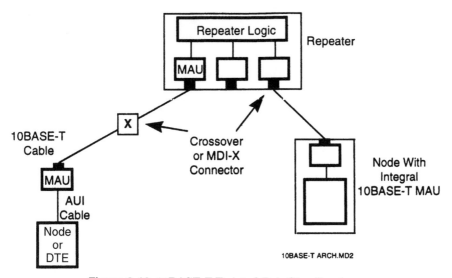

Figure 2-19 10BASE-T Twisted-Pair Star Topology

quired in each cable (although, technically, an odd number of crossovers will work, but installation and maintenance become very difficult with multiple crossovers in the signal path).

Since separate transmit and receive signal paths are employed in the UTP cable (see Figure 2-11 in the "Repeater Definition" section), the 10BASE-T MAU at each end of the link (at the DTE and the repeater) employs a Link Integrity test to monitor for end-to-end continuity. This is performed by each MAU's transmitting a "link test" pulse when the DTE has no packet data to transmit. The receiver in each MAU must detect packet data or link test pulses to remain in the "Link Pass" state. If the MAU detects neither, it will enter the "Link Fail" state, and effectively prevent the DTE from transmitting on the network. The link test pulse is passed only between 10BASE-T MAUs and is not observed on the AUI signaling between the MAU and the DTE. The 10BASE-T Standard also mandates the provision of a "Link Status" indication, which provides a useful external indication that the node is connected and operational. The specific details surrounding the need for the link test pulse are discussed in the "Technology Advantages of 10BASE-T" section.

A network based on the 10BASE-T Standard directly addresses many of the inherent disadvantages that are present in coaxial wired systems.

The point-to-point nature of the topology eases the tasks of network management, cable administration, and reconfiguration due to moves, additions/deletions, or changes.

The cable is inexpensive and commonly available telephone grade (Cat 3), 100 Ω Unshielded Twisted Pair (UTP). Simple, inexpensive RJ-45 type telephone jack connectors are used to connect the MAU to the medium. In North America, suitable UTP cable is widely deployed in existing building telephone installations. Since, in many cases, existing unused telephone cables can be used, installation costs can be minimal. Since 100 Ω cable is not universally deployed internationally, 10BASE-T has been adapted to operate on other unshielded or shielded cable grades (120 Ω and 150 Ω, for instance).[28]

Even if cable is not already available, it is simple to cable all of the work areas within an office building and make individual connections at any time on an "as-needed" basis using a patch panel typically located in a wiring closet. Unlike a coax LAN, detailed planning of the cable routing, to attempt to provide coverage of existing and potential new users, is not required at installation time (although this does not mitigate the need to keep detailed records of any LAN cabling installation).

The cable-distance target of 100 m (actual distance varies according to cable quality) covers the vast majority of wiring-closet-to-desktop requirements. Since this actually defines a spherical coverage area, with a 100-m radius from the repeater, the distance capabilities are better than for other media types (for instance, 10BASE2), where the overhead associated with cabling to and from each desktop system can significantly erode the overall end-to-end distance capability.

10BASE-T MAUs can be connected via an AUI, or both the MAU and AUI can be embedded within the DTE or repeater. This is also an important issue, since the provision of an explicit AUI directly results in a significant cost penalty. 10BASE-T allows this to be eliminated where appropriate and permits greater integration than is possible in a 10BASE2 architecture.

The specifics of these changes, why they were important and how they substantially affected the deployment of Ethernet/10BASE-T LANs in the 1990s, are covered in more detail under the heading "Technology Advantages of 10BASE-T."

2.8.3 Fiber Optic

Fiber optic cable as a communications medium offers several key advantages over typical copper-based media. The primary benefits are its very high bandwidth and low attenuation characteristics. In addition, since it is an optical medium, it is neither affected by, nor does it emit, high-frequency electrical noise (i.e., external EMI and

---

[28] American National Standards Institute/Institute of Electrical and Electronics Engineers, Information Technology—Local and Metropolitan Area Networks—Part 3: Carrier sense multiple access with collision detection (CSMA/CD) access method and physical layer specifications, ISO/IEC 8802-3:1996 (E) ANSI/IEEE Std 802.3, 1996 Edition, IEEE, New York, NY, July 29, 1996. ISBN 1-55937-555-8. Annex D.5 and D.6.

RFI). This, combined with the difficulty in "tapping" into the fiber without physically breaking the connection, makes it relatively secure against eavesdropping or intrusion.

Fiber also has some disadvantages. It is generally more expensive than copper media. This differential is shrinking as fiber gains popularity, especially in very long distance communications applications, and manufacturing processes improve. Although tsome grades of fiber optic cable are substantially cheaper, such as Plastic Optical Fiber (POF), to date these have not been able to meet the relatively high data rate and long cable distance demanded for LAN implementations, and they are not yet supported by any 802.3 specification. The optical-electrical components, used to convert the electrical domain of the host system to the optical domain of the fiber communications channel, add significantly to the cost of the network interface at the node and repeater. In addition, the connectors are more expensive, and connectorization is more difficult to deal with, requiring skilled (costly) installation personnel.

In a strictly 10 Mb/s 802.3/Ethernet network environment, the enormous bandwidth capability of fiber is essentially unused, since the baseband signaling rate occupies only a small fraction of the available bandwidth. For these reasons, the fiber versions of Ethernet are primarily used where the long-distance, noise-immunity and/or security benefits are paramount and cost is secondary.

All the fiber MAU specifications are common in that they require two separate fibers to provide a transmit and receive signaling path. In all cases, the use of 62.5/125 µm multimode fiber optic cable is specified (this refers to a fiber core diameter of 62.5 µm, and a cladding diameter of 125 µm), although other types are not precluded.

Fiber Optic Inter-Repeater Link (FOIRL)

The Fiber Optic Inter-Repeater Link (FOIRL) was the first of the fiber standards to be defined. FOIRL (like 10BASE-T) requires the use of repeaters to act as a central point of concentration for a group of nodes. Figures 2-20 through 2-24 show examples of the use of FOIRL in a system topology. When originally developed, FOIRL was restricted to be a repeater-to-repeater-only link and was intended to provide a long-distance connection (up to 1 km) between remotely located repeaters. However, this was due only to a strict "legal" interpretation of the original standard and was not in any way a technical deficiency. For this reason, the FOIRL signaling scheme was commonly adopted for repeater-to-DTE-link purposes in situations where fiber was required to the desktop. The FOIRL specification was subsequently relaxed to permit repeater-to-DTE connections during the development of the 10BASE-FL Standard.

Since separate transmit and receive signaling paths are employed, the FOIRL MAU (similar to a 10BASE-T MAU) at either end of the link continuously monitors the fiber connection to ensure that continuity exists. The FOIRL Standard specifies that an "active idle" signal of 1 MHz is transmitted by each MAU in the absence of packet data traffic and used for link integrity. If the receiving MAU fails to detect this activity (defined as a "low-light" condition), it enters the "Link Fail" state and prevents the DTE or repeater from transmitting onto the network. Similar to the 10BASE-T link test pulse, the FOIRL active idle signal is passed only between MAUs and is not observed on the AUI signaling between the MAU and the DTE. FOIRL requires an F-SMA plug-and-socket connector arrangement for the fiber optic cable and the MAU, respectively.

10BASE-FL/FB/FP

The 10BASE-FL, 10BASE-FB, and 10BASE-FP Standards were developed to address different market requirements.

10BASE-FL was specified to supersede the original FOIRL specification, allowing both repeater-to-repeater and repeater-to-DTE links. It is compatible in all functions, including the 1 MHz active idle, and with the idle signal and packet data asynchronous to each other. In addition, it provides some improvements over the original FOIRL system:

1. The maximum distance between MAUs is extended to 2 km.

2. The cheaper BFOC (Bayonet Fiber Optic Connector, also commonly referred to as an ST[a] connector) plug and socket connectors are specified for the fiber optic cable and MAU, respectively.

3. The signaling specifications for rise/fall times are relaxed, which enables reduced drive power requirements (this is important for embedded MAU applications).

4. As an interesting side note, the MAU state machines were adopted directly from the 10BASE-T MAU Standard. This meant that implementers had to understand only one additional set of requirements to implement both MAUs.

See Figures 2-20 through 2-24 for examples of the use of 10BASE-FL in a system topology.

10BASE-FB was designed to provide a more optimized interface for inter-repeater links. The 10BASE-FB MAU is essentially defined as embedded within a repeater, with no exposed AUI. A 2.5 MHz active idle signaling technique is used to indicate that the transmit path is idle. In addition, the transmit data from the repeater is synchronized to this idle signal, enabling the receiving MAU to remain locked to the active idle/packet data transitions. In this way, the response time of the receiver is improved, since a PLL or similar function within the MAU receiver can remain locked to the incoming signal. In comparison, for instance, the PLL in a FOIRL-based DTE or repeater would be locked to a local clock during idle, until preamble commenced, at which point it would take several bit times to acquire lock to the incoming but phase-unrelated clock). In addition, the 10BASE-FB specification supports:

1. A maximum distance between MAUs (repeaters) of 2 km.

2. The cheaper BFOC (ST^a) plug and socket connectors are specified for the fiber optic cable and MAU, respectively.

3. A "remote fault" signaling scheme, allowing the MAU at one end of the link to indicate jabber, low light, or loss of synchronization to the MAU at the other end.

Since 10BASE-FB was essentially designed as a backbone technology and gained only limited vendor support, since the existing FOIRL Standard was deemed to be adequate in almost all topologies, there is a very small installation base. See Figures 2-20 through 2-24 for examples of the use of 10BASE-FB in a system topology.

10BASE-FP uses a passive "optical star" approach. The star and fiber optic cabling effectively provides the overall medium. The star has no active components and is not a repeater, it simply provides an optical "mixing" of the received signals for all of its ports. Signals entering any port on the star are output on all other ports, including the originating port. Hence if multiple receive signals occur simultaneously at the star, the signals interfere, causing a collision.

The use of 10BASE-FP falls into niche applications, in situations where power is not available for intermediate repeaters or in hazardous areas when electrical signaling/power is impractical.

To guarantee reliable collision detection, the fiber optic passive MAU has several major differences from other types of 802.3 MAU. This means 10BASE-FP MAUs are more complicated, not widely supported by LAN equipment vendors, and hence not deployed in mainstream office environments. For this reason, 10BASE-FP is not discussed further in this overview, although Figures 2-23 and 2-24 show examples of the use of 10BASE-FP in a system topology.

2.8.4 Mixed Topologies

A network that mixes the various 10 Mb/s Ethernet/802.3 media technologies can be constructed, making use of the most advantageous attributes of each. Since only the physical-layer interface changes in each case (the type of MAU), the various implementations are fully interoperable at the DTE (MAC, PLS, and AUI) and repeater, with some practical limitations. For instance, high-density multiport repeaters are normally physically constructed with the PHYs integrated within the product. Frequently a single AUI port will be provided, but other AUI ports are normally not exposed (as in the repeater set definition in Figure 2-12). Obviously such a repeater would interface only to the media types provided by the PHYs integrated within, and would not be a general-purpose device which could be configured to interface with any media type.

Guidelines

Guidelines for the reliable operation of mixed topology networks are specified in the "Systems Considerations for Multi-Segment Networks" section of the IEEE 802.3 Standard.[29] Amendments have been made to this section to incorporate the topologies encompassed by the 10BASE-FL/FB/FP Standards. Two sets of topology rules are specified, known as the "Transmission System Model 1" and "Transmission System Model 2."[30]

A few basic rules must be obeyed to ensure that the network does not become oversized. An oversized CSMA/CD network will not operate correctly, since the detection of collisions cannot be guaranteed within the slot time. In addition, the number of repeaters between any two stations on the network must be restricted to limit the effect of the inter-packet gap shrinkage, as it propagates through the network (IPG shrinkage is discussed in the "Repeater Definition" section). These basic rules are defined by the Transmission System Model 1. The Transmission System Model 1 guidelines ensure that the network will not become oversized, so they are relatively conservative. Networks based on this model will be guaranteed to operate, although they may not allow the network to achieve its most aggressive geographic span.

For networks that need to go outside the basic rules to increase the distance and/or coverage of the LAN in a particular installation, a precise model of the LAN installation must be produced. With this accurate model, the more detailed rules that are defined by the Transmission System Model 2 guidelines can be applied to identify the exact delays for each path in the network and to guarantee that the slot time and IPG shrinkage limits are not exceeded.

Application of the detailed topology rules is considered outside the scope of this overview. However, since the basic topology rules cover virtually all normal network installations, these will be reviewed with some typical examples of mixed-media networks.

In the case of coax (10BASE2 and 10BASE5) and passive fiber (10BASE-FP) segments, the medium is referred to as a "mixing segment," since signals share the same transmission path, and they "mix" when a collision is generated. Essentially, any medium where more than two MAUs can be interconnected is classified as a mixing segment. Twisted-pair (10BASE-T) and active fiber segments (FOIRL,

---

[29] American National Standards Institute/Institute of Electrical and Electronics Engineers, Information Technology—Local and Metropolitan Area Networks—Part 3: Carrier sense multiple access with collision detection (CSMA/CD) access method and physical layer specifications, ISO/IEC 8802-3:1996 (E) ANSI/IEEE Std 802.3, 1996 Edition, IEEE, New York, NY, July 29, 1996. Section 13. pp. 244–253.

[30] Institute of Electrical and Electronics Engineers, Local and Metropolitan Area Networks—Fiber Optic Active and Passive Star-Based Segments, Type 10BASE-F (Sections 15–18), IEEE Std. 802.3j-1993 (Supplement to ISO/IEC 8802-3:1993) (ANSI/IEEE Std 802.3, 1993 Edition), IEEE, New York, NY, October 12, 1993. Section 13, pp. 25-32.

10BASE-FL, and 10BASE-FB) are referred to as "link segments," since they form point-to-point links where only two MAUs are directly connected, and collision is detected logically by the presence of activity on both the transmit and receive links.

Generalized topology rules (Transmission System Model 1) are as follows:

1. Repeater sets are required to interconnect segments.

2. MAUs that are part of repeater sets count toward the maximum number of MAUs on a segment.

3. The maximum transmission path between any two DTEs can consist of up to five segments—four repeater sets (including AUIs if provided), two MAUs, and two AUI cables.

4. AUI cables for 10BASE-FL and 10BASE-FP must not exceed 25 m (since a MAU is required at each end of the segment, the total AUI cable length will be 50 m per segment for these two implementations). All other AUI cables are permitted to be 50 m each.

5. When a transmission path consists of four repeater sets and five segments, up to three may be mixing segments, and the remaining two must be link segments (see Figure 2-20). When five segments are present, each fiber optic link segment (FOIRL, 10BASE-FL or 10BASE-FB) cannot exceed 500 m (see Figures 2-20 and 2-21), and each 10BASE-FP segment cannot exceed 300 m (see Figures 2-23 and 2-24).

6. When a transmission path consists of three repeater sets and four segments, the following additional rules apply:

   a. The maximum length of any inter-repeater segment must not exceed 1000 m for FOIRL, 10BASE-FL, or 10BASE-FB segments and must not exceed 700 m for a 10BASE-FP segment.

   b. The maximum length of any repeater-to-DTE segment must not exceed 400 m for a 10BASE-FL segment (see Figure 2-23), 400 m for any segment terminated using a 10BASE-FL MAU (such as an FOIRL link connected to a DTE), and 300 m for a 10BASE-FP segment (see Figures 2-23 and 2-24).

   c. The number of mixing segments is not restricted.

Figures 2-20 through 2-24 show some examples of maximally configured networks for various types of mixed media.

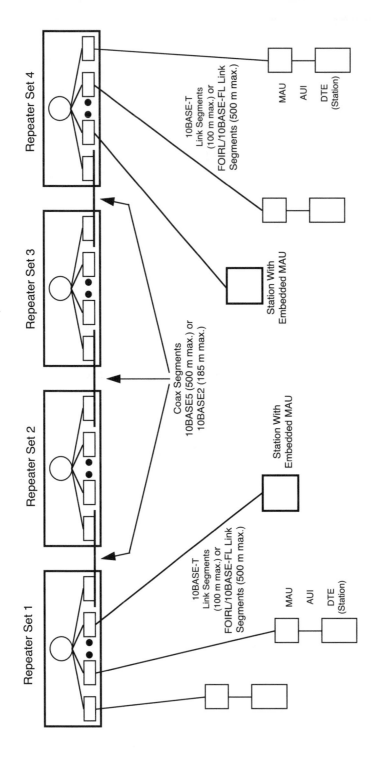

Figure 2-20 Example of 10 Mb/s Maximum Transmission Path with Three Coax Segments and Two Link Segments (From IEEE Std. 8802-3:1996, ©1996, IEEE. All rights reserved.)

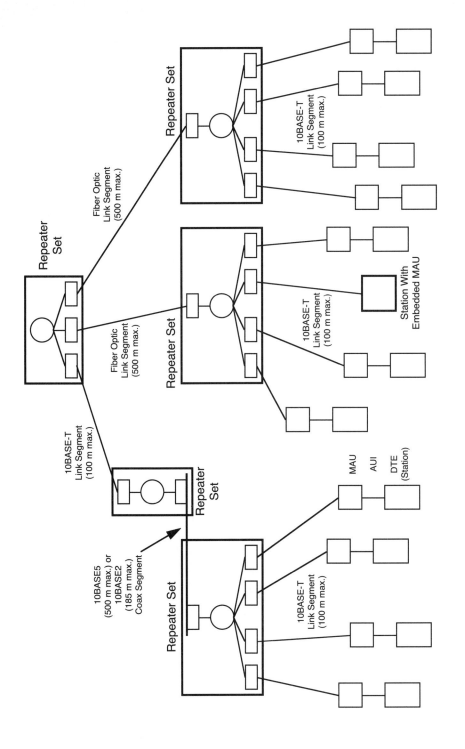

Figure 2-21 Example of Maximum Transmission Path Using Coax Segments, 10BASE-T Link Segments and Fiber Optic Link Segments

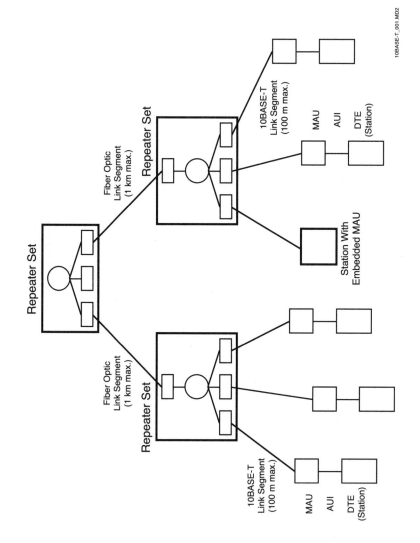

Figure 2-22 Example of Maximum Transmission Path with Three Repeater Sets and Four Link Segments (Two 100 m 10BASE-T and Two 1 km Fiber) (From IEEE Std. 8802-3:1996, ©1996, IEEE. All rights reserved.)

68

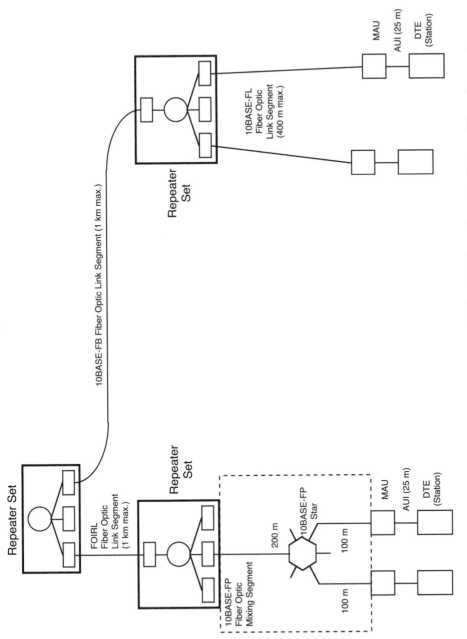

Figure 2-23 Example of Maximum Transmission Path with Three Repeater Sets and Four Segments (One 1 km 10BASE-FB, One 1 km FOIRL, One 400 m 10BASE-FL and One 300 m 10BASE-FP) (From IEEE Std. 8802-3:1996, ©1996, IEEE. All rights reserved.)

69

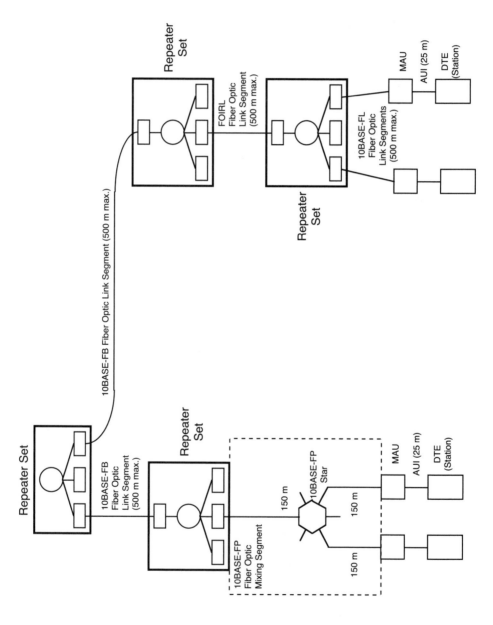

Figure 2-24 Example of Maximum Transmission Path with Four Repeater Sets and Five Segments (Two 500 m 10BASE-FB, One 500 m FOIRL, One 500 m 10BASE-FL and One 300 m 10BASE-FP) (From IEEE Std. 8802-3:1996, ©1996, IEEE. All rights reserved.)

70

2.9 Management

Like the standards-development process, network management generally gets left until last! Initially, management for 10 Mb/s Ethernet was sparse. However, as the size and complexity of networks increased and technology improved, more focus was placed on providing the low-level capabilities to monitor the LAN hardware.

As the Ethernet standards have evolved, management capabilities have also been migrated, and enhanced functionality has been included to control and monitor the new functionality.

2.9.1 Station Management

Management of the DTE, referred to as Station Management, is covered in Section 5 of the Ethernet standard. Section 5 was substantially updated and republished first in 1988. Section 5 was merged with Clause 30 to form the single cohesive management description during the 100BASE-T (802.3u) development and was revised slightly by the 802.3x (Full Duplex and Flow Control), Gigabit Ethernet (802.3z) and VLAN Tagging (802.3ac) developments. For this reason, readers are referred to the Gigabit Ethernet chapter (Chapter 4), where the latest version of Clause 30 is defined.

2.9.2 Repeater Management

The specifications for the statistics to be monitored are contained in the IEEE 802.3k Supplement,[31] which was defined as Section 19 and was first included in the complete ISO 8802-3 Specification in 1996.[32] Section 19 was merged with Clause 30 to form the single cohesive management description during the 100BASE-T (802.3u) development and was revised slightly by the Gigabit Ethernet (802.3z) development. For this reason, readers are referred to the Gigabit Ethernet chapter (Chapter 4), where the latest version of Clause 30 is defined.

---

[31] Institute of Electrical and Electronics Engineers, *Local and Metropolitan Area Networks— Layer Management for 10Mb/s Baseband Repeaters (Section 19)*, IEEE Std. 802.3k-1993 (Supplement to ISO/IEC 8802-3:1992) (ANSI/IEEE Std 802.3, 1992 Edition), IEEE, New York, NY, November 2, 1992.

[32] American National Standards Institute/Institute of Electrical and Electronics Engineers, Information Technology—Local and Metropolitan Area Networks—Part 3: Carrier sense multiple access with collision detection (CSMA/CD) access method and physical layer specifications, ISO/IEC 8802-3:1996 (E) ANSI/IEEE Std 802.3, 1996 Edition, IEEE, New York, NY, July 29, 1996. ISBN 1-55937-555-8. Section 19.

2.9.3 MAU Management

The specification for the statistics to be monitored are contained in the IEEE 802.3p Supplement,[33] which was defined as Section 19 and was first included in the complete ISO 8802-3 Specification in 1996.[34] Section 20 was merged with Clause 30 to form the single cohesive management description during the 100BASE-T (802.3u) development and was revised slightly by the 802.3x (Full Duplex and Flow Control) and Gigabit Ethernet (802.3z) development. For this reason, readers are referred to the Gigabit Ethernet chapter (Chapter 4), where the latest version of Clause 30 is defined.

2.10 Technology Advantages of 10BASE-T

10BASE-T redefined some of the key attributes of the physical-layer interfaces for 802.3/Ethernet networks. These changes directly allowed enhancement of the ability to add network management and they reduce the initial installation and long-term cost of ownership of LANs.

The next section will focus on the key technology differences between thick coax (10BASE5), thin coax, (10BASE2) and twisted pair (10BASE-T), which were the three competing implementations of 802.3/Ethernet at the time that the 10BASE-T specification was completed and mainstream products were introduced (in 1990). It will also describe how these differences have led to the widespread adoption of 10BASE-T as the office network of choice, which in turn has fueled the development and adoption of 100BASE-T.

2.10.1 Collision Detection

All 802.3-based networks rely on the fact that all devices are permitted to listen to the channel, but only one may transmit at any given time. If two or more devices transmit simultaneously, a "collision" is sensed, and the nodes involved are forced to reschedule their transmissions after a random interval.

The Medium Attachment Unit (MAU) is responsible for the detection of collisions. Early 10BASE2 (Figure 2-25), 10BASE5 (Figure 2-26), and 10BASE-T (Figure 2-27) MAU implementations consisted largely of a separate transceiver integrated

---

[33] Institute of Electrical and Electronic Engineers, Local and Metropolitan Area Networks— Guidelines for the Development of Managed Objects (GDMO) (ISO 10164-4) Format for Layer-Managed Objects (Section 5) and Layer Management 10 Mb/s Baseband Medium Attachment Units (MAUs) (Section 20), IEEE Std. 802.3p-1993 and IEEE Std. 802.3q-1993 (Supplements to ISO/IEC 8802-3:1993 [ANSI/IEEE Std. 802.3:1993 Edition.])

[34] American National Standards Institute/Institute of Electrical and Electronics Engineers, Information Technology—Local and Metropolitan Area Networks—Part 3: Carrier sense multiple access with collision detection (CSMA/CD) access method and physical layer specifications, ISO/IEC 8802-3:1996 (E) ANSI/IEEE Std 802.3, 1996 Edition, IEEE, New York, NY, July 29, 1996. ISBN 1-55937-555-8. Section 20.

circuit, with additional passive components, power supply and connectors etc. Serial data originating from the LAN controller in the Data Terminal Equipment (DTE) is passed to the MAU using the Attachment Unit Interface (AUI). If the MAU detects a collision, it reports this back to the controller using the AUI.

With a coaxial topology, all nodes are connected to the center conductor of the cable. The transceiver can detect two or more devices transmitting on the network, since the voltage seen on the center conductor will exceed a "collision threshold" (–1.6 V nominally). In order to drive the coax cable, the transceiver requires a relatively high negative supply voltage (typically –9 V), making it an unsuitable candidate for most of the mainstream CMOS semiconductor processes available.

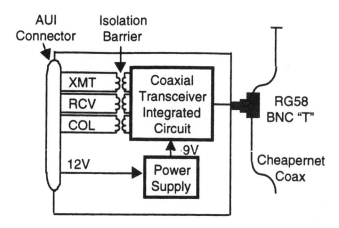

Figure 2-25 10BASE2 MAU

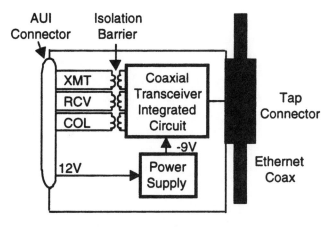

Figure 2-26 10BASE5 MAU

Since 10BASE-T uses a separate transmit and receive signal path, "logical" collision detection is implemented. While data is transmitted from the node to the repeater on the transmit wire pair, the receive pair should remain idle. If both the transmit and receive pairs become active simultaneously, the 10BASE-T transceiver detects a collision. The voltage levels employed in 10BASE-T (5.0 V ± 0.6 V peak-to-peak) can be met using standard 5 V CMOS logic, or 3.3 V logic with an appropriate transformer winding ratio.

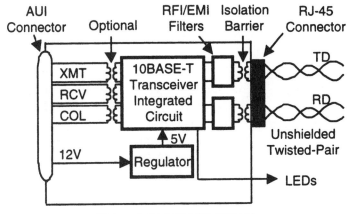

Figure 2-27 10BASE-T MAU

2.10.2 Electrical Isolation

An isolation barrier is required in all long-distance network topologies to protect the DTE from potentially hazardous voltages which may be present during fault conditions on the medium.

In a coax-based network, this DC isolation is located in the AUI path, since the coax transceiver must be DC-coupled to the center conductor to permit collision detection. This isolation requirement means that 10BASE2/5 implementations cannot integrate the MAC/PLS functions with those of the MAU, since CMOS processes do not provide the necessary electrical isolation (on the order of 2 kV). Figure 2-28 illustrates this limitation, where even if the Ethernet controller chip (integrated circuit) is located on the same circuit board as the Cheapernet transceiver, the isolation requirement of the AUI makes it impossible to merge all of the end-station functions into a single chip.

With 10BASE-T, the logical collision-detection scheme eliminates the need for the DC path to the medium (see Figure 2-2), and the MAU (hence transceiver chip) is AC coupled to the UTP cable, using an isolation transformer (actually two trans-

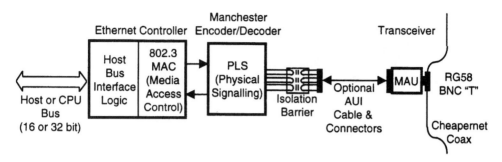

Figure 2-28 Typical Ethernet Node–Coax Chip Set

formers, one each in the transmit and receive signal paths). Given that the isolation barrier can be relocated to the medium side of the 10BASE-T transceiver, adding the same isolation function in the AUI path is redundant. The removal of the isolation requirement in the AUI path allows the 10BASE-T transceiver to be integrated with the remainder of the 802.3 node components (MAC, PLS, and host-specific interface logic) as a single piece of silicon, as shown in Figure 2-29.

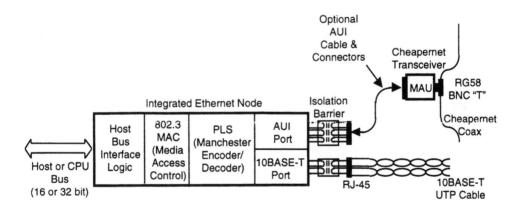

Figure 2-29 Typical Ethernet Node–Integrated 10BASE-T Chip Set

Many 10BASE-T implementations retain the ability to provide a full 50-m AUI drive capability, providing a compatibility path for legacy coax or fiber installations, using an appropriate transceiver. Frequently, the capability to automatically sense the active network port (10BASE-T or AUI) is also provided.

2.10.3 Link Integrity

In a coax system, when the node transmits, the MAU simultaneously receives the transmission (since both the transmitter and receiver are connected to the coax center tap) and returns it to the controller as an indication of transmit-to-receive path integrity. The separation of the transmit and receive paths in 10BASE-T has two potential drawbacks. The first is that the DTE cannot sense its own transmission. The second is related to this, in that it cannot detect a failed link.

In a 10BASE-T system, separation of the transmit and receive cable pairs, combined with logical collision detection, means that when driving the transmit twisted pair, the transceiver will not see activity on the receive pair (unless a collision occurs). Since the transceiver can no longer observe its own signal transmission (unlike the coax system), the loopback path to the controller is implemented internally to the MAU. So the controller is made to believe that the transmit-to-receive integrity is present, and no difference is detected between a coax or a twisted pair medium. However, a mechanism is necessary to ensure that a failure in the transmit or receive path can be detected.

In the case of a broken transmit path, the node would be unable to send data over the network—an important point. However, a broken receiver (or receive cable) has far more serious implications, which affect the network as a whole rather than just the node exhibiting the problem. The node loses its ability to monitor the network for activity or collisions. A node with data to transmit would do so regardless of current network activity and might cause a collision with an existing message.

Since correct recovery from a collision is a fundamental property of the 802.3 Media Access Control (MAC) function, it would appear that this is not a serious problem. However, in a correctly configured and operating network, collisions are guaranteed to occur within a defined window after transmission commences, defined as the "slot time." A transmission experiencing a collision within the slot time will be automatically retried by the sending node. Up to 15 retries (16 attempts total) are permitted before the node aborts the transmission. A collision after the slot time (512 bits or 51.2 μs), on the other hand, will result in a "late collision," and the node will abandon the transmission immediately. Most 802.3 LAN controllers incorporate a late-collision indication to advise the host processor of this condition. Upper-layer software then has the responsibility to recognize this and reschedule the transmission. False indications of late collision are very undesirable, since the late-collision statistic is used as an indication that the network has become oversized (the round-trip propagation delay is too large). A network administrator might therefore become concerned if late collisions were to start appearing. Further, the fact that a packet transmitted by a normally operating device could suffer a late collision due to the failed device, and that this transmission attempt is abandoned, to be rescheduled by upper-layer (slower) protocols, means the overall performance of the LAN would be degraded by such a situation. Since none of these conditions were acceptable, the 10BASE-T Standard included a mechanism to prevent such events.

A feature defined as "link test" is used to ensure network integrity. In the absence of network traffic, a simple heartbeat pulse is sent periodically (every 16 ms ± 8 ms) by the transmitter of all 10BASE-T MAUs, both at the repeater and the DTE (see Figure 2-30). The link test pulse is a unipolar pulse (positive only), unlike the normal 10BASE-T differential signaling used for packet data. If the receiver of a MAU does not see either packet data or a link test pulse within a defined time window (50–150 ms), it will enter a "link fail" condition, which disables the data transmit, data receive, and loopback functions. Disabling the transmit function prevents the disturbance of existing network traffic, preventing the false late-collision scenario. Disabling the loopback path warns the DTE that there is a failure, since the transmit (DO) to receive (DI) loopback path is interrupted. So, if the receive pair is disconnected, the MAU will enter the link-fail state, and further transmission will be disabled. During link fail, the transmission and reception of link test pulses continues. To reestablish the link, at least two consecutive link test pulses or a single packet must be received.

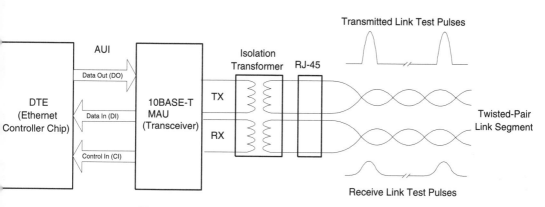

Figure 2-30 Link Test Transmission/Reception

Note that the link test pulses are exchanged only between the 10BASE-T MAUs. There is no discernible activity across any of the AUI circuits during the transmission and/or reception of the link test pulses.

2.10.4 Status Indication

Most 10BASE-T transceivers incorporate additional status features to allow simple diagnosis of the network, station, or repeater port state.

The external indication of the link status is mandated by the 10BASE-T Standard. Transmit, receive, and collision activity can all be separately indicated (whereas, in the coax MAU, receive is always active during transmit), to provide a simple display of network activity. In addition, since the link test pulse is unipolar (see Figure 2-30), unlike the normal differential data transmissions, it is possible to detect the polarity of the receive signal path. This is a useful feature, which most vendors incorporate to automatically detect and correct simple wiring installation errors.

2.11 User Benefits of 10BASE-T

10BASE-T products had a major impact on the networking industry, firmly establishing Ethernet as the dominant networking technology for business office environments during the early-to-mid 1990s. Coupled with the technical advantages outlined previously, 10BASE-T solved several key user requirements, which fueled its acceptance within the user community,

2.11.1 Installation Cost

The cost of LAN cable installation far outweighs the cost of the cable itself. If existing unused telephone cabling can be used, savings are significant. Even if new cabling has to be installed, costs are generally lower since identical connection technology is widely used in telecommunication applications, so it is inexpensive and familiar to installation personnel.

2.11.2 Cost of Ownership

During the lifetime of a LAN, the long-term cost of ownership may far outweigh the original equipment cost. Addition or movement of users is more difficult in coax-based Ethernet. Connection to the coax cable requires specialized tools, and the coax bus is generally not easily accessible. 10BASE-T is literally "plug and play." Reconfiguration is as simple as adding a new, or plugging into a prewired, connection from the repeater. When the user is moved (or switches off their system), link test pulses stop being transmitted, and the repeater port effectively shuts down.

2.11.3 Fault Isolation, Management and Security

In large corporate networks, the ability to manage and maintain the network is vital. Many businesses depend on their communications facilities. The LAN is required to be a utility, much like the telephone system. When a person picks up the telephone, they expect to hear a "dial tone." In the same way, when a user accesses a networked service, it is expected to be available.

On a coax bus, faults are difficult to analyze, since all nodes are connected to the cable at all times. With 10BASE-T, only one DTE (or repeater) is connected to any port on a repeater, so the behavior of any connection can be individually monitored. A failure can be isolated quickly, and the remainder of the network can operate unimpaired while the problem is corrected.

Access control and network security can be readily administered through the repeater. For instance, the manager can instruct the hub to shut down a particular link on Friday at 5:00 PM and reenable it on Monday at 8:00 AM. More sophisticated security features are described in the section titled "Vendor-Differentiated Repeater Functions" earlier in this chapter. Other features, such as configuration mapping, can also be monitored at the hub, since each 10BASE-T link will in general only be connected to a single node. Connections to repeaters (and coax segments) do not obey this rule, since they appear connected to a group of nodes, but this characteristic also allows these links to be identified.

Even in small or low-cost installations, where a "network manager" job function is not warranted, the single point of concentration, point-to-point connectivity, and the addition of rudimentary status indicators makes diagnosing a problem on a 10BASE-T network a far less daunting task than checking the entire coax for a potential connection problem.

The fact that each 10BASE-T station requires a repeater port increased enormously the importance of the role the repeater undertook in a network. System and silicon vendors responded to this by developing the 802.3Repeater Management Standard (the work of 802.3k[35] in the standards group). This standardized the statistics that a repeater gathered and presented to the network manager. Refer to the "Repeater Management" section in this chapter for additional detail.

2.11.4 Volume Manufacturing

The 10BASE-T topology enables cost-effective silicon integration. Despite the maturity of Ethernet technology at the advent of 10BASE-T, this allowed a continued reduction in 10BASE-T system costs in two principal areas. First, the high demand for integrated circuits and board-level products has generated fierce competition for market share from both semiconductor and systems companies. Second, the sheer size of the Ethernet market, and specifically 10BASE-T market opportunity, has mandated the use of high-volume manufacturing techniques to both meet demand and maintain cost competitiveness.

---

[35] Institute of Electrical and Electronics Engineers, *Local and Metropolitan Area Networks—Layer Management for 10Mb/s Baseband Repeaters (Section 19)*, IEEE Std. 802.3k-1993 (Supplement to ISO/IEC 8802-3:1992) (ANSI/IEEE Std 802.3, 1992 Edition), IEEE, New York, NY, November 2, 1992.

2.11.5 Interoperability and Standardization

The overwhelming demand from the user community is for interoperability based on open standards. 10BASE-T, in itself a standard, also drove the creation and adoption of additional standardization. The lack of a centrally located point for monitoring and/or management has always been a criticism leveled at coax-based 802.3/Ethernet. The 10BASE-T hub-based star architecture removed this as an obstacle.

Due to the widespread adoption of hub-based topologies supporting Ethernet, Token Ring, and FDDI, the standardization of network-management information and its exchange has also received significant attention. Currently, Simple Network Management Protocol (SNMP)[36] is the de facto standard employed in Ethernet networks for the management of infrastructure components (e.g., bridges, routers, etc.). Several standards organizations and network vendors have been actively working on the definition of standards to allow the management of repeaters—particularly 10BASE-T repeaters. This is discussed briefly under the earlier heading "Repeater Management."

---

[36] J.D. Case, M.S. Fedor, M.L. Schoffstall, and J.R. Davin, *A Simple Network Management Protocol*, Request for Comment 1157, DDN Network Information Center, SRI International, May, 1990.

The Second Generation:
100 Mb/s and Switched Ethernet

3.1 Overview

Many of the advantages that were gained in the implementation of 10BASE-T were again leveraged in the 100BASE-T standards and product developments. Structured, star-wired cabling was retained, in fact there is no support for mixing segments in 100BASE-T, since buildings and businesses had endorsed the 10BASE-T "hub-and-spoke" architecture, with the repeater (or "hub") at the central point of the wring scheme, with end stations (users) connected to their own individual twisted-pair cable (at the end of each "spoke").

Figure 3-1 shows the enhanced 802.3 layered model, showing the addition of several new sublayers and modified interfaces. Compare this with the simple 10 Mb/s only representation previously depicted in Fig. 2-11. These modifications will be discussed later in this chapter.

In addition to the technical changes involved in making Ethernet run at ten times its original data rate, there were also interesting and highly charged political power struggles between major network vendors in the industry. Two factions were competing in the standards and product development processes (and ideologies!).

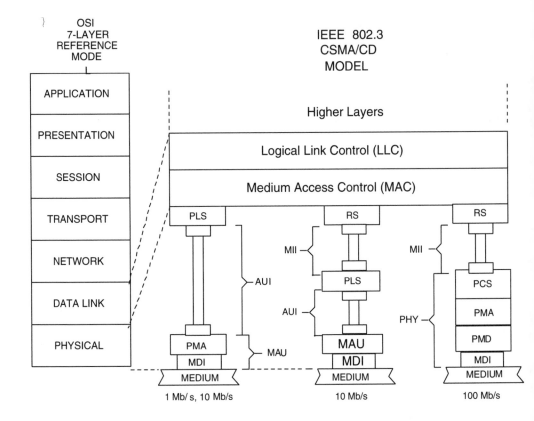

Figure 3-1 100BASE-T Architectural Relationship of 100BASE-T DTE and Repeater to OSI Reference Model (From IEEE Std. 802.3u-1995, ©1995, IEEE. All rights reserved.)

One group wanted to retain the Ethernet MAC protocol, making minimal changes to enhance operation of the MAC at 100 Mb/s, and to add repeater and physical-layer definitions to support operation over various categories of UTP and fiber, but focusing on Category 5 (Cat 5) UTP cable initially. The rationale for this approach was that it leveraged the excellent "brand-name recognition" that Ethernet enjoyed in the user community as well as the large base of hardware, software, and systems engineering expertise that knew and understood Ethernet due to a long association with it. This group went on to become the 802.3u Task Force, and developed the 100 Mb/s enhancement to the Ethernet standards suite. The group was also backed by a huge marketing and public relations effort funded by a large collaborative group of vendors, known as the "Fast Ethernet Alliance" (FEA).

The other group wanted to define a new MAC protocol, again augmented with repeater and physical-layer definitions, to support a range of UTP and fiber-based topologies. Their rationale was that there were more efficient mechanisms than the original Ethernet CSMA/CD access method, and that Category 3 (Cat 3) grade cable was an absolute necessity for support by the standard, to upgrade the installed based of 10BASE-T that was specified to operate on UTP Cat 3. This group went on to form the new 802.12 Task Force and developed a new MAC protocol for the Demand Priority Access Method (DPAM).

Both factions fought an embittered technical, marketing, and press campaign during the standards development process. Many people (in the hundreds) contributed to the development of both standards, culminating in both 802.3u and 802.12 being passed by the IEEE Standards Board as official standards on June 13, 1995.[1]

However, while both 802.3u (known as 100BASE-T or Fast Ethernet) and 802.12 were completed in the same time frame, the brand name of Ethernet and 802.3 was a powerful message in the marketplace and overcame any minor technical advantages that 802.12 touted. Although a small set of vendors have consistently offered 802.12 products, virtually all mainstream LAN vendors coalesced around 100BASE-T products and effectively won in the marketplace over a relatively short time period.

In addition to the directly applicable MAC, repeater and physical-layer standards work that was ongoing within the 802.3u standards group, several other related standards developments and industry trends significantly influenced the adoption of and interest in 100BASE-T. Primarily, these were all related to the deployment of a new class of network device, referred to as a "switch." Switches are basically multiport bridges (see "Bridge Definition" in Chapter 2 and "Switch Definition" in this chapter for more details), but implemented with dedicated hardware to substantially increase performance. Standards developments which augmented the value proposition of switches were in the Full Duplex/Flow Control and Virtual LAN (VLAN) Tagging Specifications. Both of these capabilities and how they enhance the performance and usefulness of switches are discussed later in this chapter.

---

[1] Institute of Electrical and Electronic Engineers, Local and Metropolitan Area Networks, Media Access Control (MAC) Parameters, Physical Layer, Medium Attachment Units and Repeater for 100 Mb/s Operation, Type 100BASE-T (Clauses 21–30). IEEE Std 802.3u—1995 (Supplement to ISO/IEC 8802-3, 1993 [ANSI/IEEE Std. 802.3, 1993 Edition]), IEEE, New York, NY, October 26, 1995, ISBN 1-55937-542-6.

3.1.1 100BASE-T Adoption Issues

The reader might assume that the advent of 100BASE-T products would have immediately caused the demise of the 10 Mb/s Ethernet marketplace and products sold into it. The answer is categorically no! Several factors allowed both 10 and 100 Mb/s products to exist in the marketplace. First, not everyone needed the additional bandwidth. Many network installations had not yet reached the point where the network was either perceived to be, or actually had become, a performance bottleneck. Second, the installed base was all 10 Mb/s only, and a massive investment had been made by the industry in this technology. With this huge installed base of 10 Mb/s Ethernet (estimates indicated in excess of 60 million 10BASE-T nodes deployed at the time the 100BASE-T Standard was completed), corporate network managers were not exactly thrilled with the prospect that their existing investment in 10 Mb/s Ethernet and star-wired UTP was unsuitable for emerging applications. So there was some natural market latency to immediate adoption. However, 100BASE-T products were rapidly developed to both interconnect and augment the installed base of 10BASE-T networks. Third, there was a cost premium associated with 100BASE-T products over 10 Mb/s devices. This was fairly significant in the first year that 100BASE-T products appeared, although this differential was quickly eroded as competition in the market increased, and products were developed and integrated into more advanced silicon process technologies.

So, despite the availability of new technologies such as switched Ethernet and 100BASE-T, in terms of total ports shipped into the market, these technologies did not exceed the quantities of standard 10BASE-T devices for some time.

In order to be considered as a viable network technology to displace the existing 10BASE-T installed base and be deployed as a mainstream desktop solution, 100BASE-T would have to meet some basic requirements, which the 803.3u committee summarized as follows:

1. Seamless integration with the installed base.
2. Be in the order of two times the cost of 10BASE-T (or less).
3. Offer increased aggregate bandwidth.
4. Be standardized and supported by multiple vendors.
5. Potentially offer a solution for time-bounded delivery.

Each of these issues is discussed in some detail in the following sections.

Seamless Integration with Installed Base

There are two primary factors in considering the installed base. The first is the physical infrastructure, mainly relating to cable plant. The second is the interoperability with existing hardware (such as adapters and internetworking equipment) and software (such as desktop and network management applications).

As already stated, 10BASE-T dominated the installed base for office applications. 10BASE-T is a star topology, with a repeater at the center of the star. The repeater performs signal amplitude and timing restoration.

Figure 3-2 and diagrams that follow show the generic topology of the network, as well as the layer model of the end station (Data terminal Equipment, or DTE).

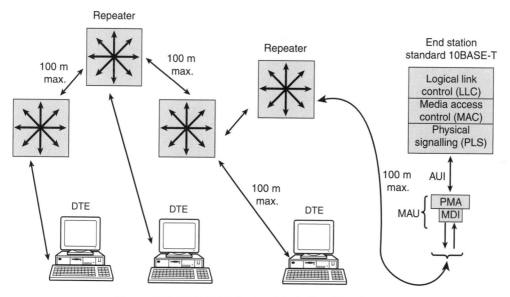

Figure 3-2 10BASE-T Twisted Pair Star Topology

The cabling employed for 10BASE-T is either Category 3 (Cat 3) or Category 5 (Cat 5) UTP. The "category" rating refers to the electrical performance of the cable. Cat 5 is better quality cable than Cat 3, having less high-frequency attenuation, lower susceptibility to external electromagnetic interference (EMI) and radio-frequency interference (RFI), and reduced self-emission of EMI/RFI. 10BASE-T requires only two pairs of Cat 3 cable to operate. Cable quality and the number of pairs required (or available) are major issues. High-speed data transmission (and reception) over UTP to meet data integrity and regulatory emissions issues is highly challenging. This generally requires either better quality cable or more pairs of lower quality cable. In addition, cable quality tends to vary geographically. For instance, in Europe, very little 4-pair cabling exists, and 2-pair UTP or Shielded Twisted Pair (STP) are common. In the United States, 25-pair bundles of UTP are sometimes used to connect 10BASE-T multiport repeaters to "punch-down" blocks (basically a telecommunications term for a terminal strip, where large numbers of cables can be connected). At the punch-down block, the 25-pair bundle (capable of carrying 12 10BASE-T connections) is broken out to the individual cable runs to the desktops (often referred to as "home-runs"). Cabling is also discussed later in relation to cost issues.

Large corporate networks are rarely configured as one single-repeater-based network, where all the stations would be connected within a single "collision domain." Devices within a collision domain observe all network activity, including both packet data and collisions (when two or more stations attempt to transmit simultaneously). Typical networks are segmented into multiple collision domains by bridges or routers. These internetworking devices forward only the traffic that is destined from a station on one network to a station on another network, and they block traffic that is local to stations on the same network, as well as collisions.

Bridges and/or routers may also be used to interconnect different network technologies, such as Ethernet to FDDI. FDDI was commonly used as a backbone to interconnect geographically distant Ethernet networks due to its high bandwidth (100 Mb/s), long-distance capability, and immunity to RFI/EMI (when operated over fiber optic cable). However, the FDDI protocol and mandatory management features make it inherently more expensive to implement than Ethernet. In addition, the difference in packet formats between FDDI and Ethernet necessitates that the internetworking device converts each packet that traverses the Ethernet/FDDI boundary, incurring a high processing overhead. These factors are part of the reason FDDI has seen minimal deployment in the cost-sensitive desktop market but is widely used in the lower-volume and less cost-sensitive backbone market.

Less Than Twice the Cost of 10BASE-T

While there is no stringent criterion which makes this a technical attribute, the mainstream desktop market is extremely cost sensitive. The cost/performance expectations for computer and communications equipment is loosely based on the rule-of-thumb "10 times the performance for twice the price."

A primary contributor to the cost of network installation is the cable type. 10BASE-T requires only 2-pair Cat 3 cable to operate, and in some installations is run within 25-pair cable bundles. Making it a requirement to use Cat 5 cable to run 100 Mb/s proved a significant obstacle for the UTP version of FDDI (often referred to as CDDI). The slow initial deployment of Cat 5 cable was based on cost, since it was significantly more expensive than Cat 3. However, the cost of Cat 3 and Cat 5 is generally a minor consideration when compared to the overall installation costs, which dwarf the actual cable material cost. It is extremely hard to quantify the installed base of Cat 3 versus Cat 5 cable, although it is fair to say that the vast majority of cable currently being installed is Cat 5 quality.

Clearly, an objective of a cost-effective upgrade to 10BASE-T should not mandate the use of Cat 5 cable.

Increased Aggregate Bandwidth

The distinction between the need for increased aggregate bandwidth versus burst bandwidth is key. In this context, aggregate bandwidth is used to define the overall instantaneous network capacity. For instance, a 10 Mb/s Ethernet network has an aggregate bandwidth of 10 Mb/s. Burst bandwidth is used to describe the bandwidth available to an individual user or station over a time period. For instance, for a repeater-based 10 Mb/s Ethernet with 10 stations attached, any station would see a burst bandwidth of between 1 and 10 Mb/s, depending on the activity of the other stations.

For most current and emerging desktop computing applications, a burst bandwidth capability of 10 Mb/s is more than adequate. There are some applications where an even higher burst bandwidth is needed. Generally these are applications where very large data files are moved across the network—for instance, for high-definition image retrieval/display. However, these applications are generally niche and are also not as cost sensitive. The primary issue for mainstream applications is not the need for additional burst bandwidth; it is the sharing of the aggregate bandwidth.

The primary ways to address this are to increase the aggregate bandwidth of the LAN, as in the case of 100BASE-T, or to reduce the sharing of bandwidth by segmenting the LAN to ever smaller groups of stations, as in the case of switched Ethernet.

Standardized and Multi-Vendor Supported

Interoperability is key to large corporate networks, as is the ability to select optimal components from different vendors. Although typical LANs do not mix every different vendor for the same equipment, they frequently use one vendor for internetworking equipment, a different vendor for adapter cards, and possibly another vendor for stackable repeaters. Without broad support from multiple vendors, interoperability and cost competitiveness cannot be guaranteed.

The large base of vendors that developed the 100BASE-T Standard and provide products for 10 and 100 Mb/s Ethernet make this a nonissue.

Time-Bounded Delivery

Future applications will emerge that value guaranteed time variance more than guaranteed data integrity. This is contrary to the way LANs have always been optimized. The assumption for a data network is that the data itself is the all-important deliverable, and the timing, relative ordering, or timing variability of data delivery is much less important. From this assumption have grown highly robust signaling and protocol schemes which generally attempt to guarantee the data delivery, handle out-of-order issues, and even retransmit the data if it does not arrive (or arrives corrupted) at the destination. However, emerging voice and video applications operate on a different paradigm. They need the next piece of data, in order, and within a defined time window. For instance, consider a digitized voice data stream being received over the network and then decompressed at the station. The voice data must be received in order and at a (relatively) constant rate, otherwise pitch and content of the decoded voice signal will become unintelligible. If the data is delayed, it is useless, and it is better to discard it than try to retransmit it.

Some network protocols are already incorporating these capabilities natively, and some are retrofitting them using higher-layer functions. Note, however, that in general, voice/video conferencing will not be very useful if constrained to the local environment (building or campus, for instance). What is needed is wide area support, which implies end-to-end paths that encompass conversions from LAN to WAN and back to LAN. Any protocol support that is provided for time-sensitive delivery must be translated and passed intact across these boundaries to ensure that the priorities of time critical traffic can be preserved.

The debate still rages on whether isochronous (i.e., voice/video) traffic will be handled by a single hybrid network also capable of providing "bursty" data traffic services, or whether these will remain separate. In either case, other standards and industry initiatives have been initiated to address these issues in order to allow time-bounded delivery mechanisms to be overlaid onto existing data networks. One such initiative, for VLAN Tagging, is discussed later in this chapter.

3.1.2 Major Differences Between 10BASE-T and 100BASE-T

The 100 Mb/s Ethernet ("Fast Ethernet") standard built on the tremendous success of the existing developed 10 Mb/s suite of 802.3 standards. However, there were some substantial differences, which are outlined below, in order to provide a quick-reference comparison for those familiar with either the 10 Mb/s or 100 Mb/s versions. Additional detail of the actual functionality of the 802.3u 100 Mb/s Standard is given later in this chapter.

Media Independent Interface (MII) Versus AUI

The Media Independent Interface (MII) for 100 Mb/s replaces the AUI for 10 Mb/s operation, although essentially it provides the same function—namely, to decouple the MAC layer from the different requirements of the various PHY layers. The AUI provided exactly this function, although this was not an original design objective for Ethernet devices. What became clear in later years, as the PHY layers were developed for the original Ethernet, was that rather fortuitously the AUI provided an excellent interface to allow the MAC to remain constant but to change the PHY devices below to accommodate new technologies, permitting other cable types such as fiber and twisted-pair to be supported. However, the AUI proved unsuitable for this function at data rates of 100 Mb/s, due to the very high frequencies involved. Instead of the bit-serial interface of the AUI, the data path for the MII was modified to allow a 4-bit (nibble) interface in both transmit and receive directions, lowering the required speed of operation (from a 100 MHz requirement if a bit-serial implementation were retained) to 25 MHz. In addition, the MII provided some additional enhancements to allow dedicated error and management signaling between the MAC and PHY. One of the biggest issues with the MII, from an implementation point of view, is the number of signal pins required between the MAC and PHY. It should be noted that the MII is capable of operating at both 10 Mb/s and 100 Mb/s data rates, whereas the AUI is only applicable to 10 Mb/s operation.

Another key difference between the AUI and the MII is that of distance, since the AUI was permitted to be up to 50 m in length, whereas the MII is restricted to a distance of 0.5 m.

Addition of Reconciliation Sublayer (RS)

The Reconciliation Sublayer (RS) is essentially a "standards-etiquette" layer. As Figure 3-1 shows, it resides between the original MAC layer and the MII. In practice, the RS provides no actual function and is implemented as an integral function of 100 Mb/s MAC devices. In terms of the 802.3u Standard, the RS provides the mapping between the original Ethernet MAC, which provided a bit-serial-only interface, and the MII, which provides a nibble-wide transmit/receive data interface.

The rationale for the RS was basically driven by the concept that the Ethernet MAC should be preserved as a standards entity, since it was the MAC that defined the "DNA" of Ethernet. (While the PHY layers could change under the MAC layer, the MAC layer provided the overall identity of the Ethernet protocol.) To accommodate this belief, the RS was added as a "shim" to convert the original bit-serial MAC interface to that defined by the MII.

Dual-Speed 10/100 Mb/s MAC Operation

While 10 Mb/s Ethernet components operated at this single data rate, even though a 1 Mb/s data rate option was developed (StarLAN[2]), building a device to operate at both speeds was not a popular option. However, during the development of 100BASE-T, it was a specific goal of the vendors involved in developing the standards to allow a single device to operate at either 10 or 100 Mb/s. This was driven by simple economics and a determination to preserve Ethernet's "plug-and-play" image. By the time 100BASE-T was being developed, there were literally tens of millions of 10 Mb/s Ethernet devices deployed in the marketplace. Vendors realized that in order

---

[2] American National Standards Institute/Institute of Electrical and Electronic Engineers, Information Technology—Local and Metropolitan Area Netowrks—Part 3: Carrier Sense Multiple Access with Collision Detection (CSMA/CD), IEEE, New York, NY, July 29, 1996. Section 12.

to maintain the market momentum of Ethernet, users would have to have a "backward compatibility" path. This would allow users to gradually install 100BASE-T devices, but not necessarily upgrade the whole network. In many cases, a new installation may use all 100-Mb/s-capable devices and operate at this data rate, whereas legacy networks might need devices to operate at the 10 Mb/s data rate for compatibility. What was really needed was a mechanism to automatically detect what speed the network devices were capable of operating at, before connecting to the network. This was the driving need that resulted in the development of the Auto-Negotiation protocol, which is also discussed in this section, since it was developed specifically for 100BASE-T.

The economics and practical realization of 10/100-Mb/s-capable devices is covered later in this chapter.

Deletion of Manchester Encoding

Manchester Encoding was described in Chapter 2. It provides the ability to combine a data bit in a serial stream with the appropriate clock information and is therefore efficient in that it requires no separate clock signal (an important issue in long-distance communications). However, Manchester encoding has a side effect that causes high frequencies to be generated. See "Physical Signaling Specification" in Chapter 2 for details. This aspect becomes less desirable as data rates increase, since the issues of electromagnetic interference (EMI) and radio-frequency interference (RFI) become very significant (EMI and RFI emissions and susceptibility become more of an issue as frequencies increase). Hence, encoding techniques more suited to high-speed signaling over various media types were required. The Manchester encoding of the AUI was replaced, and simple Non-Return-to-Zero (NRZ) was used over the nibble-wide interface for the MII transmit and receive data paths.

There was an additional benefit of moving from a Manchester encoded interface at the primary interoperability interface—namely, the AUI. Anything that connected to the AUI had to receive data from, and pass data back to, the MAC/PLS via the AUI, in Manchester encoded format. Hence, all 10 Mb/s transceivers had essentially used this Manchester data, with different voltage levels and current drives appropriate to each media type, and so Manchester Encoding was the approach used over the network medium as well as the AUI. As stated above, more complex coding techniques were required to operate at the 100 Mb/s data rate, and more coding choices were needed, to better suit these media types individually. These coding techniques are covered in much more detail in the "Media" and "Topology" sections of this chapter. Suffice it to say that the nibble-wide data interface with separate clock information is much better suited to these coding schemes than Manchester encoded serial data with its embedded clock information.

Class I and II Repeater Specifications

Unlike 10 Mb/s Ethernet, which had a single repeater definition for all media options, 100 Mb/s defines two different "classes" of repeater. The reason is the need to optimize the signal delays for 100BASE-T and the significant differences between the coding techniques employed for the different media types. The Class I repeater allowed more generous delays, to allow conversion between the two coding schemes, allowing all media types to be connected to the repeater. The Class II repeater was defined with much more stringent timing specifications, requiring it to be optimized to one specific coding scheme, meaning that it could not support all media types. This is discussed in more detail in the "100 Mb/s Repeaters" section later in this chapter.

An additional difference between the standards definitions for the 10 and 100 Mb/s repeaters is the way in which the delays through the repeaters are specified. In essence, a 10 Mb/s repeater has two defined conformance test interfaces where parameters such as delay can be measured. A 10 Mb/s "repeater unit" (the standards definition for the repeater without its physical-layer devices) has its delay measured at the AUI ports. Alternatively, a 10 Mb/s "repeater set" (the repeater function with the PHY component included) has its delay measured at the PHY interfaces.

In contrast, a 100 Mb/s repeater does not have any defined intermediate conformance test point, other than with its attached PHY devices. This is essentially an implementation issue. The delays through 10 Mb/s repeaters were readily achievable, so all repeater units could be easily constructed. This is not to say all 10 Mb/s repeaters have AUIs (the majority do not have exposed AUIs). The issue is a realization of the difficulty in meeting the delays of a repeater for 100 Mb/s if implemented using an explicit MII. The MII allows any kind of PHY to be attached, and the various PHYs have very different delays which are inherent to their native coding schemes.

It was understood from the beginning of the 100BASE-T development that operation of a CSMA/CD network would mandate a central repeater, since there was no support for mixing segments. This provided an opportunity not to repeat the redundant-timer situation present in the 10 Mb/s repeater definition (jabber in the 10 Mb/s PHY, and MJLP in the 10 Mb/s repeater). 100BASE-T optimized this so that a single jabber function is located only in the repeater, protecting the network from a faulty station that may transmit for excessive duration.

Addition of Auto-Negotiation

With the considerable sharing in functionality between the Ethernet MAC, RS, and MII, which are designed to support both 10 Mb/s and 100 Mb/s operation, there was an obvious requirement for vendors to support both 10 and 100 Mb/s operation with one device, especially in adapter-card and switch applications. 100BASE-T specifies an "Auto-Negotiation" function which allows "speed-agile" devices to be implemented. Such devices are interoperable with the installed base of 10 Mb/s and new or upgraded 100 Mb/s installations. Additionally, the Auto-Negotiation mechanism was developed to also determine half-duplex (CSMA/CD) or full-duplex capability.

Automatic configuration occurs without user intervention and will negotiate the optimal mode at which the devices at both ends of a link can commonly operate. In the event the devices share no common mode, the Auto-Negotiation scheme ensures that operation of the rest of the network is not disrupted, allowing the absence of a shared operational mode to be reported via network management.

Auto-Negotiation was defined only for twisted-pair cable media using the RJ-45 connector. There was a need to protect the installed base of 10BASE-T as new 100BASE-T devices were deployed, and also to take advantage of the new capabilities as network components were upgraded, without requiring manual intervention. It was not included on fiber optic versions, since fiber generally is deployed in much smaller volumes. In addition, it is not generally deployed where the user can gain physical access, so the network does not require protection from the uninitiated!

Accommodation for Full-Duplex Operation

While 10BASE-T had the ability to support full-duplex operation, since the 2-pair twisted-pair medium provided a full-duplex physical channel, there was no accommodation to define this in the standards documents, and so interoperability was not assured. Although several vendors offered full-duplex-capable 10 Mb/s products based on 10BASE-T, configuration had to be performed at both ends of the link to assure interoperability, and so this capability was rarely invoked in real installations. Full-duplex operation is discussed in detail in the "Full Duplex and Flow Control" section.

The 100BASE-T Standards were developed with the acknowledgement that full-duplex (versus the half-duplex CSMA/CD protocol) operation was not only desirable from an increased bandwidth perspective, it was actually a needed function. Since the round-trip propagation-delay limit sets the maximum network diameter for a CSMA/CD network, when the slot time is reduced by a factor of ten (since the bit rate is ten times as small as for 10 Mb/s), then the network diameter decreases by a factor of ten. Hence 100BASE-T networks have a much smaller geographic limit, as will be discussed later in the "Topology" section. Full-duplex operation removes the round-trip-delay limitation, allowing larger physical topologies to be supported.

Although not all the physical layers for 100BASE-T can support full-duplex operation, the RS, MII, and Auto-Negotiation additions defined in the 100BASE-T suite all were written to be "full-duplex aware."

Different Cable Categories and Numbers of Pairs Used

100 Mb/s Ethernet does not support any "mixing segments" as did the 10 Mb/s version—there are no provisions for coaxial cables with multiple devices attached, as

was the case for "Thick Ethernet" and "Cheapernet." All cabling is point-to-point, between DTEs and/or repeaters, using UTP, STP, or fiber optic cable as the allowable link segments.

Support for three types of twisted-pair media was initially developed, two UTP versions for Cat 3 and Cat 5 cable and one version for shielded twisted pair (STP). The 100BASE-TX specification defines operation over 2 pairs of Cat 5 UTP or 150 Ω STP. The 100BASE-T4 specification defines operation over 4 pairs of Cat 3 UTP. Fiber optic cable is also supported. The 100BASE-FX specification defines operation over a pair of 50/100 μm or 62.5/125 μm graded-index multimode fibers.

Soon after these initial PHY developments were commenced as integral parts of the overall Fast Ethernet suite, another physical layer effort was initiated. This effort, known as 100BASE-T2, developed a 100 Mb/s signaling scheme that operated over only two pairs of Cat 3 cable.

The rationale for developing this extensive suite to support multiple cable types, as well as the exact differences between each of these specifications, are defined in detail throughout this chapter.

Updated Management

The evolution of the 10 Mb/s 802.3 standards had primarily been focused on the addition of new MAUs at the Physical Layer, and new management capabilities (see the "Network Management" section in Chapter 2). This evolution had led to management features being added gradually, first to the DTE, then to the repeater, and finally to the MAU (in Sections/Clauses 5, 19, and 20, respectively). Since 100 Mb/s devices were intended to offer a superset of the existing 10 Mb/s management capabilities, with some 100 Mb/s specific additions, this was a natural place to integrate the management requirements into a single clause. Hence 802.3u Clause 30[3] integrated the 10 Mb/s applicable Sections 5 (DTE), 19 (Repeater), and 20 (MAU) into a single place in the document, and deprecated these predecessors.

Note: Deprecate had a has a special meaning in terns of the standards community. The American Heritage Dictionary definition states:

> deprecate: 1. To express disapproval of; deplore. 2. To belittle; depreciate, to ward off by prayer.

Usage Note: The first and fully accepted meaning of deprecate is "to express disapproval of." But the word has steadily encroached on the meaning of depreciate. It is now used, almost to the exclusion of depreciate, in the sense "to belittle or mildly

---

[3] Institute of Electrical and Electronic Engineers, Local and Metropolitan Area Networks, Media Access Control (MAC) Parameters, Physical Layer, Medium Attachment Units and Repeater for 100 Mb/s Operation, Type 100BASE-T (Clauses 21–30). IEEE Std 802.3u—1995, (Supplement to ISO/IEC 8802-3, 1993 [ANSI/IEEE Std. 802.3, 1993 Edition]), IEEE, New York, NY, October 26, 1995, ISBN 1-55937-542-6. Clause 30.

disparage" as in "he deprecated his own contribution." In an earlier survey, this newer sense was approved by a majority of the Usage Panel.]

Topology

The network span (or diameter) of 100BASE-T networks is considerably reduced over those permitted for 10 Mb/s topologies. This is due to the tenfold reduction of the bit time, and the direct effect of this on the round-trip-delay parameter. In an attempt to mitigate the topology restrictions, two types of repeaters were defined, allowing either single Class 1 repeater or dual Class II repeater configurations. These aspects are discussed in detail in the "Mixed Topologies" section later in this chapter.

3.2 Functional Overview of the 802.3u Standard Suite

100BASE-T was approved as an official IEEE Standard (as the 802.3u supplement to the original 802.3 Standard) in June 1995.[4]

100BASE-T retains the same Ethernet CSMA/CD Media Access Control (MAC) protocol, effectively scaling the data rate from the original 10 Mb/s to 100 Mb/s. The topology is a repeater based star, with two repeater types supported (defined as Class I and Class II repeaters).

As an aside, there were some minor terminology changes in the 802.3u standard. One of the least important was that "sections" in the previous 10Mb/s documents (Sections 1–20 at the time, the 100BASE-T effort commenced) were now referred to as "Clauses" Clauses 21–30 when the initial 100BASE-T Standard was ratified). A concise table in Appendix A provides a quick reference guide between section/clause number, subject matter, and publication title.

3.2.1 Reconciliation Sublayer (RS) and Medium Independent Interface (MII)

100BASE-T defined a new sublayer under the MAC, called the Reconciliation Sublayer (RS). The RS essentially maps the behavior of the MAC to the electrical signals of the Medium Independent Interface (MII) (Figure 3-3). More precisely, it maps the new nibble-wide[5] data path and associated control signals of the MII to the original PLS

---

[4] Institute of Electrical and Electronic Engineers, Local and Metropolitan Area Networks, Media Access Control (MAC) Parameters, Physical Layer, Medium Attachment Units and Repeater for 100 Mb/s Operation, Type 100BASE-T (Clauses 21–30). IEEE Std 802.3u—1995, (Supplement to ISO/IEC 8802-3, 1993 [ANSI/IEEE Std. 802.3, 1993 Edition]), IEEE, New York, NY, October 26, 1995, ISBN 1-55937-542-6.

[5] A nibble is 4 bits.

service interface definitions (the MAC/PLS interface), which were originally defined as bit-serial.

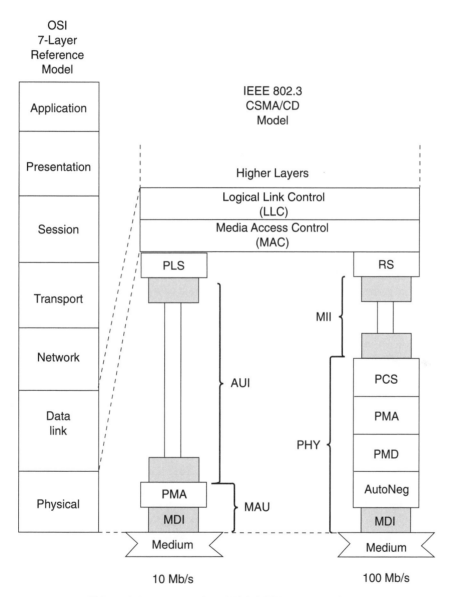

Figure 3-3 802.3u 10/100 Mb/s DTE Layer Model
(From IEEE Std. 802.3u-1995, ©1995, IEEE. All rights reserved.)

The MII is a logical equivalent to the Attachment Unit Interface (AUI) of the original 10 Mb/s Ethernet. The AUI allowed different media types to be supported under the original Ethernet MAC and Manchester encoder/decoder (the Physical Layer Signaling sublayer, or PLS, as in Figure 2-1). Unlike the AUI, which required a 6-pin (3-pair) serial interface between the DTE and the MAU, the MII is an 18-pin signal interface. Data is moved across the MII at the rate of one nibble (4 bits) for each clock cycle, hence the transmit and receive clocks operate at one-quarter of the 100BASE-T data rate of 100 Mb/s. Since the interface supports both 10 and 100 Mb/s data rates, the clocks operate at either 2.5 or 25 MHz, respectively. The MII signal pins consist of the transmit and receive data nibbles, clocks, data valid and error signals. In addition, carrier (network) activity, collision detect, and management interface signals are provided.

The MII can be used as an interconnect at the chip (integrated circuit), board, or physical device level. As an inter-chip connection, it is typically implemented as printed-circuit board traces. As an inter-board connection, it is typically implemented as a motherboard-to-daughterboard connection with suitable mating connector(s). As an inter-device connection, it is required to be implemented as a cable and connector interface. For this purpose a 40-pin connector is defined and accommodates the 18 signals, common return paths, and +5.0 V power. The cable consists of individual twisted pairs for each signal, with an overall shield. The connector on the MAC/RS function requires a female connector, and the mating cable, normally attached to the PHY device, requires a male connector. Due to the relatively high frequency and synchronous nature of the interface, the total cable length is restricted to 0.5 m. For inter-chip or inter-board connectivity, it is assumed that distance is always shorter than this limit.

The 18 pins of the MII are divided into 4 groups: transmit data, receive data, network status, and device management. All of the interface signals operate at TTL levels and are defined to be compatible with both 3.3 and 5.0 V CMOS ASIC processes (unlike the 10 Mb/s AUI, which uses Pseudo-ECL (PECL) levels, much less commonly available in ASIC libraries).

The nibble-wide data transmit and receive paths, as well as their associated control signals, operate synchronously to their respective clocks. The reason for a dedicated nibble-wide path for both transmit and receive is primarily to allow future full-duplex operation. However, for traditional half-duplex Ethernet operation, a single data path suffices. Figure 3-4 shows the relationship between bytes passed to and from the MAC to the nibbles to and from the MII.

A simple serial management interface is defined to communicate with an underlying physical layer or PHY device (or devices) to allow control and status information to be exchanged and management information to be gathered. This aspect is somewhat unusual in terms of 802.3, in that the RS defines the management register requirements of the PHY, which is a separate sublayer, although still within the Phys-

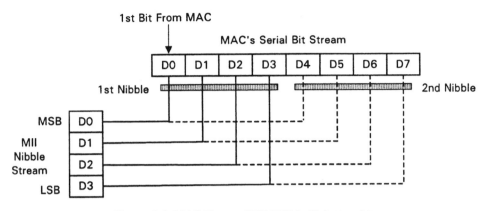

Figure 3-4 MAC Byte to MII Nibble Relationship
(From IEEE Std. 802.3u-1995, ©1995, IEEE. All rights reserved.)

ical Layer. Note that the MII Management Interface is defined to support multiple PHYs under a single RS (up to a maximum of 32). This feature is useful in implementations such as multiport repeaters and/or switches, where multiple PHYs can be serviced by a single instantiation of the management interface.

In the following descriptions of the signals, note that in terms of the 802.3u Standard, the RS and MII are defined with respect to a DTE, and no such interface is defined for a repeater. However, in practical terms, a repeater has to implement a logically similar interface.

MII Transmit Interface Signals

Refer to Figure 3-5.

Transmit Clock (TX_CLK)

The transmit clock is a continuous clock provided by the PHY and passed to the DTE (or repeater if it implements an MII). The TX_CLK signal provides the timing reference to the Reconciliation Sublayer, which drives the TXD, TX_EN, and TX_ER signals synchronously with this clock, in order to transmit data and issue status. TX_CLK runs at either 2.5 MHz (for 10 Mb/s network operation) or 25 MHz (for 100 Mb/s operation), depending upon the PHY's selection criteria.

Transmit Data (TXD <3-0>)

This group of four pins is used to transfer nibbles of transmit data issued by the DTE (or repeater), to be appropriately encoded and conditioned prior to transmission by the PHY on the medium. Data nibbles presented by the RS when TX_EN is inactive are ignored.

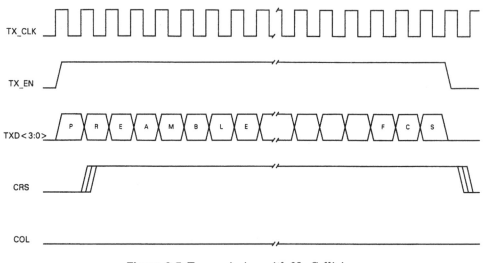

Figure 3-5 Transmission with No Collision
(From IEEE Std. 802.3u-1995, ©1995, IEEE. All rights reserved.)

Transmit Enable (TX_EN)

This signal is asserted by the DTE (or repeater) to indicated that valid data is being presented on the TXD pins and should be transmitted by the PHY onto the network medium.

Transmit Error (TX_ER)

This signal is asserted by the DTE (or optionally the repeater) to indicate to the PHY(s) that a coding violation was detected in the received signal stream. When the TX_ER signal is active for one or more TX_CLK periods at any time that TX_EN is active, the PHY is responsible for generating an invalid transmit frame on the medium, by generating any encoding that is neither normal data nor delimiter information. The relative position of the error condition in the transmitted frame does not need to be retained. The intent is to ensure that a receiving PHY will always detect this frame as having an error. An MII implementation on a DTE or repeater need not implement the TX_ER pin, if an alternative method is provided to guarantee that the distant receiver will always detect an error in the frame. Typically this is performed within a multiport repeater or switch implementation, where the retransmission process can be implemented to enforce the generation of an invalid transmit frame prior to passing it to the PHY over the MII. TX_ER has no effect on PHYs operating at 10 Mb/s. The valid encodings of TX_ER, TX_EN, and TXD are shown in Table 3-1.

Table 3-1 MII Transmit Interface Signal Encoding[a]

TX_EN	TX_ER	TXD<3:0>	Indication
0	0	0000–1111	Normal Inter-Packet Gap
0	1	0000–1111	Reserved
1	0	0000–1111	Normal Transmit Data
1	1	0000–1111	Transmit Error Indication

[a](From IEEE Std. 802.3u-1995, ©1995, IEEE. All rights reserved.)

MII Receive Interface Signals

Refer to Figure 3-6.

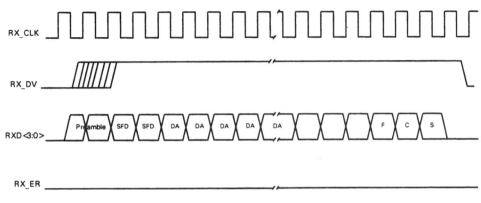

Figure 3-6 Reception with No Errors
(From IEEE Std. 802.3u-1995, ©1995, IEEE. All rights reserved.)

Receive Clock (RX_CLK)

The receive clock is a continuous clock provided by the PHY and passed to the DTE (or repeater if it implements an MII). The RX_CLK signal provides the timing reference that the PHY uses to synchronously drive the RXD, RX_DV and RX_ER signals, in order to pass receive data and/or status decoded from the medium, back to the Reconciliation Sublayer. RX_CLK runs at either 2.5 MHz (for 10 Mb/s network operation) or 25 MHz (for 100 Mb/s operation), depending on the PHY's selection criteria.

The clock is recovered by the PHY from the incoming data stream.

Receive Data (RXD <3-0>)

This group of four pins is used to transfer nibbles of receive data decoded from the medium by the PHY to the DTE (or repeater). Data nibbles presented to the RS when RX_EN is inactive are ignored.

Receive Data Valid (RX_DV)

This signal is asserted by the PHY to indicate to the DTE (or repeater) that valid data decoded from the medium is being presented on the RXD pins. As shown in Figure 3-6, RX_DV must be asserted prior to the first SFD nibble (although it is permitted to be asserted during preamble) and must be deasserted immediately at the end of the last nibble of the received frame's CRS (prior to the next rising edge of RX_CLK).

Receive Error (RX_ER)

This signal is asserted by the PHY to indicate to the DTE (or repeater) that a coding violation was detected in the data received from the medium by the PHY. It may be the detection of an illegal code or any other error detection that the PHY is capable of performing, that would otherwise be undetected by the MAC sublayer.

When the RX_ER signal is activated for one or more RX_CLK periods at any time that RX_DV is active, the PHY indicates to the RS that an error has been detected somewhere in the current receive frame. When RX_ER is asserted and RX_DV is inactive, the value of the RXD<3:0> pins indicate whether this is a False Carrier event or a normal Inter-Packet Gap condition. A False Carrier event is a medium-specific PHY detected error, which indicates generally that a false start-of-frame was detected on the medium. The relative position of the error condition within the received frame is not guaranteed. The intent is to ensure that a receiving RS/MAC will always detect this frame as containing an error. An MII implementation on a DTE or repeater should use the RX_ER indication to drive the TX_ER pin when the frame is retransmitted, or else use an alternative method to guarantee that a distant receiver can always detect that there was an error in the frame. Typically this is performed within a multiport repeater or switch implementation, where the retransmission process can be implemented to enforce the generation of an invalid transmit frame prior to passing it to the PHY over the MII. The valid encodings of RX_ER, RX_DV, and RXD are shown in Table 3-2.

Table 3-2 MII Receive Interface Signal Encoding[a]

RX_DV	RX_ER	RXD<3:0>	Indication
0	0	0000–1111	Normal Inter-Packet Gap
0	1	0000	Normal Inter-Packet Gap
0	1	0000–1101	Reserved
0	1	1110	False Carrier Indication
0	1	1111	Reserved
1	0	0000–1111	Normal Receive Data
1	1	0000–1111	Receive Error Indication

[a](From IEEE Std. 802.3u-1995, ©1995, IEEE. All rights reserved.)

MII Network Status Interface Signals

Refer to Figure 3-7.

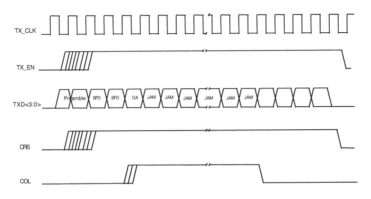

Figure 3-7 Transmission with Collision Detection

Carrier Sense (CRS)

CRS is asserted by the PHY to indicate that either the transmit or receive medium is active, and it is deasserted when both the transmit and receive media are idle. Note that this definition of active versus idle is based on whether the PHY is detecting valid packet data. Depending upon the particular medium and associated PHY, there may be signaling on the medium even though there is no packet data (in other words, the Inter-Frame Spacing has a specific signal associated with it). CRS is required to be asserted throughout the duration of a collision condition. CRS has no synchronous relationship to either TX_CLK or RX_CLK. Figures 3-5 and 3-7 show the behavior of CRS for a normal transmission without collision and with a detected collision, respectively.

Collision (COL)

COL is asserted by the PHY to indicate that a collision condition has been detected on the medium, and remains asserted while the collision condition persists. COL has no synchronous relationship to either TX_CLK or RX_CLK. Figures 3-5 and 3-7 show the behavior of COL for a normal transmission without collision, and with a detected collision, respectively. If full-duplex operation is selected, the COL signal is undefined. Since full-duplex operation has no concept of collision, the state of this signal is meaningless.

MII Management Interface

Management Data Clock (MDC)

The clock signal is provided by the DTE (or repeater) and used to synchronously transfer data in and out of the PHY using the MDIO pin. MDC operates at a maximum frequency of 2.5 MHz as specified by the 802.3u standard. However, RS and PHY integrated-circuit implementations exist which will run at significantly increased rate (i.e., 10 MHz). This is typically used to optimize the polling of the MII management registers when multiple PHYs are implemented on a single MII Management Interface. This is shown in more detail in Figure 3-8.

Management Data Input Output (MDIO)

This is a bidirectional signal that allows serial data to be clocked in and out of the PHY device. A management entity (the standards term is "Station Management Entity," mysteriously abbreviated to "STA") is assumed to be present somewhere in the DTE (or repeater) implementation, and resides above the MII.[6]

Control and configuration data from the management entity is driven onto the MDIO line synchronously with MDC and sampled synchronously by the PHY. Status information provided by the PHY, in response to a request to read a management register by the management entity, is driven onto the MDIO line synchronously with MDC by the PHY and sampled synchronously by the management entity.

The PHY that uses an exposed MII connector must provide a pull-up resistor on the MDIO line. The DTE (or repeater) must incorporate a weak pull-down resistor. Hence, if there is no PHY plugged into the MII connector, the MDIO pin will be in a low state. When the PHY is plugged in, the condition of the pin changes to a high state.

MII Management Protocol

Management data is written and read using a defined frame format, passed serially over the MDIO line, synchronous to MDC. The frame format is shown in Table 3-3 for write transactions to the PHY and read transactions from the PHY. Bit transmission order is from left to right.

Table 3-3 Management Frame Structure[a]

	Management Frame Fields							
	PRE	ST	OP	PHYAD	REGAD	TA	DATA	IDLE
Read	1...1	01	10	AAAAA	RRRRR	Z0	DDDDDDDDDDDDDDDD	Z
Write	1...1	01	01	AAAAA	RRRRR	10	DDDDDDDDDDDDDDDD	Z

[a](From IEEE Std. 802.3u-1995, ©1995, IEEE. All rights reserved.)

---

[6] From a practical standpoint, the management entity is typically a software task that resides on a processor.

Note that in the following text, fields or values are expressed in the form <ST> or <00>. For instance, <00> is equivalent to the binary sequence "0, 0."

PRE (Preamble)

The management entity commences each management frame transaction with a preamble sequence of 32 consecutive 1s on MDIO during 32 consecutive clocks on MDC. This allows the PHY to synchronize to the new frame. A "preamble suppression" option is permitted which allows this sequence to be eliminated, but only if the management entity determines that all PHYs connected to the MDIO line are capable of supporting this option.

ST (Start Delimiter)

A <01> transition indicates the start of the management frame and ensures that the MDIO line can be driven both high and low.

OP (Operation Code)

The operation code for a write (<01>) indicates the management entity will supply the address of both the PHY and management register to be written, as well as the data itself. An operation code for a read (<10>) indicates that the management entity will supply the address of both the PHY and management register to be read, and the PHY will supply the data.

PHYAD (PHY Address)

This is a 5-bit address unique within an individual MDIO/MDC implementation, allowing up to 32 PHYs to be addressed. The address is transmitted MSB first. A PHY that is provided with an exposed MII connector is required to respond to the address <00000>. In an implementation that integrates multiple PHYs, the management entity must have prior knowledge of the addresses that are present.

This apparently simple requirement has generated significant issues for PHY silicon implementers. Consider a silicon supplier who wishes to make a general-purpose PHY chip. Prior to 100BASE-T, such chips were not required to respond to a specific address. However, 100 Mb/s PHYs require a specific 5-bit address. Generally, the silicon implementers have no knowledge of how the PHY will be used by a system manufacturer, whether as an integrated PHY within a DTE, a separate PHY with an MII connector, or as one of multiple PHYs integrated in a multiport device. This means the only option is to allow the manufacturer of the end system product to be able to program the address of the PHY. The simplest way is to read the address from some pins on the chip, typically configured by strapping these high or low at power-up. As silicon suppliers provided more integrated PHY products, such as quad-channel devices, shown in Figure 3-8, only the upper bits of the PHYAD were programmed externally, while the individual PHY address selection was performed internally by means of the physical channel number.

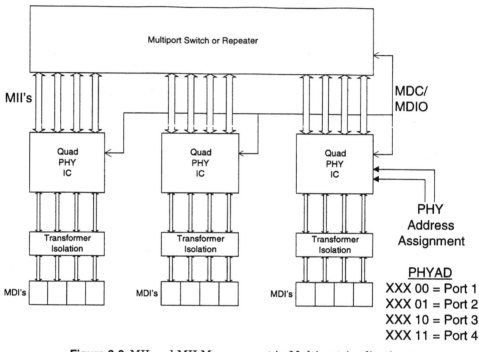

Figure 3-8 MII and MII Management in Multiport Applications

REGAD (Register Address)

This is a 5-bit address which selects the internal management register within the specified PHY that is to be addressed, allowing up to 32 PHYs to be addressed. The address is transmitted MSB first. Address <00000> is defined as the Control Register and <00001> is defined as the Status Register in all implementations (see the "MII Management Registers" section for more details).

TA (Turnaround)

During read operations from the PHY, the MDIO line must be turned around from being driven by the management entity, which drives the sequence <PRE><ST><OP><PHYAD><REGAD>, prior to the PHY driving the 16-bit <DDD...DDD> field. During the first bit of the <TA> field for a read operation, both the management entity and the PHY place their MDIO drivers in a high-impedance state, and during the second bit time the PHY drives the MDIO line to a low state, indicated by <Z0>. During a write operation to the PHY, the management entity drives the <TA> field with a <10> field.

DATA (Management Frame Data)

This is a 16-bit data field, transmitted MSB first, containing the value to be written into or read from the specified register address of the addressed PHY.

IDLE (Inter-frame Spacing)

Between management frames, both the management entity and the PHY place their drivers in the high-impedance state. The weak pull-up resistor on the PHY will cause MDIO to go to a logic one state.

MII Management Registers

The MII defines a set of management registers that are read and written by the management entity (i.e., an adapter card, or the management process in a managed repeater) via the MDIO/MDC management interface pair. These registers are broken into four fundamental groups, as shown in Table 3-4. *Basic* registers are essentially the mandatory minimum set that any PHY must support. *Extended* registers are used for enhanced features, such as support for Auto-Negotiation. *Reserved* registers are essentially intended to remain under IEEE administration to be allocated if additional features are added in the future (100BASE-T2 was allocated some of this group when it was defined, which subsequently redefined these to the Extended group). *Vendor* registers allocate the upper 16 register addresses to be used in a vendor-specific manner.

This section will restrict discussion to the mandatory registers actually defined in the RS/MII clause (registers 0 through 3). The other registers are specific to either the Auto-Negotiation function or the 100BASE-T2 medium type and are therefore described in those sections.

Note that the convention for referring to a specific register bit is "RegisterNumber.BitPosition." So, for instance, 0.15 would be register 0 (Control), bit position 15 (Reset). Multiple bits grouped as a field are referenced in the form 0.6:0, indicating register 0 (Control), bits 6 through 0 (Reserved).

Control (Register 0)

The Control Register is generally written by the management entity. It may be read after power-up or on detection of a change in the number of PHYs present. Bit definitions are given in Table 3-5.

Table 3-4 MII Management Register Map[a]

Register Address	Register Name	Requirement	Type	Defined in Clause
0	Control	Mandatory	Basic	22
1	Status	Mandatory	Basic	22
2	PHY Identifier	Mandatory (may return all zeroes)	Extended	22
3	PHY Identifier	Mandatory (may return all zeroes)	Extended	22
4	Auto-Negotiation Advertisement	Mandatory with Auto-Negotiation	Extended	28
5	Auto-Negotiation Link Partner Ability	Mandatory with Auto-Negotiation	Extended	28
6	Auto-Negotiation Expansion	Mandatory with Auto-Negotiation	Extended	28
7	Auto-Negotiation Next Page Transmit	Auto-Negotiation with Next Page only	Extended	28
8	Auto-Negotiation Link Partner Received Next Page	Auto-Negotiation with 100BASE-T2 only	Extended	32
9	100BASE-T2 Control Register	Mandatory for 100BASE-T2	Extended	32
10	100BASE-T2 Status Register	Mandatory for 100BASE-T2	Extended	32
11–15	Reserved	Unspecified	Reserved	N/A
16–31	Vendor Specific	Vendor Specific Extensions	Vendor	N/A

[a](From IEEE Std. 802.3u-1995, ©1995, IEEE. All rights reserved.)

Table 3-5 Control Register Bit Definition[a]

Bit(s)	Name	Description
0.15	Reset	Reset the PHY
0.14	Loopback	Data presented on the MII transmit data path is looped back to the receive data path
0.13	Speed Selection	Manual speed select when Auto-Negotiation is disabled
0.12	Auto-Negotiation Enable	Enable Auto-Negotiation for PHY technology, speed, and half-/full-duplex selection
0.11	Power Down	Place the PHY in a low power mode (data path disabled, management path enabled)
0.10	Isolate	Isolate PHY from MII pin, except MII management (used for implementations with more than one PHY)
0.9	Reset Auto-Negotiation	Forces Auto-Negotiation to be restarted
0.8	Duplex Mode	Manual half-/full-duplex selection when Auto-Negotiation is disabled
0.7	Collision Test	Configures PHY to activate COL pin when TX_EN enabled
0.6:0	Reserved	Undefined (write as 0, ignore on read)

[a](From IEEE Std. 802.3u-1995, ©1995, IEEE. All rights reserved.)

Status (Register 1)

The Status Register is a read-only register that returns the configuration and condition of the PHY. Bit definitions are defined in Table 3-6.

Table 3-6 Status Register Bit Definition[a]

Bit(s)	Name	Description
1.15	100BASE-T4	Indicates PHY incorporates 100BASE-T4 capability
1.14	100BASE-X Full Duplex	Indicates PHY incorporates 100BASE-TX/FX full-duplex capability
1.13	100BASE-X Half Duplex	Indicates PHY incorporates 100BASE-TX/FX half-duplex capability
1.12	10 MB/s Full Duplex	Indicates PHY incorporates 10BASE-T/F full-duplex capability
1.11	10 MB/s Half Duplex	Indicates PHY incorporates 10BASE-T/F half-duplex capability
1.10:7	Reserved	Undefined (ignore on read)
1.6	MF Preamble Suppression	Indicates PHY can accept management frames with preamble suppression
1.5	Auto-Negotiation Complete	Indicates the Auto-Negotiation process has completed
1.4	Remote Fault	Indicates the remote device at the other end of the link has a fault condition
1.3	Auto-Negotiation Ability	Indicates the PHY incorporates the Auto-Negotiation capability
1.2	Link Status	Indicates link pass or link fail state
1.1	Jabber Detect	Indicates jabber condition detected (10 Mb/s MAUs only)
1.0	Extended Capability	Indicates Extended Registers are implemented

[a](From IEEE Std. 802.3u-1995, ©1995, IEEE. All rights reserved.)

PHY Identifier (Registers 2 and 3)

The PHY Identifier is a 32-bit value, intended to store a unique value, in order to determine the exact vendor, model number, and version number of a particular PHY. Since it is part of the extended register set, the 802.3u standard allows a PHY to return an all-0s value in this field, so its value is somewhat compromised. In order to make the storage and recreation of this value as trivial as possible, it is based on the Organizationally Unique Identifier (OUI), which is a unique 32-bit value assigned to vendors who wish to manufacture 802-based network equipment; it is assigned by the IEEE.[7] For more information on the OUI field, see Appendix B. The mapping of the OUI bits into the PHY Identifier registers is shown in Figure 3-9.

A key point regarding the value of the PHY Identifier is that it should contain the OUI of the end system manufacturer (i.e., an adapter-card manufacturer). It should not contain the OUI of an intermediate component manufacturer (i.e., a silicon vendor who supplied the embedded PHY integrated circuit on an adapter card). This is the primary reason that the PHY is permitted to return a zero value for the PHY Identifier. It is assumed that a vendor may be able to create the PHY Identifier value from duplicate information stored in a system product.

---

[7] Inquiries related to the assignment of OUIs should be made to the IEEE Standards Department, Institute of Electrical and Electronic Engineers, 445 Hoes Lane, P.O. Box 1331, Piscataway, NJ 08855-1331, USA.

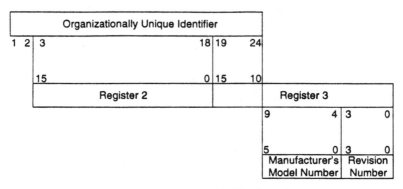

Figure 3-9 Format of PHY Identifier

3.2.2 "Reduced" MII

Ethernet/802.3 repeaters and switches have become extremely integrated, including the transceiver (or MAU) functionality. This is due mainly to the predominant deployment of 10BASE-T, the UTP star-wired version of 10 Mb/s Ethernet. However, as Ethernet has been upgraded to support 100 Mb/s operation, some of the previous definitions and assumptions for being able to make an inexpensive, single-chip, low-pin-count package that houses the entire repeater or switch functionality have changed.

The 802.3u Standard defined two UTP physical media types, these being Cat 3 and Cat 5. The 100BASE-TX specification defines operation over two pairs of Cat 5 UTP. The 100BASE-T4 specification defines operation over four pairs of Cat 3 UTP. A further 100BASE-FX specification allows operation over dual fiber optic cabling. In order to allow a switch or repeater to use whichever medium is more suitable, the PHY in 100BASE-T (which includes the encoder decoder) is segregated by a Medium Independent Interface (MII), which is essentially analogous in function to the AUI of 10 Mb/s Ethernet. However, while the AUI is only a 6-pin (three differential pairs) interface, the MII consists of 16 data and control signal pins.

Since a repeater for 100BASE-T would ideally be constructed so that some or all of its ports could be connected to any MII-based PHY, the 16-pin-per-port overhead is extremely costly, especially in modern high-density silicon process technologies. This overhead may be such as to make a repeater chip which has all MII ports "pad limited." There will be so many pads for interconnect to the external device pins, the repeater state machines being of moderately low complexity, that the spacing of the pads will determine the die size of the chip, and there will be inadequate additional complexity in the logic of the chip to fill the available silicon "real estate" enclosed by the pad ring. This is extremely undesirable. Clearly the objective is to reduce the pin overhead, while still allowing the repeater chip to connect and operate with any MII-based PHY device.

The Reduced MII or RMII[8] was a result of the realization that ever-reducing silicon geometries and ever-increasing port densities for repeaters and switches were bound to make a pin-count reduction for the MII function a pressing issue. The primary reason this specification was not developed within 802.3 was that the 802.3z Gigabit Ethernet development was in full swing at the same time. Vendors felt that it might defocus the Gigabit Ethernet standardization efforts if the development of another 100 Mb/s electrical interface were attempted at the same time.

As stated previously, the MII has a significant implementation "tax" in terms of the number of pins required. A standard MII uses a total of 16 pins for data and control along with two management pins. In devices incorporating several MACs with external PHY interfaces, such as integrated switches or repeaters, the number of pins becomes very large. For example, in a typical switch product that provides 24 ports, an MII-based solution uses a total of 384 data and control pins just for the physical-layer interface—clearly unacceptable. The RMII provides the same characteristics as the existing IEEE 802.3u MII while providing an interface that is independent of PHY port densities and saves a total of nine data and control pins per port. Therefore, a 24-port switch product requires a total of 168 pins, not including the management function—a substantial reduction.

The RMII supports both 10 Mb/s and 100 Mb/s data rates, full-duplex operation and uses TTL-compatible signals in order be compatible with common CMOS processes. Unlike the original MII, the RMII was designed only as a chip-to-chip interconnect, and both connector and cable connections were not specified. Since most multiport devices require connections to their attached physical layers to be in close proximity, this was an acceptable compromise. In addition, unlike the MII, the RMII operates synchronously. This allows the transmit paths and the receive paths to operate based upon the same clock as the switch and repeater, saving both clock pins. However, in order to provide a substantial pin reduction, the data and control paths were reduced by specifying that the RMII operate at 50 MHz, twice the data rate as the MII. This allowed the transmit and receive data paths to be reduced from nibble-wide, to di-bits or two bits wide in each direction, saving four pins. Altering the functions of Carrier Sense, Collision, Receive Data Valid and the RX_ER, TX_ER MII signals by remapping them saved the remaining three pins to complete the RMII. The new pins are described in Table 3-7, while the architecture is shown in Figure 3-10 with reference to the existing MII. The original MII signals are shown on the left and right of the figure, with the new RMII mappings in the center.

---

[8] AMD, National Semiconductor, TI, et al., *Reduced MII Interface, Rev. 1.0*, September 1997.

Table 3-7 Reduced MII Signals

Signal Name	Direction (with respect to the PHY)	Direction (with respect to the switch or repeater)	Description of Use
REF_CLK	Input	Input or Output	Synchronous clock reference for receive transmit and control interface. REF_CLK is provided by the switch or repeater or an external source. REF_CLK is a 50 MHz signal.
CRS_DV	Output	Input	Carrier Sense/Receive Data Valid. CRS_DV is asserted asynchronously to REF_CLK when the medium is not-idle. Loss of carrier shall cause CRS_DV to deassert. RXD[1:0] is considered valid when this signal is asserted.
RXD[1:0]	Output	Input	Receive Data. Two bits of recovered data synchronous with REF_CLK.
TX_EN	Input	Output	Transmit Enable. When this signal is asserted, the data on TXD[1:0] is valid.
TXD[1:0]	Input	Output	Transmit Data. Two bits of transmit data synchronous with REF_CLK.
RX_ER	Output	Input (Not required)	Receive Error. Similar signal to IEEE 802.3u Clause 24. To be asserted on error conditions.

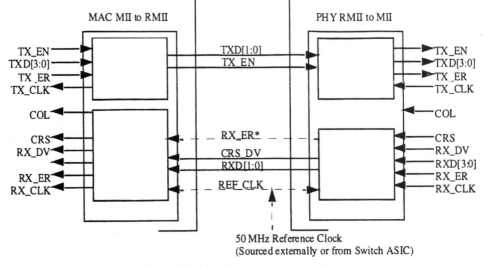

50 MHz Reference Clock
(Sourced externally or from Switch ASIC)

Figure 3-10 Reduced MII Architecture

* RX_ER is a required output of the PHY. The switch ASIC may choose to use this input.

3.3 Media and Topology Options

Like the 10 Mb/s standards that preceded, 100 Mb/s Ethernet was developed with an expansive view of the media types required to support the dissimilar topology and market needs of the networking industry.

100BASE-T supports two UTP versions, defined as 100BASE-T4 (four pair, Cat 3 and above) and 100BASE-TX (two pair, Cat 5). Both of these were focused on desktop connectivity and are restricted to cable length of 100 m. A 100BASE-FX fiber optic version is also specified, although this is generally used for longer-distance communications, such as between floors in a building, or even between buildings. Both 50/100 m and 62.5/125 m fiber cables are specified.

The topologies of Figures 3-11 and 3-13 illustrate representative topologies using Class II repeaters. A Class I mixed-media topology is shown in Fig. 3-15. Repeater "classes" are discussed later in this chapter under the "100 Mb/s Repeaters" heading. For the purposes of looking at the different PHY technologies, simply assume that a repeater function is present in a CSMA/CD network topology (although a bridge or switch could also be use to interconnect half- and/or full-duplex links).

3.3.1 100BASE-T4—Category 3 UTP

100BASE-T4, as shown in Figure 3-11, operates over four pairs of Cat 3 (or better) cable. Cat 3 bundles (such as the 25-pair bundles supported in 10BASE-T) are not permitted. DTE-to-repeater distances are restricted to 100 m. 100BASE-T4 is defined in Clause 23 of the 100BASE-T Specification.

The 100BASE-T4 PHY uses a block-coding scheme specifically developed to enable signaling at 100 Mb/s to be achieved over this type of cable, defined as 8B/6T encoding, as shown in Figure 3-12a. In this scheme, three of the four pairs are used for data transmission by either the DTE or the repeater and the remaining pair is used to detect simultaneous activity from the device at the other end of the link indicating a collision condition. Figure 3-12a shows the basic transmit operation of the 100BASE-T PHY. When the DTE transmits, the PHY takes two nibbles from the MII to form a byte, and converts this to a 6-bit ternary symbol on the medium. Each symbol (data byte) is sent over one of the three pairs, with each byte being encoded and transmitted on the pairs in a round-robin sequence.

The 8B/6T encoding technique maps the 256 possible 8B data-byte values to a subset of the available 6T ternary codes available (there are $3^6 = 729$ possible values available). Each of the 6-bit positions in the ternary code is permitted to take one of three values, defined as +1, 0, and −1. This allows the data code values to be carefully selected from the available options, such that additional benefits can be achieved. These include maintaining good clock transition density to simplify receive clock recovery, minimizing high-energy transitions (from +1 to −1, or −1 to +1) to limit

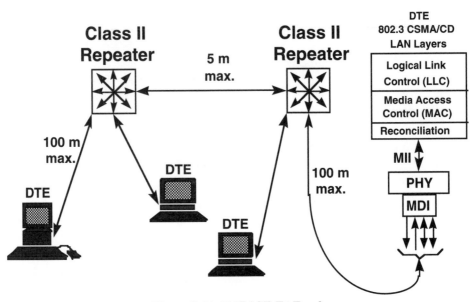

Figure 3-11 100BASE-T4 Topology

RFI/EMI effects, maintaining good DC balance on the lines by dynamically modifying the transmitted code group, and building-in error detection and robustness by using knowledge of the received code-group characteristics.

Figure 3-12b shows a detailed example of the encoding on the three transmit pairs. The Channel 1 pair (designated the TX_D1 pair) is a unidirectional output from each device used for data symbol transmission and collision resolution when transmitting. The Channel 2 pair (designated the RX_D2 pair, although not shown in Figure 3-12b) is a unidirectional input to each device used for data symbol reception when receiving, and collision detection when transmitting. The Channel 3 and Channel 4 pairs (designated ad BI_D3 and BI_D4) are bidirectional lines used to transmit and/or receive data symbols. The crossover function required between two 100BASE-T devices makes the pair allocation clearer, and is shown in Figure 3-18b.

When a 100BASE-T4 device transmits, although the data rate on each of the three pairs is 33 Mb/s, the increased efficiency of the 8B/6T coding means the frequency on the lines is only 25 MHz. A DTE or repeater uses three pairs for packet-data transmission while listening for collision on the remaining pair. While transmitting, a DTE or repeater monitors the Channel 2 pair (RX-D2) for activity that indicates a collision. If a collision condition is detected, it is resolved (using the standard jam and backoff sequences) between the unidirectional pairs and the bidirectional pairs become idle.

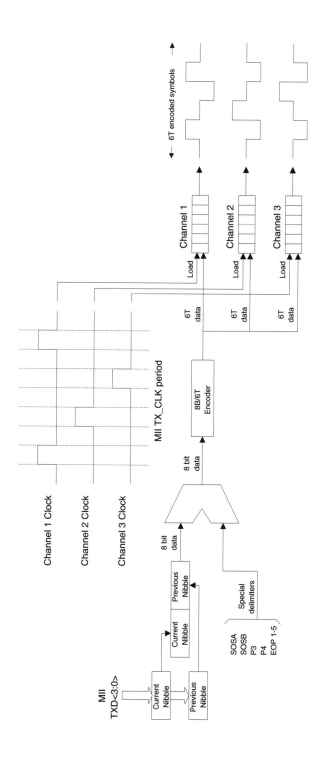

Figure 3-12a 8B/6T Encoding for 100BASE-T4 PHY

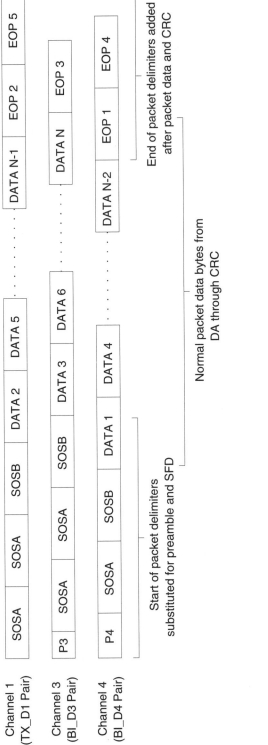

Figure 3-12b Transmit Encoding Sequence for 100BASE-T4 Pairs

Figure 3-12b shows the resulting transmission sequence over the three pairs. The 100BASE-T4 PHY replaces the preamble sequence from the MII with the special ternary "start-of-stream" delimiters SOSA and SOSB. The first 5 bytes of preamble are replaced with SOSA and the remaining 3 preamble/SFD bytes are replaced with SOSB, which is output on each line immediately prior to the encoded data. SOSB acts as a start-of-data delimiter for the receiving device. The ordering of which pair the first SOSA is output on is arbitrary, but once started, continues in a round-robin manner, as shown. The P3 and P4 patterns are essentially the same as the SOSA pattern, but only two and three ternary symbols in length, respectively, and are used for alignment. The receiving device reverses this process and removes the SOSA/SOSB code groups and replaces the preamble/SFD sequence, passing this back to the receiving MAC via the MII. Immediately following the last byte of data at the end of frame transmission, the special "end-of-packet" delimiters EOP1 through EOP5 are appended to the stream, again in an identical round-robin fashion. The start of the IPG is defined as the boundary of the last data byte and EOP1, even though the pairs are not physically idle at this point.

At a 100BASE-T4 receiver, the incoming streams received on each of the three pairs may not be aligned exactly as they left the transmitter due to a phenomenon known as "pair skew." This is due to the fact that each of the three UTP channels may be a different length (due to factors such as a different number of twists-per-inch). The 100BASE-T4 receiver is designed to handle the pair skew associated with normal cable variations. However, 100BASE-T4 should not be deployed over pairs split across different cables, since this may lead to excessive pair skew. All pairs for 100BASE-T4 cabling must reside in the same overall cable jacket.

Note that when 100BASE-T4 is not transmitting packets, the data drivers are inactive (and link test pulses, similar to 10BASE-T, are transmitted). However, in order for the 100BASE-T4 ternary signaling to maintain the same signal-to-noise ratio (SNR) that 10BASE-T enjoys with binary signaling, the output voltage is boosted by 20% (nominally 7 V instead of 5 V). This leads to significant implementation and regulatory (RFI/EMI) challenges.

While 100BASE-T4 was well supported in the standards development process, the fact that it employed a completely new PHY layer coding and signaling protocol meant that special-purpose integrated silicon had to be developed in order to permit technically and economically feasible implementations. This fact slowed its deployment relative to 100BASE-TX, which was able to leverage existing silicon for the PHY previously developed (though not mass-deployed) for FDDI over copper.

3.3.2 100BASE-TX—Category 5 UTP

The overall 100BASE-TX topology, as shown in Figure 3-13, is identical to that of 100BASE-T4. Differences are buried within the signaling and cable-type supported.

100BASE-TX is based on a unified set of specifications that use a 4B/5B block coding technology, specified in the common 100BASE-X Physical Coding Sublayer (PCS) and Physical Medium Attachment (PMA) sublayer, defined in Clause 24 of the 100BASE-T Standard (see Figure 3-1 for details of the sublayers within the PHY). 100BASE-X defines the common PCS and PMA functions that are used on top of the media-specific Physical Medium Dependent (PMD) sublayers for 100BASE-TX and 100BASE-FX.

100BASE-TX essentially marries the best qualities of the 100 Mb/s 802.3/Ethernet MAC with those of the ANSI/ PHY for TP-PMD (Twisted-Pair PMD, often referred to as CDDI), thus reusing the existing standards efforts for the physical signaling technology.

100BASE-TX operates over two pairs of Cat 5 cable, with DTE-to-repeater distances restricted to 100 m. 100BASE-TX employs a PMD that is optimized for UTP cable, defined in Clause 25 of the 100BASE-T Specification and the ANSI TP-PMD Specification.

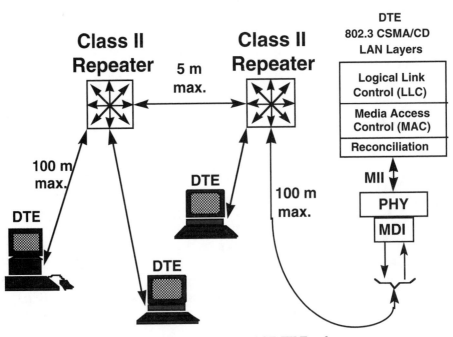

Figure 3-13 100BASE-TX Topology

The 100BASE-X PHYs uses a 4B/5B block coding technique. This scheme is inherently full duplex (unlike 100BASE-T4, but identical to 10BASE-T), with one pair dedicated to transmit and a second pair dedicated to receive.

The transmit encoding process is shown in Figure 3-14a. When the DTE transmits, the PHY takes a nibble from the MII and converts this to a 5-bit binary symbol. For 100BASE-FX, this 5-bit symbol is transmitted serially on the medium. Since all data is transmitted over a single fiber, the full data rate of 100 Mb/s is present, with a frequency of 125 MHz due to the code conversion. This type of frequency is of no consequence over fiber optic cables. For 100BASE-TX, RFI/EMI effects from these data rates on UTP are unacceptable, so additional steps are taken to reduce the spectral content of the transmission. First, the transmitted code is scrambled (the transmitter and receiver are kept in lock-step to ensure that the data can be descrambled at the receiver). The scrambling process helps smooth the spectral content of the resulting transmitted waveform. Subsequently, an MLT-3 code (multilevel transmit) is applied to the transmitted serial bit stream. This converts the binary 5B symbol to a ternary code and further reduces the spectral content. The data rate on the single pair is 100 Mb/s but the scrambling and coding steps reduce the frequency on the line to only 31.25 MHz. While transmitting, the DTE checks the receive pair for data symbols from the repeater that indicate a collision.

The 4B/5B encoding technique maps the 16 possible 4B data nibble values to a subset of the 5B binary code groups available (within the total of 32). Since this coding scheme was already defined for FDDI, a close mapping of data codes and control codes was maintained. Normal MII data-nibble values are mapped to data codes. An "IDLE" (/I/) code group is used to continuously signal between packets during IPG. The remaining 15 code groups are used for special control signaling functions (the /J/, /K/, /T/, /R/ and /H/ code-groups), or are reserved (considered invalid).

Figure 3-14b details the physical encapsulation of the Ethernet packet over the single transmit pair. The 100BASE-T PHY replaces the first byte of the preamble sequence from the MII with a special "start-of-stream delimiter," defined as the /J/K/ pattern. /J/K/ acts as a start-of-data delimiter for the receiving device. The receiving device reverses this process and removes the /J/K/ code groups and replaces them with a single byte of preamble, passing this back to the receiving MAC via the MII. Immediately following the last byte of data at the end of the frame transmission, the special "end-of-packet" delimiters /T/R/ are appended to the stream. The transmit pair will subsequently transition to the IDLE fill code, and does not become physically idle. The start of the IPG is defined as the boundary of the last data byte and the /T/ code group.

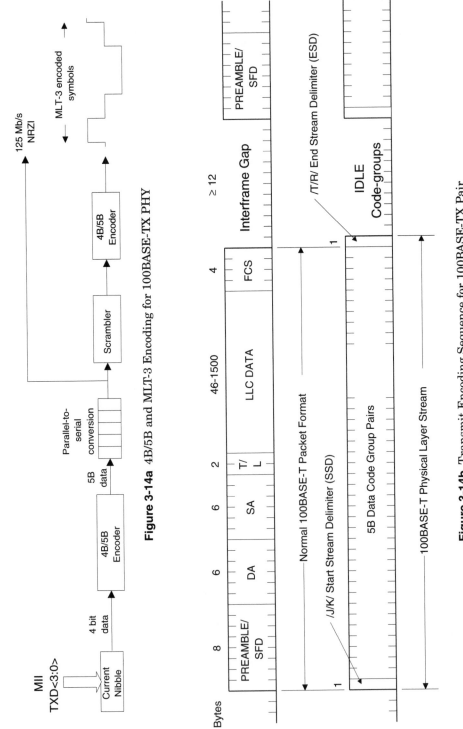

Figure 3-14a 4B/5B and MLT-3 Encoding for 100BASE-TX PHY

Figure 3-14b Transmit Encoding Sequence for 100BASE-TX Pair

For 100BASE-TX, the additional scrambling and MLT-3 (multilevel transmit) encoding steps are taken prior to transmission on the UTP medium. Each of the 5-bit positions are encoded into a ternary level code. This ternary coding is used somewhat differently, since only one bit of information is conveyed within each bit period. The line state continuously cycles between the values of +1, 0, –1, 0, +1, 0, and so on The value is permuted to change only by one level, to the next closest level (i.e., from +1 to 0, or from 0 to +1, but not from –1 to +1). Each change in level represents a logical 1; maintaining the same level represents a logical 0.

This encoding provides reasonable clock transition density (some initial implementation problems were associated with TP-PMD, where maximum frame sizes are much longer and can result in long runs without transitions), minimizes high-energy transitions to limit RFI/EMI emissions, and maintains good DC balance on the line.

Note that both pairs of the PHY are constantly operational. When 100BASE-X is not transmitting packets, idle symbols are continuously transmitted (unlike 10BASE-T, there are no link test pulses between data packets). The superior characteristics of Cat 5 cable allow 100BASE-TX to only transmit a nominal 2 V signal. Regulatory (RFI/EMI) issues are well understood from earlier CDDI implementations.

100BASE-TX has become the dominant Fast Ethernet technology deployed in the marketplace, far outstripping the deployment of 100BASE-T4. This is largely due to the early availability of silicon initially developed for the TP-PMD version of FDDI, which was adapted for use in 100BASE-TX and allowed much earlier availability from multiple vendors than was the case for 100BASE-T4. The expected entry barrier due to the Cat 5 cable requirement quickly dissipated due to the availability of switched 10 Mb/s Ethernet solutions to increase bandwidth in Cat 3 environments and widespread rewiring to take advantage of existing 100 Mb/s and future higher bandwidth technologies.

3.3.3 100BASE-FX—Fiber Optics

100BASE-FX operates over two individual (multimode) fiber optic cables, with DTE-to-repeater distances of various lengths above the 100 m UTP restriction, based on topology (more later). Like 100BASE-TX, 100BASE-FX is based on a common set of PCS and PMA specifications, defined as 100BASE-X and specified in Clause 26 of the 802.3u Standard. A typical topology using 100BASE-FX is shown in Figure 3-15.

100BASE-FX PHY uses the same 4B/5B block-coding technique as 100BASE-TX, allowing native full-duplex operation of the link (although the use of full duplex depends on the MAC, as well as other components in the network).

The DTE transmits nibbles to the PHY over the MII. The 199BASE-FX PHY converts this to a 5-bit binary symbol. The transmit encoding process is shown in Figure 3-14. For 100BASE-FX, this 5-bit symbol is transmitted on the medium at the full

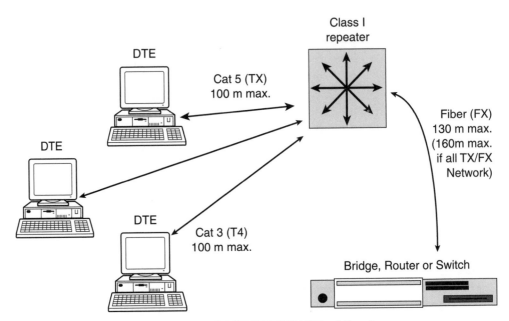

Figure 3-15 100BASE-FX/TX/T4 Mixed Topology

data rate of 100 Mb/s (125 MBaud). The additional scrambling and encoding stages required to minimize EMI/RFI over UTP cable are unnecessary in the case of fiber optic cables.

Fiber optic cable, optical/electrical converters, and connectors are substantially higher in cost and more difficult to install than copper media counterparts. Hence fiber is generally used only where necessary—typically in long-distance, high-bandwidth, or security-conscious applications. For these reasons, the application shown in Figure 3-15 is typical of a network installation, where the fiber link would be used to connect geographically distant LANs.

Full-duplex operation permits link distances to be extended considerably, to a maximum of 2 km for multimode fiber. The use of single-mode fiber is supported by some vendors to substantially increase distance even beyond this 2 km distance, again using full-duplex operation. However, repeaters are not capable of full duplex, so the topology of Figure 3-15 would not support such link distances.

Fiber optic cable distances for different configurations are summarized in Table 3-9 in the "Mixed Topologies" section. The differences between single mode and multimode fiber are discussed in Chapter 4, in the Gigabit Ethernet "Physical Medium Dependent (PMD) Sublayer" section.

3.3.4 100BASE-T2—Category 3 UTP

A third PHY for UTP was developed, although not as part of the initial 802.3u Fast Ethernet specification. When the 100BASE-T Task Force was established, proposals were heard for many signaling schemes which attempted to address the difficult problem of data transfer at 100 Mb/s over Cat 3 cable. Eventually a conservative approach was taken, and the 4-pair 100BASE-T4 solution was adopted. However, during the 100BASE-T development, several vendors started a parallel activity to attempt to allow operation over two pairs of Cat 3 cable. This was defined as the 100BASE-T2 specification, which was eventually completed in 1997, some two years after the initial Fast Ethernet specification.

To achieve the 100 Mb/s data rate over two pairs of Cat 3 cable, sophisticated multilevel coding, equalization, and noise-cancellation techniques were employed. Since full-duplex operation was required, 100BASE-T2 used both twisted pairs simultaneously in both directions, as shown in Figure 3-16. The 100BASE-T2 PHY implementation requires extensive use of Digital Signal Processing (DSP) techniques to allow the bidirectional signaling to operate reliably—especially given the restricted bandwidth of the cable, the presence of external noise, and the link partner's simultaneous transmission over the same pairs. A complex 2-dimensional constellation code was selected for data transmission, referred to as PAM 5x5 (Pulse Amplitude Modulation). This technique takes nibbles from the MII, applies a scrambler stage, and subsequently maps the 4-bit block of data into a pair of "quinery" symbols (Figure 3-17). Since there are 25 valid data-code representations, this allows redundancy and error detection capabilities to be included in the basic symbol code. The quinery symbols are transmitted using both pairs of the cable, . This yields a 25-Mbaud line rate, identical to the MII clock rate.

Although the 100BASE-T2 work was completed, vendor interest in the technology waned due to the complexity and cost of the PHY implementation. Without dedicated custom silicon being made available, there was no way to economically implement the solution. In fact, it was extremely difficult to even realize a representative test circuit. Most of the analysis had to be performed using simulation techniques. In addition, by the time the details of 100BASE-T2 were stable enough to begin implementation, it was clear that 100BASE-TX was being widely accepted, and that the requirement for Cat 5 cabling was not as big an obstacle as many vendors had originally believed.

Due to the lack of implementations, there is essentially no installed base of 100BASE-T2. For this reason, the description of the technology here has been restricted to the basic concepts.

100BASE-T2 did require additional Auto-Negotiation parameters to be exchanged, but made no change to the operation of the Auto-Negotiation algorithm.

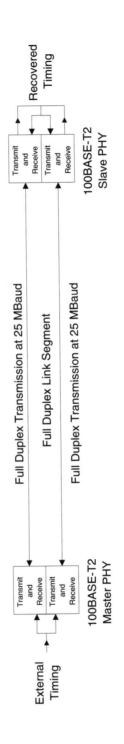

Figure 3-16 100BASE-T2 Topology

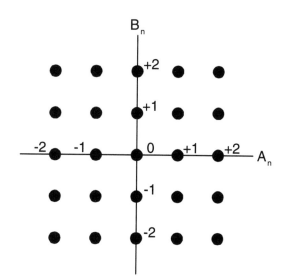

Figure 3-17 PAM 5x5 Symbol Code for 100BASE-T2 PHY
(From IEEE Std. 802.3x&y-1997, ©1997, IEEE. All rights reserved.)

3.3.5 Cable Requirements

Like 10BASE-T, the 100BASE-T cabling plant requires a crossover function at some point in each link segment to swap the cable from the transmitter of the source to the receiver of the destination. This is performed by a crossover function implemented in the signal path, such as at a punch-down block, or it may be implemented in the connector of a hub product (repeater, switch, etc.). When implemented in a hub product, the connector should be labeled as an MDI-X connector, indicating the crossover function is embedded. Figure 3-18 shows the crossover for 100BASE-TX and 100BASe-T4 cabling schemes.

Note that many product implementations incorporate circuitry to swap an individual pair in order to ensure that "Transmit+" is connected to "Receive–," and so on, for each pair. However, these do not remove the requirement to swap the complete pair. If a simple one-to-one mapping of the cable pairs were used, this would result in two transmitters and two receivers at either end of the link being connected together.

100BASE-FX also requires a crossover function, which is assumed to be performed by swapping the cable/connectors.

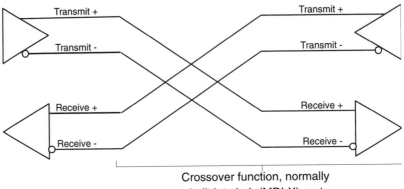

Figure 3-18a 100BASE-TX/T2 Twisted Pair Cable Crossover

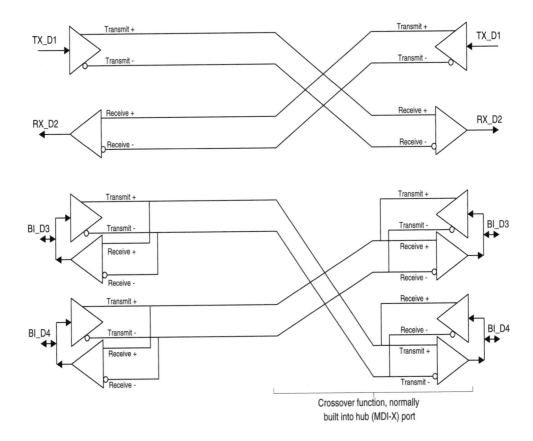

Figure 3-18b 100BASE-T4 Twisted Pair Cable Crossover

Table 3-8 Cable Pair and Line Voltage Comparison

Technology	Transmit	Receive	Voltage
10BASE-T	1, 2	3, 6	2.5V ± 0.3V
100BASE-TX	1, 2	3, 6	1.0V ± 50mV
100BASE-T4	1, 2/4, 5/7, 8	3, 6/4, 5/7, 8	3.5V ± 0.35V
100BASE-T2	1, 2/3, 6	1, 2/3, 6	1.81V ± 0.1V

3.3.6 Mixed Topologies

The diameter of a CSMA/CD network is directly related to the round-trip propagation delay. In order for reliable collision detection, a signal must be able to travel to the most distant station on the network, just as that station starts to transmit, causing a collision at the far point. However, the originating station must wait until the signal from the far end returns, before it can detect the collision. This round-trip delay must be short enough to ensure the originating station can complete a minimum-size frame (512 bit times). If this were not the case, a station could send a packet which suffered collision at the remote location, but it would not detect the collision itself and would believe the transmission was successful. Since the round-trip delay is measured in bit times (ultimately the number of bits in a minimum valid frame), as the bit time is reduced, correspondingly, so is the real time of the round-trip delay. This directly reduces the span of the network, given that the speed of light and the cable delays are essentially identical, regardless of the data rate. Hence for 512 bit times, the approximate span for 10 Mb/s is 2 km, whereas for 100 Mb/s operation it is approximately 200 m.

As with 10 Mb/s Ethernet, networks for 100 Mb/s can be constructed that mix the various 100BASE-T/F media technologies, to make use of the most advantageous attributes of each. Since only the PHY component changes in each case, the various implementations are fully interoperable at the DTE (MAC, PLS and MII) and repeater. Practical implementations may obviously not allow the PHY device to be replaced, since it is likely to be physically integrated within a product and may not be attached by an exposed MII which would allow an alternate PHY to be connected.

Guidelines

Guidelines for the reliable operation of mixed-topology networks are specified in "Systems Considerations for Multi-Segment 100BASE-T Networks" of the IEEE 802.3u Standard.[9] As is the case for 10 Mb/s topologies, two sets of topology rules are specified, known as the "Transmission System Model 1" and "Transmission System Model 2."

The rules ensure that the network does not become oversized. An oversized CSMA/CD network will not operate correctly, since the detection of collisions cannot be guaranteed within the slot time.

In addition, the number of repeaters between any two stations on the network must be restricted to limit the effect of the inter-packet gap shrinkage, as it propagates through the network (IPG shrinkage is discussed in the "Repeater Definition" section of Chapter 2).

These basic rules are guaranteed to be met when constructing a network using the Transmission System Model 1 topologies. The Transmission System Model 1 guidelines ensure that the network will not become oversized, so they are relatively conservative. Networks based on this model will be guaranteed to operate, although they may not allow the network to achieve its most aggressive geographic span. Figures 3-11, 3-13, and 3-15 show examples of maximally configured repeater topologies for Class I and II repeaters.

For networks that need to go outside the basic rules to increase the distance and/or coverage of the LAN in a particular installation, a precise model of the LAN installation must be produced. With this accurate model, the more detailed rules that are defined by the Transmission System Model 2 guidelines can be applied to identify the exact delays for each path in the network and guarantee that the slot time and IPG shrinkage limits are not exceeded.

Application of the detailed topology rules is considered outside the scope of this overview. However, since the basic topology rules cover virtually all normal network installations, these will be reviewed with some typical examples of mixed-media networks. Note that Fast Ethernet networks do have more topology restrictions than 10 Mb/s networks. There is only a small benefit to be gained by trying to stretch the network to its geographic extremes. The application of switching technology is a much more flexible and reliable way to extend the 100BASE-T topology.

While the topology restrictions appear significant compared with the 4-repeater (500 m) topologies offered by 10BASE-T, it will be seen later that by augmenting with switching (or bridging/routing), 100BASE-T has an adequate topology for advanced workgroups, which can then be interconnected using longer-distance 100 Mb/s Ethernet derivatives. Since 100BASE-T preserves the Ethernet packet format, it eliminates the packet segmentation and reassemble process required in Ethernet-to-FDDI internetworking devices and enables very easy interconnection of existing 10 Mb/s Ethernet LANs to new 100 Mb/s Ethernet technologies. Further, Ethernet's more economical protocol and management requirements make the implementation fundamentally simpler than FDDI.

---

[9] IEEE Std 802.3u–-1995 (Supplement to ISO/IEC 8802-3, 1993 [ANSI/IEEE Std. 802.3, 1993 Edition]), Local and Metropolitan Area Networks, Media Access Control (MAC) Parameters, Physical Layer, Medium Attachment Units and Repeater for 100 Mb/s Operation, Type 100BASE-T (Clauses 21–30). IEEE Standards Department, October 26, 1995, ISBN 1-55937-542-6. Clause 29. PP 281-287.

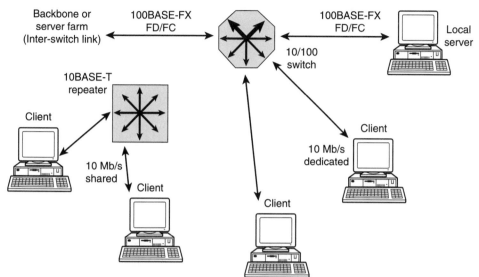

Figure 3-19 10BASE-T and 100BASE-TX/FX Mixed Topology Network

Table 3-9 Technology and Topology Comparison

Technology	Half-/Full-Duplex Operation	Minimum Cable Requirements	Maximum Distance
Switched 10	Full and half	Cat 3, 2 pair	100 m
100BASE-TX	Full and half	Cat 5, 2 pair	100 m
100BASE-T4	Half	Cat 3, 4 pair	100 m
100BASE-FX	Half and full	62.5/125 m MMF	130 m, 160 m, or 2 km[a]
100BASE-T2	Half or full	Cat 3, 2 pair	100 m

[a]100BASE-FX maximum distances depend on repeater class, number of repeaters, and half/full-duplex operation.

Additional information on the increase in topology for full-duplex operation is covered in the "Mixed Switched Ethernet Topologies" section later in this chapter.

3.3.7 Auto-Negotiation

Auto-Negotiation is located in Clause 28 of the 100BASE-T standard suite. The development of the Auto-Negotiation scheme actually started somewhat later than most of the rest of the Fast Ethernet specifications. During the early development of the standard, considerable effort was expended to maximize the commonality between the Ethernet MAC, RS, and MII, to support both 10 Mb/s and 100 Mb/s operation. One of the clear objectives was the desire by vendors to offer equipment that operated at either 10 or 100 Mb/s.

A key attribute that had made 10BASE-T so successful was its plug-and-play capability. A concern started to emerge during the Fast Ethernet development that this attribute might be compromised. As the details of the 100BASE-T PHY solutions became more defined, it became clear that the signaling solutions required for the different cable categories were incompatible with each other and 10BASE-T. It was felt that if incompatible 10 Mb/s and 100 Mb/s Ethernet components were inadvertently connected, disruptive effects should be minimized. This would be especially important, for instance, when installing a new 100 Mb/s adapter. If a 100BASE-T adapter were accidentally connected to an existing 10BASE-T network, it should not cause disruption of the entire 10BASE-T installation.

In summary, the following key issues drove the need for Auto-Negotiation:

- Manufacturers wanted to make "speed-agile" devices, which could operate at 10 Mb/s initially and would automatically upgrade to 100 Mb/s operation as the network infrastructure was upgraded.

- The 100 Mb/s signaling solutions were incompatible with each other and 10BASE-T and threatened to undermine the plug-and-play reputation of Ethernet.

- Any additional PHY solution(s) which might be developed in the future would have to take account of all other solutions that had been previously deployed, and use a signaling scheme which did not disrupt any of these schemes in the installed base (this was too hard to even contemplate!).

Principal Features of Auto-Negotiation

The Auto-Negotiation clause defines several key mandatory and optional features that a device must possess to be considered compliant with the specification.

The mandatory features are:

- The device must transmit a special pulse train to identify itself after power-up (this pulse train is referred to as a "Fast Link Pulse Burst").

- The device must recognize a similar pulse train from the "link partner" device at the opposite end of the link.

- If the local device recognizes that the link partner has compatible operating modes, the optimal mode is selected, and both devices move to their operational (link pass) state.

Optional features include:

- A device can send additional information using the special pulse train if both devices provide this feature (referred to as "Next Pages").

- A device may indicate to its link partner using the special pulse train that it has a fault, and it may further identify the type of fault.

Building on the 10BASE-T Legacy

The Auto-Negotiation algorithm builds on a key characteristic that all 10BASE-T devices provide, namely the "link test" or "link integrity" pulse.

When there is no packet data being transmitted by a 10BASE-T device, it is responsible for periodically transmitting a "heartbeat" indication. This is referred to as a link test pulse. If the receiver of a 10BASE-T device does not see either packet data or a link test pulse within a defined time window, it will enter a "link fail" condition, which disables data transmission and reception and can be locally detected by the device as a medium failure. So, if the receive pair is disconnected, the 10BASE-T device will enter the link fail state, and further transmission is disabled. During link fail, the transmission and reception of link test pulses continues. To re-establish the link, at least two consecutive link test pulses or a single receive packet must be received.

10BASE-T incorporated the link test pulse function in order to ensure end-to-end connectivity between the two devices at either end of the twisted-pair link (such as in Figure 3-20). 10BASE-T used separate transmit and receive conductor pairs in the UTP cable, unlike the original coax-based Ethernet and Cheapernet systems where transmit and receive were connected to the same single inner conductor of the coax. A mechanism was required to detect if a single pair became disconnected while the other pair remained intact. Connectivity of both pairs is fundamental to the correct operation of the CSMA/CD MAC protocol and to ensure that the Ethernet MAC observes no difference between the underlying media types (whether coax or UTP).

Additional details of how link integrity is monitored and what side benefits it provides, are discussed in Chapter 2 in the "Technology Advantages of 10BASE-T" section.

Given conservative estimates of some 60 million 10BASE-T nodes (and corresponding repeater ports) in the installed base at the time that 100BASE-T was being developed (the number is difficult to estimate, since the deployment rate at that time was on the order of 25 million adapters and repeater ports annually), the incentive to create an interoperable solution with 10BASE-T was undeniable.

Auto-Negotiation Signaling Scheme

Auto-Negotiation makes use of the timing relationship that 10BASE-T specifies for link test pulses by replacing the single link test pulse with a burst of pulses, as shown in Figure 3-20.

The link test pulse of 10BASE-T was redefined as a Normal Link Pulse (NLP) and the burst of pulses that an Auto-Negotiation device issues was defined as the Fast Link Pulse (FLP) Burst. Figure 3-21 shows the relationship of 10BASE-T NLPs to the Auto-Negotiation FLP Burst.

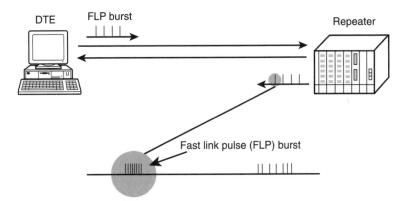

Figure 3-20 Auto-Negotiation FLP Bursts Exchanged Between a DTE and Repeater

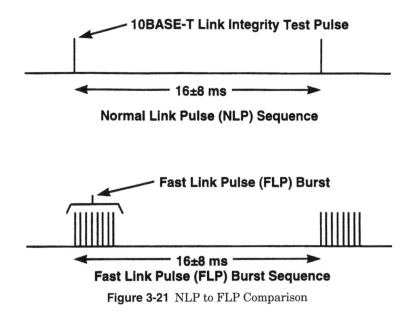

Figure 3-21 NLP to FLP Comparison

Each FLP Burst consists of a series of clock and data pulses, as shown in Fig. 3-22. The entire FLP Burst is completed within 2 ms. This ensures that existing 10BASE-T devices observe the FLP Burst as a single link test pulse (due to the timing specifications of 10BASE-T). As can be seen from Figure 3-22, odd-numbered pulse positions in the FLP Burst are designated as clock pulses and are separated by 125 µs (nominally), while even-numbered pulse positions are designated as data pulses and occur (if present) 62.5 µs from the previous clock-pulse position.

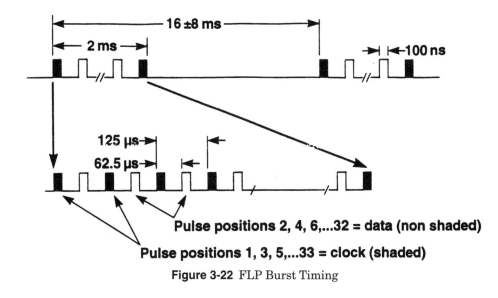

Pulse positions 2, 4, 6,...32 = data (non shaded)

Pulse positions 1, 3, 5,...33 = clock (shaded)

Figure 3-22 FLP Burst Timing

The data pulses within the FLP Burst are used to form a 16-bit Link Code Word (LCW). The clock pulses are used only for timing and recovery of the data pulses.

Figure 3-23 shows the construction of an FLP Burst in more detail. The entire FLP Burst consists of a minimum of 17 pulses (assuming all data pulses are absent) and a maximum of 33 pulses (assuming all data pulses are present). While clock pulses are always present, data pulses may or may not be. In the case that a data pulse is present, this indicates a value of 1 in the LCW, whereas absence of a data pulse indicates a value of 0 in the LCW.

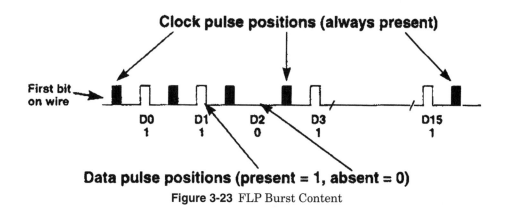

Figure 3-23 FLP Burst Content

Received signals are evaluated to ensure that an FLP Burst is correctly identified and the embedded Link Code Word is decoded. Timers are used to:

1. Detect the presence of an FLP Burst (versus an NLP).

2. Detect the presence or absence of a data pulse (between adjacent clock pulses).

3. Detect the FLP Burst repetition rate (to reject a spurious noise event as a potential FLP Burst).

Additional robustness is provided by the fact that three identical Link Code Words must be received before the contents are considered reliable and are used for the negotiation process.

Base Link Code Word

Figure 3-24 defines the bit positions of the initial Link Code Word that is exchanged between Auto-Negotiation devices. This is defined as the Base Link Code Word and is transmitted after power-on, reset, or renegotiation is requested by one of several mechanisms.

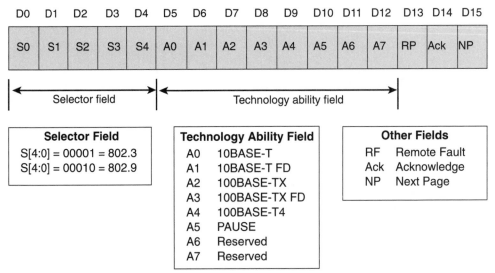

Figure 3-24 Base Link Code Word Definition
(From IEEE Std. 802.3u-1995, ©1995, IEEE. All rights reserved.)

Selector Field

This 5-bit value indicates the device type. Even though Auto-Negotiation was specifically developed for 802.3 devices, extensibility to other technologies was incorporated. Other technologies need only obtain a unique Selector Field value. When another technology uses the Auto-Negotiation function, the contents of certain fields in the LCW are permitted to be redefined to contain data appropriate to that technology.

Technology Ability Field

This field identifies the subset of technologies that are supported (i.e., 10BASE-T, 100BASE-TX/T4, full duplex, etc.). All technologies are simultaneously advertised in the Base Link Code Word. Currently, three additional bits are available for expansion, with additional expansion provided by the Next Page function (explained later). Each device maintains a prioritization table, used to ensure that the highest-common-denominator ability is chosen. The priority is assigned by technology type and administered by 802.3 and is not based on the bit ordering in the Link Code Word. The priority was initially defined as shown in Table 3-10.

Note that the PAUSE bit was added by the 802.3x Full Duplex Flow Control Standard.[10] PAUSE functionality is discussed later in the chapter in the "Full Duplex and Flow Control" section. PAUSE operation is supported only for the full-duplex technologies and is not used for half-duplex operation. Completion of Auto-Negotiation with both devices indicating that they implement the PAUSE function for a full-duplex technology is always considered a higher priority than the corresponding full-duplex technology without PAUSE.

Table 3-10 Priority Resolution Table

Priority	Technology	Minimum Cabling Requirement
1 (Highest)	100BASE-TX (Full Duplex)	2 Pair, Cat 5
2	100BASE-T4	4 Pair, Cat 3
3	100BASE-TX (Half Duplex)	2 Pair, Cat 5
4	10BASE-T (Full Duplex)	2 Pair, Cat 3
5 Lowest)	10BASE-T (Half Duplex)	2 Pair, Cat 3

New technologies can simply be inserted at any point in the priority table. Existing devices which have no knowledge of these new technologies will ignore the bits in the Link Code Word and so will not have their priority hierarchy altered. For instance, when the 100BASE-T2 PHY technology was completed, Table 3-10 was modified to that shown in Table 3-11.

Remote Fault Bit

This bit indicates the presence of a fault detected by the remote link partner. In addition, the Next Page bit may be set to identify the precise type of remote fault. One of the simplest uses of Remote Fault is to set this bit if the device enters the "link fail"

---

[10] Institute of Electrical and Electronic Engineers, Local and Metropolitan Area Networks—Specification for 802.3 Full Duplex Operation and Physical Layer Specification for 100 Mb/s Operation on Two Pairs of Category 3 or Better Balanced Twisted Pair Cable (100BASE-T2), IEEE Std. 802.3x-1997 and IEEE Std. 802.3y-1997 (Supplement to ISO/IEC 8802.3:1996 [ANSI/IEEE Std. 802.3, 1996 Edition]), IEEE, New York, NY, November 18, 1997, Annex 31B.

Table 3-11 Priority Resolution Table Modified by 100BASE-T2

Priority	Technology	Minimum Cabling Requirement
1 (Highest)	100BASE-T2 (Full Duplex)	2 Pair, Cat 3
2	100BASE-TX (Full Duplex)	2 Pair, Cat 5
3	100BASE-T2 (Half Duplex)	2 Pair, Cat 3
4	100BASE-T4	4 Pair, Cat 3
5	100BASE-TX (Half Duplex)	2 Pair, Cat 5
6	10BASE-T (Full Duplex)	2 Pair, Cat 3
7 (Lowest)	10BASE-T (Half Duplex)	2 Pair, Cat 3

state, which may the result of a broken receiver (or receive cable). Using this mechanism, for instance, a hub can be informed by a DTE that no receive path appears to exist from the hub to the DTE, although the DTE is able to report this using the intact transmit path to the hub. The Next Page bit may additionally be set to allow Next Pages to be transported, which identify the precise type of Remote Fault. A special Remote Fault message code is defined for this purpose.

Acknowledge Bit

This bit acknowledges the successful receipt of three identical LCWs from the link partner. An LCW with ACK = 1 is transmitted a minimum of 6–8 times to the link partner. This ensures the partner will detect the LCW with ACK = 1 also three consecutive times. The ACK bit is one field that is fixed across all Selector Field values.

Next Page Bit

This bit indicates a device wishes to send additional Link Code Word(s) following the current word being exchanged. In order for additional pages to be sent, both ends must be "Next Page Able" (both must set this bit in the Base LCW). Next Page information will follow the same protocol and timing as the Base LCW. Encodings for Next Pages have been defined to allow expansion of the Technology Ability Field, to more precisely define the nature of a Remote Fault, and to allow vendor-specific extensions.

Next Page Function

The Next Page function allows the exchange of LCWs in addition to the Base LCW. However, in order for any Next Pages to be exchanged, both devices must indicate they are "Next Page Able" in the Base LCW. If both devices indicate they are Next Page Able, both must send at least one Next Page. Next Page exchange occurs until both devices have no additional Next Pages. If one device has no more information, it continues to send a "Null Message Page" until the partner device has completed its Next Page transmissions.

The Next Page protocol consists of a two message sequence. A "Message Page" is transmitted first (Figure 3-25), which indicates both the number and type of "Unformatted Pages" (if any) that will follow (in the Message Code Field). Unformatted Pages (Figure 3-26) are subsequently transmitted as necessary, until the transfer completes. Unformatted Pages effectively provide the 11-bit Unformatted Code Field of the Next Page to be used for data, while the top 5 bits are protocol overhead.

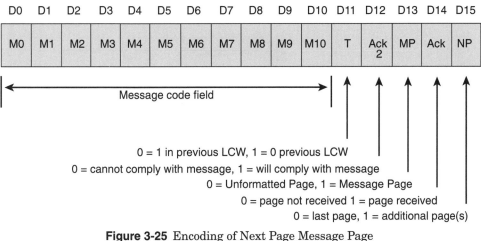

Figure 3-25 Encoding of Next Page Message Page
(From IEEE Std. 802.3u-1995, ©1995, IEEE. All rights reserved.)

Note that in order for the Next Page sequence to complete correctly, and to allow the transport of the ACK and ACK2 bits in response to the last meaningful Next Page (the last Next Page which contained user or application data), an additional Null Message Page must be used to terminate the Next Page sequence.

Management Interface

Auto-Negotiation allows for management via the MII Management Interface (or an equivalent if the MII is not provided). The mandatory Control (register 0) and Status (register 1) features provide most of the enable/disable and ability reporting for Auto-Negotiation. These are defined in the "MII Management Registers" section within this chapter. Three additional Auto-Negotiation specific registers are defined as mandatory if Auto-Negotiation is implemented. In addition, a fourth register is required if the Next Page function is implemented.

Finally, the 100BASE-T2 PHY definition added requirements for specific additional registers and mandated the use of the Next Page function to transport additional technology-specific information at start-up.[11] Given the absence of adoption of the 100BAASE-T2 technology, these are referenced, but not described here.

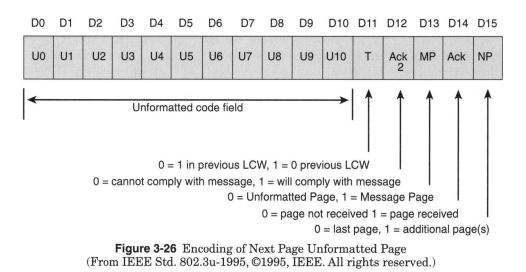

Figure 3-26 Encoding of Next Page Unformatted Page
(From IEEE Std. 802.3u-1995, ©1995, IEEE. All rights reserved.)

Advertisement Register (MII Management Register 4)

Used to store the device's LCW for transmission.

Link Partner Ability Register (MII Management Register 5)

Stores the advertised ability of the link partner device (the received LCW).

Expansion Register (MII Management Register 6)

Miscellaneous Auto-Negotiation-specific information (i.e., Link Partner Auto-Negotiation Able, Page Received, etc.).

Next Page Transmit Register (MII Management Register 7)

Required only if the Next Page function is implemented. Used to store the Next Page of information to be transmitted.

Functional Overview

Figure 3-27 shows a simple block diagram of an 802.3 device with multiple technologies supported, including 10BASE-T. The signals passed between the MDI (the RJ-45) and the Auto-Negotiation function are the transmit and receive data signals from the UTP medium, which always use the same pins of the RJ-45 for all 802.3 networks.

---

[11] Institute of Electrical and Electronics Engineers, Local and Metropolitan Area Networks—Specification for 802.3 Full Duplex Operation and Physical Layer Specification for 100 Mb/s Operation on Two Pairs of Category 3 or Better Balanced Twisted Pair Cable (100BASE-T2), IEEE Std. 802.3x-1997 and IEEE Std. 802.3y-1997 (Supplement to ISO/IEC 8802.3:1996 [ANSI/IEEE Std. 802.3, 1996 Edition]), IEEE, New York, NY, November 18, 1997,Clause 32, Annex 28B/C/D.

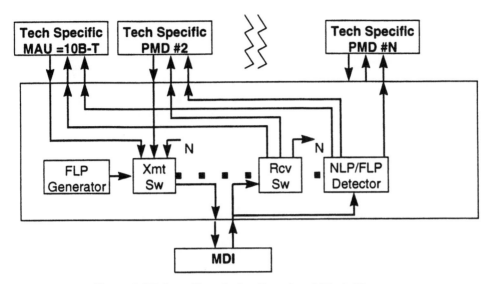

Figure 3-27 Auto-Negotiation Functional Block Diagram

Each of the technologies resides above the Auto-Negotiation layer, which polices what is transmitted from them to the medium and also directs any receive signals from the medium. Each technology must encompasses its own native detection scheme for "link good" (e.g., 10BASE-T uses normal link pulses) to provide a mechanism to verify the underlying medium, once control is handed off from Auto-Negotiation, and a single technology is enabled.

After power-up, reset, or upon a renegotiation request, the Xmt Sw (Transmit Switch) connects the FLP Generator to the MDI transmit path, and FLP Bursts are generated to advertise the device's abilities to the link partner. All other technology transmit functions are isolated from the MDI during negotiation. After negotiation, the Xmt Sw connects a single-technology transmitter to the MDI transmit, and the technology is then responsible to use its own test for link good.

The NLP/FLP Detector detects NLPs (which indicates the other device is 10BASE-T only) or FLP Bursts in which case the Base LCW is decoded to determine the optimal mode shared by both devices. Once a single technology has been chosen by the Auto-Negotiation function, it is informed and control is passed to it, to perform its own link integrity function.

During the negotiation phase, the Rcv Sw (Receive Switch) blocks MDI receive traffic to the technology receivers, passing it to the NLP/FLP Detector only (the Parallel Detection function allows a modification to this, which is explained below). After negotiation completes, the Rcv Sw connects the MDI receive to a single-technology receiver.

Parallel Detection Function

Auto-Negotiation assumes that devices generate NLP and/or FLP sequences. However, since the Auto-Negotiation work started later than the definitions of 100BASE-TX and T4, early implementations did not provide FLP compatible signaling. The "Parallel Detection" scheme was developed to permit interoperation with 100BASE-T technologies under development prior to initiation of Auto-Negotiation. Only 100BASE-TX and/or 100BASE-T4 technologies are permitted to use Parallel Detection. All subsequent 802.3 technologies (100BASE-T2, etc.) must use the FLP Burst transaction.

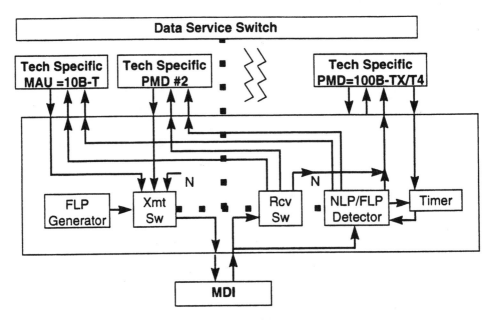

Figure 3-28 Auto-Negotiation With Parallel Detection Function

Figure 3-28 shows how Parallel Detection is incorporated into the Auto-Negotiation function. The Timer function is added, and the RCV Sw and NLP/FLP Detector are modified. Now, as signals are received from the medium, they are passed in parallel to the NLP/FLP Detector and to any 100BASE-TX or T4 PMD which exists in the implementation. If the received signal causes the TX/T4 PMD to enter the link good condition (it is a native TX or T4 signal, rather than an FLP), the link good event is detected by the Auto-Negotiation function and the timer started. When the timer expires, if only one technology indicates link good, control is passed to it. If more than one link good condition exists after the time expires, then the signal at least appeared acceptable to more than one technology. Auto-Negotiation will flag this as an error, and the device will remain in link fail, isolated from the network.

Auto-Negotiation Interoperability Examples

Interoperability with 10BASE-T Installed Base

Refer to Figure 3-29.

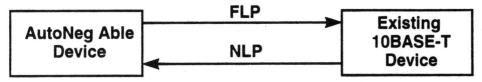

Figure 3-29 Auto-Negotiation to Existing 10BASE-T

- The Auto-Negotiation able device powers up in link fail and transmits consecutive FLPs (after "break link" time delay).

- The 10BASE-T device transmits NLPs or traffic (10BASE-T devices are allowed to power up in link good).

- The 10BASE-T device goes into link fail due to inactivity for the break link time.

- If the Auto-Negotiation device has a 10BASE-T mode, Auto-Negotiation passes control to it, the 10BASE-T MAU transmits NLPs, and the 10BASE-T mode is configured.

Protection from Incompatible Equipment

Refer to Figure 3-30.

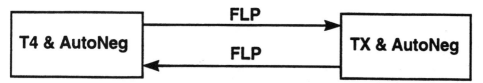

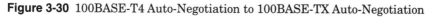

Figure 3-30 100BASE-T4 Auto-Negotiation to 100BASE-TX Auto-Negotiation

- Both devices power up in link fail and transmit FLPs.

- Upon receiving three consecutive and consistent FLP Bursts, the capabilities of the far end station are recognized.

- Based on the capabilities communicated, no common denominator exists (assumes no common 10BASE-T data service).

- Both devices remain in link fail—any network connected to either end will not be disrupted.

- The link partner's ability information is saved in local register(s) and could be used for management purposes (report incompatible device type).

Interoperability with Non Auto-Negotiation 100BASE-T

Refer to Figure 3-31.

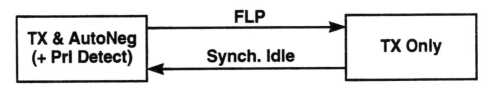

Figure 3-31 100BASE-TX Auto-Negotiation to 100BASE-TX Only

- The Auto-Negotiation able device powers up in link fail and transmits FLPs.

- 100BASE-TX/non-Auto-Negotiation device powers up and sends "idle symbols" (continuous activity during idle).

- Provided that 100BASE-TX network technologies exist at both ends, Parallel Detection will allow the NLP/FLP Detector to be bypassed.

- Devices will operate in 100BASE-TX mode.

- Auto-Negotiation could also be disabled and the mode forced by management or manually (least optimal choice) if required.

3.3.8 100 Mb/s Repeaters

During the development of the Fast Ethernet specification, the IEEE 100BASE-T Task Force established the need for two different types of repeater. Essentially, one was to be optimized for minimum delay and one for maximum flexibility. Early in the Fast Ethernet development, it was hoped to achieve up to three repeaters in the topology. This architecture allows one repeater to act as a "hub of hubs," with multiple additional repeaters connected beneath it. Eventually, it was recognized that the delays imposed by the PHY coding schemes, as well as the worst-case delays which had to be assumed for the Cat 3 and Cat 5 cables, meant that a maximum of only two repeaters could be achieved.

100BASE-T defines two "classes" of repeaters. A Class I repeater for 100 Mb/s permits only a single repeater to be present in the topology. Class II repeaters permit one or two repeaters to be used in a single CSMA/CD collision domain. Class I repeaters are often referred to as "translation repeaters," Class II repeaters are often referred to as "code-based repeaters."

The simple explanation is that Class I repeaters are allowed to have dissimilar media types connected to their ports, such that the encoding schemes on each port can be different. This allows 100BASE-X (TX and FX) to be interconnected with 100BASE-T4. This requires an extra level of translation when entering one port with one coding scheme and exiting another port with a dissimilar coding scheme. Hence Class I repeaters are defined with additional margin in their delay budget.

Class II repeaters have like media types connected to all ports This means that they are optimized to a specific coding scheme and support only the media type and PHYs that utilize this coding. So Class II repeaters are less flexible, being optimized for 100BASE-X or 100BASE-T4, but do not support the interconnection of both.

Class I Repeater

A Class I repeater is capable of support for all 100BASE-T media types, dependent on the PHY layers incorporated. This provides the flexibility of allowing 100BASE-TX, FX, T4 and T2 links to be interconnected, as shown in Fig. 3-32. However, the disadvantage of this mixed-topology environment is that only one repeater is practically possible.

As described previously, the block codes used for 100BASE-T4 and 100BASE-X and 100BASE-T2 are different. In order for a repeater to convert between the media types, it must translate from one code to another, typically using an intermediate (arbitrary) step. This decoding/encoding takes additional delay, which is a critical parameter in all Ethernet networks. This is the essential difference between Class I and Class II repeaters. Class I repeaters are permitted to be slower, which allows them to incorporate the translation step but limits the topology to a single repeater. As can be seen from the example in Figure 3-32, if all DTEs are maintained as type TX and FX, the FX link is permitted to be 160 m, whereas if any repeater port is T4, it is restricted to 130 m.

Class II Repeater

Class II repeaters permit two repeater topologies for 100BASE-TX/FX-based networks (since both employ the same 4B/5B block coding) or 100BASE-T4-only networks. To allow 100BASE-X and 100BASE-T4 links to be interconnected requires the use of a single Class I repeater (since they use different coding schemes). Examples of Class II repeaters are shown in Figures 3-11 and 3-13.

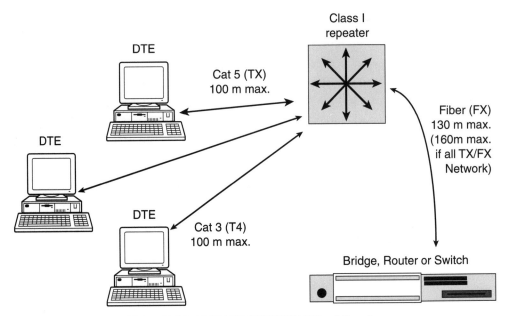

Figure 3-32 100BASE-TX/FX/T4 Mixed Topology

A Class II repeater has more stringent delays that a Class I repeater. For instance, a 100BASE-X repeater could be implemented as a simple "code-level" repeater, where the 5B symbols from the received line code would be passed within the internals of the repeater core and retransmitted at the repeater output ports, essentially with no code conversion.

While Class II repeaters allow a two-repeater topology, they essentially offer minimal advantages (other than marketing reasons) over Class I repeaters, since the allowable distance between the Class II repeaters is restricted to around 5 m. This allows some expansion capability between separate repeater products located close together (i.e., within a wiring closet) but does not really allow a large network to be constructed of multiple separate products. For implementations with a large port-density requirement, a switch is virtually mandated to act as the central hub, with half-duplex connections to the outlying repeaters.

The reduced delay in a Class II repeater can be exchanged for additional span in a single-repeater topology. For instance, the single Class II topology shown in Figure 3-33 allows a half-duplex 100BASE-FX link of 200 m to be attained.

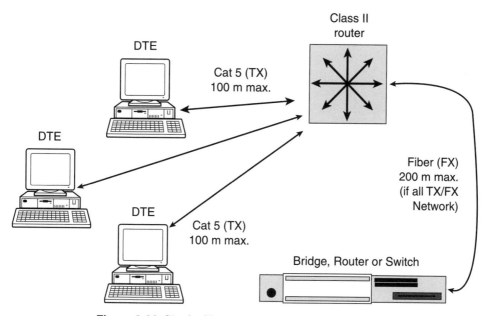

Figure 3-33 Single Class I 100BASE-TX/FX Topology

3.3.9 Management

Clause 30 of the 802.3u Standard[12] defines the entire management capabilities for 100BASE-T devices. Clause 30 condensed all of the management attributes of 802.3 together into a single place, for the first time. It also deprecated the original MAC (Clause 5), Repeater (Clause 19), and MAU (Clause 20) specifications (although Clause 5 later had to be reinstantiated, due to an oversight).

The majority of the changes to the management clauses were the result of adding new PHYs and the Auto-Negotiation capability. However, since Clause 30 was taken directly by the Gigabit Ethernet development, and enhanced to support all 10, 100, and 1000 Mb/s speeds variants, it is covered in the review of Gigabit Ethernet.

---

[12] Institute of Electrical and Electronic Engineers, Local and Metropolitan Area Networks, Media Access Control (MAC) Parameters, Physical Layer, Medium Attachment Units and Repeater for 100 Mb/s Operation, Type 100BASE-T (Clauses 21–30). IEEE Std 802.3u—1995 (Supplement to ISO/IEC 8802-3, 1993 [ANSI/IEEE Std. 802.3, 1993 Edition]), IEEE, New York, NY, October 26, 1995, ISBN 1-55937-542-6. Clause 30.

3.4 Switched Ethernet

Switched Ethernet solutions began to appear in around 1993, as Fast Ethernet was being developed. Switched Ethernet and Fast Ethernet were linked, each providing the other technology highly complementary features.

Fast Ethernet (802.3u), Full Duplex Ethernet (802.3x), and VLAN Tagging (802.3ac) were all initiated and executed as a result of the industry movement to migrate high-performance Ethernet networks from shared-medium technologies to switching.

3.4.1 Layer 2 Switch Definition

A Layer 2 switch is essentially no more than a bridge. The broad description of a bridge was covered in Chapter 2 under the "Bridge Definition" section. So, why change the name of a bridge to a switch? There were two reasons for this change—one technical and one market related.

The technical reason was that a switch performed most of the functions of a bridge in hardware. Bridges were traditionally software based, executing code to perform the filtering, learning, and forwarding processes. Switch implementations, on the other hand, were focused on moving this functionality into dedicated hardware. The continuing advances in silicon processing technology and the availability of sophisticated computer-aided design tools to allow system designers to become digital ASIC designers provided the opportunity to implement the functionality of a bridge in logic.

The market reason for the migration from bridging to switching was the fact that bridges had been severely criticized for their limitations. Issues such as broadcast storms and topology instability due to poor implementations of Spanning Tree had been cited as reasons not to employ bridges and to use routers instead. However, at the time of the Fast Ethernet developments, routers were still not practical to put into hardware, but bridges were—hence the trend to rename the venerable bridge as a switch.

A switch, like a bridge, allows multiple ports to be active simultaneously. Switches also commonly allow ports to operate in either full- or half-duplex mode, and they provide 10/100 Mb/s auto-sensing on a port-by-port basis. Other features such as full wire speed forwarding and learning performance, VLAN tagging, traffic classification, and sophisticated management are also incorporated, all primarily in hardware.

3.4.2 Deploying Switched Ethernet

Given the 100 Mb/s options previously outlined, why would anyone consider a Switched Ethernet system? There are two answers. First, there is a huge installed base of 10 Mb/s stations, some of which would benefit from segmentation to relieve bandwidth bottlenecks. Second, 100 Mb/s Ethernet systems benefit enormously from switching technology, which essentially eliminates the topology restrictions.

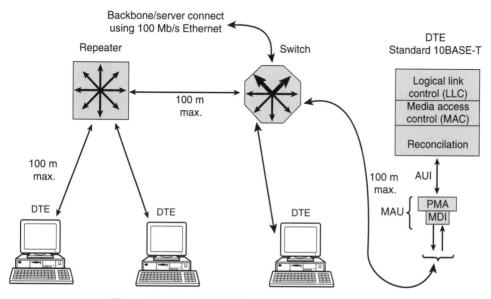

Figure 3-34 10BASE-T Switched Ethernet Topology

Figure 3-34 shows a Switched Ethernet topology based on 10BASE-T end stations. In essence, the shared repeater is replaced with a switch, which permits multiple stations to transmit simultaneously. The end stations, driver software, and cabling remain undisturbed. The switch typically acts as a multiport bridge, forwarding a received packet only to the port it is addressed to (unlike a repeater, which forwards to all ports). Switches typically operate in either a store-and-forward mode (entire packet is received before forwarding is attempted) or a cut-through mode (forwarding is commenced before packet has been entirely received) and may incorporate other criteria for forwarding, such as protocol type and/or broadcast domain (VLAN) filtering.

The solution of Figure 3-34 provides each client with a full 10 Mb/s burst bandwidth. However, to solve the aggregate-bandwidth issue (10 ports can now generate 100 Mb/s of traffic), a high-performance connection ("fat-pipe") is required for access to central resources such as a local server and/or backbone. To this end, the use of switched 10 Mb/s Ethernet to the desktop with 100 Mb/s Ethernet as a connection to a server or collapsed backbone is an excellent complementary solution.

Figure 3-34 also shows a repeater connected to the switch port. This configuration can only be supported if the switch can support multiple MAC addresses per port. Some switches are intended for a limited number of stations per port. The switch port connected to the repeater must operate in CSMA/CD mode—repeaters will not operate correctly in full-duplex operation.

3.5 Full Duplex and Flow Control

The Full Duplex/Flow Control Standard enhancements specified by 802.3x are neither limited or specific to 100BASE-T. They are described here simply because they were developed in a similar time frame to the 100BASE-T specifications and were very much driven by the acknowledgement that the restricted topologies of 100BASE-T were substantially enhanced by the incorporation of full-duplex operation.

The standards work was completed within the 802.3x Task Force. However, the document output from this effort was not ideal. First, the full-duplex specification required the update of several existing clauses, including the MAC Service (Clause 2), MAC Frame Structure (Clause 3), MAC (Clause 4), PLS Service Interface (Clause 6), 10BASE-T (Clause 14), 10BASE-FL (Clause 18), and Management (Clause 30). Second, the work also generated new clauses, namely the MAC Control specification (Clause 31). While all this seems like a dramatic change, the modifications and the overall context were modest. However, the fact was that CDMA/CD had always been half duplex only, and this had led to the multiple clauses being written with this in mind.

The 100BASE-T2 Standard was also completed in a similar time frame. Since this modified some of the same clauses with respect to 100BASE-T, it was decided to incorporate both of these to change the affected documents just once. This last decision was unfortunate, since it led to delay in merging both, and it made the resultant merged document difficult to follow (not to mention the pain entailed in producing it).

3.5.1 Summary of Full-Duplex/Flow-Control Changes

For simplicity, the changes will be summarized here at a very high level. Additional detail on the more interesting aspects of the flow-control specification are discussed later in this section. The 802.3x Standard made the following modifications (this list is not exhaustive but covers the technical impact):

1. The MAC was modified to allow simultaneous transmit and receive operation. This was accomplished by disabling the normal deferral process, based on carrier sense. Frame size and Inter-Packet Gap parameters were maintained.

2. The Type field (or "EtherType") was finally acknowledged by 802.3. Since the adoption of the original Ethernet specification, 802.3 had steadfastly ignored the fact that more networks used the EtherType field, administered by Xerox, than used the 802.3 Length field. This was a minor technical change (since it already worked!) but led to a multitude of editorial changes.

3. The various 10 Mb/s MAUs that were natively able to support full-duplex operation (those that used a full-duplex-capable medium) were modified, including 10BASE-T and 10BASE-FL. The 10 Mb/s PLS and AUI specifications were also upgraded to allow full duplex.

4. A new "standards etiquette" MAC Control Sublayer was added between the MAC Sublayer and the MAC Client Sublayer (see Figure 3-35). This was the entity that would detect special MAC Control frames and react to them. One specific MAC Control frame was defined, known as the PAUSE frame. This could be used to turn off the transmitter of a remote DTE

5. The Auto-Negotiation function was modified to allow the PAUSE capability to be advertised/exchanged in the Base Page (full duplex was already allowed when Auto-Negotiation was written).

6. Some management attributes were added to manage and control the generation of PAUSE frames.

3.5.2 Flow Control

With the deployment of 100BASE-T equipment it was realized that a simple flow-control mechanism would be highly beneficial, especially to switch implementers. One of the key concerns in building a switch is the amount of buffer memory to include in order to avoid packets being dropped, due to filling up of this memory resource (regardless of whether this buffering is at the input, output, or both).

Consider a simple example. Assume a multiport switch with finite input buffering per port (say 20,000 packets worth), such as that shown in Figure 3-34. One port is a 100BASE-T port connected to a high-performance server, the remainder are 10 Mb/s links connected either directly to users or groups of users via repeaters. A request to the server for a large file from one of the users would be a relatively short transaction and use little buffer storage in the switch. However, the reply, containing the data, might be several megabytes and could quickly overwhelm the input buffering capacity of the switch, especially with the added problem that the switch can only forward the frames to the end station at one-tenth the incoming rate. Note that this metric is a best case; if the recipient desktop machine were located on a shared repeater segment, collisions would reduce the available bandwidth still further. While up-

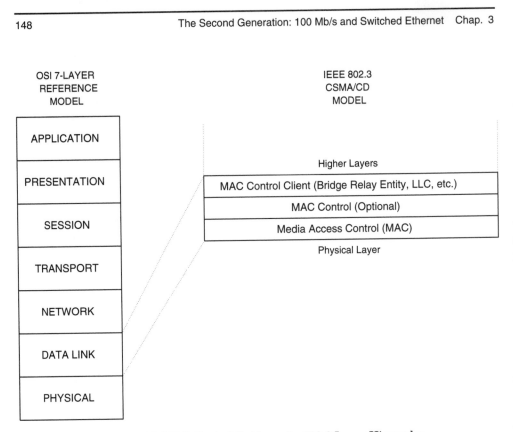

Figure 3-35 MAC Control Sublayer in 802.3 Layer Hierarchy
(From IEEE Std. 802.3x&y-1997, ©1997, IEEE. All rights reserved.)

per-layer protocols are designed for just such packet-loss situations, retransmitting the data after a specified acknowledge fails to arrive reduces efficiency substantially. In addition, this may not be the only transaction from the server, so another user or application may have suffered lost frames at the input to the 100BASE-T port of the switch, requiring multiple sessions to be repeated. In such an example, it is conceivable that by employing a switch that cannot keep up with the burst capabilities of the server, the network performance may actually be worse than by sticking with an all-10-Mb/s-repeater network. The answer is to buy a switch with lots of buffering capacity. But this makes the switch expensive (and it may exhibit more delay than is acceptable for some applications, but this is unrelated to our file-server example). If the server could be throttled, to regulate its transmission rate to the switch, the switch could be made less expensive, while maintaining good overall performance. Again, this is essentially what upper-layer protocols do, the downside being that they have long reaction times, not suitable for very responsive control.

Some vendors have implemented proprietary schemes for flow control, in order to throttle the transmitter of the device generating high traffic. However, such schemes are always a compromise, since equipment from multiple vendors may not interoperate.

3.5.3 PAUSE Frame Definition

In essence, the PAUSE frame was generated to solve exactly the type of problem outlined above. The MAC Control frame (and thereby the PAUSE frame) was an important new concept in 802.3. Prior to this definition, all Ethernet packets were treated equally. A MAC Control frame, however, can convey special information to the DTE itself, rather than just being passed transparently to the upper layers.

A MAC Control frame is a normal minimum-size (64 bytes, excluding preamble/SFD) 802.3/Etherent frame, as illustrated in Figure 3-36. The PAUSE frame is a specific encoding of the generalized MAC Control frame. The MAC Control frame has the following characteristics:

1. The DA field is the 48-bit destination address of the station(s) to which the MAC Control frame is addressed. In the general case of a MAC Control frame, the DA is permitted to be a unique physical address or a multicast address. In the specific case of the PAUSE frame, this value must be set to a special globally assigned value (the 48-bit multicast address 01-80-C2-00-00-01). This multicast address has been individually reserved for use by MAC Control PAUSE frames.

2. The SA field must contain the 48-bit address of the source/sending station.

3. The 2-byte Length/Type field contains the hexadecimal value 88-08. This value indicates a Type that has been globally assigned to indicate a MAC Control frame for 802.3 LANs.

4. The MAC Control Opcode is a 2-byte field that determines how the MAC Control Parameters are to be interpreted. For a PAUSE frame, this is defined as the hexadecimal value 00-01.

5. The MAC Control Parameters contain the opcode specific data applicable to the MAC Control frame. In the general case for the MAC Control frame, these are permitted to occupy any amount of the rest of the frame but not to extend it beyond a minimum frame, and still allow the FCS to be appended (hence a maximum of 44 bytes). For the PAUSE frame, this contains a 2-byte Pause Timer value. The timer is a 16-bit value, transmitted MS byte, LSB first. The units of time for the Pause Timer are increments of 512 bit times.

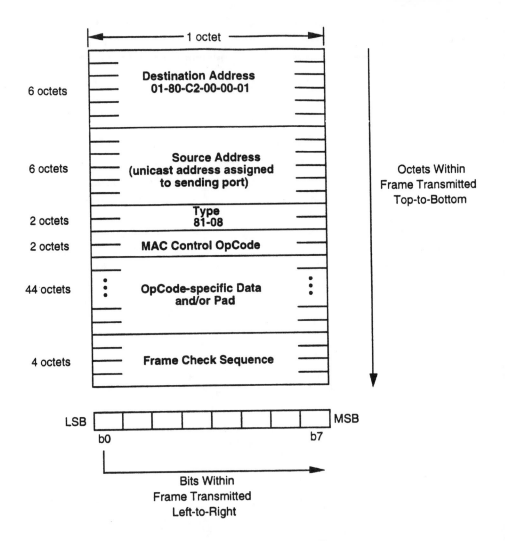

Figure 3-36 MAC Control Frame Format
(From IEEE Std. 802.3x&y-1997, ©1997, IEEE. All rights reserved.)

3.5.4 PAUSE Frame Operation and Use

The PAUSE frame is restricted to use within full-duplex 802.3 stations only. By definition, a full-duplex Ethernet station has a single point-to-point link to another single Ethernet station. Networks must be constructed using higher-layer internetworking devices, such as bridges, routers, or switches.

The 802.3x Standard does not specify at what point a MAC Control entity actually generates a PAUSE frame. This is an implementation issue that is product specific. Only the designer of an internetworking device can determine at what point the PAUSE frame must be generated, taking into account the transmission delay before it arrives at, and is acted upon by, the intended recipient.

A PAUSE frame is generated by a full-duplex station and will be received by its full-duplex link partner (assuming normal behavior of the physical link and the intermediate components). The transmitter is responsible for generating the PAUSE frame with the correct address and data fields, and an appropriate Pause Timer value.

The receiving station will decode the PAUSE frame (in the MAC Control sublayer), and will not pass the frame to its upper layers (the term frequently used for this is that the receiver will "sink" the PAUSE frame). While this is the standard's behavior, note that this does not mean that a practical implementation, such as an Ethernet MAC chip, will necessarily use the frame internally. It may pass the frame to a software or hardware process, as it does for all other frames, and expect another process to act on the PAUSE frame. An optimal implementation will, however, act on the PAUSE frame without further intervention. The receiver will extract the value of the Pause Timer contained in the PAUSE frame and load it into an internal Pause Timer. When this timer is nonzero, further transmissions for the device will be inhibited. Note, however, that transmissions in progress will continue until normal completion (there can be no collisions, hence it will only transmit any packet with a single attempt). The Pause Timer is decremented until zero (decremented by one each 512-bit time), at which point transmission is permitted to resume.

There are some additional rules.

The first is that when a transmitter is paused (its internal Pause Timer is nonzero), this does not inhibit PAUSE frame transmission. The way to look at this is that the MAC Control sublayer is the process that prevents transmissions. Once it hands a frame to the MAC, the MAC can send it. While paused, the MAC Control sublayer blocks the upper layer (the MAC client in Figure 3-35) from passing additional frames to the MAC, but it can still generate its own MAC Control frames and pass these to the MAC.

The second is that zero is a valid Pause Timer value to be transported in the PAUSE frame. A station that has been paused, and has a positive value in its Pause Timer, can have a lower value loaded into it (including zero) by simply sending this in a subsequent PAUSE frame. This has the effect that a station can be allowed to transmit again if its link partner determines there are now sufficient resources available.

Note that the reserved multicast address used for PAUSE frames is treated specially by 802.1D (Spanning Tree) bridges. 802.1D bridges will not forward a PAUSE frame sent to this multicast destination address between ports, regardless of the state of the bridge's ports, or whether or not the bridge implements the MAC Control sublayer. Therefore a bridge does not propagate PAUSE frames.

As the 802.3x Standard is currently defined, stations connected by half-duplex repeaters must not generate PAUSE frames.

3.5.5 PAUSE Negotiation

Support for PAUSE operation is optional in a full-duplex device (although highly desirable). Pause operation is determined at link start-up using the Auto-Negotiation protocol. When the pause behavior was being specified, a single symmetrical pause capability was all that was specified. This means that both devices must have the PAUSE bit set in the Base Link Code Word. To advertise this capability, a device must be capable of generation and reception of PAUSE frames. This is the symmetrical aspect—if the devices both possess the PAUSE capability, they must be able to react to a PAUSE frame generated by the opposing link partner, and they will expect the link partner to be "pause-able." The PAUSE-related negotiation is covered in the "Auto-Negotiation" section of this chapter.

However, when Gigabit Ethernet was specified, it was decided that an asymmetric PAUSE capability would be supported. This capability is an option only for 1000 Mb/s devices and is not permitted for 10 Mb/s or 100 Mb/s Ethernet operation. This is described in the "Auto-Negotiation for 1000BASE-X" and "Flow Control" sections in Chapter 4.

3.5.6 Mixed Switched Ethernet Topologies

Full-duplex Ethernet is a further derivative of Switched Ethernet. In this case, the switch is capable of allowing simultaneous transmission of both multiple stations, as well as simultaneous transmit and receive activity on each port. The key difference is that a full-duplex adapter is also required. Operating in full-duplex mode removes the need for devices to detect collision. Essentially only the packet format of Ethernet is retained. Eliminating the collision-detect timing restriction, which sets the size of the Ethernet topology (collision domain), allows longer cable distances to be permitted between full-duplex stations. Distance becomes based on cable attenuation rather than propagation delay. This does little in the case of UTP links, since their length is generally limited to 100 m by cable attenuation. But normal CSMA/CD fiber links are almost always restricted by round-trip delay, and not by attenuation.

Since virtually the entire 10 Mb/s installed base of end stations are capable only of half-duplex operation, upgrading both the adapter (or motherboard) and repeater may be prohibitively expensive for only a doubling of potential bandwidth to the desktop, especially given that the many client operating systems (and applications) are not multitasking. However, most 100 Mb/s adapters are manufactured as full-duplex capable (at least to the MII). Using a full-duplex-capable medium, such as 100BASE-FX, allows substantially larger topologies to be addressed.

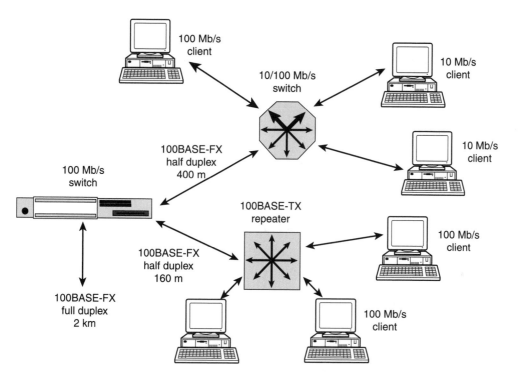

Figure 3-37 10/100BASE-T Full/Half Duplex Network

Figure 3-37 shows a hybrid 10 and 100 Mb/s Ethernet topology, employing both full- and half-duplex links. Notice that a half-duplex fiber connection to a repeater is limited to 160 m (assuming all 100BASE-X ports, as in Figure 3-32). Repeaters are shared-medium devices and cannot operate in a full-duplex mode. A half-duplex inter-switch fiber connection is capable of 400 m, and a full-duplex-capable inter-switch fiber connection can span 2 km (using single-mode fiber).

3.6 VLAN Tagging

The concept of a Virtual LAN (VLAN) is to allow network operators to configure and administer a corporate network as one single bridge-interconnected entity, while providing users the connectivity and privacy they expect from having multiple separate networks. The use of VLANs has been touted as solving a host of problems in the networking industry, including remote- and/or mobile-user connectivity, security and privacy, bandwidth management, and increased performance (by enhancing switching technology). It is fair to say that, in general, VLANs do provide solutions to some of these issues, but it is unlikely that VLANs alone can be a universal solution to all of them. There are several alternatives which offer solutions using alternate mechanisms and protocols.

The subject of VLANs is very broad and complex, with several different philosophies being adopted by network vendors. This is much too detailed a topic for our purpose here, which is to describe the underlying mechanism that is standardized for 802.3 to allow VLANs to operate.

VLANs were defined initially as a generic capability for all 802 LANs in 802.1Q[13] (802.1 looks after bridging and LAN interconnection issues). However, since the 802.1 definition required transport of information to convey the VLAN information (the VLAN Tag), which affected the frame length, a Working Group was established in 802.3 to align with the needs of this effort, defined as the 802.3ac. The 802.3ac document closely relates to the 802.1Q specification and identifies changes to existing clauses to permit the VLAN extension (the 802.3ac document introduces no new clauses).

3.6.1 VLAN Operation

The operation of VLANs is best illustrated by a simple example. Figure 3-38 shows a two-switch network, with 10 Mb/s desktop stations, interconnected over a 100BASE-TX link (or FX for longer distance). The users are divided into four logical groups, although physically connected to the same network. (Let's not yet discuss the aspect of how a particular user gets assigned to one of more of these logical groups.) Such a configuration may be useful to restrict traffic between different departments in a company, such as payroll, sales, engineering, and marketing. Each member of a group can communicate with the other members in their department but cannot access data or users in other departments (this is overly simplistic but serves as a basic example to build on). In effect, the LAN has been segmented into four logical LANs, or Virtual LANs.

The technical definition for a VLAN is that it is a logical broadcast domain. This is to say that traffic sent to the broadcast address (the DA field set to all 1s) on a particular VLAN in a bridge-interconnected network is only forwarded to other ports on

---

[13] Draft Standard P802.1Q/D10, IEEE Standards for Local and Metropolitan Area Networks: Virtual Bridged Local Area Networks, P802.3Q/D10, March 22, 1998.

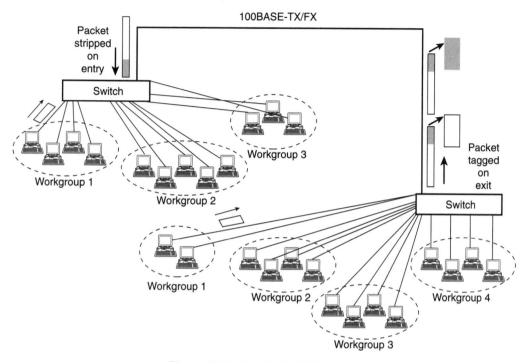

Figure 3-38 Simple VLAN Example

that bridge which have members of that VLAN attached. In contrast, a bridge that was not VLAN aware would forward broadcast traffic received on one port to all of its other ports (or at least to those ports permitted by the Spanning Tree protocol).

In order to make the association between a VLAN and its associated membership, some additional information is required by the bridge or switch. VLAN association can be performed using several different policies. For the simple example in Figure 3-38, let's assume that a station is identified as belonging to a particular VLAN by the port on the switch it is connected to. This association, referred to as "port-based" VLANs, is probably the most commonly implemented VLAN policy in the industry. So a packet received on a particular port will be "bound" to a VLAN, assigned to that port.

From the point of view of a single switch this is very reasonable. Broadcast frames received on ports associated with one VLAN are forwarded only to other ports in that VLAN. Furthermore, as an additional policy, particular station addresses appearing in one VLAN, can be prevented from either joining another VLAN or forwarding data to any member of that VLAN. This is another relatively simple association made using the DA and SA of a received frame.

However, returning to our example, how would this VLAN membership association be maintained between switches? This is the solution provided by VLAN tagging. The 100 Mb/s port connecting the two switches is a "tagged port" and is in this case a member of all of the VLANs. A broadcast frame received on one switch is flooded to all members of the VLAN, including the inter-switch port. When transmitted on the inter-switch port, it is tagged with the identity of the VLAN membership. The other switch receives the frame, strips off the VLAN while noting its association, and forwards it to the other port members of that VLAN.

This has several advantages and enhancements that can be applied. First, only one inter-switch link is required, where four would have been necessary without the VLAN Tag, if the VLAN association was to be maintained between the switches. A second link could be added, either for redundancy (in the event one failed or was cut) or for load balancing. In the load-balancing case, one link would be assigned to be in some of the VLANs, the other would be assigned as a member of the remaining VLANs. This provides a higher aggregate bandwidth connection between the VLAN members located across the switches.

3.6.2 VLAN Tag Frame Format

The VLAN Tag, defined in 802.3ac and 802.1Q, is a 4-byte field, inserted between the original Ethernet frame's Source Address field and Type/Length field. The VLAN Tag location and format are shown in Figure 3-39. Since it is inserted into the frame, it is an "intrusive tag" rather than a simple encapsulation. Insertion of this tag field means that the CRC must be recomputed whenever the tag is inserted or stripped, and the length of the frame becomes 4 bytes longer when it is present.

The change in length was really the only significant technical change that was required to the 802.3 standards, in order to accommodate the tag. This meant that legal frame sizes were modified to allow from 64 (minimum frame size) to 1522 bytes. The 1522 is allowed only for frames that have the assigned VLAN EtherType field; otherwise, 1518 is still the maximum permitted.

The VLAN Tag is split into two 16-bit fields, as follows:

VLAN Tag Protocol Identifier (TPID)

The TPID field is a globally assigned and reserved EtherType field, with a value 0x81–00.

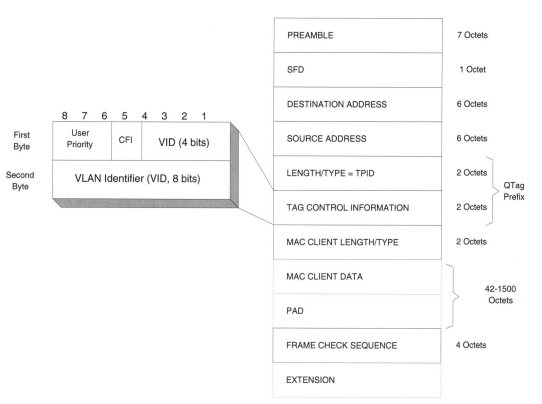

Figure 3-39 VLAN Tag Frame Format (From IEEE P802.3ac/D2.2, ©1998. All rights reserved.)

Tag Control Information (TCI)

The TCI is a 16-bit value, transmitted MS byte, LSB first, and contains 3 fields:

1. A 3-bit User Priority field. Up to eight levels of priority can be assigned to and carried within the VLAN Tag for any packet. Assignment of priorities is specified in 802.1p.[14] Realistically, most vendors will use fewer values of priority (0 is the highest, 7 the lowest). This field allows the concept of "class-of-service" to be supported across Ethernet networks.

2. A 1-bit Canonical Format Indicator (the CFI bit). This bit is not used by 802.3 devices, and it should be sent and received as 0. If it is set, the effect is undefined in 802.3. The real use of the bit was to encapsulate Token Ring frames in Ethernet, but the 802.3 vendor community basically refused to acknowledge this in an 802.3 document. Some Token Ring vendors may use this bit in a vendor-specific manner.

---

[14] Institute of Electrical and Electronic Engineers, Information Technology—Telecommunications and information exchange between systems—Local and Metropolitan Area Netwroks—Common Specifications—Part 3: Media Access Control (MAC) Bridges (incorporating IEEE 802.1p: Traffic Class Expediting and Dynamic Multicast Filtering), IEEE 802.1Q/D16, IEEE, New York, NY, March 19, 1998.

3. A 12-bit VLAN Identifier (VID). This is the actual VLAN association. Table 3-12 shows those VIDs that are reserved. All others are available and are locally admisitered.

Table 3-12 VLAN Identifier (VID) Definition[a]

VID	Meaning/Use
0x0–00	Null VLAN ID. Indicates that the tag contains no VID information, only priority information. This is referred to as a Priority Tagged Frame. A VLAN-aware bridge will forward such frames only after either classifying an appropriate TCI at the output port, or stripping the VLAN Tag and retransmitting the frame untagged.
0x0–01	The default port-based VLAN value, used for frame classification through a bridge. The value can be changed by management on a per-port basis.
0x–F–FF	Reserved.

[a]From IEEE P802.1Q/D10, ©1998. All rights reserved.

3.6.3 VLAN Administration

The port-based VLAN example, described in the "VLAN Operation" section, is the simplest form of VLAN association. A switch can apply alternate VLAN associations (often referred to as "VLAN binding"), based on looking into the Ethernet packet, at MAC, subnet, and protocol fields.

However, other than port-based VLANs, which appear to be consistently implemented in many vendors' products, MAC-based VLANs, subnet-based VLANs, and protocol-based VLANs have still to gain widespread acceptance and/or standardization. The advent of Layer 3 switches may render the issue essentially moot. Layer 3 switches are discussed in Chapter 4.

3.7 10/100 Mb/s Capable Devices

One of the paramount goals in the development of 100BASE-T was to permit the cost-effective implementation of 10/100 Mb/s capable Ethernet devices. Although most early implementations supported only 100 Mb/s, the industry very quickly moved to 10/100 auto-sensing products—first at the PC adapter and soon afterward at the switch and the repeater.

After this initial wave of 10/100 Mb/s devices in each product category, there followed the now familiar (in the Ethernet market space) price competition from multiple vendors, leading to extremely aggressive cost-reduction curves.

For the purchaser of a mainstream PC, a 10/100 Mb/s adapter choice incurs such a small price delta compared with the overall system cost that trying to save money by selecting a 10-Mb/s-only device barely warrants consideration.

10/100 Mb/s auto-sensing repeaters and switches will likely maintain a modest price (and cost) premium over 10-Mb/s-only devices. However, this price delta will continue to erode steadily for substantially equivalent functionality products (i.e., if comparing a 10-Mb/s-only managed switch versus a 10/100 Mb/s managed switch), such that the added functionality is worth the small added initial investment. This is especially true for purchases made for large corporate networks, where the purchase decision is frequently made on the basis that buying additional functionality, even if not currently required, allows the network to be "future-proofed," delaying future disruption of the network as long as possible.

The Third Generation:
1000 Mb/s (Gigabit)

4.1 Overview

The concept of running Ethernet at gigabit speeds started to gain interest in 1995. Late in 1995, sufficient interest had been garnered to request a study group to be formed within 802.3. Figure 4-1 shows the timeline for the development of the Gigabit Ethernet standard, which involved literally hundreds of individual contributors and dozens of networking companies.

Chapter 1 explains the various stages required for the development of an IEEE standard.

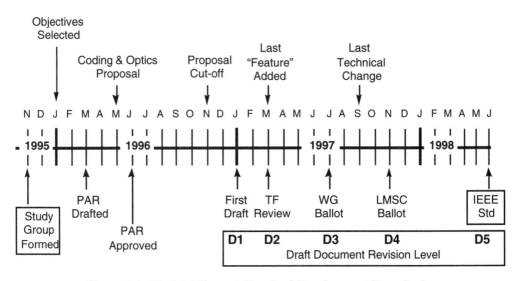

Figure 4-1 Gigabit Ethernet Standard Development Time Scale

4.1.1 Why Gigabit Ethernet?

Gigabit Ethernet was the natural evolution after the development and widespread deployment of networking equipment based on Fast Ethernet (100BASE-T) technology. During the development of 100BASE-T, many claims were made by industry analysts, observers, and vendors as to how quickly this new technology would be adopted, and whether it was needed or just perceived to be needed. However, once the 100BASE-T standard was completed, vendors immediately introduced a torrent of products based on it. Costs associated with deploying 100BASE-T quickly fell, and the installed base of latent 100BASE-T devices leaped.

While this was obviously good for the participating vendors it also had a negative effect. Few networks up to this point had been 100 Mb/s capable, and where they were, these were primarily backbones based on FDDI. Widespread deployment of 100 Mb/s to the desktop made the existing infrastructure look very feeble.

In addition, the other primary backbone network interconnection technology is ATM. ATM already has 622 Mb/s (OC-12) capable links shipping, and a plan to upgrade to OC-48 (2.4 Gb/s) links in the early adoption phase.

But ATM and/or FDDI in the backbone require frame formats to change. For high-speed switching and routing (discussed in Chapter 5), segmentation, reassembly, encapsulation/decapsulation and frame format conversions are very expensive, in terms of efficiency of implementation and speed of operation, for the silicon, software and systems capabilities to perform these operations at line rates.

Backbone Technology—Bandwidth Aggregation

Few (if any) applications or users currently need the bandwidth capabilities of Gb/s technologies at the desktop (whether Ethernet or any other). However, backbone technologies, where aggregate bandwidth needs coalesce, will need these Gb/s capabilities, as user demands migrate to use the 100 Mb/s technologies that are being rapidly deployed to the desktop.

New and Emerging Bandwidth-Intensive Applications

New and emerging bandwidth-intensive applications will continue to drive the need for raw bandwidth, especially as Internet-related browser and "push" content capabilities continue to deliver enhanced services from a user perspective. As Internet, intranet, and Web content traffic continues to expand, and as the cost of 10/100 Mb/s capable equipment is driven down, there is a growing potential that corporate backbones and aggregation points will be overwhelmed by bandwidth requirements alone.

Gigabit Ethernet offers the potential to upgrade the core of the network simply and efficiently.

4.1.2 Major Differences Between 100 Mb/s and 1000 Mb/s

Gigabit Media Independent Interface (GMII) Versus MII

When Ethernet moved from 10 to 100 Mb/s operation, a new media-independent interface was required, principally because the original AUI at 10 Mb/s would not easily scale to 100 Mb/s operation. Similarly, in the move to 1000 Mb/s, the MII defined for 100 Mb/s operation was unsuitable. While many of the MII signaling concepts were maintained, the GMII transmit and receive data paths were widened to 8 bits (from the 4-bit paths provided by the MII) to allow reasonable frequency clocks and data path transition frequencies. Even with this modification, the transmit and receive data paths and clocks were required to operate at 125 MHz in order to achieve the 1 Gb/s data rate.

Adoption of Fibre Channel Encoding

As the speed requirements for Ethernet have steadily increased, so has the challenge of providing a reliable signaling scheme over the media at these increasing rates. The IEEE Gigabit Ethernet committee looked for an existing signaling system at Gb/s data rates, in order to speed the standard development cycle and to leverage existing industry experience at these high data rates. As a result, Fibre Channel (ANSI X3.230-1994) was adopted as the physical signaling scheme, similar to the way in which 100BASE-TX merged the FDDI PHY and Ethernet MAC.

Fibre Channel uses an 8B/10B line code, encoding each 8 bits of data payload into a 10-bit line code, incorporating additional bits for error-checking robustness. The coding technique was initially developed by IBM (who licensed the patents for use in Fibre Channel initially, and later Gigabit Ethernet), for high-speed signaling over fiber optic cable. The Gigabit Ethernet PHY specifications based on 8B/10B coding are generically referred to as 1000BASE-X, with derivatives for short-wave-length optics (1000BASE-SX), long-wavelength optics (1000BASE-LX), and copper media (1000BASE-CX).

At the time the Fibre Channel signaling scheme was initially presented to the Gigabit Ethernet committee, the closest appropriate signaling rate was 1.0625 Gb/s, yielding an effective data rate of 850 Mb/s. The requirement to achieve a data rate of 1 Gb/s meant the signaling rate had to be increased to 1.25 Gb/s and caused most existing silicon implementations to be reworked.

Return to a Single-Repeater Specification

While 100BASE-T moved to two classes of repeaters, Gigabit Ethernet returned to a single repeater type. As discussed in the 100BASE-T overview, the CSMA/CD access method is sensitive to round trip delay, so increasing the data rate directly affects the round-trip delay, and hence the distances that can be achieved. To combat this, various attempts were made to define different types of repeater during the Gigabit Ethernet development. This included a device defined as a "Buffered Repeater", which is discussed in Chapter 5. However, the committee eventually chose not to specify such a device in the standard.

Even though modifications were made to the Ethernet MAC when operating at Gb/s to extend the distance limitations, there was a realization that most Gb/s Ethernet networks would utilize full-duplex operations, and so a single simple repeater definition was considered acceptable.

Modification of Auto-Negotiation for Fiber

Auto-Negotiation was originally defined for 10/100 Mb/s capable devices, in order to allow self-configuration after power-on or reset. The original Auto-Negotiation signaling scheme was optimized for UTP cable and not suitable for fiber optic media, due to the signaling mechanism employed. While the Auto-Negotiation protocol was retained, the Fibre Channel 8B/10B signaling scheme was adopted to permit the exchange of configuration information (such as half- or full-duplex capability), prior to data transfer.

Modified CSMA/CD Operation and Preference for Full Duplex

The round-trip-delay constraint of CSMA/CD directly affects the network diameter, since a MAC must be able to detect a collision within the slot time. For the previous 10 and 100 Mb/s versions of Ethernet, the slot time was 512 bit times. For Gb/s Ethernet, retaining this slot time reduces the network topology to such an extent that it is not a very useful network. So for gigabit operation, the CSMA/CD operation of the MAC was modified, increasing the slot time to 512 bytes. Considerable effort was expended during the development of the standard to tune the performance of the MAC in CSMA/CD mode. This is examined in detail later in this chapter.

In full-duplex mode, since no concept of collision is present, the operation of the MAC was unchanged, except for the speed increase, over the previous 10 and 100 Mb/s full duplex modes. This was the first significant change to the CSMA/CD MAC since the original Ethernet specification in 1980.

From an industry perspective, there was general acceptance that full-duplex operation in conjunction with switching had compelling advantages.

Prioritization of Fiber over Copper Media Types

Previous generations of Ethernet had been focused on providing a cost-effective network solution to interconnect typical office computer and peripheral equipment. This meant that there was always great focus on operating over an inexpensive, simple, and readily available cabling scheme—hence the developments to allow operation over UTP for the 10 and 100 Mb/s versions. However, at each increase in speed, operating over limited-bandwidth cable becomes more difficult. Recognizing this, and that gigabit technology would be initially be demanded in less cost-sensitive applications, such as switch-to-switch or switch-to-server links, the IEEE 802.3z committee decided to initially focus on solutions over fiber optic cable. The 1000BASE-T version of gigabit Ethernet, which focussed on providing a solution over 4 pairs of Cat 5 cable, was started later and was not complete when the initial fiber and twin-axial cable versions were approved as the first Gigabit Ethernet standard.

Updated Management

Network-management capabilities for Ethernet had migrated consistently as new functionality had been incorporated, which was also the case for gigabit operation. The Clause 30 specification for 100BASE-T, with additional changes to incorporate full duplex, were merged with the gigabit requirements, so the result was not an amended version of Clause 30.

Topology

As stated previously, each increase in speed for a CSMA/CD network leads to a reduction in the network span, if no other parameters of the MAC are scaled. In very approximate terms, this meant that going from 10 Mb/s to 100 Mb/s reduced the network diameter from around 2 km to 200 m. If this were continued in the move to gigabit speeds, the effective network diameter would reduce to 20 m—not a particularly attractive distance for a large network topology. For this reason, the MAC was modified to operate at the gigabit rate, increasing the span of a gigabit CSMA/CD network (using a single repeater) to a practical value of around 200 m. Full-duplex operation provides significantly enhanced distance capabilities.

4.2 Layer 3 Switch Definition

Concurrent with the development of the Gigabit Ethernet standard, many network equipment vendors started to apply hardware-implemented switching schemes to network layer devices (traditionally considered routers), similar to those previously applied to MAC layer devices (traditionally considered bridges). Hence, as the definition of a bridge with a predominantly hardware-based forwarding and learning table had migrated to be reclassified as a "Layer 2 Switch," certain classes of routers became redefined as "Layer 3 Switches."

Typically, first-generation Layer 3 Switches were limited in the number of network layer protocols that were accelerated using hardware. Only one or perhaps two protocols were normally accelerated, with other protocols effectively being treated as exceptions, and routed using conventional software-based routing algorithms.

Optimization for a restricted number of protocols was a direct result of trends in the network industry to focus on the Internet Protocol (IP) suite as the primary protocol for corporate and World Wide Web (WWW) based traffic. The enormous growth of IP-based traffic in the mid-to-late 1990s fueled the need for very fast IP-optimized routers to handle the aggregation of traffic from, and forwarding of traffic to, multiple gigabit data links.

Layer 3 switching, and various optimizations to assist hardware-based acceleration of routing functions, are discussed in significant detail in Chapter 5.

4.3 Gigabit Ethernet Technology: Introduction

Figure 4-2 shows a layered model for gigabit technology in relation to the OSI 7-layer model. The MAC operation for shared gigabit was enhanced to allow a reasonable topology of 200 meters. The physical-layer technology was adopted from the Fibre

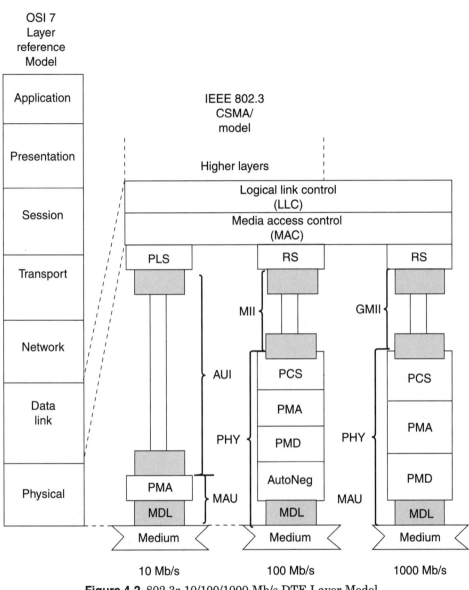

Figure 4-2 802.3z 10/100/1000 Mb/s DTE Layer Model
(Redrawn from IEEE Std. P802.3z, IEEE. All rights reserved.)

Channel standards. The MII interface for gigabit became 8 bits wide running at 125 MHz to allow gigabit operation. A new coding scheme (also used in Fibre channel standards), 8B/10B, was used for coding signals before transmission onto the physical layer.

4.4 Gigabit MAC Operation

4.4.1 Overview

One of the goals of the IEEE 802.3z standards task force was to maintain compatibility with the existing standards for 10 Mb/s and 100 Mb/s operation. Seamless operation was required to forward frames between segments running at different speeds, between segments and switched networks, etc. Therefore, the existing Ethernet format, the minimum and maximum frame lengths, and the truncated Binary Exponential Backoff (BEB) algorithm were unchanged for backward compatibility. However, in Gigabit Ethernet half-duplex networks, because of large propagation delays, some changes to the Carrier Sense Multiple Access with Collision Detection (CSMA/CD) Medium Access Control (MAC) protocol were required. The following section explains what those changes were for half-duplex operation.

4.4.2 Half-Duplex Operation

Before we start discussion on the MAC operation in half duplex, it is important to understand the MAC operation in 10 Mb/s and 100 Mb/s (See the section on "Media Access Management" in Chapter 2). It is important to understand the relationship between slot time and minimum frame size in half-duplex operation. When a DTE transmits a frame, the absence of a collision within a slot time is assumed as an implicit acknowledgment that no other DTE is transmitting at the same time. Likewise, receivers can detect collision fragments by comparing the fragment lengths to the minimum frame size. If the fragment at the receiver is less than the minimum frame size, it is interpreted as a collision fragment and therefore filtered out. However, if shorter frame transmissions were allowed, two frames that collide while transmitting may not be detected by the receivers in time before the transmitter goes idle. In 10BASE-T and 100BASE-T operation, collisions are detected at the sending DTEs if the receiver goes active while the transmitter is active. With shorter frames, it is possible that a receiver might go active well after the transmitter has become idle, and the receiver might interpret this as a new frame. Of course, this frame will not be a complete one and will be eventually discarded. There is also a possibility a new frame transmission might collide with the remnants of a previous collision. Needless to say, the minimum frame size must be at least 512 bits to ensure proper operation of half-duplex networks.

The relationship between minimum frame size and slot time can be further illustrated with the help of the timing diagram in Figure 4-3. Consider two DTEs A and B in a network, separated by a maximum distance such that the round-trip time for a bit is a slot time. Let us assume that A and B have frames whose lengths are less than a

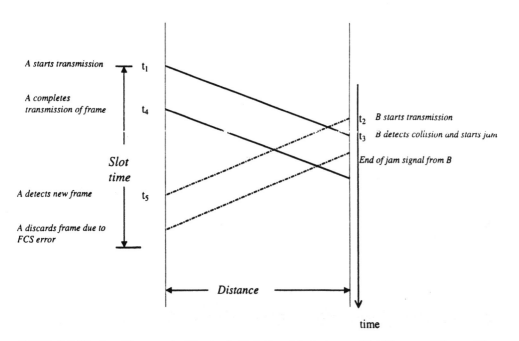

A starts transmission — t_1

A completes
transmission of frame — t_4

t_2 B starts transmission

t_3 B detects collision and starts jam

Slot time

End of jam signal from B

A detects new frame — t_5

A discards frame due to
FCS error

Distance

time

Figure 4-3 Timing Diagram to Illustrate Relationship between Slot Time and Frame Size

slot time. At time t_1, A starts transmitting a frame, the first bit of which will reach B at t_3. However, at time t_2, B starts sending a frame, since it senses the network to be inactive. Since B started transmitting at t_2 and its receiver goes active at time t_3, B recognizes that a collision has occurred, aborts its transmission, sends jam signals and then stops. The first bit from B reaches A at time t_5, well after the transmission from A ended (which happened at t_4). Since A's receiver goes active at t_5, A will now interpret the frame as a new frame. Of course, this frame will be eventually be discarded because of FCS error, since B has already aborted the transmission. It is also possible that A could start transmission of another frame just before time t_5, which would then collide with the previous collision fragment. Needless to say, this would render the operation of the network infeasible. Therefore the minimum transmission time of a frame on the network must be at least a slot time.

Since the minimum frame size is 512 bits and the minimum transmission time should be at least a slot time, this would imply that the network size should be decreased to 20 m to make the CSMA/CD operation viable at gigabit speed. However, decreasing the network size to 20 m would not be practical. The IEEE 802.3z task force therefore specified the slot time as 512 bytes (i.e., 4096 bit times) for 1000 Mb/s networks.

4.4.3 Extensions for Shared Gigabit Networks

Carrier Extension

Increasing the slot time to 512 bytes for shared gigabit networks was a first step in developing a version of CSMA/CD for use. Simply increasing the slot time has no real unwanted effect. Since the backoff delay is an integral multiple of slot times, each DTE backoff delay is higher, thereby allowing other DTEs to attempt to transmit. However, the minimum frame length was still kept at 64 bytes. Increasing the minimum frame length also to 512 bytes would break the compatibility with lower-speed networks. In a bridged network, a bridge will have to segment a frame from gigabit network to 64-byte chunks. If a server had gigabit links, then each acknowledgment would be eight times longer than necessary. The IEEE 802.3z task force decided to adopt a technique called 'carrier extension' to decouple the minimum frame length from the slot time for gigabit half-duplex operation.

Transmit Operation

Under carrier extension, the minimum frame size is unchanged and is 512 bits. When a DTE transmits a frame, if the frame is longer than slot time (i.e., 4096 bits), the MAC returns the *'transmitdone'* status to the upper layer as before. However, if the frame length is less than the slot time, the transmit status is withheld and the physical layer transmits a sequence of special 'extended carrier' symbols until the end of slot time.[1] These special symbols are transmitted after the Frame Check Sequence (FCS) which delimits the frame. The special symbols are not considered part of the frame and are handled in a special way at the receiver. If a collision were to occur during frame transmission, i.e., during data transmission or while transmitting extended carrier symbols, the transmitter would abort transmission and transmit 32 bits of jam signals in the usual way.

Receiver Operation

Each receiver will synchronize with the transmitter after detecting preamble and will then strip the Start-of-Frame Delimiter (SFD). The receive buffer collects incoming data bits that are not extension bits until the frame ends. After the frame ends, if the incoming data bits are less than the minimum frame size, the frame is discarded, even though the receive buffer has a perfectly valid frame. If the received frame is valid and slot time has passed, the receive buffer is passed to the MAC layer for address match and frame-check sequence. A transmitter that detects collision during extended carrier may retransmit the frame. Therefore, even though a perfectly valid frame was transmitted, it must be discarded to avoid duplication.

---

[1] See section on GMII and Physical Coding Sublayer (PCS).

Media Access Control Frame Format

Figure 4-4 shows the frame format[2] for shared gigabit operation. Notice that the frame format is similar to 10BASE-T and 100BASE-T except that if the frame is less than 512 bytes, then extension bits are sent after the FCS. The FCS covers only the data portion of the frame and does not include the extension symbols. The maximum length of the extension is equal to 448 bytes, which is (slot time) – (minimum frame size).

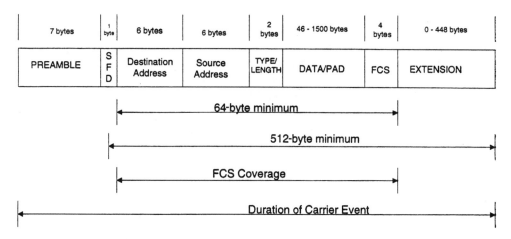

Figure 4-4 Frame Format with Carrier Extension

The MAC will monitor the medium while transmitting extension bits, and any collision after the slot time is interpreted as a late collision. In a gigabit network, the IEEE 802.3z explicitly specifies that the DTE shall not retransmit after a late collision. Since a valid frame could be transmitted well before the slot time ends, the receiver would have passed on the valid frame to the upper layer at the end of slot time. If a late collision occured and the DTE chose to retransmit the frame, duplication would occur. To avoid this, the IEEE 802.3z specifies no retransmission of a frame after late collision. Note that, however, the decision to retransmit in 10BASE-T and 100BASE-T networks is left as optional.

While carrier extension solves the problem of maintaining the same network diameter as 100 Mb/s, without increasing minimum frame length, it increases the transmission time for short frames. In general, for a 64-byte frame, the transmission time is increased by a factor of 8 although the bits are transmitted 10 times faster. Therefore, in a network consisting of only 64-byte frames, the effective throughput[3]

---

2 IEEE 802.3z—Media Access Control (MAC) Parameters, Physical Layer, Repeater and Management Parameters for 1000 Mb/s Operation.

achieved is only 25%. However, network traffic rarely consists of only short frames. Therefore, the overhead per frame is generally smaller. A technique called Frame Bursting, described below, was developed to address the issue of improving performance in shared gigabit, especially if the network traffic consists of short frames.

4.4.4 Frame Bursting

A number of approaches[4,5] were proposed before the IEEE 802.3z Task Force to improve the efficiency of transmitting short frames on shared gigabit networks. Packet packing,[6,7] in particular, received serious consideration. This approach required packing multiple frames within a slot time and using carrier extension to fill up the slot time if there are no more frames available. With packet packing, most of the efficiency lost by simple carrier extension can be recovered. However, the implementation requires substantial changes to the MAC interface since a block of frames are transmitted in a slot time as opposed to one frame in a slot time. This poses numerous changes—viz., retransmitting several frames when there is a collision, multiple updates of statistical counters, etc. Packet packing was considered too complex from the perspective of implementation and was dropped.

Frame Bursting Overview

The principle of Frame Bursting is as follows. A DTE tries to transmit a frame, which may or may not require carrier extension. At the same time a burst timer is started. If the first frame transmission is successful (i.e., without collision) then the DTE has the option of transmitting additional frames under the following conditions: (i) There is another frame to transmit and (ii) the "burst timer" has not expired. Note that subsequent frames within the burst are not extended. This is because the slot time has passed and the DTE has control of the medium. Once the burst is terminated, the DTE contends for the medium all over again.

---

[3] Note the terms *throughput* and *efficiency* are used interchangeably.

[4] M. Molle, "Reducing the effects of propagation delay on CSMA/CD networks," IEEE 802.3 High-Speed Study Group Plenary Meeting, San Diego, CA, Mar. 1996,
http://grouper.ieee.org/groups/802/3/z/public/presentations/mar1996/Mmredpd.txt.

[5] M. Weizman, "HSSG CSMA/VCD proposal," IEEE 802.3 High-Speed Study Group Plenary Meeting, Enschede NL, July 1996,
http://grouper.ieee.org/groups/802/3/z/public/presentations/july1996/MWvcdprp.txt.

[6] M. Kalkunte, J. Kadambi, "Packet Packing and mTBEB Simulation Results," IEEE 802.3 High-Speed Study Group Plenary Meeting, Enschede NL, July 1996,
http://grouper.ieee.org/groups/802/3/z/public/presentations/july1996/Mksim.pdf.

[7] S. Haddock, "Carrier Extension Issues," IEEE 802.3 High-Speed Study Group Plenary Meeting, Enschede NL, July 1996,
http://grouper.ieee.org/groups/802/3/z/public/presentations/july1996/SHcareext.txt.

Transmitter Operation

A transmitter first checks to see if a frame is in the middle of a burst or is the first frame of the burst. If the burst timer is running, this indicates that it is in the middle of the burst. Otherwise, it is considered as the first frame and the normal CSMA/CD operation is followed—defer if there is carrier activity, backoff after collisions, etc.

If the frame transmitted is a first frame, then the transmitter checks to see two things: (i) Is there another frame to transmit? (ii) Has the burst timer expired? If the burst timer has not expired, the transmitter sends another 96 bits of extended carrier. Note that the extended carrier during the burst is considered as inter-frame gap. Only the first frame in the burst is extended if necessary.

If there is another frame to transmit, the transmission starts after the inter-frame gap. If there is no frame to transmit, the burst is terminated, the burst timer is cleared, and the host gives up the medium and starts the process all over again when the next frame arrives. Figure 4-5 shows a flow chart of transmit operation for frame bursting.

Figure 4-6 shows an example of the sequence of events in a frame burst. The figure shows the first frame in the burst being extended, since it is a short frame. Although the first frame is extended, an inter-frame gap still follows to allow the receivers some time to process the next frame. Figure 4-6 shows that the start of the last frame must occur before the burst timer expires, but the transmission may extend beyond the burst timer limit. The decision to use a starting-time threshold for burst timer instead of an ending-time threshold makes implementation very easy.

Receiver Operation

A receiver starts synchronizing with the transmitter after detecting valid preamble and then strips the Start-of-Frame Delimiter (SFD). An extending flag is set to indicate that this is the first frame in the burst and the normal rules of carrier extension apply. The receiver collects incoming data bits into a receive buffer to form the incoming frame until it finds either (a) end-of-carrier or (b) an extension bit when the extending flag is cleared. The receiver compares the incoming bits with the slot time after each bit is received. The extending flag is cleared when the incoming number of bits (data bits + extension bits if any) is equal to slot time.

When the receiver has received a frame it checks to see if the extending flag is still set. In this case, the frame is considered as a collision fragment and discarded. If the received frame has an invalid FCS, it is discarded. If the transmitter terminates a burst, the receiver returns to looking for the next burst. However, if the burst has not ended, the receiver starts collecting incoming bits to form the next frame, which is terminated by one of two events as described above.

In a properly configured network, there should be no collision after the slot time has passed. Therefore, the familiar one-at-time interface is still preserved while improving the efficiency for short frames.

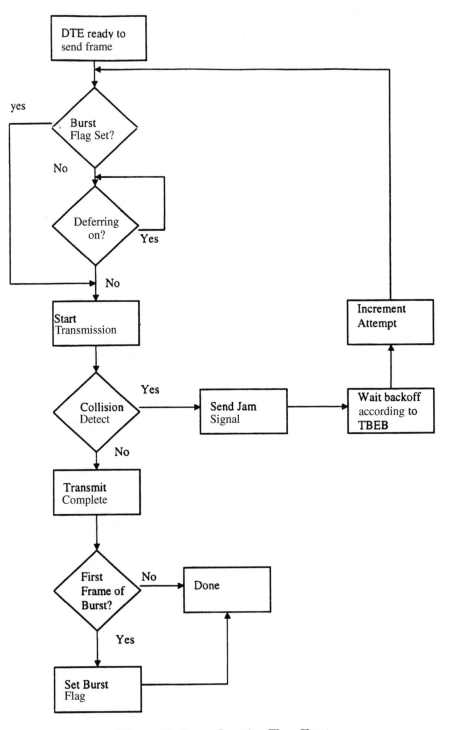

Figure 4-5 Frame Bursting Flow Chart

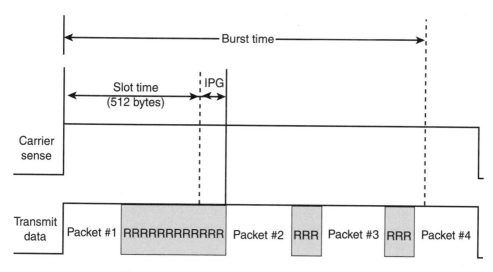

Figure 4-6 An Illustration of Frame Bursting

Parameters for Gigabit Operation

Table 4-1 shows the operational parameters for gigabit network implementation.[8] The inter-frame gap for 1000 Mb/s is one-tenth of Fast Ethernet and the slot time is increased to 4096 bits. When the frame-bursting option is enabled, the maximum burstLimit is set at 65,536 bits.[9] All other parameters are identical to Fast Ethernet. Note that the bit time at 1000 Mb/s is 1 nanosecond.

Table 4-1 Operational Parameters for 1000 Mb/s implementation
(Data from IEEE Std. P802.3z, IEEE. All rights reserved.)

Parameters	Values
slotTime	4096 bit times
inter-framegap	0.096 μs
attemptLimit	16
backoffLimit	10
jamsize	32 bits
maxFrameSize	1518 octets
minFrameSize	512 bits
burstLimit	65,536 bits

---

[8] IEEE 802.3z—Media Access Control (MAC) Parameters, Physical Layer, Repeater and Management Parameters for 1000 Mb/s Operation, Clause 4.

[9] Setting the burstLimit to 65,536 bits changes the definitions of maxDeferTime and jabber timer, which are dependent on the length of carrier activity.

4.4.5 Performance

The performance of shared gigabit networks employing frame bursting really depends on the traffic mix. Frame bursting may reduce the overhead of carrier extension by reducing the number of times it must be applied. Performance of a network is generally characterized by network throughput and end-to-end packet delay. In addition, measures quantifying capture effect, such as access latency and number of consecutive transmits by a DTE, are important to assess fairness. The capture effect is explained in more detail in later sections.

Worst-Case Efficiency Comparison

The efficiency of a single DTE can be mathematically calculated. This represents the theoretical maximum throughput efficiency that can be achieved. A network consisting of several nodes will have a throughput less than this theoretical maximum because of collision overhead.

For 100 Mb/s CSMA/CD, the normalized efficiency η can be expressed as

$$\eta = \frac{P}{P + I + p}$$

in which

P = the length of the packet (bits),

I = inter-frame gap (96 bits), and

p = length of preamble (64 bits).

The worst-case normalized efficiency occurs at $P = 512$ bits. Therefore,

$$\eta = \frac{512}{512 + 96 + 64} \approx 76\%$$

For 1000 Mb/s CSMA/CD with carrier extension only, the normalized efficiency can be expressed as

$$\eta = \frac{P}{\max(S, P) + I + p}$$

in which

S = slot time (4096 bits).

The worst-case efficiency occurs for small frames ($P = 512$ bits) and is calculated as

$$\eta = \frac{512}{4096 + 96 + 64} \approx 12\%$$

Clearly, there is a reduction of 64% in worst-case normalized efficiency for 1000 Mb/s CSMA/CD with carrier extension only.

The normalized efficiency for 1000 Mb/s with frame bursting is expressed as [Molle et al.]

$$\eta = \frac{(n+1)\,P}{\max(S,P) + n(P + I + p)}$$

in which

n = the number of consecutive frames transmitted in the burst after the first frame.

As before, the worst-case normalized efficiency occurs at $P = 512$ bits, with the burst timer[10] set at 65,536 bits. The number of frames that can be transmitted within the burst is calculated as $(65{,}536 - 4096) / (512 + 64 + 96) \approx 92$. Therefore, the worst-case efficiency achieved is

$$\eta = \frac{93 * 512}{4096 + 92 * 672} \approx 72\%$$

which is almost 95% of the worst-case normalized efficiency for ordinary CSMA/CD.

Effect of Burst Timer on Worst-Case Efficiency

Figure 4-7 illustrates the effect of the burst timer on the worst-case efficiency of a single DTE for 64-byte frames. As the burst timer increases, the throughput efficiency increases as well. This is because the overhead for a 64-byte frame (which is 448 bytes) is shared by more rames as the burst timer increases. For instance, at a burst-timer value of 12,000 bits, the 448 bytes of overhead is shared by 12 frames, whereas

---

[10] Note that the terms burst limit and burst timer are used interchangeably

the same overhead is shared by 92 frames at a burst-timer value of 65,536 bits. The efficiency gained beyond 65,536 bits is minimal, since the per-frame overhead becomes negligible.

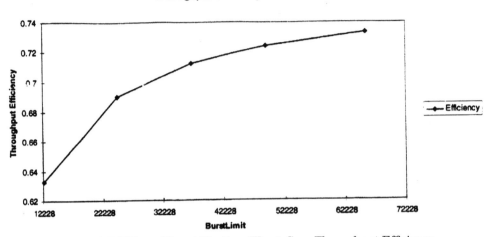

Figure 4-7 Effect of Burst Limit on Worst-Case Throughput Efficiency

Performance Simulations

Molle, Kalkunte, and Kadambi[11] conducted extensive simulations to compare the performance of 100 Mb/s, 1000 Mb/s with carrier extension, and 1000 Mb/s with frame bursting. They conducted simulations on a 15-host system, with open traffic with the packet lengths following a workgroup average distribution [see Appendix A3].

Figure 4-8 shows the percentage throughput as a function of percentage offered load for a 15-host network. For the workgroup average traffic the maximum network efficiency for 100 Mb/s system is 86%, while for the basic 1000 Mb/s with carrier extension the maximum network efficiency is about 61% (a 30% reduction). With frame bursting of 12,000 bits, the maximum throughput achieved is 72%. With 8 kbits of frame bursting, the throughput increases to 80%, which is within 8% of the 100 Mb/s Fast Ethernet system. It is clear that with increase in the burst timer in frame bursting the performance of the 1000 Mb/s approaches that of the 100 Mb/s. This is because, while the data rate increases by a factor of 10 and the slot time by a factor of 8, in-

---

11   M. Molle, M. Kalkunte, and J. Kadambi, "Frame Bursting—A Technique for Scaling CSMA/CD to Gigabit Speeds," *IEEE Network Magazine,* Aug. 1997.

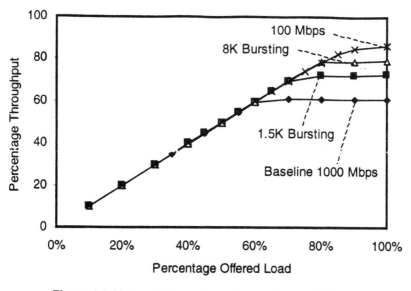

Figure 4-8 Network Throughput Comparison at Various
Offered Loads (© 1997, IEEE)

creasing the burst timer is tantamount to effectively increasing the maximum frame transmission per host, so that the resulting operation of 1000 Mb/s is a scaled operation of 100 Mb/s.

Figure 4-9 shows the mean end-to-end delay as a function of offered load for a 15-node network using the workgroup average traffic [Molle et al.]. The end-to-end delay includes waiting time in the queue as well as access latency. Figure 4-9 shows that with frame bursting, a substantial improvement in mean delay is achieved.

Effect on Collisions

Figure 4-10 shows the probability that a frame transmitted experiences at least one collision. The peakedness of the curve indicates the beginning of congestion in the system, but not enough to form queues at each DTE. In 1000 Mb/s, the peakedness of the collision-likelihood curve occurs sooner than in the 100 Mb/s network. This is because of longer slot time, which causes each DTE to retransmit less aggressively. However, the limiting value of the collision likelihood in 1000 Mb/s is lower than in 100 Mb/s, because the longer slot time causes longer backoff. Therefore, each DTE can transmit more frames when it captures the network.

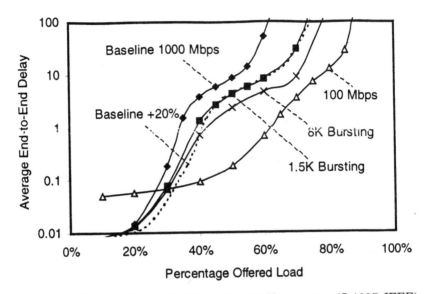

Figure 4-9 Average End-to-End Delay in a 15-Host system (© 1997, IEEE)

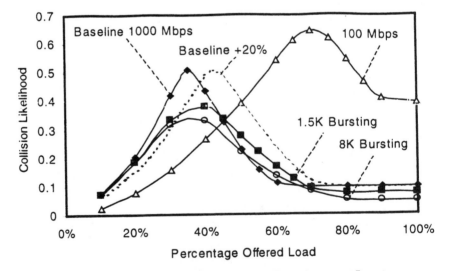

Figure 4-10 Probability that a Frame Experiences at Least
One Collision (© 1997, IEEE)

Capture Effect

Capture effect is a phenomenon in which a DTE that transmits successfully after a collision has a higher chance of transmitting new frames than a DTE which has lost the collision resolution.[12,13] In a busy network, this results in a DTE having a long period of transmission while other DTEs are unable to transmit. Capture effect, although it makes the network throughput more efficient does not bode well for latency-sensitive applications because of long variable access latencies. Further, packet loss could occur because of excessive collisions.

In Gigabit Ethernet, with the slot time increased by a factor of 8, the collision backoff delay increases at a faster rate with each attempt. This allows other DTEs to transfer for longer periods, while a DTE that loses collision resolution will have to wait a long time. With frame bursting, there was a concern that capture effect would be amplified.

One way to examine the effect of capture in 1000 Mb/s network is to examine access latency of packets and number of consecutive transmission by a single DTE. Access latency is defined as the waiting time experienced by a frame when it is at the head of the transmit FIFO in the MAC. If the network is experiencing capture effect, it is possible to have lower access latency for the packets that were transmitted when the DTE has captured the medium. It is also conceivable that a few packets will experience longer access latencies, because DTEs are unable to transmit them for a long time. So, in order to determine the effect of capture, we need to look at the distribution of the access latency. Figure 4-11 shows the mean and 95th percentile of access delay, and Figure 4-12 shows the number of consecutive transmissions by a single host as a function of offered load.

What is surprising is the result that frame bursting actually helps reduce the capture effect, as evident from Figures 4-11 and 4-12. The explanation fis quite simple. In frame bursting only the first packet of the burst can potentially experience collision. Subsequent packets in the burst do not experience collision. Frame bursting improves the efficiency of a single host by allowing it to transmit multiple frames, thereby emptying the transmit queues much faster. Further, other DTEs experience fewer collisions during frame bursting; therefore their backoff delays do not increase rapidly.

---

[12] M. Molle, "A new binary logarithmic arbitration method for Ethernet," Technical Report CSRI-398, University of Toronto, April 1994 (Revised July 1994).

[13] K. Ramakrishnan and H. Yang, "The Ethernet Capture Effect: Analysis and Solution," 19th IEEE Local Computer Networks Conference, Minneapolis, MN, Oct. 1994, pp. 228–240.

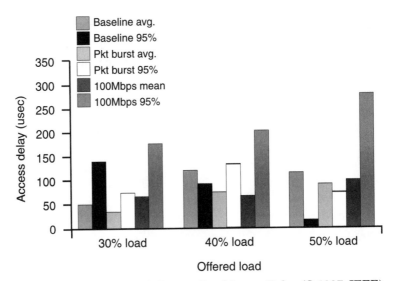

Figure 4-11 Mean and 95th Percentile of Access Delay (© 1997, IEEE)

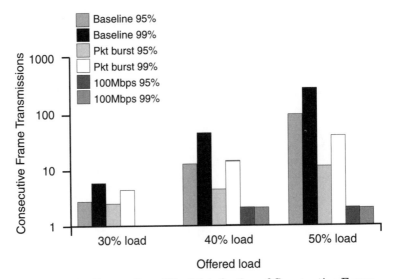

Figure 4-12 Percentiles of the Distribution of Consecutive Frame
Transmissions by a Single DTE (© 1997, IEEE)

Effect of Frame Bursting on Lightly Loaded Hosts

A natural concern with frame bursting is that some DTEs might experience longer delays, because a DTE that acquires the medium could send a burst of frames until the burst timer expires. This could be especially true in a network when there is uneven loading between the hosts. Figures 4-13 and 4-14 show the mean and 95th percentile

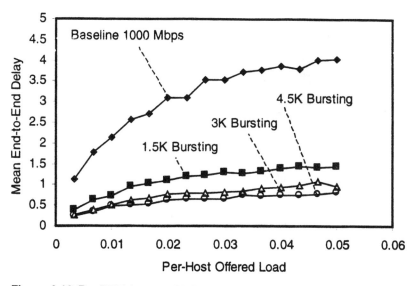

Figure 4-13 Per-DTE Average End-to-End Delay, 40% load, Nonuniformly Assigned to the DTEs (©1997, IEEE)

of end-to-end delay of a frame in a network with uneven loading. The loading was such that the maximum load on a DTE was 15 times the minimum load. The overall network offered load was maintained at 40%. The figures show that frame bursting actually improves the performance of the network over the baseline carrier extension. As the burst length is increased, the end-to-end delay actually reduces, which is quite surprising. This is because, by increasing the burst timer, the DTEs with heavy load become more efficient in transmitting frames, thereby improving the overall efficiency of the network. However, such a result may not occur if the traffic is bursty in nature.

A Note on Performance Simulations

The above set of performance simulations gives a general idea of performance of shared gigabit with workgroup average packet-length distribution. However, the actual performance of shared gigabit will really depend on the network configurations,

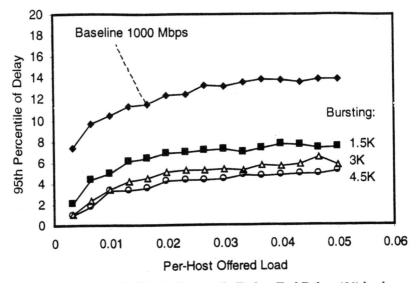

Figure 4-14 Per-DTE 95th Percentile End-to-End Delay, 40% load,
Nonuniformly Assigned to the Hosts (©1997, IEEE)

network protocol, and burstiness of the application traffic. The performance of the
network in general deteriorates as more DTEs are added. This is because each DTE
is contending for access to the medium. For a given offered load, it is expected that a
network with fewer DTEs will have higher network throughput efficiency than a network with a larger number of DTEs. The collision likelihood increases as more DTEs
are added to the collision domain.

Shared Gigabit Ethernet is likely to find market acceptance when gigabit speeds
are required at the desktop. Initial deployment of Gigabit Ethernet will be in backbone
networks using full-duplex connections only.

4.4.6 Ethernet Performance (A Hierarchical View)

Figure 4-15 gives an indication of relative comparison of performance and cost for 10
Mb/s, 100 Mb/s, and 1000 Mb/s shared and switched networks. In general, switched
networks give a higher performance than shared networks but at a higher cost. Further, some QoS (Quality of Service) parameters can be supported in switched networks, which, in general, are not possible in shared networks. It is expected that
Buffered Distributor (See Chapter 5) will perform better than shared gigabit. However, the cost per port for a Buffered Distributor will be more than for the shared gigabit.

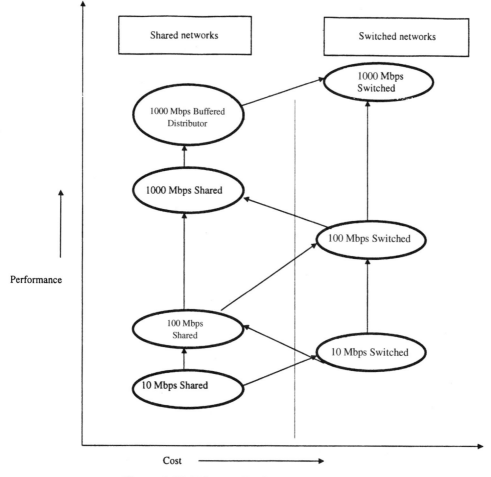

Figure 4-15 Ethernet Performance Hierarchy

4.5 Full-Duplex Operation

A link operating in full-duplex mode allows simultaneous transmission and reception of data. (See the "Full Duplex" section in Chapter 3.) A MAC operating in full-duplex mode requires the following changes from a CSMA/CD MAC.

- The transmission of a frame is not deferred during active reception.
- The inter-frame gap counting in back-to-back transmission is started when the transmission of the first packet ends. In half-duplex mode, the IPG counting is started when transmission and carrier activity ends.

- Collision indication in full-duplex mode is ignored

Full-duplex links are point-to-point connections only. So, in order to network two or more hosts, a switching hub is necessary. In order for full duplex to work, the host, link, and switch must all support full-duplex mode.

In a full-duplex switched network, if many ports send traffic to a single output port, then buffer overflow could occur. In such instances, packets could be dropped. Alternatively, if a switch employs flow control, congestion could be minimized. The IEEE 802.3x has specified a mechanism for flow control on point-to-point full-duplex links (see the next section, "Flow Control").

4.5.1 Flow Control

When the traffic exceeds the nominal capacity of the network, throughput degradation results. For instance, in a switch, if the traffic is bursty and is directed to single port, the buffers overflow and will result in loss of throughput and packet loss. Flow control is a mechanism by which the switch or a congested entity limits access to the network by placing thresholds on buffers, modifying transmission rates, or shutting the sending source for a prescribed amount of time. The parameters that trigger the flow control procedure can be static or dynamically adjusted, depending on the traffic flow.

Loss of packets has a deleterious effect on throughput performance, especially for applications using access methods such as TCP/IP. In TCP/IP, when a packet is dropped, the sending TCP/IP source will eventually realize that a packet is not delivered and will retransmit the frame. This results in substantial throughput loss, even for a small packet loss rate. Therefore, it is better to delay a packet by flow control rather than drop the packet.

Flow control can be implemented at different levels—link level, network level or higher levels. The IEEE 802.3x flow control specified is at link level and as such is useful to reduce congestion in switches, which operate at layer 2. Figure 4-16 illustrates the use of IEEE 802.3x flow control (also referred to as PAUSE control) in a full-duplex switch. Port D is shown to be congested. Therefore, the switch will initiate PAUSE frames of specified duration to be sent out on ports A, B, and C. Obviously, sending PAUSE frames to all the ports other than the congested port would be inefficient. Intelligent schemes, such as identifying the input port which causes congestion at the output port, can be used for more efficient flow control.

In shared segments, the CSMA/CD algorithm forces each DTE on the network to reduce the offered load by way of collisions. Each DTE involved in a collision is forced to retransmit after a random backoff. This has the effect of reducing the load that each DTE can send. However, in a switch, congestion can occur if the switch cannot forward packets at a rate faster than the arrival. In such instances, flow control can

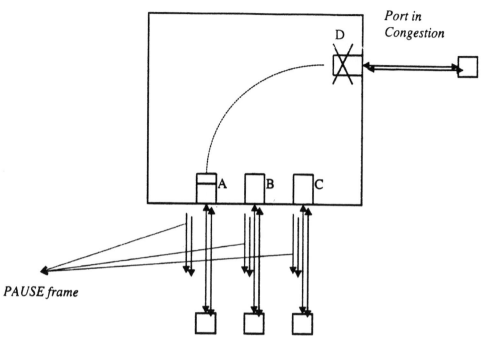

Figure 4-16 Illustration of PAUSE Flow Control in a Switch

be employed to reduce the load on the switch. The idea of flow control is to throttle the source traffic for a specified period of time so that the congestion eases. If the switch port is in half-duplex mode, two methods—backpressure and carrier sense extension—can be used to throttle the traffic into the switch port.

Flow Control Performance Measures

Flow control performance measures are required to compare alternative flow control policies. In addition, parameters of flow control policies can be tuned to optimize performance measures. Three commonly used performance measures are *throughput efficiency*, *packet delay,* and *packet loss rate*.

Throughput efficiency, which is usually measured in packets/sec, represents the ability of a device to handle the offered load. At low offered loads, the throughput efficiency is equal to the offered loads. However, at higher offered loads, the throughput efficiency is reduced because of contention of resources. *Packet delay* as a function of throughput is another good measure of flow-control performance. A particular flow control policy might be such that the delay characteristics are optimized at high loads, whereas at low offered loads the delay characteristics may not be optimal. *Packet loss* rate is a measure of number of packets dropped due to retransmission timeouts, excessive collisions, buffer overflow, etc. As packet loss rate increases, the throughput efficiency becomes lower and the packet delay increases.

Head-of-Line Blocking

The idea behind flow control is to inhibit the sending station or host from sending additional frames to a congested port for a predetermined amount of time. While a flow control scheme is expected to ease congestion, it also aggravates the Head-of-Line (HOL) blocking problem. HOL blocking is a phenomenon that occurs in an input-buffered switch wherein a packet is temporarily blocked by another packet either at the input buffer or at the output buffer.

Figure 4-17 shows a multiport switch, which has packets at, ports A, B, and C. Port A has two packets, d and e, destined for ports D and E, respectively. Port B has one packet, d, destined for port D, while port C has one packet, f, destined for port F. The packets at port A are temporarily blocked because the packet from B is currently at the output port D. Although port E is currently not busy, the packet e at port A is temporarily blocked by the packet at the head of the queue. This is called the Head-of-Line (HOL) blocking, which effectively reduces the line rate of transfer.

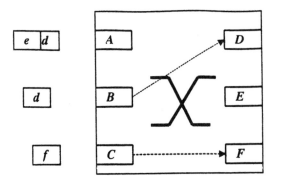

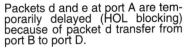

Packets d and e at port A are temporarily delayed (HOL blocking) because of packet d transfer from port B to port D.

Figure 4-17 Illustration of Head-of-Line Blocking

Flow control further aggravates the HOL blocking. Figure 4-18 shows that packet d from port A to D is blocked because port D is congested. Port D cannot accept any more packets until the congestion is reduced. Packet e will experience longer delays, although port E is not congested due to HOL blocking and flow control.

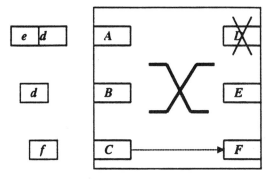

Port D is congested. Packet e at port A experiences HOL blocking.

Figure 4-18 Illustration of Head-of-Line Blocking under Congestion

Backpressure Flow Control

Congestion in a switch could be either at the input port or at the output port. Input-port congestion is easy to handle in most situations. When a frame starts arriving at the input port, a collision is forced on the arriving frame. This forces the remote DTE to abort, jam, and retransmit after the backoff interval. It is expected that during this interval the congestion will ease. However, if the congestion still persists, the backpressure mechanism is used again. Figure 4-19 illustrates backpressure flow control when an input port is congested.

If the congestion occurs on the output port, when a frame starts arriving at an input port, the destination address of the packet is decoded. If DA is that of congested port, then a collision is induced so that the source station or DTE can abort, jam, and backoff. The source will retransmit traffic after backoff. It is expected that the congestion may be relieved during this period. If not, backpressure is used, causing further backoff delay followed by retransmission. A less sophisticated method is to jam all source ports without decoding the destination address of the packet. This will degrade the performance of other nodes on the network. It is important to insure that the decision to apply backpressure should be done in less than one-half *slot time*. This is to make sure that late collisions are not caused because of backpressure. Figure 4-20 illustrates backpressure flow control when an output port is congested.

The advantage of this mechanism is that a collision can be forced after detecting that the DA of the arriving frame is for the congested port. However, the backpressure flow control has a few disadvantages. The backoff time can grow exponentially if there are repeated forced collisions. This might lead to dead time if the congestion eases and the DTE is waiting for the backoff timer to expire before sending frames.

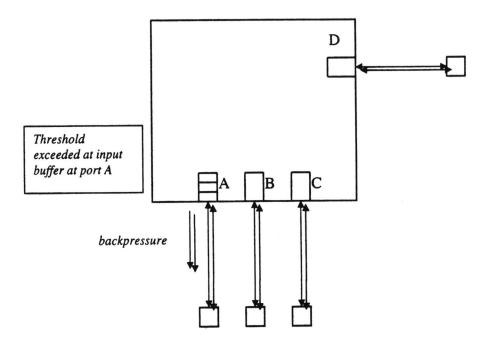

Figure 4-19 Illustration of Backpressure Flow Control (Input-Port Congestion)

If the number of forced-collision attempts exceeds 16, then the DTE will drop the frame. Dropping the frame has a deleterious effect on the performance.

Carrier Extension Flow Control

In this method,[14] the switch will assert carrier sense whenever the switch is congested. The DTE will defer as long as the carrier sense is asserted. The DTE will see the link as busy, since the MAC at the switch port has asserted the carrier sense. Since the DTE defers, no backoff is necessary. The advantage of asserting carrier sense is that the switch can deassert carrier sense as soon as the congestion eases. However, the DTE will have to support this feature. The switch will have to send valid bits to assert the carrier sense during congestion.

---

[14] R. Seifert, "The Use of Carrier Sense for Congestion Control in Half-Duplex Switched LANs," Technical Report, Networks and Communications Consulting.

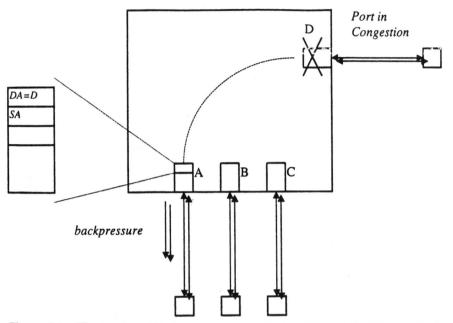

Figure 4-20 Illustration of Backpressure Flow Control (Output-Port Congestion)

4.5.2 Flow Control Symmetry

The IEEE 802.3x defines the configuration for the PAUSE frame format that supports PAUSE capability in both directions (see "Auto-Negotiation," in Chapter 3). By setting the PAUSE bit, both ends of the link are capable of transmitting and receiving PAUSE frames. Setting this bit to zero implies that the device or DTE cannot transmit PAUSE frames, nor will it understand a PAUSE frame on reception. The PAUSE functionality is enabled only when both ends of the link have the PAUSE bit set during Auto-Negotiation. Figure 4-21 shows a pictorial description of PAUSE frame transmission.[15]

While the PAUSE functionality provided *symmetric flow control,* a need was recognized for *asymmetric flow control* (AFC). The idea behind asymmetric flow control is to stop traffic at the source so that additional buffering is not needed in intermediate devices such as switches. Asymmetric flow control makes sense especially in configurations where an end station is connected to a switch port, as shown in

---

[15] H. Hsiaw and C. Nelson, "Flow Control for Gigabit Ethernet," IEEE 802.3z Plenary Meeting, Vancouver, Nov. 1996,
http://grouper.ieee.org/groups/802/3/z/public/presentations/nov1996/flow40.ppt.

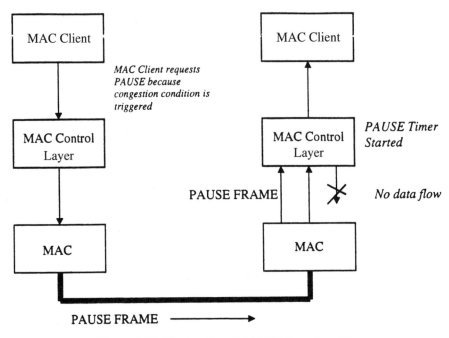

Figure 4-21 Illustration of PAUSE Functionality

Figure 4-22. In this configuration, the switch has the capability to flow-control the end station, while the end station cannot flow-control the switch. By allowing AFC in this case, the potential for network congestion is minimized. This implies that end stations will have to buffer the frames until the congestion conditions are alleviated. In general, end stations have large buffers, and by doing AFC there is no need to provide large buffers in the switch.[16]

Asymmetric flow control is very useful in Buffered Distributor (BD) (see Chapter 5 for a description of BD). A Buffered Distributor could be connected to many end stations, as shown in Figure 4-23. If symmetric flow control were allowed in such a configuration, the TX FIFOs in the BD's would overflow, which in turn would effectively lead to stopping transmissions on all DTEs. However, this poses a problem if a BD is to be connected to switch. It is desirable to have symmetric flow control when connecting the BD to a switch and AFC when the BD is connected to end stations.

---

[16] B. Bunch, "Asymmetric Flow Control (AFC) and Gigabit Ethernet," IEEE 802.3z Plenary Meeting, Vancouver, Nov. 1996,
http://grouper.ieee.org/groups/802/3/z/public/presentations/nov1996/asym.pdf.

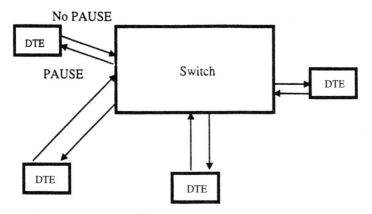

Figure 4-22 Asymetric Flow Control Illustration

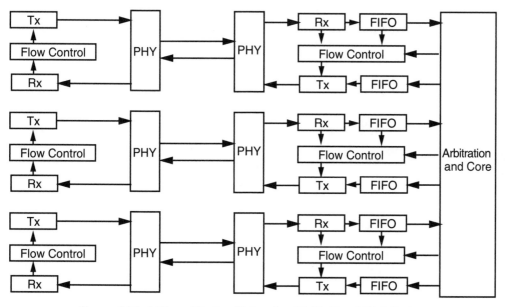

Figure 4-23 A Three-Station Network with Buffered Distributor

Implications of AFC between Switches

AFC, in general, is not desirable between switches.[17] Consider the configuration shown in Figure 4-24. Switch A cannot initiate PAUSE frames, whereas switch B can send PAUSE frames, which switch A can understand. In this arrangement,

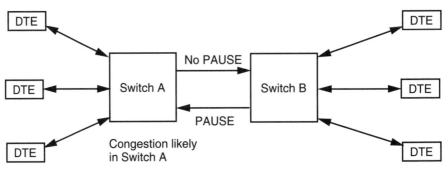

Figure 4-24 Illustration of Problems Associated with
AFC between Switches

switch A is likely to get more congested than switch B. Additionally, a switch designer will have to take into consideration the likelihood of congestion and design the
buffer sizes accordingly. By allowing AFC between switches, the user will have to be
aware of the individual switch capabilities and determine if topology will create any
bottlenecks.

4.5.3 Flow Control Policies

While the IEEE 802.3x has defined the mechanism for point-to-point flow control,
the question of when or under what conditions to initiate flow control and how long
to flow-control is totally dependent on the vendor or the user. Many different policies
could be used, depending on the complexity of the implementation.

Issues in Flow Control Policy

When determining the type of flow control policy to be implemented in switches, the
following factors should be kept in mind.

- The amount of pause time specified in the PAUSE frame should be such that the congestion is expected to ease during that time. If the PAUSE frame time is too large, then star-
  vation could occur. If the PAUSE frame time is too low, then additional PAUSE frames
  need to be sent. Sending too many PAUSE frames will adversely affect throughput.

- Another problem in initiating flow control is the selection of threshold. The threshold
  values should be selected such that congestion is very likely when these thresholds are

---

[17] B. Bunch, "Asymmetric Flow Control (AFC) and Gigabit Ethernet," IEEE 802.3z Plenary
Meeting, Vancouver, Nov. 1996,
http://grouper.ieee.org/groups/802/3/z/public/presentations/nov1996/asym.pdf.

reached. Also, the thresholds should be set such that additional frames can be received without dropping, since the initiation and transmission of a PAUSE frame take some time.

- When networks employ fiber links, it is conceivable that several frames might be on the link before a PAUSE frame is received at the end station. Therefore, adequate buffering capacity should be provided, keeping in mind the PAUSE frame latency and the likelihood that the end station might have sent several frames before it receives the PAUSE control frame.

PAUSE Frame Maximum Latency

When a congested entity issues a PAUSE frame to the sending source, it takes a certain amount of time before the sending source stops sending new frames. The components of this latency are as follows (Figure 4-25):

1. Initiation delay when the congestion occurs (for example, in the switch).
2. Link delay for sending and receiving PAUSE frame.
3. Transmission delay for PAUSE frame between the switch and the end station.
4. End-station processing delay of received PAUSE frame.
5. End-station transmission delay of packet in-progress when PAUSE frame was received.

Clearly, the maximum latency occurs when the end station has just begun to transmit a maximum-length frame at the time a PAUSE frame is received.

Implications of IEEE 802.3x Flow Control in Gigabit Switches

When a switch detects congestion in a buffer—for example, exceeding a predefined buffer threshold—the switch will initiate a PAUSE frame. The detection of congestion, formulation of PAUSE frame and insertion of the PAUSE frame into the transmit FIFO of the port takes a certain time. Figure 4-26 illustrates the components of time before a PAUSE frame can be sent out.

The buffer size should be such that there is additional space in the buffer to receive new frames until the PAUSE frame is received by the remote-end DTE. At gigabit speed this buffer size requirement may increase significantly (compared to 100 Mb/s)[18]. System design considerations call for faster processing within the switch connected to a gigabit link, since frames are transmitted and received at 1000 Mb/s.

Advantages of PAUSE frame control

1. It is simple and relatively easy to implement.

---

[18] H. Hsiaw and C. Nelson, "Flow Control for Gigabit Ethernet," IEEE 802.3z Plenary Meeting, Vancouver, Nov. 1996,
http://grouper.ieee.org/groups/802/3/z/public/presentations/nov1996/flow40.ppt.

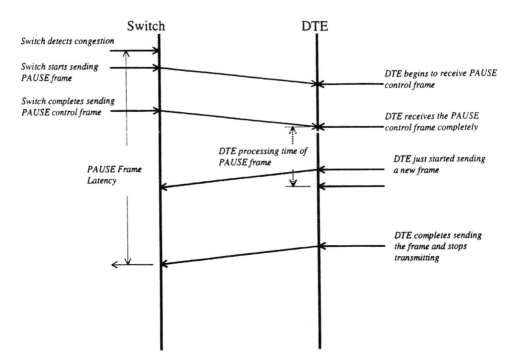

Figure 4-25 PAUSE Frame Flow Control: Sequence of Events

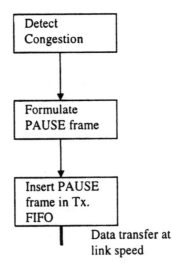

Figure 4-26 Delay Components before PAUSE Frame Transmission

2. Relieves congestion at the link level.

Disadvantages of PAUSE frame control

1. PAUSE frame control does not distinguish between application streams. All data traffic transmission is stopped upon reception of PAUSE frame.

2. PAUSE frame control does not distinguish priorities. Therefore, latency-sensitive applications will be adversely affected by PAUSE control.

3. The implications of large PAUSE frame duration on upper-layer protocol performance (e.g. TCP/IP) are not clear.

Watermarks

The most common policy to initiate flow control is the use of watermarks. Generally, buffers inside the switch will have a high watermark and a low watermark. Associated with these watermarks are certain PAUSE times, during which the congestion is expected to ease. Upon exceeding the low-watermark threshold, the switch will generate a flow control frame with a user-programmed PAUSE time. The PAUSE frame is sent to the DTE, which will then stop sending new frames for a time period specified by the PAUSE frame. After the PAUSE time has elapsed the DTE will resume sending frames again. If the congestion is not relieved, the frames in the buffer will reach the high watermark. At this point, the switch will send a PAUSE frame with a pause time higher than that associated with the low watermark. Generally, there will be another watermark, at which point the transmitting station is shut down until the congestion is relieved. One way to do this is to send a PAUSE frame with a very large pause time, resending a PAUSE frame with time zero when the congestion eases.

Credit-Based Flow Control

Credit-based schemes operate on the principle that a DTE can send a frame if it has an adequate number of credits. Credit-based schemes are implemented in ATM networks. In frame-switching networks, credit-based schemes can still be employed. Such a scheme is really dependent on the vendor. The principle of a credit-based scheme is as follows. Consider a switched network as shown in Figure 4-27. A DTE can send a frame to the switch if it has positive credit. The switch will advertise to the DTE about the number of credits available for the DTE to send frames. In Ethernet, the maximum credit needed to send one frame is 1518 bytes. When a switch goes into congestion, the switch will signal to the DTE with an appropriate number of credits. The advertising of the credits to the DTE can be accomplished through the flow control frames. This would require a new opcode to be defined to differentiate between PAUSE frame and CREDIT frame.

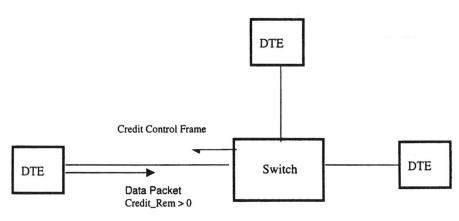

Figure 4-27 Credit Control Illustration

Rate-Based Flow Control

Rate-based flow control schemes have been successfully adopted in ATM networks. For a rate based scheme to work in frame switching network, the following things should be considered. The switch will need to signal to the end stations to send frames at desired rate. Generally, this can be accomplished using control frames. The end station can send frames either faster or slower by adjusting the Inter-Frame Gap (IPG) between the frames.[19] Typically, this can be accomplished by making the IPG programmable, which can be effected by flow control frames. When there is no congestion, the switch will indicate to the end station to send frames at the maximum rate or minimum IPG (Figure 4-28a). When the switch detects congestion, a flow-control frame with a new IPG is sent. The end station will now start sending frames separated by the revised IPG (Figure 4-28b). The IPGs for different rates have to be predefined. Depending on the complexity, several levels of congestion can be defined.

The above rate-based scheme is a nonstandard approach and is very dependent on implementation. Therefore, any rate-based scheme for flow control is proprietary and can only work if the solution is provided completely by a vendor.

Rate-based schemes have several advantages. Smoothing of the arrival of frames to the network eliminates burstiness of the data. Unlike PAUSE frame control (XON, XOFF), the control scheme does not exhibit all-or-none behavior with regard to sending frames. However, there is no guarantee that frames will not be lost due to buffer overflow in rate-based schemes.

---

[19] M. De-Leon, "Flow Control for Gigabit Ethernet," IEEE 802.3 High-Speed Study Group Plenary Meeting, Enschede NL, July 1996,
http://grg/groups/802/3/z/public/presentations/july1996/MDfcgig.pdf.

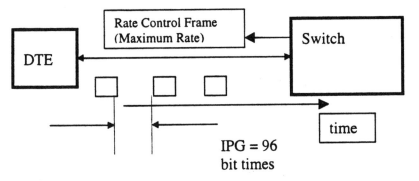

Figure 4-28a Rate Control Illustration with Maximum Rate

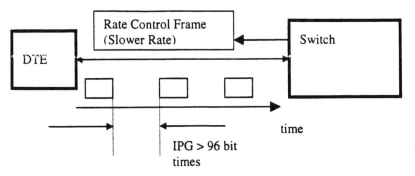

Figure 4-28b Rate Control Illustration with Slower Rate

4.5.4 Full-Duplex Performance

When a link is in full-duplex operation, simultaneous transmission and reception of data is possible. Theoretically, the throughput is doubled. However, applications may not take full advantage of full-duplex capability. In a switched network, the performance of the network depends on a number of factors—switching capacity to support all the ports, buffer capacity, and the flow control policy. Generally, most switches are nonblocking; that is, the switch capacity can handle full traffic on all ports, provided the traffic at the output port is not contentious. The buffer sizes play a major role in latencies. Larger buffer sizes tend to increase latency while reducing packet loss and vice versa. In a nonblocking switch, performance can be degraded if most of the traffic is directed to one or few ports, which could cause output port congestion. As a result, packets have to be dropped, or, if flow control is employed, the throughput is reduced.

Switch Performance

Switching Capacity

Switching capacity is the necessary bandwidth required by the switch fabric to support full-load traffic on all of its ports. Figure 4-29 shows a workgroup switch (100/1000 switch) that has eight downlinks (100 Mb/s ports) and one uplink (gigabit ports). The uplink is generally connected to a server or to a backbone switch. The downlinks could be DTEs or 100 Mb/s shared segments or an uplink from another 10/100 workgroup switch. The links could be either full-duplex or half-duplex or a mix of both. Assuming all links as full-duplex, the necessary bandwidth to support all ports is calculated as follows:

$$8 * 2 * 100 + 1 * 2 * 1000 = 3.6 \text{ Gb/s}$$

The capacity of the example switch should be at least 3.6 Gb/s for the switch to be non-blocking. In reality, the bandwidth required is slightly higher because of overheads involved.

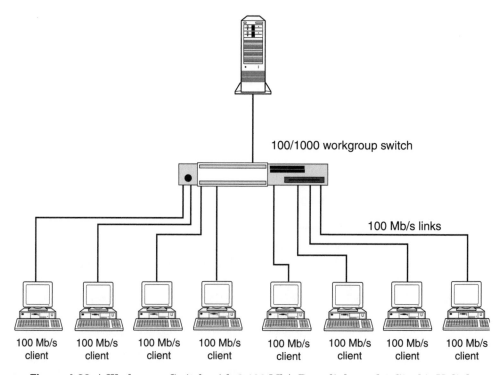

Figure 4-29 A Workgroup Switch with 8 100 Mb/s Downlinks and 1 Gigabit Uplink

Switching Latency

The advent of gigabit workgroup switches also poses the issue of making a filtering and forwarding decision in a short period of time. This is especially true if Layer 3 switching or cut-through switching is to be supported. The worst-case maximum time limit within which a filtering and forwarding decision is to be made can be calculated as follows:

forwarding decision time = Interarrival time for minimum frame at full load /
   Σ port speed

The interarrival time between frames is the time interval between start of two frames in a back-to-back transmit mode. The shortest time occurs for minimum frame size (64 bytes). Therefore, at 100 Mb/s speed, the interarrival time between back-to-back 64 byte frames is (64 + 12 +8) * 0.08 μs or 6.72 μs. In the example switch (Figure 4-29), the equivalent number of 100 Mb/s ports is 28.[20] Therefore,

forwarding decision time = 6.72 / 28 = .24 μs or 240 nanoseconds

To switch the frame at wire-speed, the forwarding decision has to be made in less than 240 nanoseconds. This would imply efficient storing and retrieval of the addresses in the forwarding table.

4.6 Reconciliation Sublayer (RS) and Gigabit Medium-Independent Interface (GMII) (Clause 35)

The function of the Reconciliation Sublayer (RS) is similar to that of RS in Fast Ethernet (see Chapter 3: RS and MII). The RS maps the octet-wide data paths and associated control signals of the GMII to the original PLS service interface definitions (the MAC/PLS interface).

The GMII interface provides the logical interface between the gigabit MAC and the physical layer. GMII and Reconciliation Sublayer allows a GMAC to be connected to different physical media. Currently, GMII interface is not really a necessity because of the physical medium used—fiber and short copper use the same coding/decoding scheme. However, before Gigabit Ethernet can migrate to the desktop, low-cost solutions such as UTP physical media should be available. The IEEE 802.3ab task force has defined a solution using UTP Cat 5 cable.

Figure 4-2 shows the relationship of Reconciliation Sublayer and GMII to the ISO (IEEE) OSI reference model. The GMII interface is similar to the MII interface with some additions/modifications. The data path in GMII is specified to be octet-

---

[20] Equivalent number of 100 Mb/s ports = 8 + 2 * 10 = 28. Each Gigabit uplink is equivalent to ten 100 Mb/s ports.

wide instead of nibble-wide. During each cycle data is moved across the GMII at the rate of one octet/sec, hence the transmit and receive clock operate at 125 MHz to provide a total data rate of 1000 Mb/s. Since the GMII interface can also operate at 10 Mb/s and 100 Mb/s data rates, the clocks operate at 2.5 or 25 MHz, respectively. While it is not necessary to support all the three data rates, the PHY must advertise the rates they support through the station management entity. The operation of the GMII at 10 Mb/s and 100 Mb/s is identical to MII.

The GMII interface is not an exposed interface. The GMII can be used to connect chip-to-chip (IC to IC) level, which is typically implemented as printed circuit board traces or a motherboard-to-daughterboard connection between two or more printed circuit boards.

4.6.1 GMII Signals

The GMII signals are similar to the MII signals with one exception. In GMII a separate clock, GTX_CLK, is used for operation at 1000 Mb/s. The Reconciliation Sublayer interface allows a variety of higher speed PHYs (1000BASE-SX, 1000BASE-LX, 1000BASE-CX, 1000BASE-T, etc.) to be attached to the gigabit MAC engine without future upgrade problems. The GMII interface consists of two independent data paths, receive (RXD<7:0>) and transmit (TXD<7:0>), control signals for each data path (RX_ER, RX_DV, TX_ER, TX_EN), network status signals (COL, CRS), clocks (RX_CLK, TX_CLK, GTX_CLK) for each data path, and a two-wire management interface (MDC, MDIO). Figure 4-30 shows the direction of signals at the interface.

GMII Transmit Interface Signals

Transmit Clock (GTX-CLK)

The transmit clock at 1000 Mb/s operations is a continuous clock sourced by the Reconciliation Sublayer. The GTX-CLK is used as a timing reference to drive TXD, TX_EN, and TX_ER signals synchronously with clock, in order to transmit data and/or issue status. GTX_CLK runs at 125 MHz.

Transmit Clock (TX_CLK)

The TX_CLK is used when the GMII operates at 10 Mb/s or 100 Mb/s data rate (see Chapter 3: RS & MII). TX_CLK is not used in 1000 Mb/s operation.

Transmit Data (TXD< 7:0>)

Data issued by the DTE is transmitted as a group of eight data signals (TXD<7:0>) by the RS to the PHY after proper coding and conditioning for transmission. The data octets presented by the RS when TX-EN and TX_ER are inactive are ignored.

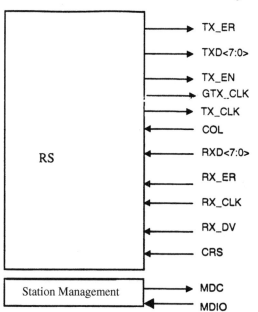

GMII Signals

Figure 4-30 Gigabit Media-Independent Interface Signals

Transmit Enable (TX_EN)

This signal is asserted by the DTE to indicate that valid data (octets) is being present-ed by the RS and should be transmitted by the PHY onto the network medium. Figure 4-31a shows a frame transmission with no collisions and without carrier extension or errors.

Transmit Error (TX_ER)

TX_ER is a signal asserted by the DTE (or optionally a repeater) to indicate to the PHY that a coding violation was received on the input signal stream. When the TX_ER signal is activated for one or more GTX_CLK periods at any time TX_EN is active, the PHY is responsible for sending one or more code-groups that are not nor-mal data or delimiter information. Table 4-2 shows valid encodings of TX-ER, TX-EN and TXD.

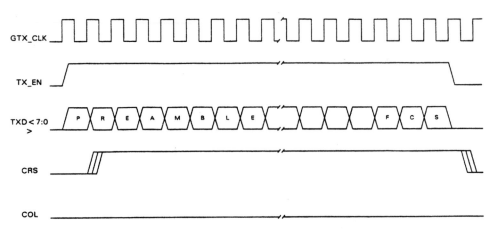

Figure 4-31a Basic Frame Transmission
(From IEEE Std. P802.3z, IEEE. All rights reserved.)

Table 4-2 Permissible Encodings of TXD<7:0>, TX_EN, and TX_ER[a]

TX_EN	TX_ER	TXD<7:0>	Description
0	0	00 through FF	Normal Inter-Frame
0	1	00 through 0E	Reserved
0	1	0F	Carrier extend
0	1	10 through 1E	Reserved
0	1	1F	Carrier extend error
0	1	20 through FF	Reserved
1	0	00 through FF	Normal data transmission
1	1	00 through FF	Transmit error propagation

[a] Source: IEEE 802.3z—Media Access Control (MAC) Parameters, Physical Layer, Repeater and Management Parameters for 1000 Mb/s Operation, Clause 35.

GMII Receive Interface Signals

Receive Clock (RX_CLK)

The description of RX_CLK signal is similar to that given in the MII section. RX_CLK runs at 125 MHz for 1000 Mb/s operation.

Receive Data (RXD<7:0>)

Data received by the PHY is passed as a group of eight data signals (RXD<7:0>) to the RS after proper decoding. Figure 4-31b shows RXD<7:0> behavior during frame reception.

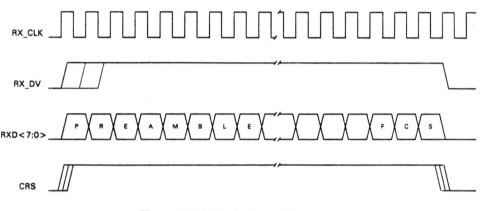

Figure 4-31b Basic Frame Reception
(From IEEE Std. P802.3z, IEEE. All rights reserved.)

Receive Data Valid (RX_DV)

This signal is asserted by the PHY to indicate to the DTE that valid data decoded from the medium is being presented on the RXD signal. Figure 4-31b shows the behavior of RX_DV during frame reception.

Receive Error (RX_ER)

The operation of this signal is similar to that of MII (see Chapter 3: RS & MII). Figure 4-31c shows the behavior of RX_ER during frame reception with errors. Two errors are illustrated: when RX_DV is active, RX_ER becoming active indicates an error within the data octets of the frame. Error indication in the carrier extension of the frame is indicated by proper encoding of RXD<7:0> while RX_ER is active.

Table 4-3 shows valid codings of RX_ER, RX_EN, and RXD.

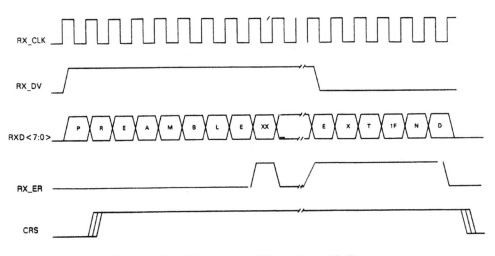

Figure 4-31c Illustration of Reception with Errors
(From IEEE Std. P802.3z, IEEE. All rights reserved.)

Table 4-3 Permissible encodings of RXD<7:0>, RX_DV, and RX_ER[a]

RX_DV	RX_ER	RXD<7:0>	Description
0	0	00 through FF	Normal Inter-Frame
0	1	00	Normal Inter-Frame
0	1	01 through 1D	Reserved
0	1	0E	False carrier indication
0	1	0F	Carrier extend
0	1	10 through 1E	Reserved
0	1	1F	Carrier extend error
0	1	20 through FF	Reserved
1	0	00 through FF	Normal data reception
1	1	00 through FF	Data reception error

[a] Source: IEEE 802.3z—Media Access Control (MAC) Parameters, Physical Layer, Repeater and Management Parameters for 1000 Mb/s Operation, Clause 35.

GMII Network Status Interface Signals

The signals **CRS** (carrier sense) and **COL** (collision sense) operate identically to MII counterparts (See Chapter 3: RS and MII). Carrier sense is used to detect a beginning of transmission on the network. Collision sense is used to indicate that simultaneous transmission has occurred in a half-duplex network. Figures 4-31d and 4-31e show the behavior of CRS for a normal transmission without collision and with detected collision, respectively.

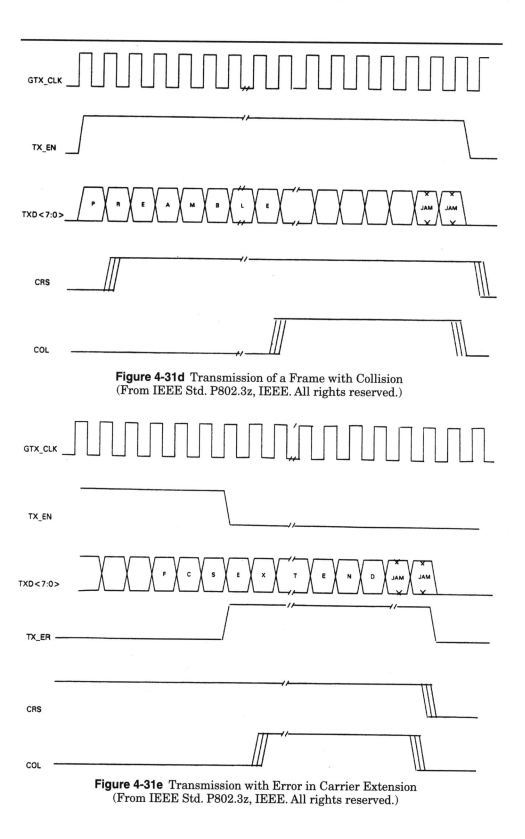

Figure 4-31d Transmission of a Frame with Collision
(From IEEE Std. P802.3z, IEEE. All rights reserved.)

Figure 4-31e Transmission with Error in Carrier Extension
(From IEEE Std. P802.3z, IEEE. All rights reserved.)

GMII Management Interface

Operations of two signals, **MDC** and **MDIO,** used for management are described in MII (see Chapter 3: RS & MII).

4.6.2 Carrier-Extension and Frame-Bursting Signaling

Carrier extensions, carrier-extension errors, and interframe spacing between and within bursts occur even though no packet data is transmitted by the RS. The PHY has to send valid code-groups during these events for accurate delivery of information. The combination of signals and proper encoding of TXD or RXD signals accomplish this signaling.

During frame transmission, indication to the PHY to transmit extension symbols (Carrier Extend) by RS is accomplished by TX_EN being inactive and TX_ER becoming active with proper encoding of TXD<7:0>. Another specific coding of TXD <7:0> signals an error during carrier extension. Table 4-2 shows the values for encoding of TXD. Figures 4-31f and 4-31g show the behavior of signals during transmission of a frame with carrier extension and error within carrier extension respectively.

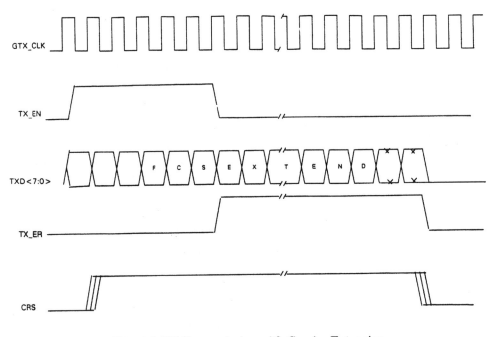

Figure 4-31f Transmission with Carrier Extension
(From IEEE Std. P802.3z, IEEE. All rights reserved.)

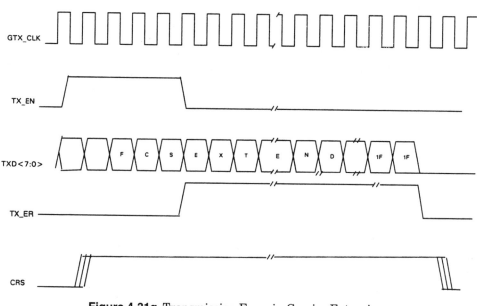

Figure 4-31g Transmission Error in Carrier Extension
(From IEEE Std. P802.3z, IEEE. All rights reserved.)

During frame reception, Carrier Extend is provided by RS while RX_DV is inactive and RX_ER becomes active with a specific coding of RXD <7:0>. Errors within carrier extension during frame reception are signaled by another specific coding to RXD. Table 4-3 shows the values of encoding for RXD. Figure 4-31h shows the behavior of signals during frame reception with carrier extension.

The interframe period between frames within a burst is signaled as carrier extend on the GMII. On the transmit side, this is done by asserting TX_ER with appropriate encoding of TXD<7: 0> along with the deassertion of TX_EN. On the receive side, the interframe within a burst is recognized by the assertion of RX_ER with the appropriate encoding of RXD<7:0> along with the deassertion of RX_DV (see Tables 4-2 and 4-3). The normal interframe between bursts is signaled as in the MII. Figures 4-31i and 4-31j show the behavior of signals during burst transmission and reception.

4.6.3 GMII Management Protocol

GMII will use the MII management register set specified under MII—i.e., a basic register set and an extended register set (see "RS & MII" in Chapter 3). In addition, a third basic register set is defined for GMII. The frame format and protocol specification for exchanging management frames are similar to those of MII and will not be repeated here.

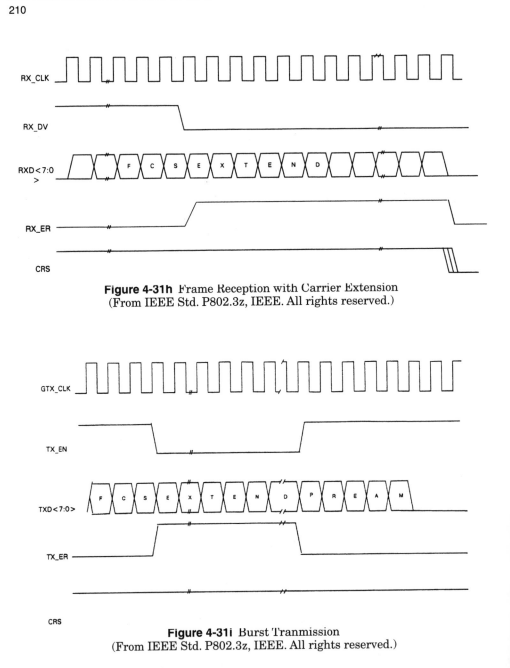

Figure 4-31h Frame Reception with Carrier Extension
(From IEEE Std. P802.3z, IEEE. All rights reserved.)

Figure 4-31i Burst Tranmission
(From IEEE Std. P802.3z, IEEE. All rights reserved.)

GMII Management Registers

PHYs that provide a GMII shall incorporate the following mandatory register set: (1) Control register (register 0), (2) Status register (register 1), and (3) Extended status register (register 15). Table 4-4 gives a brief description of the GMII management registers. Registers 0, 1, and 15 are defined here, while registers 4 through 7 pertain to Auto-Negotiation. Registers 8, 9, and 10 are specific to 100BASE-T2 and are not discussed here.

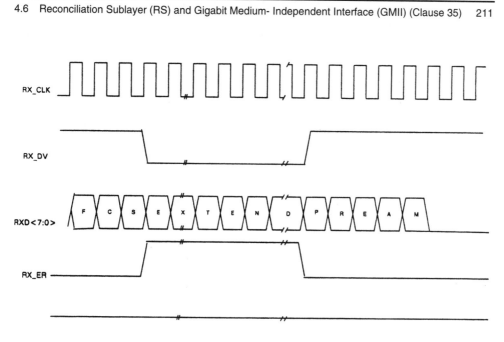

Figure 4-31j Burst Reception
(From IEEE Std. P802.3z, IEEE. All rights reserved.)

Table 4-4 GMII Management Register Map[a]

Register Address	Register Name	Requirement	Type	Defined in Clause
0	Control	Mandatory	Basic	22
1	Status	Mandatory	Basic	22
2	PHY Identifier	Mandatory (may return all zeroes)	Extended	22
3	PHY Identifier	Mandatory (may return all zeroes)	Extended	22
4	Auto-Negotiation Advertisement	Mandatory with Auto-Negotiation	Extended	37
5	Auto-Negotiation Link Partner Ability	Mandatory with Auto-Negotiation	Extended	37
6	Auto-Negotiation Expansion	Mandatory with Auto-Negotiation	Extended	37
7	Auto-Negotiation Next Page Transmit	Auto-Negotiation with next page only	Extended	37
11–14	Reserved	Unspecified	Reserved	N/A
15	Extended Status	Mandatory	Basic	22
16–31	Vendor Specific	Vendor-specific extensions	Vendor	N/A

[a]Source: IEEE 802.3z—Media Access Control (MAC) Parameters, Physical Layer, Repeater and Management Parameters for 1000 Mb/s Operation, Clause 35

Control (Register 0)

The Control register definition is similar to that of MII with minor modifications. Bit 0.13 and a new bit 0.6 were defined as LSB and MSB, respectively, to select speeds of 10 Mb/s, 100 Mb/s, or 1000 Mb/s when Auto-Negotiation is disabled (bit 0.12 is cleared to zero). Bits 5:0 are undefined. Table 4-5 shows the Control-register bit definitions for GMII. Table 4-6 shows the combinations of bits for 0.6 and 0.13 indicating different speeds.

Table 4-5 Control-Register Bit Definitions for GMII[a]

Bit(s)	Name	Description
0.15	Reset	Reset the PHY
0.14	Loopback	Data presented on the GMII transmit data path is looped back to the receive data path
0.13	Speed Selection	Manual speed select when Auto-Negotiation is disabled (least significant bit)
0.12	Auto-Negotiation Enable	Enable Auto-Negotiation for PHY technology, speed, and half/full-duplex selection
0.11	Power Down	Place the PHY in a low power mode (data path disabled, management path enabled)
0.10	Isolate	Isolate PHY from GMII , except GMII management (used for implementations with more than one PHY)
0.9	Reset Auto-Negotiation	Forces Auto-Negotiation to be restarted
0.8	Duplex Mode	Manual half/full-duplex selection when Auto-Negotiation is disabled
0.7	Collision Test	Configures PHY to activate COL signal when TX_EN enabled
0.6	Speed Selection	Manual speed select when Auto-Negotiation is disabled (most significant bit)
0.5:0	Reserved	Undefined (write as 0, ignore on read)

[a]Source: IEEE 802.3z—Media Access Control (MAC) Parameters, Physical Layer, Repeater and Management Parameters for 1000 Mb/s Operation, Clause 35

Table 4-6 Bit Combinations for Manual Speed Selection

Bit 0.6	Bit 0.13	Speed Indication
1	1	Reserved
1	0	1000 Mb/s
0	1	100 Mb/s
0	0	10 Mb/s

Status (Register 1)

The Status-register definitions for GMII are similar to those of MII with a minor exception. Bit 1.8 is defined as the Extended Status register, while bit 1.7 is reserved. Setting this bit indicates that the base register status information is extended into register 15. Extended Status register is mandatory for 1000 Mb/s operation.

Extended Status (Register 15)

The Extended Status register is a read-only register, which returns the configuration and condition of the PHY. Bit definitions are defined in Table 4-7.

Table 4-7 Extended Status-Control Register Bit Definitions[a]

Bit(s)	Name	Description
15.15	1000BASE-X Full-Duplex	Indicates PHY incorporates 1000BASE-X full-duplex capability
15.14	1000BASE-X Half-Duplex	Indicates PHY incorporates 1000BASE-X half-duplex capability
15.13	1000BASE-T Full-Duplex	Indicates PHY incorporates 1000BASE-T full-duplex capability
15.12	1000BASE-T Half-Duplex	Indicates PHY incorporates 1000BASE-T half-duplex capability
15.11.0	Reserved	Undefined (write as 0, ignore on read)

[a]Source: IEEE 802.3z—Media Access Control (MAC) Parameters, Physical Layer, Repeater and Management Parameters for 1000 Mb/s Operation, Clause 35

4.6.4 Comparison of GMII with MII

Table 4-8 gives a summary comparison of the GMII and the MII interfaces.

Table 4-8 Comparison Summary between GMII and MII

Description	MII	GMII
Data Width	4 bits	8 bits
Transmit Clock Rate	25 MHz for 100 Mb/s	125 MHz
Interface	Exposed, IC-IC interface	IC-IC interface
Mandatory Registers	Control, Status	Control, Status, and Extended
Encoding	4B/5B coding	8B/10B coding

4.7 Physical-Layer Technology

The physical layer provides the means to transform data bytes provided by the data link layer into appropriate signals for transmission on the media. Likewise, it converts signals received from the media into appropriate data bytes before passing them to the data link layer.

The physical-layer technology for Gigabit Ethernet is drawn heavily from the ANSI NCITS T11 Fibre Channel. Fibre Channel is a technology for interconnecting workstations, supercomputers, storage devices, and peripherals at gigabit speeds. Figure 4-32 illustrates the components that are used in Gigabit Ethernet. The lowest two levels of Fibre Channel, FC-0 (interface and media) and FC-1 (encode/decode) are

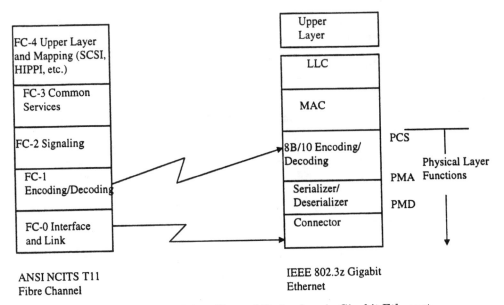

Figure 4-32 Use of Fibre Channel Technology in Gigabit Ethernet

used in Gigabit Ethernet. Since Fibre Channel technology has been in use for several years, the IEEE 802.3z standards committee decided to adopt this technology to greatly reduce development time and risk for a Gigabit Ethernet standard.

The physical layer in Gigabit Ethernet consists of three sublayers:

- Physical Coding Sublayer (PCS)
- Physical Medium Attachment Sublayer (PMA)
- Physical Medium Dependent Sublayer (PMD)

The Physical Coding Sublayer (PCS) provides the functions of data coding and decoding, which are usually independent of the physical medium used. However, in Gigabit Ethernet, the encoding scheme used for fiber media and short shielded cables (the Fibre Channel 8B/10B code) is different from that of UTP copper media.

The Physical Medium Attachment sublayer performs symbol serialization and deserialization (SERDES). The encoded stream of 10-bit symbols is serialized before transmission, and the received stream is deserialized and passed as 10-bit symbols to the PCS layer.

The Physical Medium Dependent (PMD) layer performs the function of converting signals from the PMA layer into signals appropriate for the specific media. If the medium is fiber, the electrical signals are converted to optical signals and vice versa. The Media Dependent Interface (MDI) defines the connector between the PMD layer and the media.

4.8 Physical Coding Sublayer (PCS) (Clause 36)

The PCS is located between the Reconciliation Sublayer (via the GMII) and the Physical Medium Attachment (PMA) sublayer, as shown in Fig. 4-2. The PCS is defined in Clause 36 of the 802.3z standard.

The PCS essentially performs a similar function as did the same layer for 100BASE-X, mapping the well-defined functionality of the Ethernet MAC to that of an already developed encoding and physical-layer signaling system. 100BASE-X is based on the FDDI physical layer. Gigabit Ethernet used a slightly modified version of the Fibre Channel Specification.[21] Note that "Fibre" is spelt correctly. When originated, the goal was to make Fibre Channel an international standard. The International Standards Organization is based in Europe, hence the European spelling.

The 1000BASE-X PCS leverages the FC0 and FC1 (Fibre Channel levels 0 and 1) sections of the specifications. FC-0 defines the physical link, including fiber specification, connectors, and optical and electrical interfaces. FC-1 defines the transmission encoding/decoding, error control and special control characters.

Fibre Channel specifies several data rates. The most optimal at the time of the 802.3z effort was specified for operation at 1.0625 Mb/s, using an 8B/10B block code. This coding scheme yielded a potential data rate for the Ethernet application of 850 Mb/s (1.0625 Mb/s $\times$ 8/10). At an early stage of investigation the 802.3z participants felt this was unacceptable, even though existing physical-layer chips and optics were available for this data rate. Suppliers of silicon and optical components quickly investigated the issues and reported that a speed increase to 1.25 Gbaud to achieve the desired data rate of 1 Gb/s (or 1000 Mb/s) was a manageable technical challenge.

The 1000BASE-X PCS supports three different media types:

- 1000BASE-CX—specifies operation over two pairs of 150-ohm balanced copper cable.

- 1000BASE-SX—specifies operation over a pair of optical fibers using short-wavelength optics.

- 1000BASE-LX—specifies operation over a pair of optical fibers using long-wavelength optics.

Each of the above media types requires an appropriate corresponding PMD, discussed in more detail in the "Physical Medium Dependent" section of this chapter. Note that an additional PHY, specifying an alternate PCS, PMA, and PMD, was still in development after the 802.3z standard was completed. This PHY and associated signaling scheme is designated as 1000BASE-T and supports Gb/s transmission over four pairs of Cat 5 UTP.

---

[21] ANSI X3.230-1994 Fibre Channel Physical and Signaling Interface, Clauses 6 and 7.

The interface to the RS/MAC above is provided by the GMII, and to the PMA below using the PMA service interface. No connectors are specified for the GMII. While signals for both these interfaces are mandatory, neither interface need be physically exposed to achieve a compliant implementation. The GMII is described in the "Gigabit Medium Independent Interface" section in this chapter. An optional physical implementation of the PMA service interface called the Ten-Bit Interface (TBI) was defined to assure that an interoperable interface was provided, and because pre-existing chips were already available with this interface for Fibre Channel.

4.8.1 PCS Functional Description

A functional block diagram of the PCS is shown in Fig. 4-33. The PCS masks the RS/MAC sublayers from the specialized signaling required to support Gb/s transmission and reception over the various media types. The functions are described in more detail in the following block descriptions.

Transmit

Packet data for transmission is presented by the RS over the GMII, using the byte-wide TXD<7:0> path, and is framed by the TX_EN and TX_ER signals. These signals are defined in detail in the GMII section. The PCS Transmit process continuously generates 10-bit code-groups and passes these to the PMA layer below for transmission. The exact specifics of the 8B/10B coding scheme are described later in this section. However, the basics are described here in order to define the attributes of the Transmit function. The code-groups passed to the PMA will provide one of the following indications:

1. *Idle.* When no packet data is presented on the GMII (TX_EN and TX_ER are inactive), such as between frames, an IDLE (/I/) code-group indication is issued.

2. *Start_of_Packet delimiter (SPD) or End_of_Packet delimiter (EPD).* When the GMII indicates a start-of-frame condition (when TX_ER is first sampled active and TX-ER is inactive), the PCS generates SPD. When the GMII indicates the end-of-packet, the PCS generates EPD.

3. *Packet data.* Packet data presented on the TXD<7:0> bundle (when TX_EN is active and TX_ER is inactive) is encoded directly by the 8B/10B encoder and passed to the PMA, with the exception that the first byte of preamble is replaced with the SPD code-group.

4. *Carrier Extension.* When the MAC is providing the carrier-extend indication over the GMII (TX_EN inactive, TX_ER active, and TXD<7:0> = 0F), the PCS generates a carrier-extend (/R/) code-group for each GTX_CLK period that the indication remains.

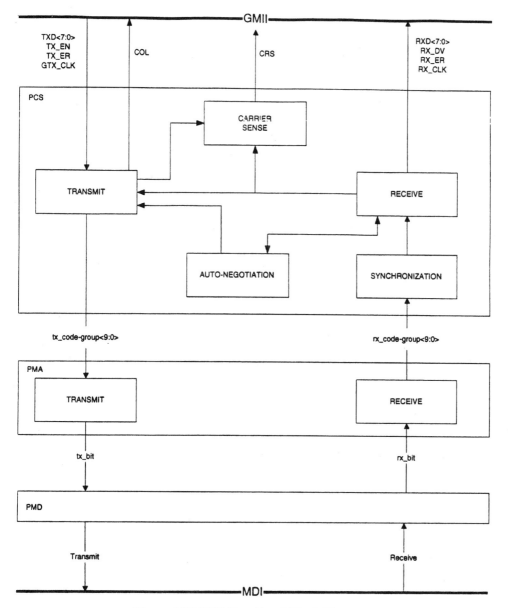

Figure 4-33 PCS Functional Block Diagram

5. *Error indication.* When the GMII indicates the transmit-error condition (TX_EN active and TX_ER active), the PCS generates an error-propagation (/V/) code-group for one or more GTX_CLK periods during the frame transmission.

6. *Configuration.* The Transmit process will encode the 16-bit Configuration register or Next-Page Transmit register provided by the PCS Auto-Negotiation process, in order to configure itself and its corresponding link partner to a compatible mode of operation.

Some of the above code-groups are in fact a set of 10-bit code-groups in a specified order, referred to as ordered-sets. These ordered-sets are described in more detail in the "8B/10B Coding" section.

The PCS Transmit function is also responsible for generation of the collision indication (COL) to the GMII, if it detects simultaneous transmit and receive packet activity. Note that there will always be simultaneous physical signaling activity on the medium, since IDLE or Configuration is always sent in the absence of packet activity; however, only simultaneous packet-data activity constitutes a collision.

The Transmit process also generates an internal indication of transmit packet activity used by the Carrier Sense block.

Finally, the Transmit process monitors the Auto-Negotiation function to determine whether packet-data transmission is permitted, or the link requires (re-)configuration.

Receive

The PCS Receive function decodes the received 10-bit code-groups passed to it from the Synchronization process and passes the decoded data to either the GMII receive signals or the Auto-Negotiation process. When the link is operating correctly and Auto-Negotiation has completed, the GMII RXD<7:0> are driven when packet data is decoded. In this case, the decoding process is essentially the reverse of the transmit encoding process. Configuration code-groups or IDLE code-groups are not passed to the GMII but are directed instead to the Auto-Negotiation process.

Synchronization

The Synchronization block in the PCS is responsible for ensuring lock to the code-group boundaries and passing the received code-groups to the Receive process. Since the code-groups are transmitted in a continuous bit stream over the medium at a 1250 Mbaud, the Synchronization process must determine whether the PMA sublayer is functioning dependably by detecting the boundary of the code bits and code-groups within this continuous stream.

The Synchronization process requires that a series of three consecutive comma code-groups be received, with no invalid code-groups between them, in order to achieve synchronization of the receiver to the link partner's transmitter. This ensures that code-groups and ordered-sets can be correctly detected and passed to the Receive process.

Synchronization is maintained while good code-groups continue to be detected. The Synchronization process provides a hysteresis function such that in the event that invalid code-groups are detected, it will take a succession of invalid code-groups to cause loss of synchronization. This ensures that a short error burst, such as a noise event corrupting the data on the medium, which affects only a small number of code-groups, will not cause loss of synchronization. However, longer error bursts, indicating a significant error condition or complete loss of received signal, cause loss of synchronization, and code-group contents can no longer be considered reliable.

Carrier Sense

The Carrier Sense function monitors the transmit and receive packet data activity and asserts the GMII CRS pin, depending on the condition of these events and whether the PCS is implemented in a repeater or a DTE application. If the PCS is implemented in a repeater, CRS is asserted only for receive-packet activity. The repeater will use the fact that multiple ports exhibiting CRS activity indicates a collision. In a DTE application, the CRS signal is asserted for either transmit or receive packet activity to assure the CSMA/CD protocol is observed at the MAC.

Auto-Negotiation

Auto-Negotiation for Gigabit Ethernet performs the same functions as for 100BASE-T, namely determining the capabilities of the remote-link partner device and determining the optimal common mode of operation shared by the two devices.

The 100BASE-T Auto-Negotiation mechanism was specified only for use on equipment using the RJ-45 connector. It was specifically excluded from fiber links, because the Fast Link Pulse (FLP) burst used to convey the information between the link partners was not well suited to fiber-signaling schemes. Gigabit Ethernet specifically defines Auto-Negotiation to be used on all media types, including the 1000BASE-X copper and fiber media, as well as the 1000BASE-T UTP version.

While Auto-Negotiation for 100BASE-T is defined as a separate sublayer within the PHY, in Gigabit Ethernet it is defined as a functional block within the PCS. However, since the functionality is significant enough to warrant its own clause in the 802.3z standard (clause 37), it is described in its own section in this chapter. See the "Auto-Negotiation" section in Chapter 3 for an understanding of the overall scheme, and see the "Auto-Negotiation for 1000BASE-X" section in this chapter for additional details on how it is optimized for Gigabit Ethernet.

4.8.2 8B/10B Coding

The 8B/10B coding scheme maps groups of 8 binary bits to a code-group of 10 binary bits. This is actually accomplished as a combination of two separate block codes, a 5B/6B coding and a 3B/4B coding (although implementations may not physically perform these as separate operations). The code has good transition density, is run-length limited, and is DC balanced. This facilitates clock recovery and error detection of most single- and multiple-bit error conditions, making it an excellent choice for optical and copper media types. The code was initially developed by IBM.[22] Figure 4-34 shows the bit-ordering relationship between the byte interface of the GMII and the bit stream from the PCS and ultimately from the PMA to the PMD. The nomenclature used to describe the code requires some explanation, which follows.

D and K Codes

Two types of 10-bit code-groups are defined. Examples are shown in Table 4-9. Each code-group is referred to in the form /Zx.y/, where Z indicates the code-group type, D indicates a data code-group, and K indicates a special code-group. Each unencoded byte is given the notation A, B, C, D, E, F, G, H, for each of the bits. The x.y identification is the decimal representation of the unencoded bits, where x = E, D, C, B, A, and y = H, G, F. When encoded, the 10-bit code-group representation is given the notation a, b, c, d, e, i, f, g, h, j. Complete encoding tables for all 8B/10B data and special code-groups can be found in the 802.3z document.[23]

Table 4-9 Example Data (D) and Special (K) Codes[a]

Code Group Name	Octet Bits HGF EDCBA	Octet Value	Current RD– a b c d e i f g h j	Current RD+ a b c d e i f g h j	Notes
K28.5	10 111100	BC	0011111010	1100000101	1
D5.6	11 000101	C5	1010010110	1010010110	2
D2.2	01 000010	42	1011010101	0100100101	3
D21.5	10 110101	B5	101010110	1010101010	2

[a]Source: IEEE 802.3z—Media Access Control (MAC) Parameters, Physical Layer, Repeater and Management Parameters for 1000 Mb/s Operation, Clause 36.

Notes:
1. /K28.5/ is the only code-group containing a comma used-for Gigabit Ethernet.
2. Code-groups with identical RD+ and RD– encodings and neutral disparity subblocks.
3. Code-groups containing nonneutral disparity subblocks which change the current running disparity.

---

[22] A DC-Balanced, Partitioned-Block, 6B/10B Transmission Code. A. X. Widmer and P. A. Franaszek, IBM Publication.
[23] American National Standards Institute/Institute of Electrical and Electronics Engineers, Information Technology—Local and Metropolitan Area Networks - Part 3: Media Access Control (MAC) Parameters, Physical Layer, Repeater and Management Parameters for 1000 Mb/s Operation. 1998, IEEE, New York, NY, Clause 36, Table 36-1b.

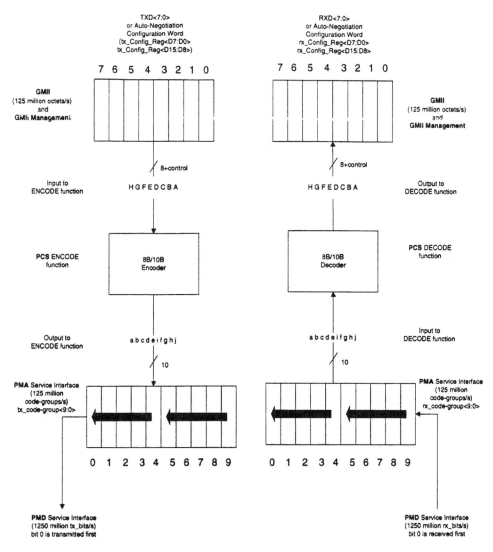

Figure 4-34 Coding and Decoding Ordering Conventions
(From IEEE Std. P802.3z, IEEE. All rights reserved.)

The 8-bit unencoded value is effectively broken into two subblocks. A 5-bit subblock, represented by the bits ABCDE of the input byte, is encoded into a 6-bit subblock represented by the bits abcdei; and a 3-bit subblock, represented by the bits FGH of the input byte, is encoded into a 4-bit subblock represented by the bits fghj. Each subblock has a "disparity" value associated with it. Disparity is the difference between the number of zeroes or ones in the encoded subblock and code-group.

Running Disparity

As stated previously, each 6-bit and 4-bit encoded subblock within a 10-bit code-group has a disparity value associated with it. Many of the 256 code-groups that represent the 8-bit values are disparity neutral; that is, both the 6-bit and 4-bit subblocks have the same number of zeroes and ones. Running disparity at the end of each code-group is continuously maintained as either positive or negative in the transmitter and checked at the receiver of an 8B/10B implementation.

The value of running disparity is calculated by using the disparity of each subblock and the running disparity value of the previous subblock. Each 4-bit or 5-bit subblock is permitted to have a disparity value of +2, 0, or −2 within the subblock and +1 or −1 (positive or negative, respectively) at the beginning and end of each subblock.

The transmitter assumes a negative value for its running disparity at start-up. It calculates a new value for running disparity based on each code-group it transmits. Code-groups that are disparity neutral do not change the value of running disparity (e.g., D5.6 in Table 4-9, etc.). Nonneutral disparity code-groups flip the value of running disparity.

8B/10B encoding tables are used to determine the proper encoding of the next data byte. For example, assume that the current running disparity is positive, and the next byte to be transmitted is D2.2 (the byte value 42). The encoding for D2.2 must be taken from the "Current RD+" column.

A receiver will assume either a positive or negative value of running disparity at start-up. On receipt of code-groups, it will determine the validity of the code-group and calculate a new value of running disparity based on the received code-group.

The running disparity value is used as an additional error check at the receiver, since the transmitted value is defined to ensure running disparity will be maintained as either positive or negative (i.e., never zero or greater than +1 or less than −1).

Comma

A comma is a bit pattern that, in the absence of transmission errors, cannot appear within a transmitted code-group, and cannot occur across the boundaries of two adjacent code-groups. The comma is used to find transmission code-group boundaries and ordered-set boundaries in the received bit stream.

A comma is either the abcdeif sequence 0011111 (comma+) or 1100000 (comma−). /K28.5/ is the only code-group containing a comma defined for normal 1000BASE-X use (although /K28.7/, which also contains a comma, is reserved for diagnostics usage).

Ordered-sets

An ordered-set is either a single special code-group or a sequence of code-groups consisting of an initial special code-group followed by additional special or data code-groups. Ordered-sets are always 1, 2 or 4 code-groups in length. Table 4-10 shows the eight different ordered-sets that are defined for 1000BASE-X. Code-groups that commence an ordered-set sequence containing multiple code-groups always start on an even-numbered code-group position. The first code-group position after power-on is considered even numbered, with subsequent positions alternating between odd and even.

Table 4-10 Ordered-Set Definitions[a]

Code	Ordered-set	Number of Code-groups	Encoding
/C/	**Configuration**		**Alternating /C1/ and /C2/**
/C1/	Configuration 1	4	/K28.5/D21.5/Config_Reg/
/C2/	Configuration 2	4	/K28.5/D2.2/Config_Reg/
/I/	**IDLE**		**Correcting /I1/, Preserving /I2/**
/I1/	IDLE 1	2	/K28.5/D5.6/
/I2/	IDLE 2	2	/K28.5/D16.2/
	Encapsulation		
/R/	Carrier_Extend	1	/K23.7/
/S/	Start_of_Packet	1	/K27.7/
/T/	End_of_Packet	1	/K29.7/
/V/	Error_Propagation	1	/K30.7/

[a]Source: IEEE 802.3z—Media Access Control (MAC) Parameters, Physical Layer, Repeater and Management Parameters for 1000 Mb/s Operation, Clause 36.

Valid/Invalid Code-groups

Valid data code-groups (D) are defined for the 256 values required to fully encode the 8-bit data values, as well as additional special code-groups (K) for the required additional information. As seen by the examples in Table 4-9, each code-group has two encodings, with the current running disparity determining which encoding is used.

From a receiver's point of view, if a received code-group is in the correct column of the 8B/10B encoding tables, dependent on the current received running disparity, it is considered valid and is decoded and action taken dependent on its contents. If a received code-group is in the incorrect column, it is considered invalid. Invalid code-groups can result in loss of synchronization if enough of them are detected. However, regardless of the validity of the code-group, it is used to compute the new value of the receiver's running disparity. The new code-group is used as is, to compute the new value of the receiver's running disparity, to be used to check the next code-group.

4.8.3 Frame Encapsulation and Line-State Encoding

The PCS sublayer accepts packets from the Reconciliation Sublayer via the GMII and encodes the packet before passing it to the PMA sublayer. The PCS decodes the bit stream received from the PMA sublayer and passes it to the MAC via the GMII and Reconciliation Sublayer. Figure 4-35 shows PCS encapsulation of a MAC frame based on GMII signals. The following are the defined ordered-sets (see also Table 4-10)

Configuration (/C/)

The ordered-sets /C1/ and /C2/ are used to convey to the link partner the 16-bit Configuration Register. Table 4-10 defines these ordered-sets.

For an identical value of the Configuration Register, the /C1/ ordered-set will change the running disparity at the end of the transmitted /C1/ to the opposite running disparity at the start. The /C2/ ordered-set will keep the running disparity at the end of the transmitted /C1/ the same running disparity at the start.

Data (/D/)

Data code-group /D/ defines an octet of arbitrary data between the GMII and the PCS. Sequencing of data code-groups is arbitrary. The data code-groups are not interpreted by the PCS.

IDLE (/I/)

The idle ordered-sets, /I/ are transmitted whenever there is no transmit activity from the GMII (TX_EN and TX_ER are both inactive). The idle ordered-sets /I1/ and /I2/ are continuously transmitted to maintain clock synchronization and are required to delimit packet data. Table 4-10 defines these ordered-sets.

An /I1/ ordered-set will change the running disparity at the end of the transmitted /I1/ to the opposite running disparity at the start. The /I2/ ordered-set will keep the running disparity at the end of the transmitted /I1/ the same running disparity at the start.

Start_of_Packet (/S/)

The Start_of_Packet delimiter (SPD) is used to indicate the start of the data-transmission sequence. When the GMII TX_EN signal goes active, the PCS replaces the current octet of the preamble with the /S/ ordered-set (Figure 4-35). At the start of data reception, the /S/ ordered-set is replaced by the first octet of the preamble.

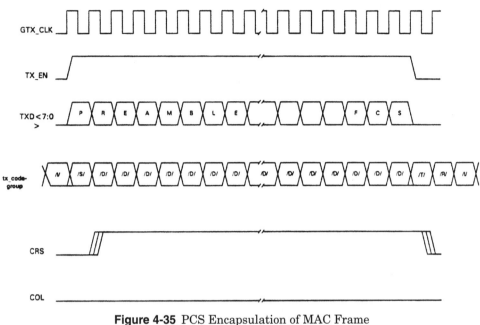

Figure 4-35 PCS Encapsulation of MAC Frame
(From IEEE Std. P802.3z, IEEE. All rights reserved.)

End_of_Packet (/T/)

End_of_Packet (EPD) delimiter is used to indicate the end of data transmission sequence. When the GMII TX_EN signal goes inactive, the PCS replaces the last octet of the frame with a /T/R/R/ or /T/R/K28.5/ code-group (Figure 4-35). The receiver considers that the MAC interpacket gap begins two octets prior to transmission of the first /I/ after the EPD..

Carrier Extend (/R/)

The /R/ ordered-set is used by the MAC to indicate carrier extension during a burst and packet separation within a burst. It is also used by the PCS to indicate an EPD delimiter and to maintain alignment of an even-numbered code-group after EPD.

Error_Propagation (/V/)

Error_Propagation is used by the PCS to indicate transmission of an error to its peer entity. The normal use of this is to allow a repeater to propagate a receive error. Error_Propagation consists of /V/ ordered-sets. When the TX_ER signal is asserted by the GMII, the PCS interprets this as an Error_Propagation event. The PCS indicates reception of /V/ or an invalid code-group (the result of a collision or an error condition) by asserting the GMII RX_ER signal and driving the appropriate value onto RXD<7:0> (see Table 4-3).

4.9 Physical Medium Attachment (PMA) Sublayer (Clause 36)

The PMA sublayer provides the serialization service interface between the PCS and PMD layers. The connection to the PCS sublayer is called the PMA Service Interface. The transmit section of the PMA sublayer converts the 10-bit symbols into a serial bit stream before passing them to the PMD. The receive section of the PMA sublayer converts a received serial bit stream into 10-bit symbols before passing them to PCS. In addition, the PMA sublayer extracts the symbol-timing clock from the received bit stream for correct symbol alignment (framing) of the received data.

4.9.1 Physical Implementation of the PMA

A block diagram of the PMA Service Interface adapted from the Fibre Channel Ten-Bit Interface (TBI) ANSI Technical Report[24] is shown in Figure 4-36. This implementation is optional. However, when the interface is implemented as a TBI at an observable point, the data path has to be 10 bits wide and must meet all other requirements specified in the 802.3z PMA sublayer.

The figure shows the input and output signals used:

tx_code_group<9:0>

This is the 10-bit parallel data presented to the PMA by the PCS after 8B/10B encoding. The PMA layer serializes the data for transmission of the data.

PMA_TX_CLK

PMA_TX_CLK is the 125 MHz transmit symbol clock. This clock is used to latch 10-bit symbols in the PMA for transmission. A clock multiplier unit is used to generate the 1250 MHz clock required for transmission of serialized 10-bit symbols on the media. If the _LCK_REF signal is active, the receiver also uses PMA_TX_CLK.

EWRAP

When high, this signal allows the loopback of serialized transmit data to the deserializer to assist in link diagnostics. Most commercial SERDES integrated circuits place the serial transmit data output signals (TX+ and TX-) into an inactive state.

---

[24] Fibre Channel—10 bit Interface, ANSI Technical Report TR/X3.18, 1997.

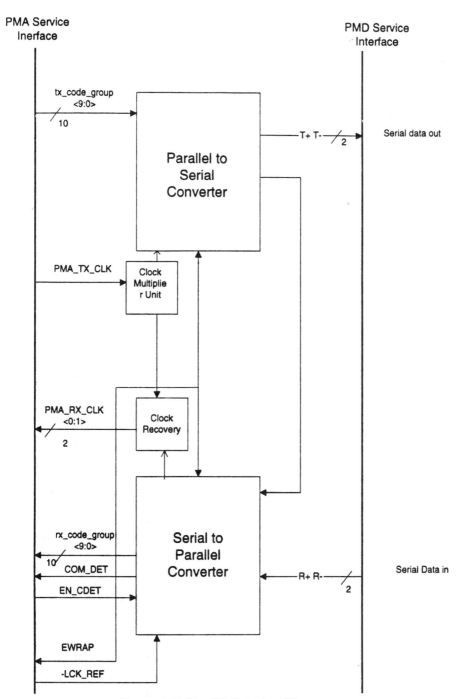

Figure 4-36 Ten-Bit Interface Diagram

PMA_RX_CLK<0>

This is the 62.5 MHz recovered receive clock that the PMA uses to latch odd-numbered symbols reconstructed from the incoming serial bit stream. This clock may be delayed during symbol alignment, but it is never shortened.

PMA_RX_CLK<1>

This is the 62.5 MHz recovered receive clock that the PMA uses to latch even-numbered symbols reconstructed from the incoming serial bit stream. PMA_RX_CLK<1> is 180° out of phase with PMA_RX_CLK<0>. This clock may be delayed during symbol alignment, but it is never shortened.

COM_DET

This is an indication that the code-group or symbol received with the current PMA_TX_CLK<1> contains a valid comma symbol. The TBI is required to detect and align to the comma sequence for packet delineation.

-LCK_REF

This causes the clock recovery unit to lock to PMA_TX_CLK (i.e., a local clock rather than a clock recovered from incoming serial data) within 500 μs. This mode of operation is mostly used for testing by the manufacturer.

EN_CDET

When high, the code-group alignment function is operational; that is, COM_DET signals will be generated. This is the normal setting for this signal. If EN_CDET is low, the incoming data is considered to be an unformatted and unframed bit stream.

4.9.2 Functional Description of the Ten-Bit Interface (TBI)

The TBI connects to the PCS and PMD sublayers as shown in Figure 4-36.

The PMA transmit interface accepts a 10-bit-wide code-group or symbol (from PCS after 8B/10B encoding) on parallel lines tx_code_group <9:0>. The symbols are timed and strobed into the PMA by the associated PMA_TX_CLK. An internal clock multiplier unit uses the PMA_TX_CLK to generate a 1250 MHz clock to sequence the serialized data onto the media. The PMA service interface latches symbol data on the rising edge of PMA_TX_CLK. The serialized data is transmitted in the order least significant bit (TXD[0]) to most significant bit (TXD[9]).

The PMA accepts 1250 Mb/s serial data from the PMD. The received serial data is de-serialized and delivered by the PMA to the PCS in TBI format on rx_code_group<9:0>. The clock recovery unit extracts two symbol clocks,

PMA_RX_CLK<0> and PMA_RX_CLK<1>, that operate at 62.5 MHz and are out of phase by 180°. The 10-bit wide code-group is presented to the PCS layer relative to the rising edge of each receive clock. Even-numbered symbols are presented on rx_code_group<9:0> during PMA_RX_CLK<1> while odd-numbered symbols are presented on rx_code_group<9:0> during PMA_RX_CLK<0>.

In addition, there are two more signals in the TBI, EWRAP and -LCK_REF. EWRAP or the loopback signal is an input signal to the PMA layer and causes the serialized transmit data to be looped back to the receiver. -LCK_REF, which is the optional lock to reference signal, is an input signal and is used to lock the clock recovery unit to PMA_TX_CLK instead of the incoming serial stream. Table 4-11 shows the possible combination of control signals on the TBI. Please refer to IEEE 802.3z, Clause 36, for details of electrical characteristics of the TBI.

Table 4-11 Possible Combinations of TBI Signals[a]

EWRAP	-LCK_REF	EN_CDET	Interpretation
L	L	L	Undefined
L	L	H	Lock receiver clock recovery unit to PMA_TX_CLK
L	H	L	Normal Operation; COM_DET disabled
L	H	H	Normal Operation; COM_DET enabled
H	L	L	Undefined
H	L	H	Undefined
H	H	L	Loop transmit data to receiver; COM_DET disabled
H	H	H	Loop transmit data to receiver; COM_DET enabled

[a]Source: IEEE 802.3z—Media Access Control (MAC) Parameters, Physical Layer, Repeater and Management Parameters for 1000 Mb/s Operation, Clause 36.

4.10 Auto-Negotiation for 1000BASE-X (Clause 37)

The Auto-Negotiation function for 1000BASE-X is defined in clause 37 of the 802.3z standard, however, Auto-Negotiation is actually defined as a function within the PCS. The Auto-Negotiation specification for 1000BASE-X was leveraged directly from the work already in place for 100BASE-T, with some significant modifications. This section does not repeat the explanation of the basic functionality already contained in the "Auto-Negotiation" section in Chapter 3. The reader is encouraged to refer to this section for a basic understanding of the Auto-Negotiation protocol. Where there are substantive changes, these are documented in this section.

At the highest level, the differences between Auto-Negotiation for 1000BASE-X versus the corresponding capability specified for 100BASE-T are summarized in Table 4-12.

Table 4-12 Differences Summary between Auto-Negotiation for
100BASE-T and 100BASE-X

100BASE-T Auto-Negotiation	1000BASE-X Auto-Negotiation
Specified only for UTP cable using RJ-45 connector	Operates over fiber optic and copper media with variety of connector types
Uses out-of-band fast link pulse burst to exchange Base-Page and Next-Page information	Uses normal 8B/10B code words to exchange Base-Page and Next-Page information
Next Page implementation optional (except for 100BASE-T2)	Next Page implementation optional
Control and Status Registers defined in MII (clause 22)	Additional bits defined in Control and Status Registers for Gb/s operation (see GMII section)
MII Management Registers 0–10 specified (including 100BASE-T2)	Register 15 added to support Gb/s operation, defined as Extended Status Register (see GMII section)
Single bit in Base Page defines symmetric PAUSE capability	Two-bit field in Base Page defines symmetric and asymmetric PAUSE capability
Single bit in Base Page for remote fault indication	Two-bit field in Base Page for enhanced Remote Fault reporting

4.10.1 Differences in 1000BASE-X versus 100BASE-T Auto-Negotiation

In the descriptions that follow, only the noticeable differences in Auto-Negotiation (thankfully, abbreviated to AN in the 802.3z standard) are documented. Since the AN operation at 1 Gb/s performs the identical function to that at 100 Mb/s, there is no need to duplicate the description in Chapter 3.

Base Link Code Word

Figure 4-37 defines the bit positions of the Base Link Code Word (Base LCW) that is exchanged between Auto-Negotiation devices after power-on, reset, or renegotiation is requested by one of several mechanisms. Bits marked "R" are "Reserved." The Base Link Code Word has modified content and is encoded into the /C/ ordered-sets for transmission. Note that this implies that if the medium has a fault which prevents it from operating at the 1250 MBaud rate, Auto-Negotiation is unlikely to complete successfully.

Half-/Full-Duplex Bits

Support for both half- and full-duplex operation is provided. Since there are relatively few options in Gb/s for different media or capabilities, resolution of the highest-common-denominator mode is straightforward. Full duplex is higher in priority than half duplex.

LSB   MSB

D0	D1	D2	D3	D4	D5	D6	D7	D8	D9	D10	D11	D12	D13	D14	D15
R	R	R	R	R	FD	HD	PS1	PS2	R	R	R	RF1	RF2	Ack	NP

Figure 4-37 Base Link Code Word Definition

Pause Bits

The PAUSE function initially defined as a fully symmetric operation in the Full-Duplex/Flow-Control specification (802.3x[25]), was modified by the Gigabit Ethernet standard to allow asymmetric operation. Asymmetric operation and its use are described in more detail in the "Flow Control" section of this chapter. The definition of the PAUSE bits is shown in Table 4-13, with additional detail in Table 4-14.

Table 4-13 PAUSE Encoding[a]

PAUSE PS1 (D7)	ASM_DIR PS2 (D7)	Capability
0	0	No PAUSE
0	1	Asymmetric PAUSE toward link partner
1	0	Symmetric PAUSE
1	1	Both symmetric and asymmetric PAUSE toward local device

[a]Source: IEEE 802.3z—Media Access Control (MAC) Parameters, Physical Layer, Repeater and Management Parameters for 1000 Mb/s Operation, Clause 37.

Resolution of the PAUSE capability is defined in Table 4-14. The PAUSE resolution will determine whether the local device and/or the link partner can generate and/or receive PAUSE frames.

Table 4-14 PAUSE Priority Resolution [a]

PAUSE	ASM_DIR	PAUSE	ASM_DIR	Local Device Resolution	Link Partner Resolution
0	0	-	-	Disable transmit PAUSE Disable receive PAUSE	Disable transmit PAUSE Disable receive PAUSE
0	1	0	-	Disable transmit PAUSE Disable receive PAUSE	Disable transmit PAUSE Disable receive PAUSE
0	1	1	0	Disable transmit PAUSE Disable receive PAUSE	Disable transmit PAUSE Disable receive PAUSE

[25] " 802.3x&-1997. Supplement to ISO/IEC 8802-3:1996. Specification for 802-3 Full-Duplex Operation and Physical Layer Specification for 1000 Mb/s Operation on Two Pairs of Category 3 or Better Balanced Twisted Pair Cable (100BASE-T2): Part 1 and 2." Section 31, Mac Control.

Table 4-14 PAUSE Priority Resolution (Continued)[a]

0	1	1	1	Disable transmit PAUSE Disable receive PAUSE	Disable transmit PAUSE Enable receive PAUSE
1	0	0	-	Disable transmit PAUSE Disable receive PAUSE	Disable transmit PAUSE Disable receive PAUSE
1	0	1	-	Enable transmit PAUSE Enable receive PAUSE	Enable transmit PAUSE Enable receive PAUSE
1	0	0	0	Disable transmit PAUSE Disable receive PAUSE	Disable transmit PAUSE Disable receive PAUSE
1	1	0	1	Disable transmit PAUSE Enable receive PAUSE	Enable transmit PAUSE Disable receive PAUSE
1	1	1	-	Enable transmit PAUSE Enable receive PAUSE	Enable transmit PAUSE Enable receive PAUSE

[a]Source: IEEE 802.3z—Media Access Control (MAC) Parameters, Physical Layer, Repeater and Management Parameters for 1000 Mb/s Operation, Clause 37.

Remote Fault Bits

Two bits are provided to allow reporting of fault conditions detected by the remote link partner. The encoding of the bits is defined in Table 4-15. The Next-Page bit may additionally be set to allow Next Pages to be transported, which contain the precise type of Remote Fault. A special Remote-Fault Next-Page encoding is defined for this purpose.

Table 4-15 Remote Fault Encoding[a]

RF1	RF2	Description
0	0	No error (default)
0	1	Offline
1	0	Link Fail
1	1	Auto-Negotiation Error

[a]Source: IEEE 802.3z—Media Access Control (MAC) Parameters, Physical Layer, Repeater and Management Parameters for 1000 Mb/s Operation, Clause 37.

A device that has no mechanism to map fault conditions to the Base-Page register bits must return the default condition: No Error. Note this does not precisely indicate that there is an operational link, rather that either the link is operational or a remote-fault capability does not exist.

The Offline report is used by a remote link partner to advice the local device that it will become unavailable. This may be sent by a device that is going into a test mode, for example. There is no timing constraint implied as to when the device will return to an available state, and therefore Auto-Negotiation may not be able to complete if this state is detected.

The Link-Fail indication advises that the remote device is reporting a previously encountered link-failure condition. For instance, it may be used to indicate a problem with the remote device's receive path (link fail).

   Auto-Negotiation Error indicates that the remote link partner is unable to complete the Auto-Negotiation procedure. A likely cause is that it shares no common mode of operation with the local device.

Acknowledge Bit

This bit acknowledges the successful receipt of three identical LCWs, contained within /C/ ordered-sets from the link partner. An LCW with ACK = 1 is transmitted a minimum of 6–8 times to the link partner. This ensures the partner will detect the LCW with ACK = 1 also three consecutive times.

Next-Page Bit

Indicates a device wishes to send additional Link Code Words (LCWs), within /C/ ordered-sets following the current word being exchanged. In order for additional pages to be sent, both ends must be "Next Page-able" (both must set this bit in the Base LCW).

Next-Page Function

The Next-Page function operates in the same manner as the corresponding 100BASE-T function, except that Next Pages are contained within the /C/ ordered-sets of the 8B/10B encoding scheme, instead of Fast Link pulses.. Message pages and Unformatted pages are identical in format.

Management Interface

Auto-Negotiation allows for management via the GMII/MII management interface (or an equivalent if the GMII is not provided). The mandatory and optional register additions and modifications were defined as modification to the original MII management interface (Clause 22). These changes are defined in the GMII section of this chapter.

4.11 Physical Medium Dependent (PMD) Sublayer (Clauses 38, 39)

The PMD sublayer supports the exchange of serialized 8B/10B symbol code bits between the PMA sublayer and the medium. The PMD sublayer performs the functions of translating these electrical signals to a form suitable for transmission on the specified medium. Figure 4-38 shows the functional block diagram of the PMD sublayer.

   The PMD is the lowest sublayer of the physical layer that is specified by the Gigabit Ethernet standard for transmitting and receiving signals on the media. The IEEE 802.3z standard specifies three types of media: (1) 850 nm laser on multimode fiber (1000BASE-SX), (2) 1300 nm laser on single-mode and multimode fiber (1000BASE-LX) and (3) short-haul copper (1000BASE-CX). A separate working

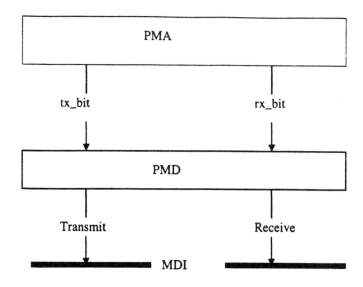

Figure 4-38 Functional Block Diagram of PMD Layer

group, IEEE 802.3ab, has defined a solution to allow gigabit operation over UTP cable as a desktop technology. Figure 4-39 shows the different physical media to be supported for Gigabit Ethernet operation.[26]

4.11.1 Media

The media specifications defined by IEEE 802.3z are for fiber optic cables and short-haul copper cables intended for wiring closet jumpers.

In general, fiber provides very high data rate over greater distances. Therefore, it is expected that Gigabit Ethernet will initially be used as a backbone connection between high-speed workgroup switches or campus switches.

Optical Fiber Transmission

Figure 4-40 shows the cross section of a typical optical fiber structure. The inner circle is called the core. Light propagates through this "core," which can be glass or plastic. A "cladding" which is also made of glass or plastic but has optical properties

---

[26] Source: "Gigabit Ethernet: Accelerating the standard for speed," White paper, Gigabit Ethernet Alliance, 1997,
http://www.gigabit-ethernet.org/technology/whitepapers/gige_0997/gigabit0997.pdf.

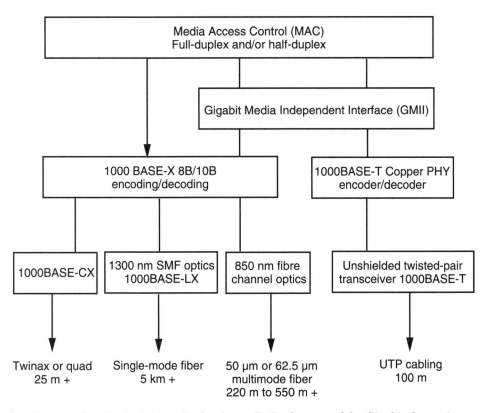

Figure 4-39 Physical-Layer Technologies To Be Supported for Gigabit Operation

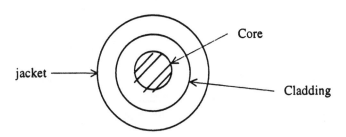

Figure 4-40 Fiber Structure

different from those of the core surrounds the core. Surrounding the cladding is the outermost layer, called the jacket, which provides protection from environmental factors such as heat, moisture, and mechanical contact.

Optical fibers transmit light by means a phenomenon known as Total Internal Reflection (TIR). Figure 4-41 shows the principle of optical fiber transmission.

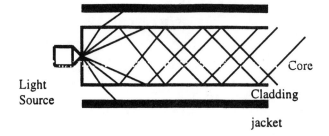

Figure 4-41 Propagation of Light in Fiber

Light from a source enters the core. Light rays entering at shallow angles are internally reflected and propagate through the fiber. The outer layers absorb rays, which have an entrance angle which is too large.

The method of propagation shown, in which rays propagate through the fiber in many ways, is referred to as **multimode.** The core size of multimode fiber typically varies from 50 to 200 μm. In multimode fibers light rays propagate through many paths, each with a different path length. These differing path lengths cause various rays to arrive at the receiver end of the fiber at different times. The overall effect is to smear or distort the light pulses in proportion to distance; eventually the pulses are sufficiently distorted to interfere with data integrity, limiting the distance to receive data accurately. However, multimode fibers are less expensive than single-mode fibers and are typically used in applications requiring moderate lengths (a few hundred meters).

Multimode fibers are of two types: **step-index** fiber and **graded-index** fiber. In step-index fiber (Figure 4-42) the refractive index of the core is different from that of the cladding but is the same throughout the core. As a result, dispersion occurs because of light-path lengths spreading with increasing distance, as described above. In graded-index fiber, the refractive index of the core varies across the cross section to reduce the differences in various path lengths through the fiber. This increases the usable distance for the fiber, allowing an intermediate signal performance characteristic between multimode (step-index) and single-mode fiber.

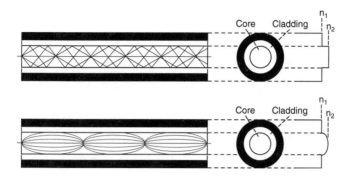

Figure 4-42a Step-Index (top) and Graded-Index (bottom) Fiber

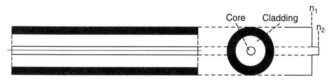

Figure 4-42b Single-Mode Step-Index Fiber

Gigabit Ethernet will be supported over two types of multimode fiber: (1) 50 μm fiber (core diameter) and (2) 62.5 μm fiber. The 62.5 μm fiber, in general, has low modal bandwidth compared to 50 μm fiber, especially for short-wave lasers. In other words, the distance traversed by light in a 62.5 μm fiber is typically less than in 50 μm fiber, especially with short-wave lasers.

When the core size of the fiber is reduced such that only a single ray along the axis can propagate, the fiber is referred to as **single-mode** fiber. The core size of a single-mode fiber typically varies from 2 to 10 μm. Single-mode fibers provide better performance than multimode fibers. Single-mode fibers can be used to transmit signals over several kilometers.

Optical Transmitter and Receiver

An optical transmitter is used to convert electrical signals to optical signals. An optical receiver converts the optical signals back to electrical signals. A combination of the two units, packaged into a single housing, is called an optical transceiver.

Optical Transmitter

Two types of light sources (transmitters), Light-Emitting Diodes (**LED**) and **laser** diodes are used to transmit light over fiber. Figures 4-43a and 4-43b[27] illustrate the launching of light into fiber by LED and laser. While LEDs spray light over a wider area into the core, illuminating many modes of propagation, lasers illuminate only a few modes of propagation. LEDs are not affected by fibers that have a notch in their index profile (Figure 4-43b). This is because the power is distributed over the entire core and very little power is concentrated in few modes that use the faulty part of the core. Lasers, which propagate light in fewer modes, are easily affected by such irregularities.

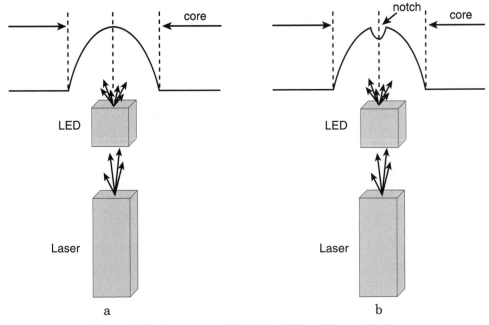

Figure 4-43 Launching of Light by LED and Laser Diodes

Laser diodes are faster than LEDs. Typical rise time for a laser is between 0.1 and 1 ns, while for LEDs it can range from a few nanoseconds to 250 ns.

For gigabit operation a laser-diode type of transmitter is required, since at the present time only a laser provides high enough bandwidth. An optical is transmitter specified by the following parameters:

---

[27] H. Frazier, "Differential Mode Delay for Dumbies," IEEE 802.3 Plenary Meeting, Montreal, Canada, November 1997,
http://grouper.ieee.org/groups/802/3/z/public/presentations/nov1997/optdumb.pdf

- Wavelength
- Spectral width
- Power
- Rise time/Fall time
- Extinction ratio
- Jitter
- Relative Intensity Noise (RIN)

Wavelength

Wavelength is defined as the ratio of wave velocity to the frequency,

$$\lambda = v/f$$

where v = the velocity of light
        f = the frequency

The frequency (and hence the wavelength) of the light depends on the transmitters used. It is desirable to select wavelengths at which the losses in the optical fiber are low. For commercially available fiber, the losses are minimal at wavelengths of 850, 1300, and 1550 nm, as shown in Figure 4-44.

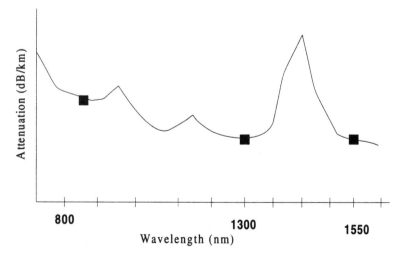

Figure 4-44 Spectral Attenuation in Glass Fibers
(Reprinted from A. Shah and G. Ramakrishnan, FDDI - A High Speed Network, Upper Saddle River, NJ, Prentice Hall, 1993. ISBN-0-13-308388-8.)

For multimode fiber using short-wave lasers the wavelength range is typically 770 to 860 nm (see Table 4-16). For multimode fiber and single-mode fiber using long-wave laser, the range is 1270–1355 nm.

Spectral Width

In practice, transmitters never emit light at a single wavelength. Instead, a range of wavelengths are produced. This range is called the spectral width. A perfect transmitter emitting light at single wavelength is said to have zero spectral width. For a laser-diode type of transmitter, the typical spectral width is 1–5 nm, whereas for LED transmitters the typical range of spectral width is 20–100 nm The low spectral width of laser allows for efficient propagation of light by reducing dispersion[28] (Figure 4-45).

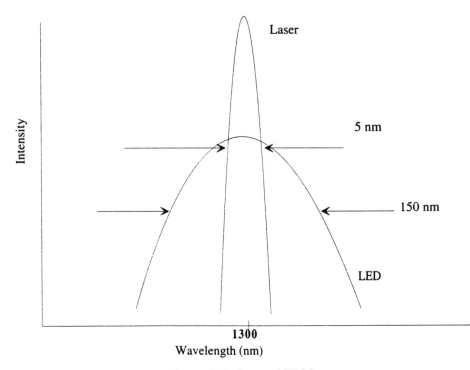

Figure 4-45 Spectral Width
(Reprinted from A. Shah and G. Ramakrishnan, FDDI - A High Speed Network, Upper Saddle River, NJ, Prentice Hall, 1993. ISBN-0-13-308388-8.)

---

[28] AMP—Introduction to Fiber Optic Networking, http://www.amp.com/products/articles/ifo_tr.html.

Power

Transmitters must have sufficient power to drive the optical signals on the fiber. Similarly, receivers must have sufficient sensitivity to reliably extract the received optical signals. In general, the higher the transmitter power, the greater the loss that can be sustained due to attenuation, connectors, and link penalties. Limiting factors on transmit power are cost and eye safety. The transmitter power minus the loss due to transmission on the fiber must be equal to or greater than the minimum acceptable receive power.

Rise Time / Fall Time

Rise time is defined as the time it takes for the output power of the transmitter to rise from 20% to 80% of its final value when the input is a step current (Figure 4-46). A perfect transmitter transmitting a square pulse of light would have a rise and fall time of zero. However, in practice, the transmitter takes certain amount of time to reach maximum power (logical 1) and a certain amount of time to reach minimum power (logical 0). These are called rise time and fall time, respectively. Generally, efficient transmitters have low rise and fall times.

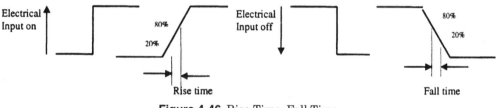

Figure 4-46 Rise Time, Fall Time

Extinction Ratio

In high-speed systems the laser diode is not turned on and off (modulated) completely, since the junction would have to be precharged each time and this would slow it down. Instead, two levels of brightness are defined, one brighter level corresponding to a logic one and a less bright one corresponding to a logic zero. Extinction ratio is defined as the ratio of the average optical energy in the logic-one value to the average optical energy in the logic-zero level.

Relative Intensity Noise (RIN)

A laser is a very highly tuned quantum-effect oscillator. When a laser source is used to transmit light through fiber, a certain amount of optical power is reflected back into the laser device due to connectors and optical lens interfaces. This reflected optical power disturbs the purity of oscillation in the laser, and this appears as optical noise. This is called relative intensity noise and is measured in dB/Hz since it has characteristics similar to thermal noise in resistors.

Jitter

When a digital signal is transmitted, random timing errors build up through the length of the optical link, and these errors can cause incorrect interpretation of the signals at the receiver. Such random timing errors are called jitter.[29] Jitter can be of two types: (1) Deterministic (that is, data content or pattern related) and (2) Random (noise). It is important to separate the two kinds of jitter when computing the total allowed jitter, because deterministic-jitter contributions add directly and random-jitter contributions add in a statistical (RMS) manner.

Tables 4-16 and 4-17 specify a partial list of specifications for the parameters described above for short-wave laser and long-wave laser transmitters.

Table 4-16 Optical Transmitter Specifications for 1000 BASE-SX (62.5 μm and 50 μm MMF)[a]

Characteristics	Value
Wavelength (λ), nm	770–860
Spectral width, nm	0.85
Trise/Tfall (max; 20–80%; λ > 830 nm)	0.26
Trise/Tfall (max; 20–80%; λ 830 nm)	0.21
Average launch power (max), dBm	Lesser of Class I safety limits or maximum receive power
Average launch power (min), dBm	−9.5
Extinction ratio (min), dB	9
RIN (max), dB/Hz	−117

[a]Source: IEEE Std. P802.3z, IEEE. All rights reserved.

Table 4-17 Optical Transmitter Specifications for 1000 BASE-LX
(62.5 μm and 50 μm MMF and 10 μm SMF)[a]

Characteristics	62.5 μm MMF, 50 μm MMF	10 μm SMF
Wavelength (λ), nm	1270–1355	1270–1355
Spectral width, nm	4	4
Trise/Tfall (max; 20–80% response time)	0.26	0.26
Average launch power (max), dBm	−3	−3
Average launch power (min), dBm	−11.5	−11
Extinction ratio (min), dB	9	9
RIN (max), dB/Hz	−120	−120

[a]Source: IEEE Std. P802.3z, IEEE. All rights reserved.

---

[29] Jeff Hecht, *Understanding Fiber Optics,* SAMS Publishing, 1993. ISBN 0-672-30350-7.

Optical Receiver Specifications

The receiver portion of the PMD (transceiver) is comprised of a high-speed photo detector and amplifier with wave-shaping and threshold circuitry. Its output is a pair of complementary positive ECL (PECL) logic signals which produce pulses at frequencies of up to 1250 MHz.

In addition, the receiver includes a signal detect (SIGNAL_DETECT) threshold circuit which indicates whether a cable is attached and is sending 8B/10B code. This threshold circuit does not actually sense 8B/10B code streams as such. Instead, it takes advantage of the fact that 8B/10B code has very strong energy content at certain frequencies such as 650 MHz. In this fashion the signal detector ignores such extraneous light sources as room lighting and sunlight.

Table 4-18 specifies the requirements for the optical receiver for short wave laser and long wave laser.

Table 4-18 Optical Receiver Specifications for 1000 BASE-SX and 1000 BASE-LX[a]

Characteristics	1000 BASE-SX	1000 BASE-LX
Wavelength (λ), nm	770–860	1270–1355
Average receive power (max), dBm	0	–3
Average receive power (min), dBm	–17	–19
Return loss (min), dB	12	12
SIGNAL_DETECT = Logic 1	–17.0 dB Min	–17.0 dB Min
SIGNAL_DETECT = Logic 0	–30.0 dB Max	–30.0 dB Max

[a]Source: IEEE Std. P802.3z, IEEE. All rights reserved.

Cabling Distance Specification

The IEEE 802.3z standards specify distances (Table 4-19) for the following:

- Multimode fibers using Short-Wave Laser (SWL) and Long-Wave Laser (LWL).
- Single-Mode Fiber using LWL.

In all cases, a Conditioned Launch (CL) as described below is required.

Table 4-19 Cabling Distance Specification

Transmitter Type	MMF (50 µm)		MMF (62.5 µm)		SMF (10 µm)
	Modal Bandwidth	Distance	Modal Bandwidth	Distance	
SX	400	500 m (internal CL)	160	220 m (internal CL)	N/A
	500	550 m (internal CL)	200	275 m (internal CL)	
LX	400	550 m (external CL)			5 km (no CL)
	500	550 m (external CL)	500	550 m (external CL)	

Differential Mode Delay and Conditioned Launch

A condition called Differential Mode Delay (**DMD**)[30] was identified by the IEEE 802.3z standards body as a condition which occurs in certain MMF fibers when using laser diodes.

As explained earlier (see "Optical Fiber Transmission" section), DMD is a phenomenon in which light rays in a multimode fiber (MMF) go through several paths. Some paths are longer than others, so that pulses launched at one end of the fiber spread out in space and time. This causes the signal reception at the receiver to be poor due to "smeared" pulses.

In graded-index MMF, the refractive index of the core varies from the center. The relationship between the index value and diameter in the core is such that rays at the center of core are slowed down and rays at the outer edge are speeded up. Ideally, all the rays would arrive at the same time at a particular point down the fiber length. In other words, the DMD phenomenon would not occur. However, due to variances in manufacturing, imperfections arise in the grading of the refractive index, and this gives rise to DMD. (The DMD phenomenon does not arise in single-mode fiber since there is only one ray or propagation mode of light.)

Multimode fibers were originally designed to be used with LED light sources. LEDs do not provide coherent (single frequency and phase) light output, but rather a range of wavelengths. This provides plenty of opportunity for the light to traverse many different paths, and the graded-index DMD correction works very well in spite of small manufacturing variances.

Unfortunately, it was found that with laser-diode systems, the highly coherent laser light tends to choose only a few paths through the fiber, and the manufacturing variances are of such a nature that the light is rapidly dispersed in high-order propagation modes. The net result is that laser light propagates through some kinds of fiber for only small distances. This is unacceptable because one of the major goals of Gigabit Ethernet is to use existing installed fiber cables at gigabit speeds.

Therefore, the IEEE 802.3z standards body decided to develop a solution that would work without reducing link distances or increasing costs substantially. The resulting solution, after study by numerous experts, was to use what is termed a **conditioned launch.**

The principle of conditioned launch is simple: spread the laser light-source output so that it looks like an LED source for which the cable was designed. By spreading the power across the core more or less equally in all modes, DMD effect can be minimized. This is substantially identical in notion to the mode-stirring paddles in microwave ovens that continually mix and change the microwave paths to avoid cold spots in cooking food.

---

[30] DMD Mode Delay Q&A, GEA,
http://www.gigabit-ethernet.org/technology/overview/dmd.html.

It turned out that majority of vendors are able to provide the required conditioning for short-wave lasers (1000BASE-SX) internal to the transceivers. However, since a 1000BASE-LX transceiver must operate both on MMF and SMF fibers, an external launch conditioner is provided when long-wave lasers are used with MMF fibers. This takes the form of a short patch cable which accepts a single-mode launch from the transceiver and mixes the light in internal fibers to provide a conversion to a conditioned multimode launch which will propagate down the (long) multimode fiber run.

Link Power Budget

Since the fiber optics link is not lossless, it is necessary to calculate the various losses when designing a fiber optics system. Link power budget is an estimating guide to account for the loss of power from the transmitter to the receiver. The worst-case link power budget is estimated as the difference between the minimum average transmitter power and the (minimum) average received power (Figure 4-47). Thus, the link power budget establishes the maximum optical range or length of a feasible fiber optic link. The power budget is allocated between channel insertion loss (coupling losses) and link power penalties (losses due to modal dispersion and such phenomena). Tables 4-20 and 4-21 give information on link power budget and penalties for 1000BASE-SX and 1000BASE-LX respectively.[31] Basically, it may be seen that the allowed losses in the fiber and connectors are 7 dB total.

Table 4-20 Worst-Case Link Power Budget (dB) and Penalties (dB) for 1000BASE-SX[a]

Parameter	1000BASE-SX			
	62.5 µm MMF		50 µm MMF	
Modal bandwidth (MHz-km)	160	200	400	500
Channel insertion loss (dB)	2.38	2.60	3.37	3.56
Link power penalties (dB)	4.27	4.29	4.07	3.57
Unallocated margin in link power budget (dB)	0.84	0.84	0.05	0.37
Total link power budget (dB)	7.5	7.5	7.5	7.5

[a]Source: IEEE Std. P802.3z, IEEE. All rights reserved.

Table 4-21 Worst-Case Link Power Budget (dB) and Penalties (dB) for 1000BASE-LX[a]

Parameter	1000BASE-LX			10 µm SMF
	62.5 µm MMF	50 µm MMF		
Modal bandwidth (MHz-km)	500	400	500	N/A
Channel insertion loss (dB)	2.35	2.35	2.35	4.57
Link power penalties (dB)	3.48	5.08	3.96	3.27
Unallocated margin in link power budget (dB)	1.67	0.07	1.19	0.16
Total link power budget (dB)	7.5	7.5	7.5	8.0

[a]Source: IEEE Std. P802.3z, IEEE. All rights reserved.

---

[31]   IEEE 802.3z—Media Access Control (MAC) Parameters, Physical Layer, Repeater and Management Parameters for 1000 Mb/s Operation, Clause 38.

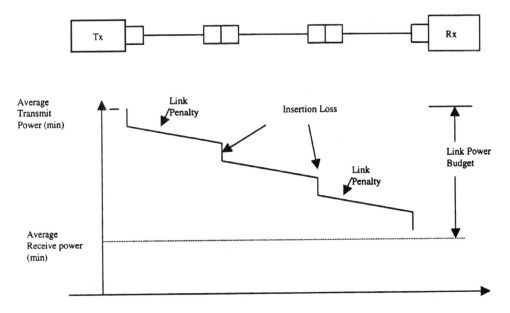

Figure 4-47 Illustration of Power Budget for Fiber

4.11.2 Media Dependent Interface (MDI)—Optical Connector

A connector (MDI) allows for coupling of the PMD (transceiver) to the physical transmission medium (fiber). The requirements for efficient coupling place stringent tolerances on the connector. Hence the connectors are difficult to design and expensive.

A good connector should meet the following requirements:

- The loss due to the connector must be minimal. This is especially critical in a system that has several intermediate connectors.

- The connector should withstand temperature changes, moisture, and other environmental challenges.

- The connector should be easy to use (mate and unmate).

- The connector should provide long life; i.e., coupling efficiency must not degrade over time and should not change with repeated mating.

The most common types of connectors used today are ST connectors and SC connectors. ST connectors use a bayonet coupling for quick release. This requires only a quarter turn to engage and disengage the connector. The connector also has built-in keys so that it will always mate in the same way (Figure 4-48). However, these connectors are quite expensive. Currently, ST connectors have given way to SC connectors.

Figure 4-48 An ST Connector
(Reprinted from A. Shah and G. Ramakrishnan, FDDI - A High Speed Network, Upper Saddle River, NJ, Prentice Hall, 1993. ISBN-0-13-308388-8.)

The specified connector for 1000 BASE-SX and 1000 BASE-LX is a duplex SC connector, which has to meet the dimensional and interface specifications of IEC 61754-4 and ISO/IEC 11801. It uses a push-pull mechanism for mating and is also keyed to always mate in the same way.[32] Figure 4-49 shows the diagram of a duplex SC connector.

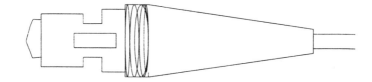

Figure 4-49 An SC Connector
(Reprinted from A. Shah and G. Ramakrishnan, FDDI - A High Speed Network, Upper Saddle River, NJ, Prentice Hall, 1993. ISBN-0-13-308388-8.)

4.11.3 Short Jumper Cable (1000BASE-CX)

A short-haul copper link (1000BASE-CX) provides interconnection between devices up to 25 meters apart. This can be useful to connect devices within a wiring closet where the distances are not large.

The 1000 BASE-CX PMDs are connected with each other through a jumper cable. The jumper cable consists of a continuous shielded balanced cable, which is terminated at each end with a polarized shielded plug. Effectively, 1000BASE-CX is simply two 1000BASE-SX or 1000BASE-LX PMAs connected directly with wires and eliminating the expense of the optical transceivers and fiber. Thus, the signals in the cables are differential Positive ECL (PECL) logic signals. It is generally necessary to build equalizer networks into the cables or connectors to allow transmission of such high-frequency signals over these cables. Tables 4-22 and 4-23 show the specification for transmitters and receivers.[33]

Two types of connectors are defined for 1000BASE-CX. A style 1 connector is a D-subminiature connector with the mechanical mating interface defined by the IEC 60807-3. A style 2 balanced cable connector is an 8-pin shielded ANSI fibre channel style 2 connector with the mechanical mating interface defined by IEC-61076-3-103.

---

[32] AMP—Introduction to Fiber Optic Networking, http://www.amp.com/products/articles/info_ch.html.
[33] IEEE 802.3z—Media Access Control (MAC) Parameters, Physical Layer, Repeater and Management Parameters for 1000 Mb/s Operation, Clause 39.

The style 2 connector is preferred ,because the D-subminiature type of connector does not have specified characteristics above 6 MHz, and there is no guarantee that all makes and variations of these connectors will operate properly.

Table 4-22 Transmitter Characteristics for 1000BASE-CX[a]

Characteristics	Value
Clock tolerance, ppm	±100
Differential amplitude (p-p): Max (worst case p-p), mV Min (opening), mV Max (OFF), mV	2000 1100 170
Rise/Fall time (20–80%): Maximum, ps Minimum, ps	327 85
Differential Skew (max), ps	25

[a]Source: IEEE Std. P802.3z, IEEE. All rights reserved.

Table 4-23 Receiver characteristics for 1000BASE-CX[a]

Characteristics	Value
Clock tolerance, ppm	±100
Minimum differential sensitivity (p-p), mV	400
Maximum differential input (p-p), mV	2000
Input impedance TDR Rise time, ps Exception window, ps Through connection, Ω At termination, Ω	85 700 150±30 150±10
Differential skew, ps	175

[a]Source: IEEE Std. P802.3z, IEEE. All rights reserved.

4.12 Repeater Operation (Clause 41)

As with 10 Mb/s and 100 Mb/s Ethernet, Gigabit Ethernet defines a 1000 Mb/s repeater to provide half-duplex connectivity between two or more Ethernet segments. Gigabit Ethernet repeaters exist in the OSI and IEEE 802.3 architectures as physical-layer devices. The 10 Mb/s Ethernet standard defined a single repeater specification for all media types. The 100 Mb/s Ethernet standard specified two different repeater types, Class I and Class II repeaters. The Gigabit Ethernet standards specify a single repeater type with the same objectives as in the previous standards: to provide an interoperable means of connecting independent Ethernet segments together independently of the underlying physical media.

Figure 4-50 provides a pictorial view of the Gigabit Ethernet repeater's relationship and standing in the IEEE 802.3 CSMA/CD model. As in the previous standards, the repeater connects multiple, independent link segments using the media independent interface specified. In the case of Gigabit Ethernet, the GMII is used. The gigabit repeat-er unit and the underlying physical layer entities constitute a repeater set. Though Figure 4-50 shows the repeater connecting only two physical layers, repeaters can connect many tens, or in some cases, even hundreds of physical layers. The limit is usually set by practical considerations, not by any specification in the standard itself.

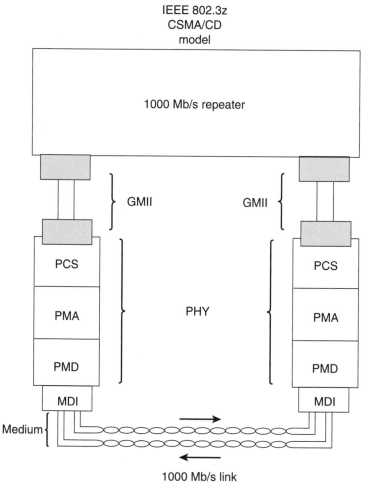

Figure 4-50 Repeater Relation to IEEE Reference Model

Figure 4-50 illustrates a repeater unit that is connected to its individual physical-layer entities using the GMII interface. As with 100 Mb/s and 10 Mb/s repeaters, it is perfectly acceptable to construct a gigabit repeater that does not expose the GMII interface. In fact, it is possible to expose the PMA interface or not expose any physical layer interface at all. In most instances this is the preferred alternative, due to the fact that the GMII consists of a large number of pins and designing a repeater with twelve exposed GMII ports is problematic for both the system and silicon designers.

Gigabit Ethernet repeater operation follows exactly the same principles of 10 Mb/s and 100 Mb/s repeaters, that the total available bandwidth is shared by all connected parties. Repeater-based networks are classic examples of shared-media networks, or networks in which all the attached stations share the total available bandwidth. The Gigabit Ethernet repeater, like its 10 Mb/s and 100 Mb/s cousins, repeats, or forwards, all incoming packets to all connected and active ports except the port on which the packets entered. The result is that all stations on the network connected to the repeater receive a copy of the packet. The repeater performs its function completely at the physical layer and does not check, alter, or disturb any of the bits in the packet unless a physical-layer coding violation is found. The gigabit repeater replaces the invalid code bits and all subsequent bits with 8B/10B code-groups indicating a receive error. This is then guaranteed to cause an error indication at all receiving stations.

Due to the lack of an MAC layer circuitry and its operation as a physical-layer device, the repeater is substantially simpler than a switch, router, or full-duplex repeater.[34] At 1000 Mb/s, however, this simplicity extracts a price. At speeds such as 10 Mb/s and 100 Mb/s, the performance and throughput characteristics of the CSMA/CD protocol allow large repeater networks to be constructed that maintain good performance characteristics. However, as explained previously, at 1 Gb/s, the shrinkage of the collision domain and the shared-media nature of a repeater significantly impact the overall performance of repeater-based networks, when compared to switch or full-duplex repeaters.

Due to the bit budget requirements imposed by the CSMA/CD protocol on repeaters at 1000 Mb/s speeds, only one repeater may exist in any one collision domain. Therefore, unlike 10 Mb/s and 100 Mb/s Ethernet networks, hierarchical or multiple repeater networks cannot be constructed. Interrepeater links are not defined by the Gigabit Ethernet standards. Therefore, only method of constructing larger Gigabit Ethernet networks is by using full-duplex or point-to-point switched Ethernet connections.

4.12.1 Repeater Features

Repeaters provide the ability to connect separate Ethernet segments of like or different topologies. The Gigabit Ethernet repeater can connect any of the standard-specified physical media (1000Base-SX, 1000Base-LX, 1000Base-CX, or 1000Base-T)

---

[34] See Chapter 5 for a discussion on full-duplex repeaters (a.k.a. Buffered Distributors).

together into one collision domain. Repeaters are therefore useful as translation devices between disparate media. They perform this function by receiving incoming bit
streams, determining when the incoming bit stream constitutes the beginning of an
Ethernet packet (by detecting preamble), and transmitting the resulting bit stream
onto all ports but the one on which the bit stream was originally detected. If multiple
incoming bit streams are detected simultaneously, repeaters handle this *collision*
event by propagating a specific jam sequence onto all ports in order to notify them
that a collision has taken place.

Repeaters also provide important error-handling features, jabber detection, partition and code-bit error detection. All Gigabit Ethernet repeaters will detect and terminate attached stations that transmit for an abnormally long duration[35] as well as
keep a record of abnormal collision activity. In both cases the repeater will inhibit the
reception of data from the offending station. In the case of jabber, the repeater also
inhibits transmissions to the offending station. When the input port becomes quiescent, the repeater will restart normal operation. The case of excessive collision detection results in the repeater *partitioning* the network. The network remains partitioned
(input data streams are ignored, output data streams are transmitted) until the excessive collision condition is removed.

As with 100 Mb/s repeaters, Gigabit Ethernet repeaters ensure that the incoming
bit stream is free of 8B/10B code violations. Any incoming bit stream that is detected
to have a code violation is replaced by an 8B/10B code-group that indicates an error.
This substitution continues until the incoming bit stream returns to the idle state.

Gigabit repeaters are specified to operate only at a single speed, 1000 Mb/s. The
operation of repeaters that support multiple speeds (100 Mb/s and 1000 Mb/s) is not
specified and is outside the scope of the standards.

On Topologies and Bit Budgets

The construction of repeater-based networks always involves a detailed analysis of
bit budgets. Due to the nature of the CSMA/CD protocol, the time taken[36] for a packet
to traverse the entire length of the network (and back) is of utmost importance. As repeater-based networks grow, this time, or propagation delay, lengthens. If the round-
trip propagation delay exceeds the maximum end-to-end delay of 512 bit times, the
CSMA/CD protocol is subject to errors, late collisions, and other misbehavior. For
Gigabit Ethernet, the propagation delay is obviously a single order of magnitude more
stringent than for 100 Mb/s Ethernet.

---

[35] Remember that the maximum transmission size on an Ethernet is limited to 1518 bytes.
[36] Usually analyzed in bits.

In both 10 Mb/s and 100 Mb/s networks, repeater-based network construction involves detailed bit-budget calculations.[37] The reason is that in 10 Mb/s networks multiple repeaters were allowed in a single collision domain. Each additional repeater used to construct the network added to the round-trip propagation delay. By restricting 1000 Mb/s repeaters to one in any single collision domain, the calculation of bit budgets becomes far simpler and easier. The round-trip propagation delay is simply the delay through one repeater, two links, and two stations. Gigabit Ethernet networks using repeaters are restricted to a single repeater per collision domain. The construction of larger networks is accomplished by using bridges, switches, or routers to partition the Ethernet network into separate, distinct collision domains. This is explained in more detail in the section on "Topology (Clause 42)."

4.12.2 Summary

Gigabit Ethernet repeaters provide the ability to connect two independent Gigabit Ethernet segments, possibly operating over different media, into a single collision domain. Like its slower counterparts, the Gigabit Ethernet repeater performs the physical-layer functions of signal restoration, signal reception and retransmission, CSMA/CD collision handling, and various error-handling functions such as jabber protection and network partitioning. Unlike its 10 Mb/s and 100 Mb/s counterparts, only a single Gigabit Ethernet repeater is allowed in any one collision domain, and no interrepeater link is defined. Therefore, the Gigabit Ethernet repeater is useful only in very small topologies where only a single repeater is required. In fact, the maximum topological extent is 100 m from the repeater to any station. Unlike half-duplex, shared-media gigabit repeater networks, the topological extent of full-duplex networks is not limited by the round-trip propagation delay. Due to topological restrictions, coupled with the throughput and performance limitations of half-duplex CSMA/CD-based protocols operating at 1000 Mb/s, gigabit repeaters will not see widespread use. They will be confined to connecting small numbers of Gigabit Ethernet stations over a very limited geography such as a wiring closet. The cost effectiveness of switching solutions, their ability to operate over full-duplex links, and their wider topological uses allow them to be used in most instances where, previously, a simple repeater would do.

---

[37] See *Fast Ethernet—Dawn of a New Network* by Dr. Howard Johnson for a detailed analysis on 100 Mb/s repeater bit budgets.

4.13 Topology (Clause 42)

Clause 42 of the IEEE802.3z standard gives information on building 1000 Mb/s networks. Specifically, this section provides models for building shared networks.

In shared gigabit networks, the slot time is specified as 512 bytes or 4096 bits
(see Chapter 4 for slot-time discussion). This provides a constraint on the network diameter, which is defined as distance between two nodes. Two or more collision domains may be interconnected with a bridge, switch, or a router. Figure 4-51 shows a
multisegment network interconnected with a bridge (see Chapter 2 for a definition of
bridge).

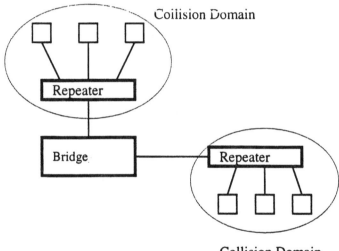

Figure 4-51 Interconnection of Multisegment Shared Networks

A switch can be considered as an interconnection of multisegment networks
with a segment size of one. The segments could be full-duplex or half-duplex or a
combination of full-duplex and half-duplex ports. Figure 4-52 shows a network with
several segments consisting of full-duplex and half-duplex ports.

4.13.1 Model 1 Topology

The following section provide information on building networks of single collision
domain. Two basic models are presented. Model 1 provides a simple template of topologies, which are shown in Figure 4-53. Figures 4-53a and b show two DTEs di-

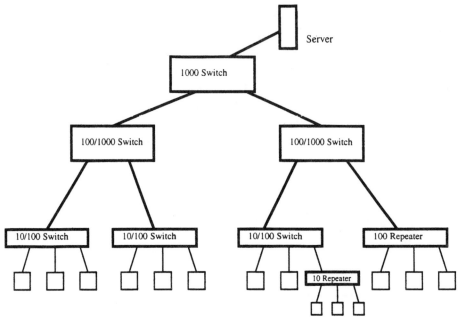

Figure 4-52 Switched Network Interconnection

rectly connected to each other without a repeater. This configuration is the simplest of all topologies. The link between the DTEs is Cat 5 balanced cable (1000BASE-T) or short copper cable (1000BASE-CX) or fiber (1000BASE-SX, 1000BASE-LX). The link lengths vary from 25 m for short copper to 316 m for fiber (Table 4-24).

Table 4-24 Maximum Collision Diameter between Two DTEs without Repeater (Model 1)

Link Type	Maximum Link Length (meters)
Cat 5 balanced copper	100
Short copper cable	25
Fiber	316

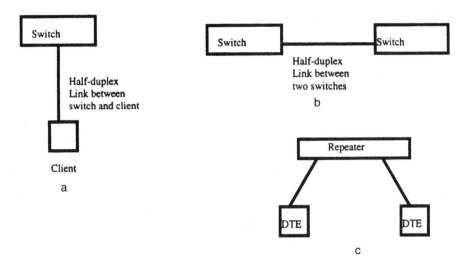

Figure 4-53 Model 1 Topologies

In Figure 4-53c a single repeater is used to connect DTEs. The maximum diameter of the network is basically limited by the collision round-trip delay. Two links of 100 m Cat 5 balanced cable, or two links of 25 m short copper cable or two links of 110 m fiber can be connected with a single repeater (Table 4-25).

Table 4-25 Maximum Collision Diameter between Two DTEs with Single Repeater (Model 1)

Link Type	Maximum Link Length (meters)
Cat 5 balanced copper	200
Short copper cable	50
Fiber	220

4.13.2 Model 2 Topology: Bit-Budget Analysis

While Model 1 topology defines simple networks that always satisfy the constraints imposed by a single collision domain, other networks need to be evaluated to see if the round-trip collision delay is satisfied. This is done by examining the round-trip collision delay between every pair of DTEs. The maximum round-trip collision delay for 1000 Mb/s operation must be less than 4096 bit times.

Network Component Delays

Figure 4-54 illustrates the components of network delays. As shown in the figure, the round-trip collision delay includes DTE delays, cable delays, and repeater delays. These delays have to be multiplied by two since we are interested in the round-trip delay. The round-trip collision delay for each path must be validated using the following formula:[38]

> Round-Trip (RT) delay = Σ link delays + repeater delay + Σ DTE delays + safety margin

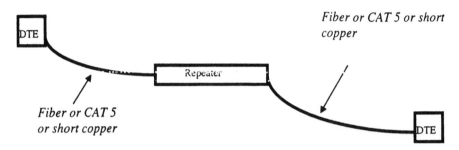

Figure 4-54 Illustration of Network Component Delays

The link delays for each segment are calculated as follows:

> link delay = Σ × segment length in meters × cable delay/meter

If the cable delays, repeater delays, and DTE delays are not specified by the manufacturer, then the default values[39] as shown in Tables 4-26 and 4-27 should be used. A safety margin is used to provide a margin for unanticipated delays in the network components. Generally, a safety margin of 32 bit times is recommended. The values are then inserted in the equation for round trip delay. If the calculated RT delay is less than 4096 bit times then the path satisfies the collision delay requirements. If the collision delay exceeds 4096 bit times, then late collision and/or CRC errors may occur in the network.

Figure 4-55 illustrates an example network configuration that needs to be validated. There are three DTEs, A, B, and C, which are interconnected to each other through a repeater with link segments of fiber, Cat 5 cable, and short copper cable,

---

[38] IEEE802.3z—Media Access Control (MAC) Parameters, Physical Layer, Repeater and Management Parameters for 1000 Mb/s Operation, Clause 42.

[39] These values are worst-case maximum. However, a manufacturer may specify a value lower than specified in Tables 4-26 and 4-27.

Table 4-26 Cable Delays

Cable Type	Round-Trip Delay (bit times/m)	Maximum Round-Trip Delay (bit times)
Fiber optic cable	10.10	1111 (110 m)
1000BASE-CX cable	10.10	253 (25 m)
Cat 5 cable	11.12	1112 (100 m)

Table 4-27 Network Component Delays

Network Component	Maximum Round-Trip Delay (bit times)
DTE	432
Repeater	976

respectively. To validate the network configuration, the round-trip collision delay between DTE pairs, A-B, A-C, and B-C needs to be calculated. Table 4-28 shows the bit-budget calculation for the DTE pairs.

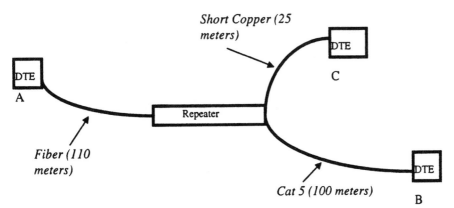

Figure 4-55 An Example Network Configuration (Half Duplex)

Table 4-28 Round-Trip Collision Delay between DTE pairs (bit times)

Network Component	A-B	A-C	B-C
DTE A	432	432	432
Link segment 1	1111	1111	1112
Repeater	976	976	976
Link segment 2	1112	253	253

Table 4-28 Round-Trip Collision Delay between DTE pairs (bit times) (Continued)

DTE B	432	432	432
Safety margin	32	32	32
Total	4095	3236	3237

In the table, we have used the default values for network component delays, which are conservative. As shown, the round-trip collision delay is less than 4096 bit times. This validates the example network configuration.

4.13.3 Full-Duplex Configuration

In a full-duplex environment, since the transmit and the receive paths are independent, there is no collision of packets between DTEs. The distances between the DTEs are primarily limited by the characteristics of the link between the DTE and the transceivers used in the PHY. Figure 4-56 gives an example configuration of a switch connected to different DTEs by different links.

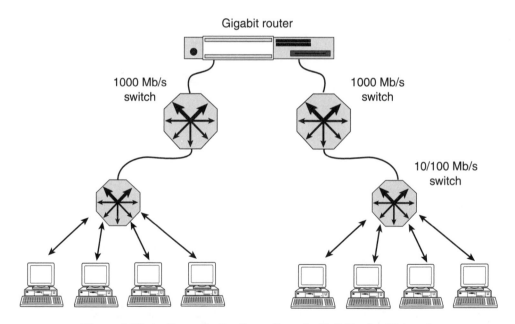

Figure 4-56 An Example Configuration of a Full-Duplex Network

4.14 Management (Clause 30)

Network management is required to handle special activities of initialization, termination, and monitoring of activities of devices in a network. Typically, network management is viewed as a distributed application which interacts with other management processes in the network. The network-management system typically consists of a "manager," which executes the managing process. The management process (local agent) within the managed device interacts with the manager and provides an interface to the resource to be managed. Figure 4-57 defines the interaction between the manager, agent, and the managed objects.[40]

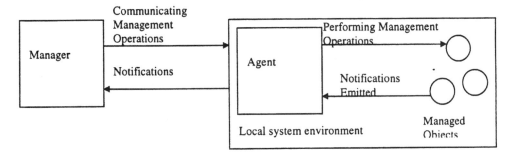

Figure 4-57 Interaction between Manager, Agent, and Objects
(From IEEE Std. P802.3z, IEEE. All rights reserved.)

A managed object is a resource from the management point of view. The resource might be physical device or a logical construct or function. A managed object provides a means to identify, control, and monitor a resource. The agent resides within the local device and collects information from the managed objects. The collection of information could be accomplished in one of several ways. The agent based on external network command could query the managed object. Alternatively, special notifications or periodic information delivery mechanisms could be used.

4.14.1 Management Protocols

A management protocol is one that is used to monitor and/or control devices and that gets information on the managed devices. Common management protocols are SNMP (Simple Network Management Protocol) and CMIP (Common Management Information Protocol). SNMP by far is the most popular management protocol in use today.

---

[40] IEEE 802.3z—Media Access Control (MAC) Parameters, Physical Layer, Repeater and Management Parameters for 1000 Mb/s Operation (Clause 30). Originally from ISO/IEC 10040, Fig. 1.

In SNMP protocol, five protocol data units (PDUs) are used to exchange network information. SNMP protocol is simple to implement on a large network. Since the design is simple, SNMP can be expanded as the network expands to accommodate user needs. Its disadvantages are lack of adequate security and of detailed information about managed objects. These issues are addressed in the newer version of SNMP, namely SNMPv2.

CMIP was designed to address several shortcomings of SNMP. In CMIP, 11 PDUs are used to exchange network information. These PDUs provide detailed information about the managed objects and are used to provide new functionality not available in SNMP. However, CMIP takes up significant resources compared to SNMP. As a result, it is not widely used.

4.14.2 Management Information Base (MIB)

A MIB specifies the different counters, status events, alarms, and notifications for each managed device. The MIBs are different for different devices. Clause 30 of IEEE 802.3z provides a standard for defining the MIB. In Fast Ethernet, Clause 30 was consolidated to include IEEE 802.3 Clauses 5, 19, and 20. Clause 30 now defines MIB objects, attributes, notifications, and behavior for (1) 10 Mb/s DTE, 10 Mb/s baseband repeater and 10 Mb/s integrated MAU (2) 100 Mb/s DTE, 100 Mb/s baseband repeater, and 100 Mb/s PHY, and (3) 1000 Mb/s DTE, 1000 Mb/s baseband repeater, and 1000 Mb/s PHY.

A managed object is defined by attributes, actions, notifications, and behavior. These are grouped into "packages" within a managed object class. Packages are either mandatory or conditional. A conditional package is present when a given condition is true. A set of packages is defined as "capabilities," which are functions of managed objects grouped logically. The capabilities defined for DTE, repeater, and MAU are shown in Tables 4-29, 4-30, and 4-31, respectively. The tables give a brief overview of the contents of the capabilities. Readers should refer to the IEEE 8023.z[41] standards document for detail information on each MIB.

Table 4-29 MIB Capabilities for DTE

Capability	Description
Basic	Detection of device, initialize device, read device ID numbers
Mandatory	Count frames transmitted and received; count frames with single collision, multiple collision, FCS errors, and alignment errors
Recommended Package (optimal)	Count frames with additional granularity in errors such as late collisions, deferred transmissions, carrier sense errors, etc.
Optional Package (optional)	Count multicast frames transmitted and received, broadcast frames transmitted and received, frame length errors, control of MAC transmit and receive operations

---

[41] IEEE 802.3z—Media Access Control (MAC) Parameters, Physical Layer, Repeater and Management Parameters for 1000 Mb/s Operation (Clause 30).

Table 4-29 MIB Capabilities for DTE (Continued)

Array Package (optional)	Histogram of collisions
Excessive Deferral Package (optional)	Count frames with excessive deferral. A high count indicates frames waiting too long, possibly congestion
Multiply PHY Package (optional)	Allows enabling and disability of a PHY, when multiple PHYs are defined per MAC entity
100/1000 Mb/s Monitor Capability (optional)	Monitor symbol errors

Table 4-30 MIB Capabilities for Repeater

Capability	Description
Basic Control Capability (mandatory)	Obtain repeater ID, type, status, and transmit collision. Also obtain port ID, port partition state, etc.
Performance Monitor Capability (optional)	Count valid frames, statistics on collisions, errors, runts—indicates partition state of a port
Address Tracking Capability (optional)	Tracks source addresses of packets
100/1000 Mb/s Monitor Capability (optional)	Monitor symbol errors, port isolation
1000 Mb/s Burst Monitor Capability (optional)	New performance attributes for 1000 Mb/s operation. Count of number of times frame bursting is employed

Table 4-31 MIB Capabilities for MAU

Capability	Description
Basic Package (mandatory)	Obtain MAU ID numbers, detect and initialize MAUs, availability of media
MAU Control Package (optional)	Reset, standby, operational, and shutdown commands
Media Loss Tracking Package (conditional)	Report count of media not available
Broadband DTE MAU Package (conditional)	This package is specific to broadband MAU such as 10BROAD36
MII Capability (conditional)	Report MII type
100/1000 Mb/s Monitor Capability	Count of false carrier events and idle errors

In addition, there is an Auto-Negotiation package which is mandatory. The Auto-Negotiation package contains the MIB for technology and link configuration between the DTE and the link partner.

4.14.3 MIB Additions for Gigabit Operation

One optional package, 1000 Mb/s Burst Monitor Capability, is added for 1000 Mb/s operation. This package is valid only at 1000 Mb/s. An MIB counter, "aBursts," is incremented every time the frame-bursting feature is used by the DTE.

Gigabit Ethernet Applications

Like any innovative networking technology, Gigabit Ethernet must be evaluated on its merits to determine whether it meets a genuine market need or is just a networking solution looking for a problem. This chapter presents an evaluation of current networking trends, applications and needs, as well as Gigabit Ethernet's applicability to fulfill these market needs. It begins by providing a brief description of the evolution of networks, followed by the application and network migration strategies for Gigabit Ethernet. This is followed by a comparison of emerging switching protocols that will be used to design and develop Gigabit Ethernet switches and routers. The chapter concludes with a comparison of Gigabit Ethernet with ATM and FDDI.

5.1 Networking Evolution

The most significant evolutionary trend in networking today is the Internet. Its use for data collection, business development, on-line shopping, and multimedia applications, based on the myriad of Web-based technologies, has transformed the Internet from its traditional roots as an e-mail and file-transfer system. These new applications have increased the number of network users that depend upon the Internet to conduct business on a daily basis. This has resulted in a geometric growth in traffic and a permanent change in the nature of enterprise networks. One of the most significant changes is the complete unpredictability of network traffic patterns that has resulted from the combination of Internet traffic, intranet traffic, and the increase in multicast applications such as videoconferencing and push-applications such as PointCast™. The 80/20 rule, which states that only 20 percent of all traffic in a network uses the backbone and 80 percent of the traffic is local, has been officially declared moribund by today's Internet. The ease with which a user can utilize a Web browser to access remote information anywhere on the corporate Internet, regardless of location, means that traffic patterns that used to be dictated by the local servers are now being dictated by the users' thirst for information.

The long-term implication of the growth of the Internet and the applications that use it for business purposes is that the users' appetite for bandwidth will grow exponentially. Specific requirements may include tens, if not hundreds of gigabits per second of total network capacity, multicast communications, and a smooth migration from today's market base that can be incrementally added anywhere in the network.

Shared 10 Mb/s Ethernet, pioneered in the 1970s, though still the most widely used network in the world, has long been unable to absorb the rapidly increasing traffic volumes in network backbones. It is for this reason that faster variations, such as switched 10 Mb/s Ethernet, shared 100 Mb/s Ethernet, and, more recently, switched 100 Mb/s Ethernet have emerged to dramatically improve performance for corporate Internet and intranet users. As organizations use increasingly complex applications, network administrators are deploying 10 Mb/s switched Ethernet and 100 Mb/s switched Ethernet connectivity at the network edges and boundaries. In fact, in some cases this advanced technology is being deployed at the desktop and server connections to service power users. However, as high-speed technology migrates toward the desktop, the bandwidth pressure on the network backbones and access points increases to a point where severe bottlenecks occur. Enter Gigabit Ethernet.

5.2 Gigabit Ethernet Meets the Challenge

Simply put, Gigabit Ethernet will maintain compatibility with the nearly 100 million strong 10 Mb/s Ethernet and 100 Mb/s Ethernet installed base, while providing a significant bandwidth increase. Tables 5-1 and 5-2 provide a comparison of Gigabit Ethernet with 10 Mb/s Ethernet, 100 Mb/s Ethernet, and the topologies in which Gigabit Ethernet can be deployed. As shown in the tables, Gigabit Ethernet allows both half and full duplex operation over a variety of physical interfaces (fiber and copper) and topologies. This wide range of topological choices will allow Gigabit Ethernet to be implemented in LANs of all sizes. The choice of topology and physical interface will depend on the particular network application. For example, switched topologies generally provide the longest distance and high throughput, whereas shared topologies provide lower cost but have shorter distance capabilities and lower throughput.

Table 5-1 Comparison of Gigabit Ethernet, 100Base-T, and 10Base-T

Feature	10Base-T Ethernet	100Base-T Fast Ethernet	1000Base-T Gigabit Ethernet
Data Rate	10 Mb/s	100 Mb/s	1 Gb/s
Category 5 UTP	100 m	100 m	100 m
STP/Coaxial Cable	500 m	100 m	25 m
Multimode Fiber	2 km	412 m (half duplex) 2 km (full duplex)	220 m (half duplex)
Single-Mode Fiber	25 km	20 km	5 km

Table 5-2 Gigabit Ethernet Topologies

Topology	Objective	Modes	Media	Application
Switched	High throughput Long distance	Full duplex Half duplex	Multimode fiber Single-mode fiber Copper	Campus backbone Building backbone Wiring closet upgrade Server farms
Shared	Low cost Short distance	Half duplex	Multimode fiber Copper	Server farms Desktops

Gigabit Ethernet's power and versatility will allow it to be configured in a variety of applications and topologies. These applications include but are not limited to the following:

- Switch-to-server connections
- Corporate backbones (intrabuilding and interbuilding) for LAN interconnection
- Intercampus backbones
- Backbones for factory automation
- Workgroup and departmental LANs.

These applications and the applicability of Gigabit Ethernet to upgrade an existing network are discussed in the forthcoming sections, keeping in mind that the majority of current networks consist of 10Base-T, 100Base-T, FDDI, and ATM.

5.2.1 Bandwidth

Gigabit Ethernet offers a dramatic increase in pure bandwidth available to the user. It offers a hundred fold improvement over 10 Mb/s Ethernet and a tenfold improvement over 100 Mb/s Ethernet. This massive bandwidth improvement translates into the ability for organizations to meet the challenges of overburdened and dramatically growing network infrastructures. Gigabit data rates will allow corporate network backbones to be scaled to relieve congestion caused by the demise of the 80/20 rule. Firms will be able to expedite large file transfers between servers and clients, servers and the Internet and other devices. Large, overnight file backups and multiprocessor applications become more feasible and less costly to perform. Manufacturers will be able to efficiently transfer large

CAD/CAM files, and marketers will be able to extract customer information from databases with more speed. In addition, the bandwidth boost will allow network managers to link increasingly powerful server farms directly to network backbones.

5.2.2 Migration

Gigabit Ethernet maintains the IEEE 802.3 and Ethernet standard frame formats as well as the network-management capabilities of IEEE 802.3. As shown in Tables 5-1 and 5-2, Gigabit Ethernet also operates over the same wiring infrastructure as 10 Mb/s and 100 Mb/s Ethernet, as well as the wiring infrastructure used by FDDI and ATM-based networks. As a result, organizations can easily upgrade to gigabit speeds while preserving all their existing software applications, operating systems, network-management applications, and network protocols such as TCP/IP, AppleTalk, and IPX. In addition, their existing network wiring infrastructure can be used by new Gigabit Ethernet hardware.

It is rarely the case that a network is installed from scratch or by removing all existing traces of the previous network. Due to its Ethernet-based architecture, Gigabit Ethernet deployment can be incremental, as will be the case for most complicated networks, so as to cause minimal disruption to the existing user base. When possible, new users, new applications, and high-performance servers can also be installed centrally at a wiring closet or data center. Gigabit Ethernet's ability to run over multiple media and varying topologies also allows network resources to be distributed over a geographic range.

5.2.3 Network Management

Gigabit Ethernet utilizes the same principles and therefore provides the same management tasks as today's 10 Mb/s and 100 Mb/s shared and switched networks. Managed objects, attributes, and actions are all defined for Gigabit Ethernet networks in a manner identical to 10 Mb/s and 100 Mb/s networks. This allows the seamless management of 10/100/1000 integrated networks. Administrators will provide additional bandwidth to users without requiring a new systemwide network management system. Total cost of ownership, an important criterion in upgrading or migrating to new networks, will be lower for gigabit-Ethernet-based networks than ATM or non Ethernet-based networks due to its heavy reliance on existing technology and standards.

5.3 Gigabit Ethernet Migration

Gigabit Ethernet is 100 Mb/s Ethernet, only 10 times faster. Therefore, the application space for Gigabit Ethernet is simply the same application space as for Fast Ethernet. As an added bonus, due to its tremendous bandwidth, ability to support single-mode fiber, and use of IEEE 802 frame formats, Gigabit Ethernet is an ideally suited for integration and migration of FDDI-based backbones

A few typical migration scenarios are described below, in chronological order of deployment. The initial applications for Gigabit Ethernet will be for campuses or buildings that require greater bandwidth between their individual routers, servers, 10 Mb/s and 100 Mb/s switches and backbones. Specific examples include switch-to-switch, switch-to-router, and switch-to-server connections. In its early phases, Gigabit Ethernet is not expected to be deployed widely to the desktop, but with the completion of the 1000Base-T standards, coupled with the inevitable price declines, this is expected to change.

5.3.1 Switch-to-Switch Upgrades

An obvious first application for Gigabit Ethernet is as a 100 Mb/s Ethernet switch upgrade. This involves replacing existing 100 Mb/s connections between switches with Gigabit Ethernet links. In such a scenario, a Gigabit Ethernet network interface card module must be installed in existing 100 Mb/s switches, and those switches should be connected together via the Gigabit Ethernet connections. If the 100 Mb/s switches do not offer the modular connections, the switches will have to be replaced completely. Figure 5-1 illustrates a typical switched network based on 10 Mb/s and 100 Mb/s switches that provided dedicated and semi-dedicated connections between the end users and servers using switches and repeaters. Due to the unpredictable nature of traffic flow, it is more than likely that the backbone link connecting the two 100 Mb/s switches is a source of congestion and is a perfect application for a short-haul, full-duplex Gigabit Ethernet link. Such high-bandwidth, switch-to-switch links enable the network backbone to support a much greater number of both switched and shared 10 Mb/s and 100 Mb/s Ethernet segments. Figure 5-2 illustrates the network after a Gigabit Ethernet upgrade. The 100 Mb/s switches have been modified by the addition of a Gigabit Ethernet link that is used to connect the switches together. The connections between Gigabit Ethernet switches will typically use a full-duplex link to maximize throughput. In addition, since it is more than likely that the switches are not collocated, 850 nm multimode fiber will be required for the connection. However, if the switches are collocated in the same wiring closet, it is possible that a 25 m short-haul copper interconnect may be used.

Figure 5-2 shows the connections between the 100 Mb/s switches being upgraded to gigabit links, though the connections to the servers remain at 100 Mb/s. Since traffic flow between the endusers is generally toward servers, these connections will also be the source of bottlenecks. They are also an ideal application for a Gigabit Ethernet upgrade.

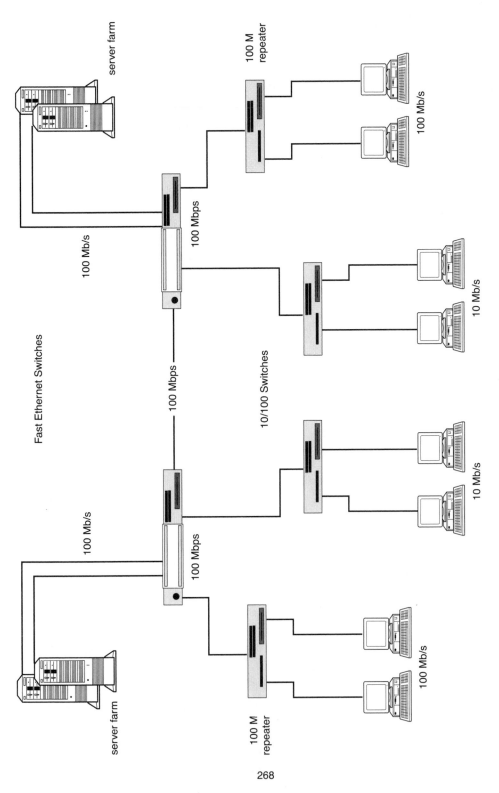

Figure 5-1 Existing Switched Network (From Gigabit Ethernet Alliance, with permission.)

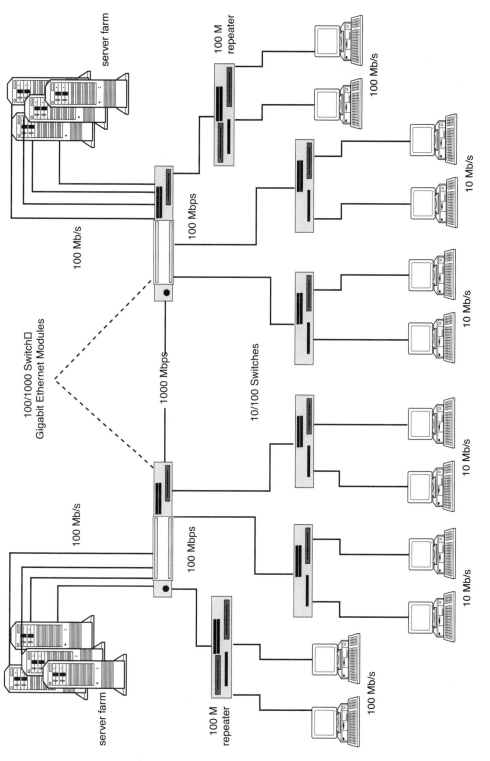

Figure 5-2 Upgraded Switched Network (From Gigabit Ethernet Alliance, with permission.)

5.3.2 Switch-to-Server Upgrades

Another application for Gigabit Ethernet is as a 1000 Mb/s upgrade for servers. Todays high-performance servers are typically connected to switches, as shown in Figure 5-3, with the use of 100Base-TX network interface cards. Upgrading to Gigabit Ethernet involves replacing the 100 Mb/s connections between the servers and switches with Gigabit Ethernet links. In such a scenario, a Gigabit Ethernet network interface card module must be installed in the existing 100 Mb/s servers and switches and connected together via the Gigabit Ethernet connections. As before, if the 100 Mb/s switches do not offer the modular connections, the switches will have to be replaced completely. Figure 5-3 illustrates a typical server/client network based on 10 Mb/s and 100 Mb/s switches that provided dedicated and semidedicated connections between the end users and servers using switches and repeaters. Figure 5-4 illustrates the network after a Gigabit Ethernet upgrade. After the upgrade, the network capacity of the server farms will allow speedier access to server-based data across the network. The connections between the switches and servers can use short-haul copper if the server and switches are centrally located together and are within 25 meters; e.g., they are collocated in a floor wiring closet. Otherwise a multimode 850 nm fiber connection will be required. Typically, in order to maximize bandwidth usage a full-duplex connection will be used.

5.3.3 Corporate Building and Campus Backbone Upgrades

Perhaps the optimal application for Gigabit Ethernet is currently the building backbone upgrade. In this application, Gigabit Ethernet is deployed for backbone links in the building risers that connect centrally located switches, routers, and network-management entities to the wiring closet that is present on each floor of a building. Each wiring closet, as well as the centrally located data center switch or router will require a Gigabit Ethernet link. Figure 5-5 shows a typical building and campus configuration after a Gigabit Ethernet upgrade. Referring to Table 5-2, we see that in the building environment, multimode fiber is used in the building riser, and in the campus environment single-mode fiber is used to connect the Gigabit Ethernet links. The server-to-switch Gigabit Ethernet connections can utilize either short-haul copper connections, if they are within 25 m of the switch, or multimode fiber connections.

5.4 Switched or Shared 100 Mb/s Ethernet and FDDI Upgrade

FDDI is still one of the dominant high-speed technologies in many campus and building infrastructures. Its inherent fault-tolerant capabilities and dependable performance characteristics ensure that it is used in both backbone and mission-critical network applications. Most FDDI campus networks have the majority of stations connected on shared or segment-switched Ethernet, therefore leveraging the existing in-

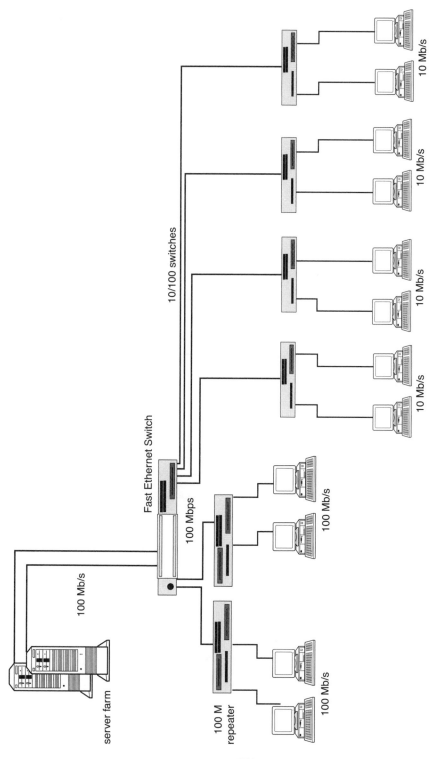

Figure 5-3 Existing Switched Server Network (From Gigabit Ethernet Alliance, with permission.)

server farm

100 Mb/s

Fast Ethernet Switch

100 Mbps

100 M repeater

100 Mb/s

100 Mb/s

100 Mb/s

10/100 switches

10 Mb/s

10 Mb/s

10 Mb/s

10 Mb/s

10 Mb/s

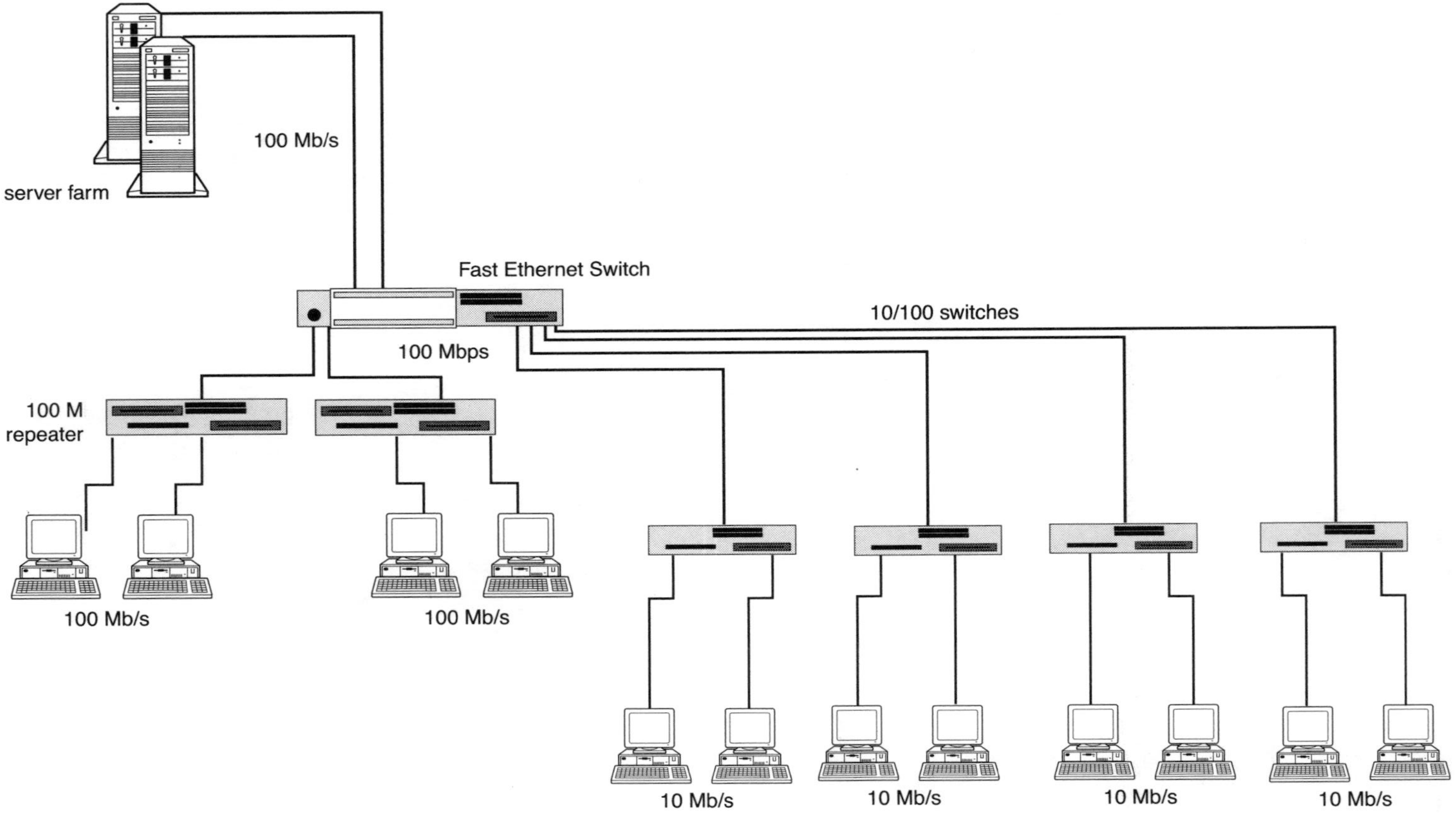

Figure 5-4 Upgraded Switched Server Network (From Gigabit Ethernet Alliance, with permission.)

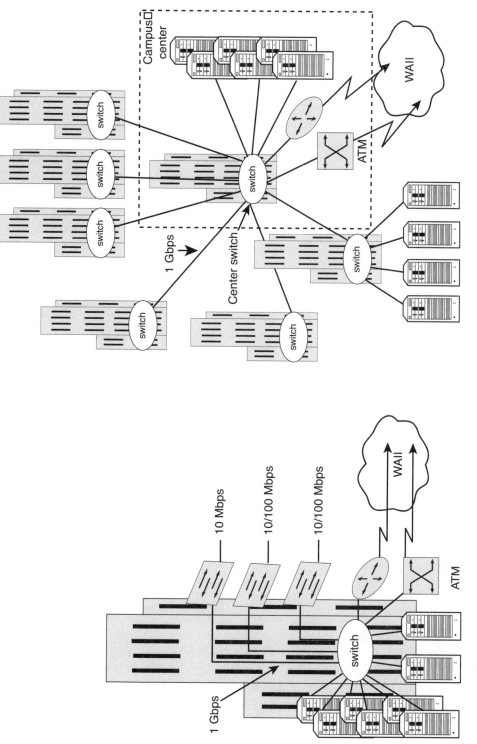

Figure 5-5 Building and Campus Gigabit Ethernet Upgrade (From Gigabit Ethernet Alliance, with permission.)

vestment toward Fast Ethernet and Gigabit Ethernet is the obvious choice. Migration is always a gradual, controlled process, balancing risk, investment, and stability. Co-existence of FDDI with 10/100/1000-Mb/s Ethernet (all speeds) is vital to achieve this end goal. Therefore, most current network backbones that use either FDDI or 100 Mb/s Ethernet are ideal candidates for Gigabit Ethernet upgrades.

A 100 Mb/s Ethernet or FDDI backbone switch aggregating multiple 10/100 switches that is upgraded to a 100/1000 switch will allow high-performance servers to be directly connected to the network backbone. This will increase the throughput to the servers and allow a faster response time for all users involved. Also, the network can support a much larger number of segments and, correspondingly, a much larger number of users. The upgrade involves replacing 100 Mb/s switches with Gigabit Ethernet switches. In such a scenario, a Gigabit Ethernet network interface card module must be installed in existing 100 Mb/s switches, and those modules should be connected to the Gigabit Ethernet backbone switch via the Gigabit Ethernet connections. If the 100 Mb/s switches do not offer the modular connections, the switches will have to be replaced completely. Figure 5-6 illustrates a typical switched 100 Mb/s network that provides dedicated and semidedicated connections between the end users and servers using switches. Figure 5-7 illustrates the network after a Gigabit Ethernet upgrade. The connections between Gigabit Ethernet switches and modules will typically use a full-duplex link to maximize throughput. In addition, since it is more than likely that the switches are not collocated, 850 nm multimode fiber will be required for the connection. However, if the switches are collocated in the same wiring closet, it is possible that a 25 m short-haul copper interconnect may be used.

5.4.1 Desktop Upgrade

In later phases of Gigabit Ethernet deployment, especially after the completion and availability of long-haul category 5 copper hardware, Gigabit Ethernet may be deployed at the desktop. In time, as desktops increase their computing power and, as a result, their thirst for bandwidth rises, they will be candidates for a Gigabit Ethernet upgrade. Currently, most desktops connect to the network using 10Base-T or 100Base-T Ethernet. Since these desktops require category 5 UTP cabling connections, the current short-haul copper cabling will be insufficient for this application. Once this capability is broadly available, it is possible that existing desktops will be upgraded to Gigabit Ethernet.

Figure 5-8 shows this application. As shown, the high-speed power-user workgroup environment can be connected with a Gigabit Ethernet switch, a Gigabit Ethernet repeater, or a buffered distributor or full duplex repeater[1]. The full duplex repeater is described in more detail in the following section, but a brief comparison of the features and uses of a repeater (shared media), a buffered distributor (full-duplex repeater), and a gigabit switch is given in Table 5-3.

---

[1] Buffered distributor and full-duplex repeater are used synonymously.

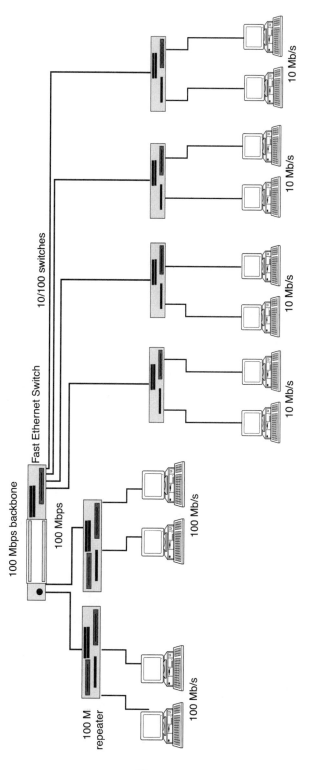

Figure 5-6 100 Mb/s Ethernet Backbone Network (From Gigabit Ethernet Alliance, with permission.)

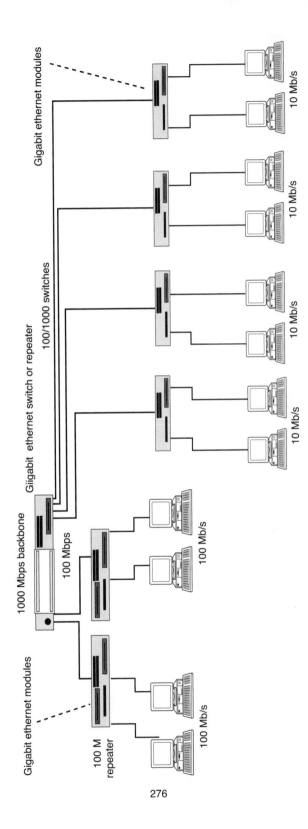

Figure 5-7 1000 Mb/s Ethernet Backbone Network (From Gigabit Ethernet Alliance, with permission.)

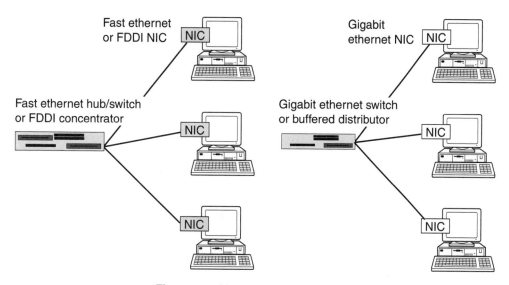

Figure 5-8 Gigabit Desktop Upgrade

Table 5-3 Comparison of Gigabit Ethernet Interconnect Mechanisms

Feature	Gigabit Repeater	Full-Duplex Repeater	Gigabit Switch
Duplex Operation	Half-duplex 1000 Mb/s is shared by all connected devices	Full-duplex dedicated 1000 Mb/s connection to all connected devices	Full-duplex dedicated 1000 Mb/s connection to all connected devices
Network Diameter	200 meters	Maximum allowed[a]	Maximum allowed[b]
Implementation Complexity/Cost	Low	Moderate to high	High
Performance	Depends upon network diameter, number of networks and loading, but less than 1000 Mb/s	1000 Mb/s	Up to a maximum of switch bandwidth, usually multiple gigabits
Congestion and Flow Control	No	Yes	Yes
QoS Guarantees	No	No	Yes
Ethernet Collisions	Yes	No	No
Layer 3 Capability	No	No	Yes

[a] See Table 5-1
[b] See Table 5-1

When connecting two or more Gigabit Ethernet Network Interface Cards (NICs), a Gigabit Ethernet repeater is the most inexpensive method. It will provide simple gigabit connectivity to two or more stations in a manner exactly similar to conventional 10 Mb/s Ethernet or 100 Mb/s Ethernet. However, due to the inherent nature of the Ethernet protocol, overall network utilization will never exceed 1000 Mb/s, though each station is capable of bursting at that rate. The full-duplex repeater provides a dedicated full-duplex Gigabit Ethernet link to every attached station to achieve point-to-point connectivity such as that of a switch. Since the connections are full-duplex, collisions are eliminated, and IEEE 802.3x flow control is utilized to monitor and control data transmissions. In cases where network expandability is of a major concern, a Gigabit Ethernet switch should be used.

Full-Duplex Repeater

Standard Ethernet repeaters are, by their very nature, half-duplex entities. In a repeater-based network, one station that begins transmission and gains control of the network is the only station that is transmitting at any given moment in time. Repeaters are generally used to connect together two or more Ethernet segments or stations. As segments exceed their maximum length, signal quality begins to deteriorate, and repeaters provide the signal amplification required to allow a segment to be extended a greater distance. A repeater takes any incoming signal and repeats it to all ports other than the port on which the signal originated. In addition, it performs a few other housekeeping functions such as preamble regeneration, error detection (jabber), and the like. It operates transparently to the data-link layer (MAC) and simply passes incoming packets through without modifications. A multiport, twisted-pair Gigabit Ethernet repeater allows several point-to-point segments to be joined into one network. One end of the point-to-point link is attached to the repeater and the other to a desktop, server, or other repeater. If the repeater is attached to a backbone, then all computers at the end of the twisted-pair segments can communicate with all the hosts on the backbone. The number and type of repeaters in any one collision domain is limited in the case of Gigabit Ethernet to one.

The main fact to note about repeaters is that they only allow users to share the Ethernet. A network of repeaters is termed a *shared Ethernet*, meaning that all members of the network are contending for transmission of data onto a single network (collision domain). This essentially forces individual members of a shared network to share a percentage of the available network bandwidth. Due to their simplicity, Ethernet repeaters have been a hugely successful method of interconnecting small workgroups.

A full-duplex repeater, shown in Figure 5-9, is similar in function and configuration to a standard Ethernet repeater. It consists of multiple Gigabit Ethernet ports that allow a simple and inexpensive aggregation of Gigabit Ethernet stations. It differs from a standard repeater in one very important respect: it is full-duplex. The full-duplex repeater consists of multiple ports, one for each attaching desktop or server. However, unlike a standard repeater, each of the ports includes a Gigabit Ethernet physical layer, a Gigabit Ethernet MAC controller, and frame buffers for incoming and outgoing frames.

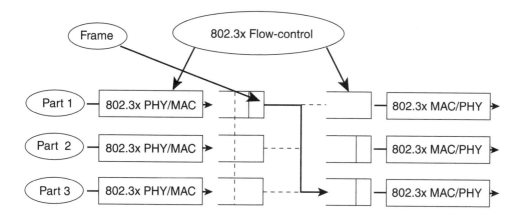

Figure 5-9 Full-Duplex Repeater Architecture

Referring to Figure 5-9, a logical flow of packets entering and leaving a full-du-plex repeater can be drawn. An incoming frame enters the full-duplex repeater at port 1. The frame waits in the input queue until it is selected for transmission to the out-puts. Once this occurs, the selected port transmits this frame to all other ports.[2] In the case of this example, the incoming frame exits on ports 2 and 3. Therefore, unlike a conventional repeater, the full-duplex repeater is a store-and-forward device that con-tains a MAC, much like a switch or router. Every frame flowing through a full-duplex repeater passes through the input Gigabit Ethernet MAC prior to being queued in a buffer for forwarding. The input PHY converts the data signal on the wire or optical fiber into a digital data stream for the MAC to process. The MAC processes this dig-ital data at the frame level to make sure that the frame is valid and has no errors. It therefore has the ability to check the incoming frame for MAC (or data-link) errors and to terminate these frames.

If multiple frames arrive at input ports simultaneously, a forwarding protocol such as round-robin is used to sequentially repeat frames in order from input ports to all output ports. Due to the internal input buffers in the full-duplex repeater, multiple incoming transmissions can be handled simultaneously. Since it is possible that mul-tiple input ports may be transmitting simultaneously and the connections are full-du-plex, the input buffers of a full-duplex repeater may become congested just as that of a switch or router. This is due to the fact that the total aggregate input rate is the num-

---

[2] In this respect, the full-duplex repeater and conventional repeater are the same. The incom-ing frame is copied to all output ports other than the input.

ber of ports multiplied by the line rate (1000 Mb/s) but the total output rate is 1000 Mb/s. The full-duplex repeater relies on IEEE 802.3x-based flow control to handle this problem of input-buffer congestion caused by multiple simultaneous transmitting stations. This is described in the following section.

Congestion Control in Full-Duplex Repeaters

When the offered load exceeds the bandwidth capability of the full-duplex repeater, in order not to drop frames, the full-duplex repeater supports IEEE 802.3x-style flow control. IEEE 802.3x flow control allows a congested entity to transmit a PAUSE indication to the directly connected source of the congestion and indicate to it to temporarily stop transmitting. Once the input-buffer congestion is alleviated, another flow-control frame can be transmitted to allow packet transmission.[3]

As an example, refer to Figure 5-9 and assume that multiple high-performance Gigabit Ethernet desktops are transmitting data to a full-duplex repeater providing an offered load in excess of one gigabit. The station attached to port #1 is transmitting at 800 Mb/s and the station attached to port #3 at 900 Mb/s for an aggregate of 1700 Mb/s. Incoming packets at the full-duplex repeater will begin to accumulate in the input buffers, since the total capacity of the repeater is only 1000 Mb/s. When an input experiences congestion, the MAC controller associated with that input buffer transmits a PAUSE indication to the sending station with a timer value that is set to the estimated time that it will take the congestion to abate. As the input buffer's congestion decreases, the MAC controller either transmits a PAUSE with a zero timeout or relies on the previous timer value's expiring. This allows the transmitting station to send frames again.

Forwarding Path

Fair treatment of all input ports depends upon the operation of the scheduler or frame forwarder. In order to determine the input port from which to extract data in a fair manner, the frame scheduler must implement an algorithm such as round-robin. An example implementation would begin at port 1.[4] If a frame is present in the input queue, then that frame is repeated (or copied) to the output ports (in this case ports 2 and 3). The forwarding mechanism then moves to port 2, and the process continues. If a frame is present at port 2's input buffer, then that frame is repeated (or copied) to the output ports (in this case ports 3 and 1). If a frame is not present at the input buffer,

---

[3] This is done by sending a PAUSE frame with a zero timer value. No explicit start-transmission indication is provided by IEEE 802.3x.

[4] The choice of port 1 here is arbitrary. Port 3 can be chosen as long as the rotation is sequential, e.g., 3->2->1->3.

the scheduler immediately moves to the next port in line, which is port 3. The frame forwarder transmits only one frame from any given input buffer to ensure and minimize latency. The process continues indefinitely.

The full-duplex repeater uses the aforementioned combination of input buffers and round-robin scheduling to forward close to a maximum of a full gigabit (1000 Mb/s or 1.48 million packets per second) of traffic. This performance is significantly better than that of conventional repeaters, which usually forward less than the theoretical maximum of one gigabit. This performance increase comes at a price: instead of being a physical-layer symbol repeater, the full-duplex repeater includes a per-port input buffer and a per-port Gigabit Ethernet MAC in addition to the per-port Gigabit Ethernet PHY. In addition, an output buffer is provided to store a frame in the event that a congestion-indication frame needs to be inserted into the data stream.

5.5 Shared, Switched and Routed Networks

Evolution of the Internet from its traditional e-mail and file-transfer roots to the current state where users trust it for business and multimedia applications, coupled with the advent of network such as Gigabit Ethernet, has made it apparent that traffic management by application or by user is, and will continue to be, essential. High-bandwidth networks such as Gigabit Ethernet allow users to overload networks at all points—at the desktop, at the backbone, and even in the core. For example, a Gigabit Ethernet transmission between two stations that are separated by a roundtrip of 40 ms may have 40 Mb/s of data in the network between the two stations. Since this amount of data far exceeds the buffering capacity of the network, data loss may be likely. Though computers have infinite patience, most users have a very limited tolerance for delay. In addition, applications such as voice and video transmission have strict requirements on reception jitter and transmission latency. This requires either the receiver to buffer the entire message and play it back locally or the network to provide some Quality-of-Service (QoS) guarantees.

Congestion may be a severe problem in enterprise, campus, and backbone networks. Traffic flow is concentrated from the edges of the network toward the core, causing multiple megabits, even gigabits, of traffic to flow through a few very concentrated choke points.

Early implementations of switches and routers used First-In First-Out (FIFO) queues for all traffic entering and leaving the switches and routers. These early units simply dropped packets in conditions where their forwarding rate was exceeded and used higher-level recovery mechanisms in TCP and other transport protocols to recover. The reason for this was simple. It was easy.

As time passed, and as network speeds increased, resource, bandwidth and over-all traffic management became more and more essential. First, Internet applications were differentiated using the IP *Type-of-Service* field. Routers and switches would examine every IP header and use special bits in the header to differentiate high-prior-ity and lower-priority traffic. This feature was rarely used. This was followed by sev-eral modifications to TCP[5] to provide end-to-end congestion control, slow-start ramps and better round-trip time determination. The net effect of these changes pro-vided users with fair access to the Internet. TCP allowed everyone equal access to the underlying network.

Other groups attempted to provide traffic management by altering and amend-ing the data-link Ethernet protocol itself. These attempts included modifications to the Ethernet Truncated Binary Exponential Backoff (TBEB) itself[6] in order to pro-vide lower latency to higher-priority or multimedia nodes. Another example is the IEEE standard for full-duplex flow control, IEEE 802.3x[7] which allowed congested Ethernet stations to force transmitting stations to temporarily halt transmission. This would allow the congested station to empty its buffers, at which point it would con-tinue accepting packets. This is the main data-link-level flow control method used for 10 Mb/s Ethernet, 100 Mb/s Ethernet, and Gigabit Ethernet.

Traffic management has evolved from its early days to the present state where QoS commitments are supported by core routers and switches using a variety of tech-niques, including RSVP (ReSerVation Protocol), IEEE 802.1Q/p and rate and credit-based flow control.

In this section, the use of shared and switched Gigabit Ethernet networks is de-scribed along with the QoS effects of each. In addition, a brief description of RSVP and its applicability to Gigabit Ethernet is provided.

5.5.1 Quality of Service

Simple prioritization of clearly defined types of traffic through the network is impor-tant at network congestion points, where decisions to delay or even drop certain pack-ets can be prioritized by switches and routers. Applications requiring differentiated prioritization are abundant and include, but are not limited to, transaction processing, streaming video and other time-sensitive traffic.

---

[5] V. Jacobson, R. Braden, et al., "TCP Extensions for High Performance," RFC1323, May 1992..

[6] K. Chang, *Making Multimedia and Real-Time Networks Possible Today,* 3Com Corporation 1995.

[7] Institute of Electrical and Electronics Engineers, *Information Technology—Local and Metro-politan Area Networks Specification for 802.3 Full Duplex Operation,* IEEE Std 802.3x—1996, IEEE, New York, NY.

The desire to provide priority is based upon globally dispersed enterprise networks and general business requirements. For example, a trading institution or brokerage firm will want to ensure that its traders always receive the fastest network response, no matter what application they may be using. As mentioned previously, prioritization capabilities have long been offered by traditional routers for LANs and WANs using IP's ToS (Type of Service) and for the Wide-Area Networks (WANs) by using the router's layer 3 intelligence to place high-priority traffic ahead of other traffic on outbound queues.

In addition to simple prioritization of traffic, Quality of Service (QoS) implies a greater guarantee of bandwidth, as well as some assurance of latency and jitter characteristics. In order for the network to deliver to a particular flow of traffic a specified QoS, like a bound in delay or a maximum jitter, it is necessary for the network nodes, switches, and routers to set aside resources for that particular flow of traffic.

Providing explicit QoS, where latency and jitter are fully predictable and guaranteed, once the sole domain of ATM technology, is now becoming possible with packet-based networks. With ATM, the combination of smaller transport units (ranging from 64 to over 1500 bytes), end-to-end per virtual circuit signaling, and flow control allows assured delay characteristics even through very large networks. This is not generally possible with packet-based networks. However, the emergence of protocols such as RSVP and switch technologies such as Tag switching and IP switching is allowing Ethernet-based QoS characteristics to be implemented in local-area networks that provide Gigabit Ethernet with the QoS guarantees that were previously the domain of ATM.

QoS Options for Gigabit Ethernet Networks

Today, protocols and switch technologies are emerging that allow Ethernet-based QoS characteristics to be implemented in LANs. One such example is the Resource ReSerVation Protocol (RSVP), an end-to-end signaling protocol that enables an end station to request the reservation of guaranteed bandwidth through the network. RSVP operates at layer 3 for IP-based data flows, RSVP-enabled layer 3 switches, and WAN routers to maintain multiple priority queues, much like 802.1Q/p-enabled switches. However, beyond simple prioritization, these devices reserve (admission control) and police (policy control) the bandwidth requested for each RSVP session. Policing means ensuring that an RSVP session uses only as much bandwidth as it requested.

While CPU-based routers have been able to perform these functions for slow WAN links, only the newest generation of layer 3 switches have implemented these algorithms in silicon, ensuring that performance remains unaffected. These switches and routers can classify traffic on the basis of specific policy requirements, using any number of different criteria (MAC address, IP address/subnet/port, protocol type, etc.) and apply the configured bandwidth and/or security constraints.

RSVP and other advanced bandwidth-management capabilities do not offer explicit QoS capabilities, as in the cell-based world. But when combined with scalable bandwidth (such as Gigabit Ethernet), they are more than adequate for many emerging applications.

Reservation Protocol (RSVP)

The Resource ReSerVation Protocol RSVP[8] was designed to enable the senders, receivers, and routers of communication sessions to communicate with each other in order to set up the necessary router state to support QoS services such as guaranteed service. These communication parameters include bandwidth, jitter, burstiness, latency, etc. RSVP can be thought of as providing a similar set of specifications with respect to packet traffic as ATM UNI signaling provides for cell flows. It should be noted, however, that though RSVP and ATM UNI signaling services are similar, in RSVP the receiver indicates to the transmitter the nature of the traffic flow, and in ATM the transmitter indicates to the receiver the nature of the cell flow.

A host uses RSVP to request a specific Quality of Service (QoS) from the network on behalf of an application data stream. RSVP control packets carry the request through the network, touching each intervening router along the path from source to destination. At each such router, RSVP is used to make a resource reservation for the application data stream. To make a resource reservation at a router or multilayer switch, RSVP uses two control mechanisms: admission control and policy control. Admission control determines whether the router has sufficient available resources to supply the requested QoS. Policy control determines whether the user has administrative permission to make the reservation. If either check fails, the RSVP protocol returns an inadequate-resource indication to the original requester. If the router has sufficient resources and is allowed to honor the resource request, special parameters are set in the RSVP packet to obtain the desired QoS.

RSVP identifies a communication session by the combination of destination address, transport-layer protocol type, and destination port number. Each RSVP operation only applies to packets of a particular session, and as such every RSVP message must include details of the session to which it applies. Figure 5-10 shows an example of RSVP for a multicast session involving one sender and three receivers. The primary messages used by RSVP are the Path message, which originates from the traffic sender, and the Resv message, which originates from the receivers. The primary function of the Path message is to provide the receivers with the information regarding the

---

[8] R. Braden, L. Zhang, et al., *Resource ReSerVation Protocol (RSVP)—Version 1 functional specification,* August 1996.

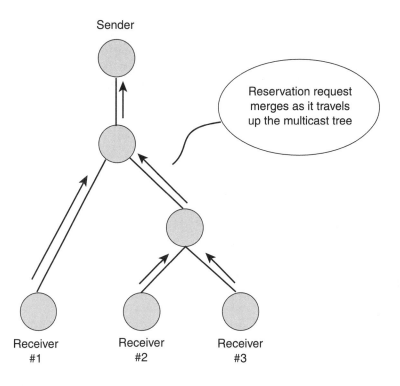

Sender

Reservation request
merges as it travels
up the multicast tree

Receiver
#1

Receiver
#2

Receiver
#3

Figure 5-10 RSVP Message Direction

characteristics of the senders traffic as well as the end-to-end path, so they can allocate the necessary resources to handle the traffic. All intervening switches and routers also allocate the necessary information regarding the transmitted traffic. The primary function of the Resv message is to carry the reservation request back to the routers or switches along a distribution tree that is formed between the transmitting source and the receiving sources.

RSVP is a unique resource reservation protocol, since it accommodates multicast, not just one-to-many or point-to-multipoint reservations. In addition, RSVP is quite straightforward in packet format and operations, and so is relatively low cost in terms of implementation in end systems, switches, and routers. RSVP is not a routing protocol and doesn't support features such as QoS-dependent routing.

It is worth noting that RSVP is not the only IP reservation protocol that has been designed for this purpose. Others include ST-II[9]and ST-I. However, the RSVP is the QoS reservation protocol that seems destined for widespread use.

---

[9] L. Delgrossi, and L. Berger, *IETF RFC 1819, Internet Stream Protocol: Version 2 (ST-II)— Protocol Specification.* August 1995.

5.6 Layer 3 Switching

Multilayer switching is a practical evolution of today's LAN switching and routing technologies. An inherently lower-cost solution than routing, switching removes the scalability and throughput restrictions that limit network growth, while also building the foundation for an emerging generation of gigabit-networked applications. There are numerous approaches to multilayer switching, and all strive to meet the same objectives, but each approach differs in its execution. In March of 1996, Ipsilon announced IP Switching, allowing high-speed forwarding of IP packets on ATM networks. Ipsilon claimed that their approach was much simpler than ATM Forum's Multiprotocol over ATM (MPOA). In a matter of six months, Cisco announced Tag switching, IBM announced Aggregate Route-based IP switching[10] (ARIS), and Toshiba announced Cell-Switched Router[11] (CSR). Eventually, all the debate in the industry led to the formation of a Multiprotocol Label Switching (MPLS) working group at the Internet Engineering Taskforce. In this section, the different approaches proposed are explained in some detail. Specifically, layer 3 switching is described in detail, including IP switching, Tag Switching, and Aggregate Route-based IP Switching (ARIS).

Over the past few years, LAN switching has greatly increased network performance by replacing shared media with dedicated bandwidth. Users benefit from direct access to their networks, and the bottlenecks of shared Ethernet disappear as point-to-point switching is deployed.

But as applications arrive to take advantage of switching's improved throughput, bottlenecks emerge at a higher level of the network. These new bottlenecks stem from the fact that, as a layer 2 bridging technology, switched networks are flat domains that must be subnetted just like bridged networks to alleviate broadcast overhead and to provide some measure of security. Without subnetting, or logically partitioning into smaller networks, a function normally provided by layer 3 routers, LAN and switching infrastructures do not scale very well. Large, flat switched networks are subject to the broadcast storms, spanning-tree loops, and inefficient addressing, not to mention suffer severe security problems, all very well known limitations that brought routers into bridged networks in the first place in the 1980s.

Routing is as important to switched networks as it ever was, and therein lies a predicament: high-performance LAN switches are pumping millions of packets per second across campus backbones, served by routers that can at best handle half a million packets. Wherever layer 3 functions have to be invoked in the switched campus backbone, the potential arises for a major bottleneck. Millions of packets from high-

---

[10] A. Viswanathan, and N. Feldman, *ARIS specification. IETF draft-feldman-aris-spec-00.txt,* March 1997.

[11] H. Esaki, et al., *Cell Switch Router,* Toshiba Corp. White Paper, November 1996.

performance desktops are funneled through routing engines that may not handle the total aggregate throughput of the desktop. In addition, by and large, routers remain expensive to buy and manage, so deploying enough switches and routers to handle the overload is usually not an effective option.

Switching allows networks to be designed with greater centralization of servers and other resources, helping to streamline network administration and increase overall security. This recentralized topology means that a greater proportion of traffic has to cross the network backbone, which entails more traffic being routed beyond a local subnet. As mentioned previously, the old 80/20 rule that used to accurately predict that 80 percent of network traffic stayed within a given workgroup or subnet is no longer applicable, since the advent of the Internet resulted in the majority of desktops having access to resources located across the backbone.

Corporate intranets further exacerbate the problem with increased network usage and by granting easy access to resources deployed widely across the enterprise. A common estimate is that roughly one-half of all intranet traffic travels between subnets. Wide-area Internet usage has a similar effect, as every Web session has to be routed to the Internet from the user's local network by an IP router. LAN switching and the applications that leverage its performance are quickly arriving at the limits of their improved capacity in many applications. Because layer 2 scalability depends entirely upon layer 3 routing, the throughput of traditional backbone routers is today's new network bottleneck. As this market continues its rapid growth, the layer 3 bottleneck will get worse.

The coalescing of layer 2 switching and layer 3 routing functionality in a single unit is what multilayer switching achieves. Integrating layer 2 (MAC layer) switching, with its high performance and traffic engineering capabilities, and layer 3 network-layer routing (or switching) with its proven scalability of network size and its special services, meets the requirements for Internet core scalability. Built on a core of Gigabit Ethernet technology, this solution can switch campus traffic at wire-speed, simultaneously satisfying IP and IPX layer 3 routing requirements. This combination not only solves today's throughput problems, but also removes the conditions under which layer 3 bottlenecks form.

Multilayer switching provides three key benefits for user applications in campus networks:

- *Scalability:* Multilayer or layer 3 switching scales with the integration of ATM with layer 3 routing. Label swapping enables ATM switches to be fully integrated into Internet packet-based, core networks without the scalability problems of a pure layer 2 network ringed by a router overlay.

- *Traffic management:* Layer 3 switching simplifies traffic management in router-based Internets by integrating layer 2 circuit capabilities. The ability to control the flow of packets across a layer 2 infrastructure to support load balancing has been one of the attractions of using ATM or frame relay switches in Internet cores. Layer 3 supports this capability. This increases the control that network managers have over the flow of packets in router-based Internets.

- *Performance:* Finally, multilayer switching enables higher-performance platforms by simplifying packet-forwarding and switching decisions. This simplification allows future switch platforms to support multigigabit, high-speed interfaces.

5.6.1 The Details

Layer 2 switches (in essence, multiport bridges[12]) deployed across LANs today are self-learning bridges. They discover the topology that surrounds them by learning and storing all the IEEE Ethernet layer 2 MAC addresses that identify all attached Ethernet devices. The function of bridges is to connect physically separate networks together. Bridges can connect different networks types (such as Ethernet and Fast Ethernet) or networks of the same type. Ethernet bridges map the Ethernet addresses of the nodes residing on each network segment and then allow only the necessary traffic to pass through the bridge.

When a packet is received by the bridge, the bridge determines the destination and source segments. If the segments are the same, the packet is dropped; if the segments are different, then the packet is forwarded to the correct segment. Additionally, bridges generally prevent packets received in error from being propagated across networks. Bridges are sometimes called store-and-forward devices because they may look at the whole Ethernet packet before making their filtering or forwarding decisions. Filtering of packets, and the regeneration of forwarded packets, enables bridging technology to split a network into separate collision domains. This allows for greater distances and more repeaters to be used in the total network design.

Most bridges are self-learning bridges, meaning that they determine the user Ethernet addresses on the segment by building a table as packets are passed through the network. This address self-learning capability dramatically raises the possibility of creating network loops in networks that have many bridges. As each device learns the network configuration, a loop presents conflicting information on the segment on which a specific address is located and forces the device to forward all traffic. The spanning tree algorithm[13] describes how switches and bridges can communicate to avoid network loops.

---

[12] The terms *switch* and *bridge* are used interchangeably in this section.
[13] Institute of Electrical and Electronics Engineers, *Standard for Local and Metropolitan Area Networks: Media Access Control (MAC) Bridges,* IEEE Std 802.1D—1991, IEEE, New York, NY.

When a switch receives a packet with a familiar destination MAC address, it forwards the packet to the proper output port; this is usually done in hardware without the multiple software-driven processing steps used by a router.

The host devices attached to these switches have their own network addresses as well, known as IP[14] addresses. An IP host that wishes to send traffic to another IP host or server must first know the other's IP (layer 3) address and then determine the corresponding layer 2 MAC address. The Address Resolution Protocol (ARP)[15] is used within IP for this purpose.

Within its layer 3 protocol stack, the sending host compares its IP address with the intended recipient's address and the current subnet mask and determines whether or not the source and destination belong to the same IP subnet. If they do, the host broadcasts an ARP request that names the intended recipient and asks it to respond with its MAC address. LAN switches by definition exist within a single broadcast domain, or one IP subnet, so they facilitate this ARP request.

When both hosts have each other's MAC address in hand, they begin communications, and their packets are forwarded via layer 2 switching. But if the two hosts are not on the same subnet, then routing is required. The sending host initiates the conversation by sending an ARP request to the nearest router, which responds by providing a MAC address for one of its ports. The host will send traffic to this port, and that's all it has to know about the connection. The router in turn may need to broadcast its own ARP request to learn the MAC address of the intended recipient elsewhere in the network. From router to router these ARP requests fan out until the recipient is reached and sends a response rippling back through the network.

The gateway router must now perform MAC address translation, i.e., stripping MAC addresses from the packets arriving from the source and destined for the remote end and replacing them with another MAC address for the next hop. This is a router management function, as are packet header checksums that verify data integrity, among other tasks. Meanwhile, every other router involved in the connection, and potentially hundreds, if not thousands, of other connections at the same time, have to perform IP and MAC address correlation. This information is stored in ARP caches and routing tables and is gleaned through the use of routing protocols such as RIP[16] and OSPF.[17] And because it's a datagram environment in which packets 1, 2, and 3 might each follow a different course through the network, routers have to deal with unpredictable traffic flows as well.

---

[14] The IP protocol is used throughout the book as an example of a network layer, owing to its predominance.

[15]   D.C. Plummer. *Ethernet Address Resolution Protocol: Or converting network protocol addresses to 48 bit Ethernet address for transmission on Ethernet hardware.* November 1982.

[16] C.L. Hedrick, *RFC 1058—Routing Information Protocol,* June 1988.

[17] J. Moy, RFC 2178, *OSPF Version 2,* July 1997.

Layer 3 switching optimizes the routing or layer 3 function (since it modifies the network or layer 3 headers of the packet) into a simpler and faster forwarding process that can move traffic between different subnets as quickly as layer 2 switching does within a single subnet. For multimedia applications that require guaranteed QoS, the idea is to reduce routing latency to match switching latency, so that delay-sensitive traffic can stream across subnets without disruption. Figures 5-11 and 5-12 illustrate the differences between switching and routing in subnets.

Though conceptually simple, the performance of layer 3 switches or network routers is usually limited by several tasks, the three major ones being the examination of the destination addresses of all incoming packets, using the address as an index into a routing table to determine the next hop and then modifying and copying the packet to the output interface. The routing lookup is never straightforward, it can include a match of up to 100,000 addresses per second. A variety of techniques have been proposed to accelerate routing lookups.[18] However, these techniques are not always applicable when designing real router systems. Therefore only techniques that are actually used in high-speed switches and router products are examined in this section.

Figure 5-11 Routing Between Subnets

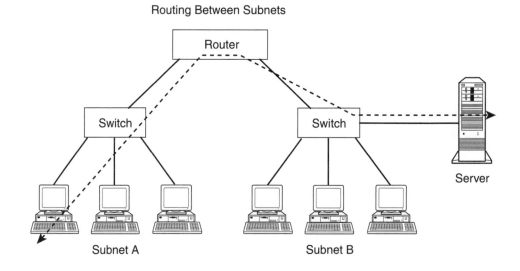

Routing Between Subnets

Subnet A

Subnet B

---

[18] W. Doeringer, G. Karjoth, and M. Nassehi. *Routing on Longest-Matching Prefixes.* IEEE/ACM Transactions of Networking. February 1996, pp. 86–97.

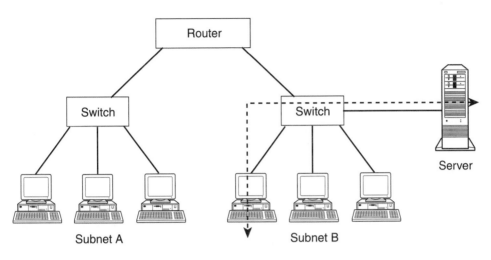

Figure 5-12 Switching Within a Subnet

These techniques fall into the general category of *label-swapping,* since they replace the long routing lookups with exact pattern matching labels. The labels are used for indexing tables which enable fast IP forwarding at close to media speeds by minimizing the need for network-layer packet processing. These include IP switching, ARIS, and tag switching. Label-swapping techniques are essential for the design and production of wire-speed Gigabit Ethernet switches and routers.

IP Switching

An IP switch maps the forwarding functions of a router onto a hardware switch matrix. This idea occurred independently and simultaneously to several people.[19,20] IP switching may be used with any application that uses IP and is not restricted to particular IP routing protocols. IP switching uses the concept of a flow. A flow is defined as a sequence of packets that are treated identically by the routing function. As example is a sequence of packets sent from a particular source to a particular destination that are forwarded through the same ports and at the same QoS. The forwarding and handling of the flow is determined by the first few packets in the flow. These packets determine the classification of the flow. The classification is cached, or stored in a highly accessible memory and used to process further packets belonging to that flow

---

[19] G. Parulkar, D.C. Schmidt, and J.S. Turner, *IP/ATM: A strategy for integrating IP with ATM.* SIGCOMM Symposium on Communications Architectures and Protocols, Cambridge, MA, September 1995.

[20] P. Newman, T. Lyon, and G. Minshal, *Flow Labelled IP: A connectionless approach to ATM.* Proceedings of IEEE Infocom, San Francisco, March 1996, pp. 1251–1260.

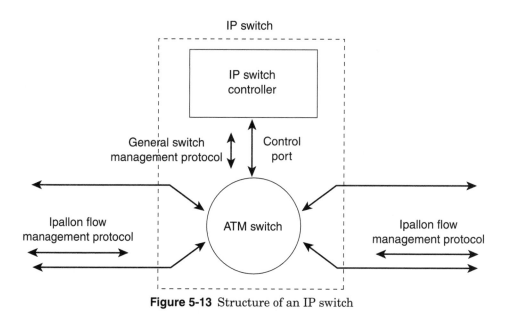

Figure 5-13 Structure of an IP switch

without full lookup times. With flow-based cut-through switching, actual routers are attached to each ATM switch in the network (Figure 5-13). Connections between source and destination are made on a hop-by-hop basis over point-to-point ATM SVCs or PVCs between pairs of routers or IP switches. The switches, using state-inspection techniques, look for flows which are likely to be long-lived. Once a flow is determined to be a candidate for cut-through switching, neighboring nodes are informed of the cut-through VC to forward the traffic on. They do this using protocols such as IFMP, or Ipsilon Flow Management Protocol.[21]

Once all nodes between the source and destination are informed of the cut-through decision, the edge devices begin delivering traffic over the ATM PVC which by-passes the intermediate routers thereby improving performance. Note that the traffic still travels hop-by-hop; performance gains are achieved by using cell switching to forward traffic instead of software-based routing.

Most IP switching solutions use ATM switch fabrics as the fabric for IP switching. Incoming flows are mapped to ATM Virtual Channels (VCs) that have been previously established. Only one or a few packets from each flow need be inspected to perform the mapping and establish an ATM virtual channel. Once the virtual channel is established for a flow, all further traffic on that flow is switched directly through the ATM switch, greatly reducing the load on the forwarding engine(s). The IP/ATM solution uses a pool of pre-established Permanent Virtual Channels (PVCs) that are

---

[21] P. Newman, W. Edwards, et al., *RFC 1953—Ipsilon Flow Management Protocol Specification for IPv4 Version 1.0,* May 1996.

taken by active incoming flows. Packets on a new flow are not forwarded until a PVC has been activated. The IP switch uses a protocol, IFMP (RFC1953), to propagate the mapping between flow and VCI upstream and forwards packets using the forwarding engine until the cut-through connection is established across the ATM switch. The Cell Switch Router[22] attempts to be more general than the IP switch in that it will permit entire classical IP over ATM (RFC1577) subnets between CSRs. It proposes using the RSVP protocol to propagate the mapping between flows and VCIs.

Flow Classification

The fundamental concept behind flow classification is based on the fact that, in most cases, data transfer usually occurs in a relatively steady flow. That is, a file or message being sent usually consists of multiple frames. For example, a 135 kilobyte file, using a typical Ethernet frame size of 1500 bytes, would require about 90 frames. Since all 90 frames would travel to the same destination, it is possible to identify the destination and establish a Switched Virtual Circuit (SVC) based on the information contained in the first frame. All 30 frames can then be segmented into approximately 2700 ATM cells (if ATM is the underlying transport medium) and transmitted over the virtual channel established by the SVC. This could be considered a shortcut, in that the entire flow of data follows a pre-established path, avoiding the default path followed by routed traffic, and greatly improving performance. In the case of steady-stream transmissions such as video, this is highly efficient and superior to simple router-to-router operation.

An important function of the flow-classification operation is to select those flows that are to be switched in the ATM switch and those that should be forwarded packet-by-packet by the forwarding engine. Long-duration flows with large amounts of traffic are generally switched. Multimedia traffic, FTP or HTTP[23] sessions, large file transfers over the Internet, etc., offer examples of long-duration flows. Short-duration flows consisting of a small number of packets should be handled directly by the forwarding engine. Domain Name Server (DNS) nameserver queries, ARP requests, and brief client-server transactions are examples of traffic that are usually not worth the effort of establishing a switched connection.

Flows can be used for bandwidth management, traffic tuning, and application monitoring as described below:

* *Traffic tuning:* Packets can be adjusted to flow along specified routes, allowing load-balancing balance connections between nodes. This is exactly the same as other IP switching techniques such as tag switching.

---

[22] H. Esaki, K-I. Nagami, and M. Ohta, *High speed datagram delivery over Internet using ATM technology.* Networld+InterOp, Las Vegas, March 1995. E12-1.
[23] R. Berners-Lee, R. Fielding, et al., *Hypertext Transfer Protocol—HTTP/1.0,* May 1996.

- *Application Flows:* This method looks at both the source and destination address, as well as other layer 3 information. This can be used to provide finer granularity in processing flows and maintain a given quality of service through the network for a specific source/destination flow of packets, such as for RSVP.

For the flows selected for switching, a virtual channel must be established across the ATM switch. ATM requires that all arriving traffic be labeled with a Virtual Channel Identifier (VCI) to indicate the virtual channel to which it belongs. Therefore, IP switching requires a protocol to distribute the association of flow and VCI label upstream across each incoming link. Every packet on a flow that is switched through a network of IP switches must be labeled with a VCI. The task of labeling each packet typically involves more effort than simple forwarding because it must examine more fields than the destination address. However, once a virtual channel is established, this flow labeling need only be performed at a single location within the IP switch network; a traditional router network would need to perform the route lookup at every hop.

In summary, IP switching provides high-speed routing by low-level switching of flows (equivalent to cached routing decisions). It defines a protocol to indicate these flows and to associate a link layer label with each flow, to the upstream network node. This enables the switching. All flows are classified, and the forwarding engine is optimized for flow classification and for forwarding packets on those flows that are decided should not be cached in the switch fabric.

Tag Switching

Another technique for high-performance packet forwarding at gigabit rates that falls into the general category of *label-swapping*, tag switching[24] assigns *tags* to multiprotocol frames for transport across packet-based or cell-based networks. Label-swapping is a concept in which Ethernet packets or ATM cells carry a fixed-length label that tells switching nodes how to process the data. This information is far easier and faster to process than the normal lookup process.

Switches at the edge of the network apply tags and perform layer 3 functions, while switches or routers at the core of the network switch packets or cells based on the information embedded in the tag. All systems use Tag Distribution Protocols (TDPs) to distribute tag information throughout the network. An example of a tag-switching network is shown in Figure 5-14.

As shown in the figure, a tag-switching network consists of the following elements:

---

[24] Y. Rekhter, B. Davie, et al., *Tag switching architecture overview. IETF draft-rekhter-tag-switch-arch-01.txt*, July 1997.

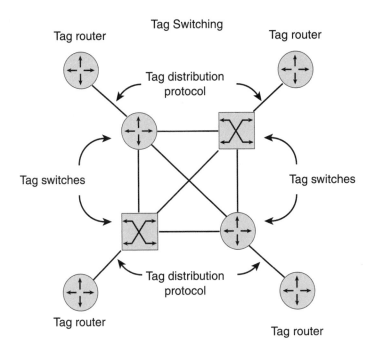

Figure 5-14 Tag Switching

- *Tag Routers:* Tag routers are located at the edges of the network and apply tags to packets flowing into the core of the network.

- *Tag Switches:* Tag switches switch tagged packets or cells based on the tags. Tag switches usually support full layer 3 routing or layer 2 switching, in addition to tag switching.

- *Tag Distribution Protocol (TDP):* In conjunction with standard network layer routing protocols, TDP is used to distribute tag information between devices in a tag-switched network.

The Details

The basic processing within a tag-switching Internetwork is described below. First, tag routers and tag switches use standard routing protocols (e.g., EIGRP, BGP,[25] OS-PF) to identify routes through the network. These fully interoperate with non-tag-switching routers. Tag switches use tables generated by the standard routing protocols to assign and distribute tag information via the Tag Distribution Protocol (TDP). Tag routers receive the TDP information and build a forwarding database that makes use

---

[25] Y. Rekhter and T. Li., *RFC 1771—A Border Gateway Protocol 4 (BGP-4)*, March 1995.

of the tags. When a tag router receives a packet from a source for forwarding across the tag network to a destination, it analyzes the network-layer header, performs any applicable network-layer services, selects a route for the packet from its routing tables, applies a tag, and forwards the packet to the next hop tag switch. The tag switch receives the tagged packet and switches the packet based solely on the tag, without reanalyzing the network-layer header. The packet reaches the tag router at the edge of the network, and the tag is stripped and the packet delivered to the final destination.

Tag Routers

Tag routers are full-function layer 3 routing devices located at the entrance or edge of a tag-switching network. Tag routers apply tags to incoming packets and remove tags from outgoing packets. Several methods are used to apply tags to packets:

- *Destination:* The tag router matches the packet's destination IP address against the destination entries in the router's forwarding tables, which determine the next hop for the packet. In a tag router, this lookup will also yield a tag value to apply to the packet. This technique allows traffic from multiple sources, going to the same destination, to share the same tag and reduces the number of total labels used by the router. Therefore, tag switching economizes on the number of tags required, relative to the number of source/destination IP address combinations seen by a router, and is a key to the scalability of tag switching.

- *Traffic tuning:* Packets can be tagged such that they flow along specified routes, allowing load-balancing balance connections between nodes. This is exactly the same as other IP switching techniques.

- *Application flows:* This method looks at both the source and destination address, as well as other layer 3 information. This can be used to provide finer granularity in processing the tagged packets and maintain a given quality of service through the network for a specific source/destination flow of packets, such as for RSVP.

Tag Switches

Tag switches operate at the core of a tag-switching network. Since lags are short, fixed-length labels, this enables tag switches to do simple and fast table lookups and implement the lookup and forwarding capabilities using fast hardware techniques, including ATM cell switching. Since tag switching decouples the tag distribution mechanisms from the data flows, a wide variety of methods of associating a tag with a packet can be used and will interoperate in a tag network including the layer 2 and layer 3 headers. This enables tag switching to be used over a wide variety of media, including Ethernet and makes tag switching a good choice for gigabit switches. Tag switching is also not specific to IP. Since the routing protocols are separate and are standard, tag switching can be used to support multiple layer 3 protocols.

Tag switching expands upon the label-swapping concept by avoiding flow-by-flow setup procedures inherent in flow-based schemes. Tag switching's destination prefix algorithm, coupled with standard routing protocols, supports an efficient use of labels and avoids flow-by-flow setup procedures altogether. This increases the scalability required for large enterprise networks, where the number of flows is enormous and the rate of change of flows may be high. By pre-establishing tag mappings at the same time as routing tables are populated, tag switching can tag switch both short-lived flows and the initial packets of long-lived flows, potentially avoiding bottlenecks in high-performance applications.

Although tag switching allows layer 2 label-swapping capabilities in IP routers, using this technology over ATM switches is problematic. Tag switching has been defined for use with ATM networks[26] such that tags are carried by the VCI/VPI fields in the ATM cell headers. This seems to be a perfect solution, since label swapping at the switch is trivial. However, an aspect of ATM switches causes trouble with this simple plan: flow merging. Tag switching allows flows to merge on their way from multiple sources to their destination. Normal ATM switches are not capable of merging virtual circuits, since, once merged, there is no inherent multiplexing information in ATM cells to separate cells into separate packets. For a network consisting of a total of M stations, tag switching uses on the order of M switched paths from source to destination over a traditional network. The requirement to map a single tag-switched stream into multiple ATM virtual circuits leads to N^2 paths for a full mesh connection for an ATM switch-based network, which is hardly scalable to Internet levels.

Aggregate Route-Based IP Switching (ARIS)

Aggregate Route-based IP Switching (ARIS) is a protocol which, in coordination with network-layer routing protocols such as BGP and OSPF, establishes data-link layer switched paths through a network of Integrated Switch Routers (ISR). ARIS proposes a slightly different approach for label switching than described above for tag switching or IP switching. The label used to route or switch packets between nodes is actually carried in the destination-address portion of the frame and, for unicast frames, is the MAC address of the egress point from the network as identified by ARIS. This, of course, as with the IEEE MAC addresses, requires that all the labels have global significance, therefore be unique. The ISR at an entry point to the switching environment performs standard IP forwarding of datagrams, with the caveat that the IP forwarding table has been extended to include a reference to a switched path

ARIS differs from tag switching in its use of a route-based algorithm instead of the flow-based switching preferred by tag switching. Unlike a flow, a route in this

---

[26] B. Davie, P. Doolan, et al., *Use of Tag Switching with ATM. IETF draft-davie-tag-switching-atm-00.txt,* November 1996.

sense is a multicast distribution tree, rooted at the egress point, and traversed in reverse. The egress point is specified by an egress identifier, such as an IP destination address or an OSPF router ID. Using the IP destination prefix, packets from any ingress point forming a leaf on the route tree and intended for that egress point's destination prefix, are switched and merged to the root egress ISR.

5.7 Gigabit Ethernet vs. Other Technologies

The emergence of Gigabit Ethernet creates the option to choose between multiple high-speed LAN technologies—Gigabit Ethernet, ATM, and FDDI—for campus-backbone, building-backbone and server-farm applications. This section provides a brief overview of ATM and FDDI and it compares and contrasts them in the application of scaling campus Internets.

In the past few years, local area networks have evolved from simple file and print sharing in a single location to applications that include large files, multimedia, and Internet access over sometimes geographically dispersed campuses. Furthermore, the numbers of users on backbone LANs are increasing owing to the lowering cost of the computer. As the volume of LAN traffic increases, typical 10 Mb/s shared Ethernet backbones are becoming insufficient to handle the traffic. This has led to the deployment of faster technologies such as Fast Ethernet and FDDI (Fiber Distributed Data Interface) in the backbone. This allows for 10 Mb/s desktop connections and 100 Mb/s in the backbone. A combination of lowering costs of Fast Ethernet adapters, and faster desktop machines, has led to the deployment of Fast Ethernet adapters in desktop machines. In fact, it was estimated that the sale of 100 Mb/s-capable network-interface cards would outnumber the sale of 10 Mb/s Ethernet cards by 1998.[27] This increased demand for bandwidth at the desktop has caused an even greater demand for bandwidth on the backbone. Several technologies have emerged to meet these demands. The two dominant technologies competing in the network backbone are ATM (Asynchronous Transfer Mode) and Gigabit Ethernet.

5.7.1 Overview of ATM

Asynchronous Transfer Mode, commonly known by the acronym ATM, is the basis for most of the world's cell-based networking. ATM is exciting, because it offers a vision of the ultimate integrated-services network, unlimited bandwidth on demand, data, voice, and video over one cost-effective infrastructure, as well as seamless interconnections between the local area and the wide area. Just sprinkle ATM on every-

---

[27] J. Smith, *1997 NIC Unit Market Shares,* IDC, March 1997

thing and watch networking problems disappear. This vision provides valuable long-term motivation, but ATM must first deal with more practical issues. In particular, one size—or one solution—does not usually fit all. Each part of an campus or enterprise network has unique characteristics. Desktop connections require the lowest possible price per port. Local area backbones must be scalable. The wide-area needs maximum bandwidth efficiency.

In response to these priorities, the application of ATM technology has evolved into three main solution spaces: local area backbone, wide area access, and wide area transport. Each space is a distinct market with its own class of ATM-based products. And, while they are interrelated, each market and class of products is developing at its own pace. Some are ready for integration into mainstream enterprise networks; others are still emerging.

The Details

ATM (Asynchronous Transmission Mode) is a connection-oriented, cell-based switching technology that uses 53-byte cells to transport information. ATM is an approach to handling information transfer within a single network or between networks that may span the globe. The ATM Forum (the ATM standards body) completed implementation agreements in mid-1993 on the cell format for transmitting user data. The ATM Forum is continuing to develop and approve standards that will allow ATM to be the bridge between different types of legacy networks, while still maintaining the ability to offer a guaranteed quality of service.

ATM does not actually transmit cells asynchronously, as the name may suggest. Fixed-length ATM cells are transmitted continuously and synchronously, with no break between cells. When no user information is being transmitted, each ATM cell is filled with a specific bit pattern indicating that it is an empty or idle cell. The asynchronous nature of ATM comes from the indeterminate time when the next information unit of a logical connection may start. Time not used by one logical connection may be given to other connections or filled with idle cells. This means that the cells for any given connection arrive asynchronously. Each cell is routed to its proper destination by addressing within that cell.

The use of small, fixed-size cells in ATM networks provides several advantages. First, high-performance hardware implementations of ATM switches are simpler and more efficient. At an OC-12 rate (622 Mb/s), 53-byte ATM cells can be switched in just over 0.68µs. ATM performance is an important consideration because of cell-oriented flows and fast hardware switching speeds allowed by fixed-length cells. Second, knowing the size of the incoming cell allows memory to be allocated in exact increments with no wastage. This allows the efficient use of memory for address lookup and storage purposes. Finally, the small size is ideal for the efficient transport of constant, low-bit-rate information such as voice.

5.7.2 ATM Protocol Stack

The ATM protocol stack can be broken down into three layers as shown in Figure 5-15: the physical layer, the ATM layer, and the ATM adaptation layer. The lowest layer is the physical layer. This layer consists of the physical transport used to transfer the ATM cells from one node to another. This includes converting the signals into the appropriate electrical or optical format and loading and unloading cells into the appropriate transmission frames. ATM has been adapted to work with the several physical transports, including 155 Mb/s SONET/STS-3c over multimode fiber and Cat 5 UTP, 622 Mb/s SONET/STS-12c over multimode fiber and single-mode fiber, and 25 Mb/s over Cat 3, 4, or 5 UTP. ATM is being extended to 2.4 Gb/s (OC-48) and possibly 10 Gb/s by the ATM Forum.

The layer above the physical layer is the ATM layer. This layer provides switching and routing of the ATM packets according to their VCI (Virtual Channel Identifier) and VPI (Virtual Path Identifier) labels. The ATM layer is also responsible for generating the headers for the ATM cells and extracting this header from incoming cells. The purpose of the ATM layer is to provide a common set of services to support higher-layer protocol functions such as data, voice, or video applications. These services include multiplexing multiple data streams and switching data over a network to the correct destination. Multiplexing allows data streams from either different sources or different applications to be sent over the same physical link. Virtual paths may be configured using UNI signaling throughout the ATM network to provide a guaranteed amount of bandwidth requested by the application. If this request cannot be guaranteed by the network, then the UNI signaling connection request is refused.

Figure 5-15 ATM Layers

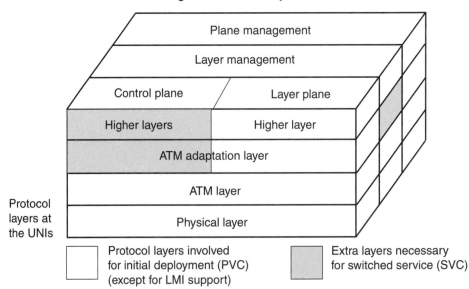

The next above the ATM layer is the ATM adaptation layer. The ATM layer moves data from the source to the destination across an ATM network. The ATM adaptation layer packages application data into cells prior to transport and extracts data from cells during reception. There are different types of adaptation layers for different traffic types. This is necessary due to the different transmission characteristics of the specific traffic. Currently there are five types of adaptation layers: AAL 1 through AAL 5. AAL 1 is used to support real-time, constant-bit-rate traffic such as voice and video traffic. AAL 2 is used to support real-time, variable-bit-rate traffic such as MPEG video traffic. AAL 3/4 is used to provide support for non-real-time data and was originally intended to carry LAN traffic. It has since been replaced by AAL 5 for LAN-traffic purposes, since AAL 5 has lower overhead per cell and a simpler encapsulation protocol. By dropping some of the features of AAL 3/4, AAL 5 provides a complete 48 payload bytes per cell.

Not shown are the ATM signaling protocols and their associated ATM addressing models. The standards for ATM signaling are described by the ATM Forum UNI 3.1 and 4.0 specifications.[28,29] The UNI specifications are based upon Q.2931, a public signaling protocol developed by the ITU-T,[30] which was based upon Q.931, the protocol used for ISDN signaling. UNI 3.1/4.0 signaling provides for connection setup, tear-down, and status inquiry. The UNI signaling stacks operate over a data-link layer protocol known as the Service Specific Connection Oriented Protocol (SSCOP),[31] embodied in Q.2100,[32] Q.2110,[33] and Q.2130.[34] These protocols provide a guaranteed delivery mechanism similar to TCP's for the ATM signaling information. ATM, in and of itself, provides no guarantee of delivery.

ATM Capabilities

ATM, unlike most other protocols, can carry voice, video, data, imaging, and graphics either separately or simultaneously on the same link. This is due to ATM's small, fixed-length cell as well as its QoS (Quality of Service) parameters. The ATM cell shown in Figure 5-16 is the key to ATM's ability to transport multimedia data efficiently.

---

[28] ATM Forum, *ATM User-Network Interface Specification V3.1*, ATM Forum Specification, 1994.

[29] ATM Forum, *ATM UNI Signaling V4.0*, ATM Forum Specification, July 1996.

[30] The ITU-T was formerly called CCITT.

[31] T. Henderson, *Design principles and performance analysis of SSCOP: A new ATM Adaptation Layer protocol,* ACM SIGCOMM Computer Communications Review, 25(2):14, April 1995.

[32] ITU-T, *Recommendation Q.2100,* Technical report, International Telecommunication Union.

[33] ITU-T, *Recommendation Q.2110,* Technical report, International Telecommunication Union.

[34] ITU-T, *Recommendation Q.2130,* Technical report, International Telecommunication Union.

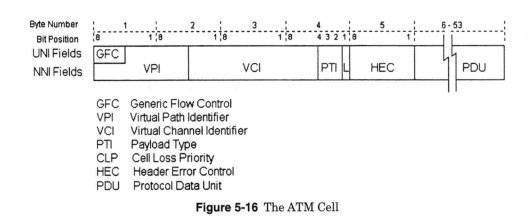

GFC   Generic Flow Control
VPI   Virtual Path Identifier
VCI   Virtual Channel Identifier
PTI   Payload Type
CLP   Cell Loss Priority
HEC   Header Error Control
PDU   Protocol Data Unit

Figure 5-16 The ATM Cell

The first 5 bytes are the header and contain the address and control information, while the next 48 bytes, called the payload, carry the revenue-bearing information or data. The ATM header is as small as possible in order to maximize efficiency. Similarly, in order to maximize efficiency, it would appear that the payload should be quite long, not just 48 bytes. However, ATM networks were designed to carry not just bursty traffic, but constant-bit-rate voice and video traffic. A long payload would have a negative impact on this type of traffic flow. The standards body was concerned not only with efficiency but also with packetization delay. Packetization delay is the time it takes to fill an ATM cell with 64 Kb/s digitized voice samples. The resulting 53-byte cell size was a compromise between payload efficiency and packetization delay.

The ATM Cell Header

The UNI cell header, as shown in Figure 5-16, provides addressing information, limited flow control, and header error checking. The first 4 bits are called the GFC (Generic Flow Control). These bits are used for local flow control for multiple users on the customer side of a switch sharing an access line over a standard UNI interface. This function is generally not used, and these 4 bits are normally set to 0. For a P-NNI (Private Network to Network Interface)[35,36] these bits are overwritten with addressing information. The UNI header provides 8 bits for the VPI (Virtual Path Identifier), while the P-NNI header uses 12 bits. This gives 255 possible paths for the UNI and 4095 possible paths for the P-NNI on the same port. The VCI (Virtual Channel Identifier) further extends the addressing with 16 more bits or 65,536 possible connections within each path address. Some addresses are reserved for specific functions such as signaling, only slightly reducing the available addresses.

---

[35] ATM Forum, *P-NNI V1.0*, ATM Forum Specification, March 1996.
[36] ATM Forum, *P-NNI v1.0 Errata and PICs*, ATM Forum Specification, July 1997.

The next three bits are the PTI (Payload Type Identifier). The PTI is used to distinguish user data cells from OA&M (Operations, Administration, and Maintenance) commands and statistics. If network congestion is experienced, the PTI is modified as it passes from switch to switch. The network can then relieve congestion by discarding any cells that are in excess of the guaranteed connection rate.

The CLP (Cell Loss Priority) bit is a two-state priority indicator telling the network which cells to discard first in the event of network congestion. All CLP bits are initially set to zero. The CLP bit may be set to 1 by the first switch in the backbone if it detects that the particular virtual circuit is congested or has exceeded the parameters specified during connection setup. Any cell with a CLP bit set to 1 will be discarded within the network before any cell with a CLP bit set to 0.

The 8-bit HEC (Header Error Control) has the capability to correct single-bit header errors and detect multiple-bit errors to ensure proper addressing. Headers that contain multiple-bit errors will simply be discarded by the switch or host that detects the error. It is important to note that the HEC does not check for errors in the information payload. This function is the responsibility of a higher-level protocol, typically in the transport layer.

5.7.3 ATM vs. Gigabit Ethernet

Any comparison of Gigabit Ethernet and ATM must also consider the respective roles the two technologies play in enterprise networks. Most desktops are 10Base-T Ethernet, and in corporate environments many have migrated and will continue to migrate towards 100Base-T. In contrast, the wide area network is becoming increasingly ATM-oriented. Many of the installed backbone frame relay switches in North America today operate with ATM switching matrices. Worldwide, private ATM services are becoming increasingly available, and public ATM services will soon become available and competitively priced. In the future, ATM will provide the fundamental infrastructure for the delivery of frame relay, ISDN, and DSL,[37] as well as native ATM services.

Within the overall enterprise network, it is not a question of either ATM or Ethernet; they coexist and complement each other. The enterprise desktop will remain Ethernet-based, while the enterprise WAN will become increasingly ATM (see Figure 5-17). The desktop and the WAN meet at the backbone—both at the campus and building backbone levels. Within the backbone, the point at which ATM and Ethernet will meet will depend on cost and the applications and services required, as well as on network size, topology, and redundancy requirements.

---

[37] Digital subscriber loop.

The choice of technology for scaling campus networks is best accomplished by establishing a set of criteria that deliver a scalable network infrastructure that meets the requirements of growing businesses. As an example, the following criteria can be used to evaluate Gigabit Ethernet and ATM technology for use in scaling the performance of campus networks:

- *Compatibility with the installed server, desktop, and network equipment.* Large enterprise networks have invested millions of dollars in server, desktop, and network infrastructure. Compatibility and leveraging of this previous investment as well as a relatively simple migration strategy are important considerations.

- *Bandwidth and latency performance.* Existing and emerging applications generally require higher bandwidth and lower latency than today's applications. Traffic patterns are changing and are less predictable, and multimedia content is increasing.

- *Compatibility with installed LAN protocols.* Protocol compatibility is important to leverage existing applications and to smooth migration.

- *Emerging needs for QoS.* These emerging needs on the campus must be addressed. Options vary from guaranteed QoS for all desktops, to no guarantee of bandwidth but large amounts of it, to all points in-between.

- *WAN compatibility.* For enterprises designing their campus backbone, WAN compatibility is important since WAN traffic and access costs dominate the overall network costs. This is especially a concern for organizations that have several geographically dispersed organizations.

- *Services integration.* Integration of data, video, and voice services can be a key objective for cost reduction. Here, consolidation of WAN services, the campus backbone, and management simplifies and lowers cost.

- *Product availability.* The availability of products is a key factor and must be consistent with the planned deployment for scaling your campus network performance. Products include networking products, embedded management agents, management applications, and test equipment.

Tables 5-4 and 5-5 summarize the capabilities for both Gigabit Ethernet and ATM with the aforementioned criteria in mind. Note that each technology has its own strengths, and the choice will ultimately depend on the existing network and the role established for the campus network in the future.

Prioritized QoS capability for Ethernet will be available with the finalization of IEEE 802.1Q/p and IETF Resource Reservation Protocol (RSVP) standards. Finally, Packet-over-SONET (POS) enables high-speed, packet-oriented WAN connections without the need to assemble/disassemble packets into cells for transmission over the

Table 5-4 Gigabit Ethernet and ATM Comparisons

Network	Installed Desktops	LAN Protocols (e.g., IP, IPX)	Scalability	WAN	QoS, Multimedia
Ethernet	Yes	Yes	Yes	Emerging	Emerging
ATM	Yes, with MPOA and LANE	Yes, with MPOA and LANE	Yes, with MPOA and LANE	Yes	Yes

Table 5-5 Gigabit Ethernet and ATM Feature Comparisons

Features	Gigabit Ethernet	ATM
Price/Performance/Bandwidth	Lower cost	Moderate cost
Quality of Service (QoS)	RSVP, IEEE 802.1Q/p, and differential services	Guaranteed QoS with traffic management
User Applications	High-speed data, voice/video over IP	Data, video, and voice
Product Availability	Since late 1997	Since early 1996
Network Applications	Building backbones, campus backbone servers and risers	WAN, building backbones, and campus backbone servers and risers

WAN. The capabilities of Ethernet are increasing toward the current capabilities of ATM while preserving the compatibility with the installed LAN nodes (80 percent of which are Ethernet) and installed protocols (which all operate over Ethernet).

Table 5-4 summarizes the key features of ATM and Gigabit Ethernet. Notice the differences in bandwidth: Gigabit Ethernet provides low-cost bandwidth, while ATM provides similar bandwidth at higher cost. This is due to the higher level of services and functionality provided with ATM technology, which requires larger amounts of silicon to implement. As mentioned above, Gigabit Ethernet will provide prioritized QoS based on emerging protocols such as differential services (diffserv), IEEE 802.1Q/p, and RS-VP, which provide differentiated service levels, while ATM provides guaranteed QoS. ATM provides voice, data, and video integration, while Gigabit Ethernet delivers high-speed data. Voice and video capabilities over Gigabit Ethernet will depend on the success of video and voice over IP. Note that there is an applications overlap between Gigabit Ethernet and ATM. Both will be used for backbone, server, and building riser applications. Presently, however, only ATM can provide WAN services.

Bandwidth Overhead

In order to carry traffic from higher-level protocols, both ATM and Gigabit Ethernet must encapsulate the traffic using the appropriate headers. When carrying typical LAN traffic, Gigabit Ethernet has lower overhead per higher-level packet than ATM. For instance, in the case of a 1500 byte IP datagram, Gigabit Ethernet adds 26 bytes of overhead, resulting in 1526 bytes[38] to transmit the IP datagram. ATM AAL 5 adds an 8-byte trailer and a variable pad size to ensure that the AAL5 protocol data unit (PDU) is a multiple of 48 bytes. For a

1500-byte IP datagram, this results in an AAL5 PDU equal to 1036 bytes. The AAL 5 adaptation layer then segments the AAL 5 PDU into 48-byte segments to be carried in 53-byte ATM cells (each ATM cell has a 5-byte header). Therefore, 32 ATM cells (1696 bytes) are required to transmit the 1500-byte IP datagram. The corresponding efficiencies when compared to the IP network layer are about 98% for Gigabit Ethernet and 88% for ATM.

Compatibility and Support for Existing Network Protocols

Since Gigabit uses the same IEEE 802.2 LLC layer as standard Ethernet, existing network protocols such as IP and IPX operate without modification over Gigabit Ethernet. In order for existing protocols to work over ATM, they must be adapted to operate directly over the ATM adaptation layer. ATM offers multiple solutions to this problem, three of which are described below: classical IP over ATM, ATM LAN Emulation (LANE), and Multiprotocol over ATM (MPOA).

Classical IP over ATM[39] predates both LANE and MPOA and has a significant installed base. IP over ATM is a considered a layer 3 routing protocol, while LANE is a bridging or layer 2 protocol. Classical IP over ATM maps IP network layer addresses to ATM addresses and enables ATM-attached devices to send IP packets over an ATM network. While this solution has the obvious advantage that it allows IP traffic to be routed on an ATM LAN, it has several disadvantages. First, classical IP only supports the IP network protocol. Second, unlike IP over Gigabit Ethernet, classical IP over ATM currently has no support for multicast traffic. This is due to the fact that ATM is a connection-oriented technology, and multicast support over connection-oriented networks is more problematic than with connectionless networks. Finally, an inherent protocol to dynamically allocate IP addresses is missing, thus causing a problem with network scaling.

LAN Emulation (LANE)[40,41] takes a different approach from that of classical IP. LANE was developed to make the ATM network invisible to the Ethernet or legacy LANs. Therefore, rather than adapting the network-level protocol to ATM, LANE emulates the MAC layer above ATM AAL5. In the case of Ethernet LANE, the LANE interface looks like a standard Ethernet interface. Therefore, all data sent across the ATM network are encapsulated in the Ethernet MAC packet format. However, no attempt was made to emulate the standard Ethernet CSMA/CD MAC protocol. The advantage of emulating the existing LAN network interfaces is that it allows all existing network-layer protocols that support Ethernet to operate over ATM. Since this solution provides the same interface to the upper layers as existing Ethernet

---

[38] The Ethernet MTU is 1518 bytes, so this packet would typically be fragmented, and the efficiency would be slightly lower than shown.

[39] *Classical IP and ARP over ATM*, M. Laubac, IETF RFC 1577, April 1994. (Note that RFCs 1483, 1626, and 1755 are also of relevance.)

[40] ATM Forum, *LAN Emulation over ATM 1.0*, ATM Forum Specification, January 1995.

[41] ATM Forum, *LANE 1.0 Addendum*, ATM Forum Specification, December 1995.

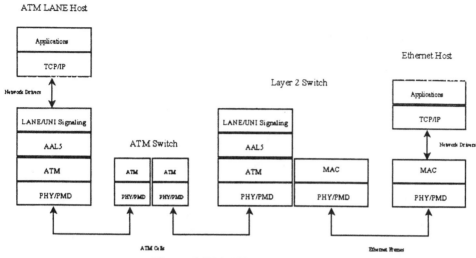

Figure 5-17 LANE Architecture

services, no driver software changes are required. Figure 5-17 illustrates the LANE protocol architecture. ATM LANE hosts use the existing protocol and driver interfaces such as NDIS to communicate with the underlying ATM hardware and software stack. To communicate with an Ethernet network a translation bridge converts the ATM cells at layer 2 into Ethernet MAC frames.

The intention of LANE was to accelerate the deployment of ATM networks. Furthermore, unlike classical IP, LANE supports multicast traffic. This is implemented by the LANE Broadcast/Unknown Server (BUS) which accepts broadcast/multicast traffic and transmits to all the ATM stations through a point-to-multipoint connection. The main disadvantage of LAN emulation is that, since it is transparent to higher level protocols, it cannot take advantage of ATM's QoS.

Lastly, Multi-Protocol over ATM (MPOA),[42] developed by the ATM Forum, aims to provide network-layer routing for multiple protocols. Multi-Protocol over ATM is an integration effort with the intention of providing a clean Internetworking of ATM networks with legacy subnetworks such as Ethernet. MPOA combines and builds upon the features of classical IP over ATM and LANE, providing a way to bridge and route IP-based applications (and in principle other protocols such as IPX) with high performance and low latency. MPOA maps routed and bridged flows of traffic to ATM switched virtual channels (SVCs), offloading traditional routers from performing packet-by-packet processing. Traffic is transported from the source to the final destination via a single-hop virtual-circuit connection. A key point of MOA is to provide the best

---

[42] ATM Forum, *Multi-Protocol Over ATM Specification v1.0*, ATM Forum Specification, July 1997.

routes for end-system connectivity over ATM networks. All of ATM's QoS features and virtual routing functions are supported. The ATM Forum's complex nomenclature obscures a fairly simple MPOA architecture, shown in Figure 5-18.

As shown in Figure 5-18, MPOA provides end-to-end layer 3 connectivity across an ATM network for hosts either attached directly to the ATM network or indirectly through routers on non-ATM IP (e.g., Ethernet) subnets. Indirectly attached hosts connect to the ATM network using so-called edge devices, which allow the formation of heterogeneous IP subnets (or subnets based on other network-layer protocols). MPOA essentially defines a distributed router. MPOA clients operate with ATM edge switches or routers at the periphery of an ATM network. These devices are responsible for forwarding packets, while the route processing takes place in MPOA routers in the core of the network. These routers supply the ATM edge switches with routing tables and routes upon request. When traffic from a desktop or server enters ATM network, it is routed directly between edge routers or switches, completely bypassing the route servers.

Figure 5-18 MPOA Architecture

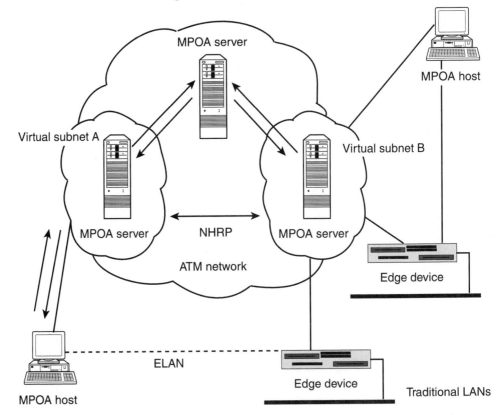

MPOA effectively allows bridging and routing in an ATM network with different protocols and underlying networks. MPOA uses both LANE concepts (for configuration purposes) and NHRP (for short-cut routing) to locate the optimal entry and exit points in an ATM network. Due to its broad scope and more effective support for layer 2 and 3 protocols than LANE, MPOA is expected to be used on a wide basis in heterogeneous ATM networks.

However, even with the advantages that classical IP over ATM, LANE, and MPOA bring to running ATM networks in a mainly Ethernet environment, Gigabit Ethernet usually offers a simpler solution when upgrading existing Ethernet networks that do not require broad-scale WAN integration. The complexity of MPOA and LANE usually lies in the integration details—that is, having to deal with heterogeneous environments. Gigabit Ethernet will operate with existing network protocols in a homogeneous fashion without the setup and installation times associated with classical IP over ATM, LANE, and MPOA.

Maturity

One disadvantage of Gigabit Ethernet is that the product maturity is less than that of other existing networks such as ATM, FDDI, and Fast Ethernet. Though ATM standards are constantly evolving to accommodate the needs of a LAN-based infrastructure, ATM has a large embedded base and is well tested. In order to implement Gigabit Ethernet, product maturity must be taken into account. That having been stated, the reliance of Gigabit Ethernet upon the existing Ethernet and Fibre Channel technologies will, in the long run, hasten the maturity of Gigabit Ethernet products.

Quality of Service and Scalability

ATM QoS is measured by an explicit set of performance parameters negotiated across a UNI interface between the attached network stations and the switch. The parameters defined by the UNI 4.0 specification include the maximum cell transfer delay, peak-to-peak cell delay variation, cell loss and error ratios, and a few others. These parameters are analogous to the latency, jitter, and peak-bandwidth parameters used in RSVP and other reservation protocols that operate over IP-based networks. Based upon these parameters, ATM QoS is classified into several service classes, such as best-effort service and guaranteed service. When using native ATM applications, ATM can offer an explicit QoS guarantee based upon the negotiated parameters. This is something that is more difficult in packet-based networks such as Gigabit Ethernet.

In a March 1997, *Telecommunications* magazine cover story, David Axner, President of DAX Associates, an Internetworking consultancy based in Oreland, Pennsylvania, stated the following about ATM's functionality.

> As a transport technology, ATM's attributes far exceed those of Gigabit Ethernet. It is an
> elegant technology. ATM is seamless, which means that it can be used in the LAN envi-

ronment as well as for WANs. Its scalability is virtually unlimited, while Ethernet is not. ATM's small, fixed-length cell and its Quality of Service (QoS) parameters make it capable of handling all forms of media, including data, graphics, imaging, video, and voice. Ethernet technology, on the other hand, is designed for data transfer. It is not designed to support multimedia applications, especially voice and video, which are sensitive to delay. Although the bandwidth of Gigabit Ethernet is sufficient to handle these applications, there needs to be some mechanism to assign priorities on a per session basis and to minimize delay for voice and video applications over data. ATM's QoS is a solution that guarantees the delivery of delay-sensitive or insensitive transmission on an end-to-end basis.

While the statement that ATM's fixed-length cells allow for easier handling of voice, video, and general multimedia traffic is true, the assertion that packet-based networks such as Gigabit Ethernet are not able to support sensitive multimedia applications is far less viable, given the enormous strides that have been made in the area of QoS assignment, IP switching, and congestion control.

It is clear that ATM offers some real advantages over Gigabit Ethernet in functionality with respect to WAN integration and explicit QoS guarantees, but this is not the only consideration users must examine when trying to determine which technology is best suited to their needs. Cost of ownership, the existing installed base, and overall ease of migration are also very important considerations.

Multimedia Performance Comparison (Voice, Video, and Data)

Voice

The standard digital voice channel currently being used by telephone networks uses 8- bit samples sampled at 4 KHz, which yields a bit rate of 64 Kb/s. When a call is placed, a fixed virtual circuit is established, guaranteeing a 64 Kb/s path through the network for the duration of the call. Usually, in the case of the telephone network, the customer or end user pays for this allocated bandwidth. In order to have uninterrupted speech that is comprehensible the network must be able to guarantee that the voice packets or cells make it to the destination in real time. Telephone customers will not tolerate significant delays in signal propagation.

Gigabit Ethernet has made huge progress over 10 Mb/s and 100 Mb/s Ethernet in delivering voice packets to the destination quickly. This improvement is due primarily to the increased network bandwidth. A customer who has upgraded from 100 Mb/s Ethernet to Gigabit Ethernet has the ability to process hundreds of voice channels and not affect network utilization. For example, a Gigabit Ethernet network with over one thousand voice calls uses far less than 1% of the network bandwidth. However, as the traffic on the network increases due to other high-performance, bursty sources, voice communication may degrade due to packet-buffering delays. Protocols such as RSVP and IEEE 802.1Q allow the reservation of bandwidth over packet-based IP networks for exactly these reasons, to allocate resources to traffic sources that require them. With the use of these protocols to preserve a QoS for the end application, Gigabit Ethernet is a viable, if not optimal solution for voice communication on a congested network. In most instance, due to its raw speed, it more than suffices.

The structure of ATM lends itself well to the implementation of voice traffic over the network. ATM will usually establish an SVC (Switched Virtual Circuit), using UNI signaling and AAL 1, throughout the network at the initiation of a session and eliminate this SVC at the end of the session. The SVC specifies a path and allocates bandwidth through the network. This guarantees that a voice session will have all of its cells delivered through the same path and in a timely fashion. If the network is too congested to guarantee the above criteria, then the session request will be denied. The SVC is very similar to the physical switching done by the telephone network and is therefore adept at carrying voice-only traffic.

Video

The transmission of video images remains the single largest bandwidth-consuming application. Even though it is usually compressed, transmitting video without flickering at 30 images per second still consumes vast bandwidth and processing times. In addition, video, like voice must be displayed at fixed intervals in order to be viewed properly. Late-arriving frames are as good as lost.

Video traffic is very similar to voice traffic because a constant stream[43] is needed to provide decent-quality pictures from source to destination. This, again, is generally problematic in Ethernet-based networks, because the link from sender to receiver is not guaranteed. If video is being sent through the network and there is not adequate bandwidth allocated, then portions of the video stream will be buffered by the network This may cause portions of the picture to arrive out of their timing window and deteriorate the displayed video quality. As mentioned earlier, Ethernet-based networks are attempting to manage this solution by using protocols such as IEEE 802.1Q/p, RSVP, and PACE™ to prioritize and reserve bandwidth. These solutions are further explained in the section on QoS.

As with voice-based traffic, the structure of ATM lends itself well to the implementation of video traffic over the network. The SVC that is established by the network along with ATM's resource-allocation capabilities will assure a constant stream that is necessary for proper playback, provided that the resources are allocated by every node along the transmitting path.

---

[43] Like voice, the rate of display is constant. However, due to compression, the amount of data per display interval may change, which is unlike voice.

Data

Data traffic is bursty in nature and not overly sensitive to delays in transmission. On a fully utilized 10 Mb/s or 100 Mb/s Ethernet network, bursty data traffic from applications such as HTTP and FTP can stand to be buffered during transmission and during transit without the destination experiencing unacceptable delays. Since data traffic does not require a constant flow of packets at specific timing intervals, as do video and voice, this buffering does not sacrifice quality.

Nothing helps the transport of raw data better than speed. Both Gigabit Ethernet and ATM have provide huge increments of speed over existing 10 Mb/s and 100 Mb/s networks. At gigabit rates, an amazing 122,100 1024- byte packets per second can be generated. At 622 Mb/s ATM rates, over 1.5 million ATM cells are transmitted into the network. Now if we could only process all this information....

Where ATM Fits

ATM is a robust technology for scaling campus networks, and a myriad of products are available—products for LAN switching, products for WAN integration, products for network adapters, just to name a few. ATM technology provides the several advantages for campus intranets and should be deployed where the foremost concerns are the following:

*   *Quality of Service (QoS) must be guaranteed.* In a large, heterogeneous environment connected over wide area networks, ATM provides a robust solution to guarantee traffic resources at every node in the network.

*   A *single network is needed infrastructure* for the integration of data, video, and voice traffic (such as voice-circuit emulation and data on the same backbone) that may require explicit guarantees for QoS.

*   *Seamless access is required* from the campus backbone to the WAN, or LAN-to-WAN switching is important.

*   *Network scalability and resiliency are needed.* ATM is eminently scalable, from 155 Mb/s to 622 Mb/s to 2.4 Mb/s.

*   *Complex topologies exist* that do not require layer 3 switching.

Where Gigabit Ethernet Fits

Gigabit Ethernet is also a robust technology for scaling campus networks. Like ATM, Gigabit Ethernet technology provides several advantages for campus intranets and should be deployed where the foremost concerns are the following:

*   Migration and upgrade simplicity as well as cost for bandwidth and installation. There is nothing simpler than installing a 1 Gb/s Ethernet network over an existing 10 Mb/s and 100 Mb/s Ethernet core network. Network-management principles remain the same; all

the existing software runs. If the bulk of the existing network is Ethernet, Gigabit Ethernet is the choice to make.

- Sufficient QoS based on the RSVP and the emerging IEEE 802.1Q/p standard. Delay-sensitive multimedia applications can operate with less stringent QoS levels than packet-based LANs can generally provide.

- Leveraging the installed base of 10 Mb/s Ethernet, 100 Mb/s Ethernet, and existing LAN protocols. Also where seamless connectivity from the desktop through to the network backbone is critical.

- Leveraging the installed base of 10 Mb/s and 100 Mb/s Ethernet knowledge for management, monitoring, and troubleshooting.

- Network traffic that is primarily data or packetized video or voice.

Conclusion

In reality, ATM and Gigabit Ethernet are not equal substitutes for each other and should not be considered as such. Each technology is appropriate for specific applications. Figure 5-19 illustrates a network infrastructure supporting both ATM and Gigabit Ethernet. Simply stated, Gigabit Ethernet will be generally be deployed in areas where 10 Mb/s and 100 Mb/s Ethernet, and other technologies like FDDI, are no longer able to provide the bandwidth needed for pure data traffic. In other words, gigabit

Figure 5-19 ATM and Gigabit Ethernet

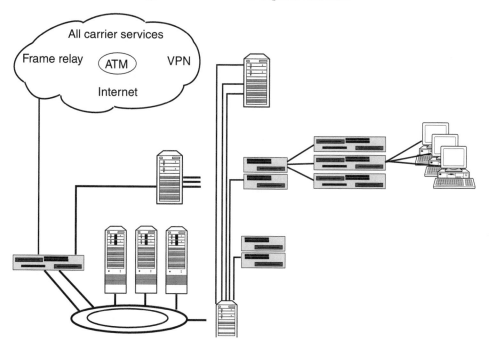

Ethernet will be used in areas where high data throughput is required, and WAN integration and strict QoS are not the main concern. ATM will be used in environments where video, voice, and other delay-sensitive traffic exists and transport across the WAN is of utmost importance. It is more often the case, however, that both networks will coexist and be used for their respective strengths.

5.7.4 Gigabit Ethernet vs. FDDI

FDDI/Copper Distributed Data Interface[44] delivers 100 Mb/s over Cat 5 unshielded twisted-pair (UTP), multimode fiber, and single-mode fiber, the same cabling infrastructure used by Gigabit Ethernet. FDDI employs a timed-token-passing arbitration method for network access. When this scheme is combined with the fact that FDDI supports two counterrotating rings, a highly reliable, fault-tolerant network is created. In addition, FDDI has a in-built network-management capability at each node, Station Management (SMT),[45] which defines an extensive set of statistics designed for troubleshooting the LAN. FDDI also supports a frame format that is based upon the IEEE 802 data-link layers. This allows simple bridging and integration of Ethernet, token ring, and FDDI networks. Due to its high-speed, reliability and distance capabilities, FDDI has become one of the dominant methods of interconnecting campus network and building backbones as well as providing high-speed server connectivity and high-speed backbones where its higher costs have been justified by delivering fast and reliable connections.

FDDI operates at a maximum rate of 100 Mb/s per second. Therefore, referring to the criteria used earlier to determine the applicability of FDDI or Gigabit Ethernet in a new or existing application, it becomes clear that bandwidth capacity for the backbone, server, or enterprise is limited by the FDDI backbone. In applications requiring more bandwidth that are based upon FDDI, Gigabit Ethernet is an attractive alternative.

---

[44] ANSI *FDDI Token Ring Media Access Control (MAC), X3.139-1987, ISO 9314-2,* 1989.
[45] ANSI *Station Management (SMT), X3.152-1990,* 1990.

Looking to the Future

6.1 Overview

Ethernet, in all its incarnations and speeds, is simply the most successful LAN networking technology in history. Its ease of use, technical simplicity, interoperability, and ability to run over existing wiring infrastructures along with its ability to scale from the original 3 Mb/s Ethernet that ran in Xerox's labs to 10 Mb/s, down to 1 Mb/s, to 100 Mb/s and now 1000 Mb/s is unparalleled. Ethernet has seen a myriad of networking technologies compete in various application spaces, from IEEE 802.5 token ring, to ANSI X3T9's FDDI, to ATM. In all cases, Ethernet has dominated in the LAN space by adapting to new media types, increasing speed, supporting heterogeneous networks, and adding multimedia and QoS support.

In this chapter we investigate the future of Ethernet. We begin by discussing the current and future trends and applications that will affect both Gigabit Ethernet and future networking technologies. Then we discuss the challenges facing Gigabit Ethernet along with the challenges that face the industry in evolving to multigigabit and terabit Ethernet networks.

6.2 Industry Trends and Technologies

6.2.1 Trends

The thirst for information and the resulting Internet growth has led to dramatic changes in the very nature of network traffic. Figures 6-1 and 6-2 illustrate the growth in
both Internet hosts and Web sites.[1,2] From a paltry three Internet hosts in 1969, the
Internet has blossomed to over 20 million hosts in 1997 and is expected to reach over
300 million by the year 2000. The growth rate of Internet hosts that support Web servers has been even more staggering, starting with just 130 Web servers in early 1993
and rising to a total of 2.5 million by the end of 1997. The World Wide Web has made
the cost of disseminating information negligible when compared to traditional services such as the post office or facsimile. In fact, a WWW address or URL is as important
as a phone number or facsimile number. Corporations are judged by the effectiveness
and completeness of their Web sites alone. The Web is a much more effective and
quicker method of retrieving and disseminating information than traditional methods.
To top it all off, the Web is not intrusive and never sleeps or closes.

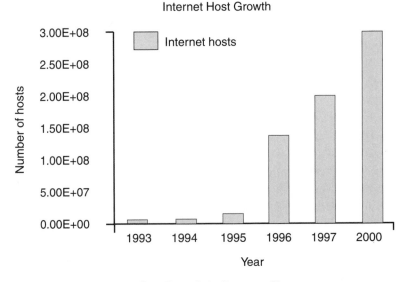

Figure 6-1 Growth in Internet Hosts

[1] Data courtesy of Mathew Gray of the Massachusetts Institute of Technology—
http://www.mit.edu/people/mkgray/net.
[2] B. Leiner, et al. *A Brief History of the Internet V3.1*, February 20, 1997.

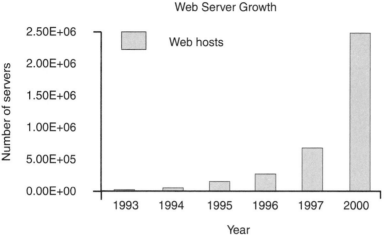

Figure 6-2 Growth in Web Servers

The rise in the ability of the underlying networks to support huge amounts of information has been directly coupled to the growth in computing power. The Sony Playstation™ contains a 200 MIPS microprocessor and has more compute power than the original IBM 360 and many PCs. Computer power is so prevalent that it is routine for families to send pictures of their children to each other over the Internet, using Web-hosting services. The digital cameras that allow the digitization of data process an amazing amount of data and digitize the data for easy information transport. Though the compute power available allows the simple transport of the information, the amount of data in a digital image can be extremely large, sometimes reaching millions of bytes. Assuming 3 bytes per pixel, a simple 320×240 pixel image occupies over 230,000 bytes of memory. MPEG motion sequences are even more demanding. A simple $1024 \times 1024 \times 24$-color graphics screen displaying data at 30 times a second will generate hundreds of megabits of data. It is therefore easy to construct applications that take megabytes of storage and therefore megabytes of network throughput to transport.

The tremendous changes in the Internet and the ability for a vast number of people across the globe to generate huge amounts of data have forced changes on the telecommunications infrastructure. Telephone networks were constructed largely to carry analog telephone calls. As the digitization of data increases, the telecommunications networks are being asked to carry computer network, Internet, and facsimile traffic. In the United States, it is estimated that over 30% of the information flowing over the telephone network is digitized data, and this traffic is growing at a far greater rate than voice traffic. This has forced a complete overhaul in the telecommunications infrastructure that is still continuing. The world's networks are evolving quickly to support gigabit technologies and transmission rates.

6.2.2 Technologies

Trends are driven in large part by technologies. Technology is constantly advancing to provide the changes required to advance networking. In the 1980s, it would never have been technically possible to produce physical layer devices in a cost-effective manner that operated at gigabit rates. In 1998, it is. Improvements in semiconductor processes such as the shrinkage of commodity CMOS densities from 0.35 μ to 0.25 μ and 0.18 μ, allow clocking rates and switching rates in the gigabit-per-second and perhaps hundreds-of-gigabits-per-second range. In addition, the capability for chip-to-chip communication across the pads and pins, along with advancements such as synchronous DRAM and RAMBUS®, have improved chip-to-memory bandwidth to keep pace with the ability of processors to perform billions of instructions per second. The latest RAID (Redundant Arrays of Inexpensive Disks) has given rise to file systems with gigabit bandwidth, allowing a seamless gigabit transfer capability from the file systems to the memory systems to the microprocessors and back to the memory systems and the networks. The future of networking systems consists of staggeringly powerful processors, capable of generating and handling gigabits of data between their memory and file subsystems and their networking subsystems.

6.3 Network Challenges to Support Gigabit Ethernet

The major challenges in Gigabit Ethernet network deployment are to take advantage of the newly developed techniques for building high-speed packet-switching networks, to find ways to evolve them to meet new applications needs, and to encourage the transition of Gigabit Ethernet into the mass market. The emergence of Gigabit Ethernet creates a series of challenges for the network infrastructure that require attention before a mass deployment of Gigabit Ethernet in a manner similar to 10 Mb/s and 100 Mb/s can occur. As explained in the previous chapter, Gigabit Ethernet products such as network adapters and switches have the capability to be deployed in a myriad of applications, starting from server connections to campus backbones and ending with desktop connections. However, the deployment of Gigabit Ethernet creates a number of challenges in addition to simple migration and evolution planning. These include the monitoring and management of gigabit networks, providing and supporting applications that can generate and handle gigabit speeds, and designing large gigabit networks that do not cause network-layer forwarding and routing bottlenecks, just to name a few.

The migration and evolution of Gigabit Ethernet should follow the same pattern of deployment as 100 Mb/s Ethernet. The initial 100 Mb/s Ethernet products were 100 Mb/s switch uplinks for 10 Mb/s routers and switches. In addition, 100 Mb/s network adapters for high-performance servers were offered. These were followed by true

100 Mb/s switches[3] and the widespread deployment of 100 Mb/s network adapters for the desktop. Gigabit Ethernet deployment will follow the same pattern. The initial Gigabit Ethernet networks will be attached to existing 100 Mb/s networks as switch-to-server or switch-to-switch or switch-to-router links. Beyond these initial applications, the industry must address several issues to use the full capacities and capabilities of Ethernet at these speeds. These are addressed briefly below:

- Network management and monitoring of Gigabit Ethernet systems. The management of the tremendous information flow demands novel new approaches to data collection and presentation. Simple software techniques to catalog and sort through data arriving at gigabit rates such as those used for RMON-based management will simply not work. Cataloging and sorting of data based on flows and other innovative techniques will be required.

- Network services at gigabit rates. The use of underlying network services such as Quality of Service (QoS), traffic shaping, policy control and redundancy will be required for operation in a backbone. Gigabit Ethernet providers will be forced to support each of these services in order to ensure that Gigabit Ethernet will be as successful as Fast Ethernet.

- Line-rate forwarding for the network layer. Physical-layer and data-link (MAC) layer forwarding at line rates is possible. The ability to sustain gigabit forwarding rates through network layers such as IP and IPX will be required due to the huge concentration of data at the core of backbone networks.

- Smooth, scalable migration and coexistence with ATM and other existing networks. Network migration is never a complete change. Networks are upgraded piece by piece, bit by bit, over time. Gigabit Ethernet must support a simple, smooth migration from existing FDDI, and 100 Mb/s networks as well as operate in a heterogeneous environment with ATM networks. Coexistence with ATM campus, metropolitan, and WAN technologies will be required. While the basic ideas of IP architecture apply to large gigabit networks, Internetworking technology needs to evolve to take advantage of the new capabilities of gigabit and faster networks.

- Connecting computers to gigabit networks. Standard personal computers will soon need gigabit capabilities in order to transport multimedia and virtual-reality applications. Though it is feasible to deliver data at gigabit rates to a network adapter, there is tremendous difficulty moving the gigabit data through the adapter into a computer's operating system and into the end-user application. Advances in memory management and PC networking stacks will be required to support Gigabit Ethernet.

---

[3] The majority of 100 Mb/s switches and adapters also support 10 Mb/s operation.

6.4 Scaling Gigabit Ethernet

Ethernet has been successfully scaled from 10 Mb/s to 100 Mb/s and finally to 1000 Mb/s. Through it all, it has retained its trademark CSMA/CD MAC protocol, albeit at shorter distances and lowered efficiencies. However, as Ethernet has been scaled, a combination of factors, including the availability of full-duplex media, cost-effective packet-switching technologies and the need for Ethernet to support a wider geographical extent have pushed Ethernet from being a simple half-duplex, shared network to being a cost-effective, full-duplex switched network. 10 Mb/s repeaters outsold 10 Mb/s switches by far. 100 Mb/s switches outsell 100 Mb/s repeaters. At gigabit rates, the trend from shared Ethernet to switched Ethernet deployment is expected to continue. We consider briefly the effect of scaling 1000 Mb/s Ethernet to 10 Gb/s Ethernet in both half and full-duplex designs.

6.4.1 Shared Ethernet

For a traditional shared Ethernet network to operate properly, it must send at least twice the total cable length in bits during any given transmission. In a 10 Mb/s Ethernet, the minimum packet size of 64 bytes allows single collision domain networks of 2 km to be constructed. At 100 Mb/s the minimum packet size allows a 200 m network to be constructed. At 1000 Mb/s, the minimum packet size of 64 bytes allows only a paltry 20 m network. It was for this reason that carrier extension was adopted for Gigabit Ethernet. By extending the carrier to 512 bytes, all stations were guaranteed to notice the transmission, and the network extent was increased to a reasonable value. During the transmission of small packets, however, the carrier-extension period was simply overhead, and performance suffered. Packet bursting increased performance back to acceptable levels by allowing packet transmissions during the carrier-extension period. Carrier extension, coupled with packet bursting, allowed reasonable-size shared Gigabit Ethernet networks to be constructed.

However, at speeds of 10,000 Mb/s, or 10 times faster than Gigabit Ethernet, without carrier extension, the network diameter will be 2 m, a clearly unacceptable diameter. In order to allow reasonable network diameters, carrier extension to around 4096 bytes will be required. This, without the addition of schemes to use the extended carrier, such as packet bursting, will reduce throughput for minimum-size packets to an abysmal 1.5 percent. Even with the addition of packet bursting, the maximum throughput will only approach 30 percent. due to Ethernet's current maximum frame size of 1518 bytes. In addition, as noted in Chapter 4, though the scaling of CSMA/CD from 100 Mb/s to 1000 Mb/s yielded a network of reasonable performance, two critical performance measures decreased: total throughput and collision likelihood. This will also be the case when scaling Ethernet from 1000 Mb/s to 10 Gb/s. The maximum throughput of the system will decrease due to a combination of increased carrier extension overhead and collisions, and the likelihood of collisions will be higher at a lower throughput. It seems that without changes to the venerable CSMA/CD protocol or the Ethernet frame size, the reign of half-duplex shared Ethernet has reached an end.

6.4.2 Switched Ethernet

The scaling of full-duplex Gigabit Ethernet does not suffer from any of the protocol-related problems that affect the scaling of shared Ethernet based upon the CSMA/CD protocol. Full-duplex networks are constructed by several point-to-point connections between stations and switches. The transmission of data is not subject to any access protocol as with CSMA/CD. The transmit channel is always available, and the receive channel is always open.[4] The rate of transmission is determined purely by the bandwidth capacity of the physical point-to-point link, the networking hardware, and the attached switch's capacity. Each is examined in some detail below.

The ability to transmit high-speed data over full-duplex media such as unshielded twisted pair and fiber continues to advance at a fast pace. Gigabit transmission over unshielded twisted pair is accomplished by splitting the transmission link into four channels and transmitting 250 Mb/s over each channel. In order to accomplish this for 10 Gb/s Ethernet, transmission over each channel will have to occur at a staggering 2.5 Gb/s. Though DSP technology is making tremendous strides, this is expected to be problematic in terms of silicon technology and of power consumption for the signal-processing implementations. Ten Gb/s Ethernet transmission will therefore probably be required to utilize fiber media in order to allow cost-effective implementations.

Light has the property that if the angle of incidence is greater than a critical angle, then all of the light is reflected. Fiber media use this property of light when transmitting signals. The bandwidth of a fiber medium is determined by the amount of light it can carry at a given wavelength. Only three wavelengths are commonly used for data transmission over fiber: 850 nm, 1300 nm, and 1500 nm. Each of these wavelengths transmits data over a 200-nm band. Each of these bands has a capacity of 25 to 50 terabits per second.[5] In addition, techniques such as Wavelength Division Multiplexing (WDM), which transmit data over several wavelengths simultaneously, allow a further gain in bandwidth capacity. It is clear that fiber media will support 10 Gb/s Ethernet transmission without the use of complicated or new methods of launching light into the fiber cable.

---

[4] This is, strictly speaking, untrue, since IEEE 802.3x flow control as well as rate and credit-based flow control schemes control access to the transmission channel. However, for the purpose of contrasting half-duplex and full-duplex schemes, this may be ignored.

[5] Remember that $f\lambda = c$. That is, the frequency multiplied by the wavelength must equal the speed of light or 3×10^8 m/s. Differentiating with respect to λ to arrive at the change in frequency with respect to the change in wavelength allows the determination of the capacity of fiber.

In order for networking hardware to scale to 10 Gb/s, both fiber transmitters and receivers and their accompanying clock and timing recovery devices must operate at 10 Gb/s. Currently Synchronous Optical Network (SONET) allows data transmission at 2.488.32 Mb/s (OC-48) rates, and there are semiconductors that support receiving and transmitting data at these rates. There are several gigabit testbeds that utilize OC-48 rates, such as LuckyNet.[6] Gigabit switch implementations exist that provide tens of gigabits of bandwidth capacity. Therefore, scaling Ethernet to 10 Gb/s seems eminently plausible over a full-duplex switched network. It is expected that future implementations of Ethernet will support full-duplex operation with sophisticated flow-control schemes over fiber networks.

6.5 Summary

The past six chapters have covered the Ethernet from its inception through its 10 Mb/s and 100 Mb/s incarnations, focusing on the 1000 Mb/s version of Ethernet. Shared-media and switched Ethernets were explored in detail in Chapters 3 and 5. Gigabit Ethernet operation was described in detail in Chapter 4, and the evolution, applications and new technologies used by Gigabit Ethernet in Chapter 5. Chapter 5 included a comparison of Gigabit Ethernet with ATM and FDDI, concluding that the networks of the future will consist of a heterogeneous mix of ATM and Ethernet networks. The current chapter looked to the future and explored the trends and technologies affecting the vibrant field of computer networks. 10 Gb/s Ethernet and perhaps terabit Ethernet will probably abandon the CSMA/CD protocol that has served Ethernet so well and migrate to a full-duplex-only version with support for frame format and management capabilities. As this book goes to press, the IEEE committee is finalizing the 802.3z Gigabit Ethernet standard, and deployment of Gigabit Ethernet networks is beginning and appears vibrant.

---

[6] R. Gitlin, et al. "Broadband Network Research and the LuckyNet TestBed." *Journal of High Speed Networks,* Vol. 1, No. 1, pp. 1–48.

Appendix A

802.3 Document Cross Reference

The following tables identify the progression of 802.3 Standard documents as published. Each Project Authorization Request (PAR) approved by the 802 Executive Committee is given an alphabetic reference. This reference also becomes the identifier for the Task Force and the documentation produced, initially as a Draft for balloting, and on successful completion of the balloting process, an official 802.3 Supplement to the latest version of the 802.3 Standard. Since the IEEE periodically reprints the base 802.3 Standard, rolling in the latest approved additions (after they new material has been approved by ISO), each edition of the Standard increases in size (and weight!). Standards are now also available via World Wide Web access and on CD ROM.

Each Supplement to the 802.3 Standard (a Supplement is the term for the approved document produced by a Working Group), is published by the IEEE and only exists as a separate document until it is rolled into the next publication of the approved standard. Because of the high level of activity in 802.3 in recent years, one unfortunate consequence is that some Supplements change previous Supplements that have not yet been rolled into the complete set. So, finding the exact latest specification for everything relies on looking at more than one document.

While this is interesting historical information, the following are the most recent and valuable published documents relating to 802.3.

Latest Base Document (8802-3: 1996)

The suite of Clauses that currently cover all of the 1 Mb/s and 10 Mb.s speed options, including Ethernet, Cheapernet, 10BASE-T and 10BASE-F, as well as the MAC, repeater, management, and system topologies.

Title: International Standard ISO/IEC 8802-3: 1996 (E), ANSI/IEEE 802.3, 1996 Edition, Information technology-Telecommunications and information exchange between systems-Local and metropoloitan area networks-Specific requirements-Part3: Carrier sense multiple access with collision detection (CSMA/CD) access method and physical layer specifications, IEEE, New York, NY. ISBN 1-55937-555-6. July 29, 1996.

100BASE-T Specification (802.3u: 1995)

The suite of Clauses relevant to the most popular Fast Ethernet versions, including the 100BASE-TX, and 100BASE-FX physical layers, 100 Mb/s repeater and management, and system topologies.

Title: IEEE Std 802.3u-1995. Medium Access Control (MAC), Physical Layer, Medium Attachment Units, and Repeater for 100 Mb/s Operation, Type 100BASE-T (Clauses 21-30). ISBN 1-55937-542-6. October 26, 1995.

Full Duplex and 100BASE-T2 Specification (802.3x&y: 1997)

The definition for full duplex and flow control operation, as well as the 100BASE-T2 physical layer (although much less popular that either TX, FX or T4).

Title: IEEE Std 802.3x-1997 and IEEE Std 802.3y-1997 (Supplement to ISO/IEC 8802-3: 1995 [ANSI/IEEE Std 802.3, 1996 Edition]). Specification for 802.3 Full Duplex Operation and Physical Layer Specification for 100 Mb/s Operation on Two Pairs of Category 3 or Better Balanced Twisted Pair Cable (100BASE-T2). ISBN 1-55939-905-7. November 18, 1997.

Gigabit Ethernet Specification (P802.3z)

The Suite of Clause that define the initial gigabit operation, including the 1000BASE-SX, 1000BASE-LX and 1000BASE-CX physical layers, 1000 Mb/s repeater and management, and system topologies.

Title: IEEE Draft P802.3z. Media Access Control (MAC) Parameters, Physical Layer, Repeater and Management Parameters for 1000 Mb/.s Operation.

Table A-1 IEEE802.3 Task Forces and Document Titles

Task Force	Common Name	Section or Clause[a]	Official 802.3 Document Title	Relevant Chapter(s) In This Book
802.3a	10BASE2	Section 10	ANSI/IEEE Std 802.3b, c, d and e-1989 Edition. Supplements to Carrier Sense Multiple Access with Collision Detection.	2
802.3b	10BROAD36	Section 11	ANSI/IEEE Std 802.3b, c, d and e-1989 Edition. Supplements to Carrier Sense Multiple Access with Collision Detection.	2
802.3c	10 Mb/s Repeater	Section 9	ANSI/IEEE Std 802.3b, c, d and e-1989 Edition. Supplements to Carrier Sense Multiple Access with Collision Detection.	2
802.3d	FOIRL	Section 9.9	ANSI/IEEE Std 802.3b, c, d and e-1989 Edition. Supplements to Carrier Sense Multiple Access with Collision Detection.	2
802.3e	1BASE5	Section 12	ANSI/IEEE Std 802.3b, c, d and e-1989 Edition. Supplements to Carrier Sense Multiple Access with Collision Detection.	2
802.3f	Multipoint Extension to 1BASE5	Section 12		N/A
802.3g	AUI Cable Conformance	1802.3 Section 4[b]	IEEE Std 1802.3-1991. Conformance Test Methodology, Carrier Sense Multiple Access with Collision Detection (CSMA/CD) Access Method and Physical Layer Specifications. Attachment Unit Interface (AUI) Cable (Section 4).	N/A
802.3h	DTE Management	Section 5	IEEE Std 802.3h-1990. Layer Management (Section 5).	2, 3, 4
802.3i	10BASE-T	Section 13-14	IEEE Std 802.3i-1990. System Considerations for Multisegment 10 Mb/s Baseband Networks (Section 13). Twisted-Pair Medium Attachment Unit (MAU) and Baseband Medium, Type 10BASE-T (Section 14).	2
802.3j	10BASE-F	Section 15-18	IEEE Std 802.3j-1993. Fiber Optic Active and Passive Star-Based Segments, Type 10BASE-F (Sections 15-18)	2
802.3k	Repeater Management	Section 19	IEEE Std 802.3k-1992. Layer Management for 10 Mb/s Baseband Repeaters (Section 19).	2, 3, 4
802.3l[c]	10BASE-T PICS Pro Forma	Section 6	IEEE Std 1802.3d-1993. Conformance Test Methodology, Carrier Sense Multiple Access with Collision Detection (CSMA/CD) Access Method and Physical Layer Specifications. Type 10BASE-T Medium Attachment Unit (MAU) (Section 6).	N/A

Table A-1 IEEE802.3 Task Forces and Document Titles (Continued)

802.3m[d]	Maintenance Ballot # 2			N/A
802.3n[e]	Maintenance Ballot # 3			N/A
802.3o[f]	Not Used			N/A
802.3p	MAU Management	Section 20	IEEE Std 802.3p and q-1993. Guidelines for the Development of Managed Objects (GDMO) (ISO 10164-4) Format for Layer-Managed Objects (Section 5) and Layer Management for 10 Mb/s Baseband Medium Attachment Units (MAUs) (Section 20).	2, 3, 4
802.3q	GDMO of Layer Management	Section 5	IEEE Std 802.3p and q-1993. Guidelines for the Development of Managed Objects (GDMO) (ISO 10164-4) Format for Layer-Managed Objects (Section 5) and Layer Management for 10 Mb/s Baseband Medium Attachment Units (MAUs) (Section 20).	N/A
802.3r	10BASE5 MAU PICS Pro Forma	Clause 8.8	IEEE Std 802.3r-1996. Carrier Sense Multiple Access with Collision Detection (CSMA/CD) Access Method and Physical Layer Specifications. Type 10BASE5 Medium Attachment Unit (MAU) Protocol Implementation Conformance Statement (PICS) Proforma (Subclause 8.8).	N/A
802.3s[g]	Maintenance Ballot # 4			N/A
802.3t	120 Ohm Informative Annex for 10BASE-T	Annex D.5	10BASE-T Use of Cabling Systems with a Nominal Differential Characteristic Impedance of 120 Ohm.	2
802.3u	100 Mb/s CSMA/CD	Clause 21-30	IEEE Std 802.3u-1995. Medium Access Control (MAC), Physical Layer, Medium Attachment Units, and Repeater for 100 Mb/s Operation, Type 100BASE-T (Clauses 21-30).	3
802.3v	150 Ohm Informative Annex for 10BASE-T	Annex D.6	10BASE-T Use of Cabling Systems with a Nominal Differential Characteristic Impedance of 150 Ohm.	2
802.3w[h]	BLAM	N/A	IEEE Draft P802.3w Supplement to 802.3 - Standard for Enhanced Media Access Control Algorithm.	
802.3x	Full Duplex/Flow Control		IEEE Std 802.3x-1997 and IEEE Std 802.3y-1997. Specification for 802.3 Full Duplex Operation and Physical Layer Specification for 100 Mb/s Operation on Two Pairs of Category 3 or Better Balanced Twisted Pair Cable (100BASE-T2).	3

Table A-1 IEEE802.3 Task Forces and Document Titles (Continued)

802.3y	100BASE-T2	Clause 32	IEEE Std 802.3x-1997 and IEEE Std 802.3y-1997. Specification for 802.3 Full Duplex Operation and Physical Layer Specification for 100 Mb/s Operation on Two Pairs of Category 3 or Better Balanced Twisted Pair Cable (100BASE-T2).	3
802.3z	Gigabit Ethernet	Clause 34-39, 41-42	IEEE Draft P802.3z. Media Access Control (MAC) Parameters, Physical Layer, Repeater and Management Parameters for 1000 Mb/.s Operation.	4
802.3aa[aa]	Maintenance Ballot #5			N/A
802.3ab	1000BASE-T	Clause 40	IEEE Draft.P802.3ab. Physical Layer Specification for 1000 Mb/s Operation on Four Pairs of Category 5 or Better Balanced Twisted Pair Cable (1000BASE-T).	4
802.3ac	VLAN Tagging	Edits to Clauses 1, 3, 4, 5, 25, 26, 30.	Frame Extensions for Virtual Bridged Local Area Networks (VLAN) Tagging on 802.3 Networks	3
802.3ad	Link Aggregation		No Draft documant at time of publication (PAR approved in March, 1998).	

[a] Prior to 100BASE-T, each chapter in 802.3 was referred to as a Section. For some reason, ISO changes this language to Clause. Older versions of the Standards still refer to Sections.

[b] Conformance Test Documents did not follow the original Section number of the base document to which they referred, since the intent was to develop a full suite of test procedures, identified with the "1802" document prefix.

[c] The 10BASE-T MAU Conformance Test document did nor follow previous conventions for numbering.

[d] Maintenance Ballots generally contain a collection of technical errata which affect multiple Clauses, so are usually not specific to a single Clause.

[e] Maintenance Ballots generally contain a collection of technical errata which affect multiple Clauses, so are usually not specific to a single Clause.

[f] Not used to avoid confusion.

[g] Maintenance Ballots generally contain a collection of technical errata which affect multiple Clauses, so are usually not specific to a single Clause.

[h] Work on the BLAM Draft was abandoned due to lack of support, and the Draft was not Balloted.

[aa] Maintenance Ballots generally contain a collection of technical errata which affect multiple Clauses, so are usually not specific to a single Clause.

802.3 Section/Clause Cross Reference

The following table identifies the primary source and content for each 802.3 Section/Clause. The initial source should be used as the basis of technical content. In many cases, later development work has modified some of the content of the original Section/Clause, the latest of which is in each case referenced.

Table A-2 Primary Source and Content for Each 802.3 Section/Clause

Section or Clause	Clause Name	First Published 802.3 Document	Last Revised in 802.3 Document	Relevant Chapter(s) in This Book
1	Introduction	Original base document[a]	1998 (by 802.3z)	Glossary
2	Medium Access Control (MAC) Service Specification	Original base document[a]	1997 (by 802.3x)	2, 3
3	MAC Frame Structure	Original base document [a]	1998 (by 802.3z and 802.3ac)	2, 4
4	Media Access Control	Original base document [a]	1998 (by 802.3z and 802.3ac)	2, 4
5	Layer Management	Original base document [a]	1998 (by 802.3z)	2, 3, 4
Section 5	Layer Management	802.3h	1998 (by 802.3z)	2, 3, 4
Section 5	GDMO of Layer Management	802.3q	1993	N/A
6	Physical Signaling (PLS) Service Specification	Original base document [a]	1997 (by 802.3x)	2
7	Physical Signaling (PLS) and Attachment Unit Interface (AUI) Specifications	Original base document [a]	1997 (by 802.3x)	2
8	Medium Attachment Units (MAU) and Baseband Medium Specification, Type 10BASE5	Original base document [a]	1985	2
9	Repeater Unit for 10 Mb/s Baseband Networks	Original base document [a]	1993 (by 802.3j)	2
9	Repeater Unit for 10 Mb/s Baseband Networks	802.3c	1993 (by 802.3j)	2
9.9	Medium Attachment Unit and Baseband Medium Specification for a Vendor Independent Fiber Optic Inter Repeater Link	802.3d	1993 (by 802.3j)	2
10	Medium Attachment Units (MAU) and Baseband Medium Specification, Type 10BASE2	802.3a	1985	2
11	Broadband Medium Attachment Unit and Broadband Medium Specifications, Type 10BROAD36	802.3b	1985	1, 2
12	Physical Signaling, Medium, Attachment, and Baseband Medium Specifications, Type 1BASE5	802.3e	1987	2
12	Multipoint Extension to 1BASE5	802.3f		N/A
13	System Considerations for Multisegment 10 Mb/s Baseband Networks	802.3i	1993 (by 802.3j)	2
14	Twisted-Pair Medium Attachment Unit (MAU) and Baseband Medium, Type 10BASE-T	802.3i	1995 (by 802.3u)	2
15	Fiber Optic Medium and Common Elements of Medium Attachment Units and Star, Type 10BASE-F	802.3j	1993	2
16	Fiber Optic Passive Star and Medium Attachment Units, Type 10BASE-FP	802.3j	1993	2

Table A-2 Primary Source and Content for Each 802.3 Section/Clause

17	Fiber Optic Medium Attachment Units, Type 10BASE-FB	802.3j	1993	2
18	Fiber Optic Attachment Units, Type 10BASE-FL	802.3j	1993	2
19	Layer Management for 10 Mb/s Baseband Repeaters	802.3k	1995 (by 802.3u)	2, 3, 4
20[b]	Layer Management for 10 Mb/s Baseband Medium Attachment Units (MAUs)	802.3p	1995 (802.3u)	2, 3, 4
21	Introduction to 100 Mb/s Baseband Networks, Type 100BASE-T	802.3u	1995	3
22	Reconciliation Sublayer (RS) and Medium Independent Interface (MII)	802.3u	1998 (by 802.3z)	3
23	Physical Coding Sublayer (PCS), Physical Medium Attachment (PMA) Sublayer and Baseband Medium, Type 100BASE-T4	802.3u	1995	3
24	Physical Coding Sublayer (PCS) and Physical Medium Attachment (PMA) Sublayer, Type 100BASE-X	802.3u	1995	3
25	Physical Medium Dependent (PMD) Sublayer and Baseband Medium, Type 100BASE-TX	802.3u	1998 (by 802.3ac)	3
26	Physical Medium Dependent (PMD) Sublayer and Baseband Medium, Type 100BASE-FX	802.3u	1998 (by 802.3ac)	3
27	Repeater for 100 Mb/s Baseband Networks	802.3u	1995	3
28	Physical Layer Link Signaling for 10 Mb/s and 100 Mb/s Auto-Negotiation on Twisted Pair	802.3u	1997 (by 802.3y)	3
29	System Considerations for Multi-Segment 100BASE-T Networks	802.3u	1997 (by 802.3y)	3
30	Layer Management for 10 Mb/s and 100 Mb/s	802.3u	1998 (by 802.3z)	3
31	MAC Control	802.3x	1998 (by 802.3z)	3
32	Physical Coding Sublayer (PCS), Physical Medium Attachment (PMA) Sublayer and Baseband Medium, Type 100BASE-T2	802.3y	1997	3
33	Not Used	N/A	N/A	N/A
34	Introduction to 1000 Mb/s Baseband	802.3z	1998	4
35	Reconciliation Sublayer (RS) and Gigabit Media Independent Intergace (GMII)	802.3z	1998	4
36	Physical Coding Sublayer (PCS) and Physical Medium Attachment (PMA) Sublayer, Type 1000BASE-X	802.3z	1998	4
37	Auto-Negotiation Function, Type 1000BASE-X	802.3z	1998	4

Table A-2 Primary Source and Content for Each 802.3 Section/Clause

38	Physical Medium Dependent (PMD) Sub-layer and Baseband Medium, Type 1000BASE-LX (Long Wavelength Laser) and 1000BASE-SX (Short Wavelength Laser)	802.3z	1998	4
39	Physical Medium Dependent (PMD) Sub-layer and Baseband Medium, Type 1000BASE-CX	802.3z	1998	4
41	Repeater for 1000 Mb/s Baseband Net-works	802.3z	1998	4
42	System Considerations for Multi-Segment 1000 Mb/s Networks	802.3z	1998	4
40	Physical Layer Specification for 1000 Mb/s Operation on Four Pairs of Category 5 or Better Balanced Twisted Pair Cable (1000BASE-T)	802.3ab	TBD	4
Various	Frame Extensions for Virtual Bridged Local Area Networks (VLAN) Tagging on 802.3 Networks	802.3ac	1998	3

[a] Original base document approved June 23, 1983, published December 31, 1984.

[b] Current ISO/IEC 8802-3 base document contains all of Sections 1-20.

Appendix B

802.3/Ethernet Frame and Address Formats

Canonical Address Format

Ethernet/802.3 (as well as 802.4, Token Bus) devices transmit bytes with least-significant-bit-first ordering, whereas 802.5 (Token Ring) and FDDI use a most-significant-bit-first ordering convention. The significance of this would be relatively minor were it not for the complication that the indication of individual or multicast address within the destination address field is defined as the first bit on the wire, rather than the most significant or least significant bit of the address. Hence a multicast address on an Ethernet network may not appear as a multicast address on 802.5 or FDDI. This has led to considerable confusion, interoperability problems, and much complication in such equipment as bridges, routers, and switches, which may have to convert between the two conventions.

A canonical format is used in an attempt to reduce this confusion, which assumes hexadecimal notation and least-significant-bit-first ordering. For example, the address c2-34-56-78-9a-bc is not a multicast address, since the least significant bit of the first byte (c4, which is 1100 0010 in binary) is 0.

| 1100 0010 | 0011 0100 | 0101 0110 | 0111 1000 | 1001 1010 | 1011 1100 |

↳ Least significant bit of least significant byte transmitted first

Figure B-1 Canonical Address c2-34-56-78-9a-bc Stored for
Least Significant Bit First Transmission

| 0100 0011 | 0010 1100 | 0110 1010 | 0001 1110 | 0101 1001 | 0011 1101 |

↳ Most significant bit of least significant byte transmitted first

Figure B-2 Canonical Address c2-34-56-78-9a-bc Stored for
Most Significant Bit First Transmission

The Ethernet Version 2.0 Frame Format

The Ethernet V2.0 frame format remains the most widespread formal in use in most networks. From the initial invention of Ethernet to 1997, Xerox administered the EtherType field, which acts as the protocol multiplexing field. In 1997, IEEE 802 took over the administration of the EtherType field from Xerox

The protocol identifier information carried in this 2-byte field allows a transmitting device to indicate the protocol it is using and a receiving device to determine if it can understand such a protocol. With a 16-bit field, there is adequate space for a large number of protocols to be supported.

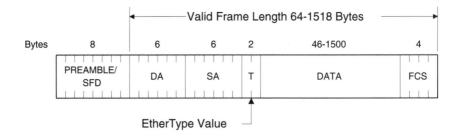

Figure B-3 Ethernet Frame Format

In order to prevent EtherType values clashing with valid 802.3 Length values (both carried in the same field), valid EtherType values start at. 0600 h. This equates to a corresponding length value of 1536 bytes, which is illegal in terms of an 802.3 frame length. Hence 802.3 and Ethernet devices can coexist.

Some early protocols were assigned EtherType values below the 0600 h range prior to 802.3 adopting the Ethernet protocol but these have subsequently either become obsolete or have been reassigned.

The IEEE 802.3 Frame Format (LLC)

802.2 defined the Logical Link Control (LLC) header, which was intended to allow protocol information to be exchanged independent of the underlying MAC technology. While this was a good idea, the result was less than perfect. Service Access Points (SAPs) were defined to indicate the destination and source protocols, providing the flexibility of assigning different numbers to the same protocol in different machines. This flexibility came at the expense of the number of protocols that could be supported, with only a single byte field for the destination SAP (DSAP) and source SAP (SSAP). This was compounded by the fact that individual/group and local/global bits were also reserved, reducing the SAP field to 6 bits. IEEE 802 administers the assignment of the small pool of global SAPs.

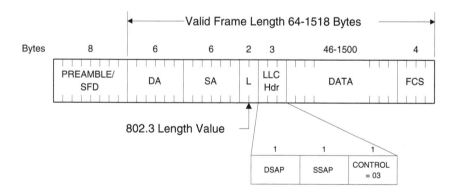

Figure B-4 802.3 Frame Format with 802.2 LLC Header

The Control field is also contained with the LLC header and allows the LLC type and additional information to be passed. LLC type 1 is almost exclusively used for Ethernet LANs, which indicates a "datagram" service. LLC type 2 is used for "connection-oriented" service. LLC type 3 is used for "semireliable" service.

The 802.3 SNAP Encapsulated Frame Format

The SNAP (Sub-Network Access Protocol) extension to the globally administered SAP address scheme was developed to support the reasonable demands for a larger number of protocols. By using a globally administered SAP value (AA h), protocols that do not have a globally assigned SAP value (from IEEE 802) extend the protocol type field by an additional 5 bytes following the LLC header field.

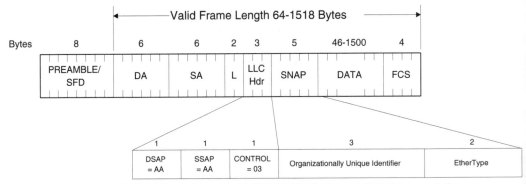

Figure B-5 802.3 Frame Format with 802.2 LLC Header and SNAP Encapsulation

This requires setting the DSAP and SSAP to the globally assigned value of AA h, indicating the SNAP SAP extension is in use, and setting the control field to 03 h (indicating "unnumbered information," simply a datagram). The first 3 bytes of the SNAP extension are set to the 24-bit OUI value uniquely assigned to Ethernet manufacturers and the remaining 2 bytes carry the EtherType value.

Appendix C

The simulation model was run with a simple empirical traffic model, known as the *workgroup average distribution* (Figure C-1). The data was derived from traffic measurements performed on several 10 Mb/s and 100 Mb/s networks at Sun Microsystems, Advanced Micro Devices and 3Com and presented to the IEEE 802.3z group in the spring of 1996.

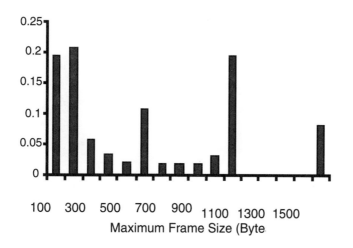

Glossary

4B/5B Code

The 4B/5B code is a binary block code used by both the FDDI and 100BASE-TX physical layers. In 100BASE-TX, 4 bits of data are encoded into 4 bits and transmitted at 125 Mb/s, yielding an effective data rate of 100 Mb/s. See Block Code.

8B/6T Code

The 8B/6T code is used by 100BASE-T4. 100BASE-T4 uses different physical layers than 100BASE-X. 100BASE-T4 combines and optimizes block coding and ternary signaling into an encoding scheme called 8B6T. 8B6T replaces each 8-bit byte with a code of only six ternary-state symbols. To represent 6 ternary bit bytes, 729 ternary symbols are possible. Of the 729, only 256 symbols have been chosen as a one-to-one remapping of every possible byte. See IEEE 802.3 Annex 23A.

8B/10B Code

The 8B/10B code is a binary block code used by both the Fibre Channel and 1000BASE-T physical layers. In 1000BASE-T, 8 bits of data are encoded into 10 bits and transmitted at 1.25 Gb/s, yielding an effective data rate of 1 Gb/s. See Block Code.

10BASE2 - 10 Mb/s Baseband 200 m (Cheapernet)

A low cost version of 10BASE5 (frequently referred to as Cheapernet), it eliminates the external AUI requirement, relaxes the network electrical interfaces and allows use of thin 50 Ω coaxial cable. Maximum 30 nodes (or mating connectors) on cable segment, 185 m per segment. Defined in Section 10 of ISO/IEC 8802-3 : 1996 (ANSI/IEEE Std 802.3).

10BASE5 - 10 Mb/s Baseband 500 m (Ethernet)

Based on the original Ethernet specification proposed by DEC, Intel and Xerox, for multi-drop communication scheme using the CSMA/CD access protocol, over thick 50 Ω coaxial cable. 802.3 is the corresponding IEEE standard which varies in minor electrical and protocol specifications. Maximum 100 nodes on cable segment, 500 m per segment. Defined in Section 8 of ISO/IEC 8802-3 : 1996 (ANSI/IEEE Std 802.3).

10BASE-FB - 10 Mb/s Baseband Fiber Optic Backbone

Covered by Section 17 of IEEE 802.3. Uses 802.3 protocol, dual fiber point-to-point cabling with synchronous signaling to provide an interrepeater "backbone" link. No defined maximum node count, maximum fiber distance 2 km, depending on system configuration.

10BASE-FL - 10 Mb/s Baseband Fiber Optic Link

Covered by Section 18 of IEEE 802.3. Uses 802.3 protocol, dual fiber point-to-point cabling and repeaters to provide the network architecture. No defined maximum node count, maximum fiber distance 1–2 km, depending on system configuration.

10BASE-FP - 10 Mb/s Baseband Fiber Optic Passive

Covered by Section 16 of IEEE 802.3. Uses 802.3 protocol, dual-fiber point-to-point cabling and passive optical star to provide the network architecture. No defined maximum node count, maximum fiber distance 0.5 km, depending on system configuration.

10BASE-T - 10 Mb/s Baseband Twisted Pair

Covered by Section 14 of IEEE 802.3. Uses 802.3 protocol, point-to-point twisted pair cabling and repeaters to provide network services. No defined maximum node count, maximum cable distance 100 m. Defined in Section 13 and 14 of IEEE Std 802.3i-1990 (Supplement to ISO/IEC 8802-3 : 1996 (ANSI/IEEE Std 802.3)).

25-Pair Cable

In the U.S., 25-pair bundles of UTP are sometimes used to connect 10BASE-T multiport repeaters or switches. Initially, 25-pair cable (and the associated connectors) was only commonly available to Cat 3 rating. Cat 5 rated 25-pair cables and connectors are now available. The 25-pair bundles are normally broken out at a "punch-down" block, where the connection to the individual 2- or 4-pair user cable is made.

50/125 μm Multimode Fiber

The most popular core/cladding size of fiber in Europe and Japan and also recommended by ISO. This size of fiber has superior transmission properties when compared to 62.5/125 μm, but due to its smaller size, requires more complicated and expensive optics.

62.5/125 μm Multimode Fiber

The most popular core/cladding size of fiber in North America and recommended by ISO.

100BASE-FX - 100 Mb/s Baseband Fiber Optic

The IEEE 802.3 Physical Layer signaling specification for a 100 Mb/s CSMA/CD LAN over two 62.5/125 μm or 50/125 μm fibers. 100BASE-FX is based on the FDDI Physical Layer. Defined in Clauses 24 and 26 of IEEE Std 802.3u-1995 (Supplement to ISO/IEC 8802-3 : 1996 (ANSI/IEEE Std 802.3)).

100BASE-T2 - 100 Mb/s Baseband Twisted Pair

The IEEE 802.3 Physical Layer signaling specification for a 100 Mb/s CSMA/CD LAN over two pairs of Category 3, 4, or 5 UTP or STP cable. Defined in Clause 32 of IEEE Std 802.3y-1997 (Supplement to ISO/IEC 8802-3 : 1990 (ANSI/IEEE Std 802.3)).

100BASE-T4 - 100 Mb/s Baseband Twisted Pair

The IEEE 802.3 Physical Layer signaling specification for a 100 Mb/s CSMA/CD LAN over four pairs of Category 3, 4, or 5 UTP or STP cable. 100BASE-T4 uses an 8B/6T coding scheme to transmit and receive data on the physical medium. Defined in Clause 23 of IEEE Std 802.3u-1995 (Supplement to ISO/IEC 8802-3 : 1996 (ANSI/IEEE Std 802.3)).

100BASE-T - 100 Mb/s Baseband Twisted Pair

The IEEE 802.3 Physical Layer signaling specification for a 100 Mb/s CSMA/CD LAN. Defined in Clauses 22 to 30 of IEEE Std 802.3u-1995 (Supplement to ISO/IEC 8802-3 : 1996 (ANSI/IEEE Std 802.3)).

100BASE-TX - 100 Mb/s Baseband Twisted Pair

The IEEE 802.3 Physical Layer signaling specification for a 100 Mb/s CSMA/CD LAN over two pairs of Category 5 UTP or STP cable. 100BASE-TX is based upon the FDDI Physical Layer. Defined in Clauses 24 and 25 of IEEE Std 802.3u-1995 (Supplement to ISO/IEC 8802-3 : 1996 (ANSI/IEEE Std 802.3)).

1000BASE-CX - 1000 Mb/s Baseband Copper Cable

The IEEE 802.3z Physical Layer signaling specification for a 1000 Mb/s CSMA/CD LAN over two pairs of 150 ohm balanced copper cable. 1000BASE-CX is based upon the Fibre Channel Physical Layer. Defined in Clause 39 of IEEE Std 802.3z (Supplement to ISO/IEC 8802-3 : 1996 (ANSI/IEEE Std 802.3)).

1000BASE-LX - 1000 Mb/s Baseband Long Wavelength Fiber

The IEEE 802.3z Physical Layer signaling specification for a 1000 Mb/s CSMA/CD LAN over a pair of optical fibers using long wavelength optics. 1000BASE-LX is based upon the Fibre Channel Physical Layer. Defined in Clause 38 of IEEE Std 802.3z (Supplement to ISO/IEC 8802-3 : 1996 (ANSI/IEEE Std 802.3)).

1000BASE-SX - 1000 Mb/s Baseband Short Wavelength Fiber

The IEEE 802.3z Physical Layer signaling specification for a 1000 Mb/s CSMA/CD LAN over a pair of optical fibers using short wavelength optics. 1000BASE-SX is based upon the Fibre Channel Physical Layer. Defined in Clause 38 of IEEE Std 802.3z (Supplement to ISO/IEC 8802-3 : 1996 (ANSI/IEEE Std 802.3)).

1000BASE-T - 1000 Mb/s Baseband Twisted Pair

The IEEE 802.3z Physical Layer signaling specification for a 1000 Mb/s CSMA/CD LAN over four pairs of Category 5 Unshielded Twisted Pair cable. Defined in IEEE Std 802.3ab (Supplement to ISO/IEC 8802-3 : 1996 (ANSI/IEEE Std 802.3)).

AAL

A set of internationally standardized protocols and formats that support circuit emulation, packet video, data, and audio services over either connection-oriented or connectionless networks.

AppleTalk

A networking protocol used primarily to connect Apple computers.

ARIS

A form of topology-based switching originated by IBM that uses one virtual circuit per egress router.

ASIC - Application-Specific Integrated Circuit

An ASIC is a chip designed for a particular application. Generally ASICs utilize verified and proven building blocks that have been used previously.

ATM - Asynchronous Transfer Mode

A high-speed connection-oriented network that utilizes fixed-length (53 byte) cells to support multiple classes of service.

ATM Forum

An industry group the supports ATM standards. Information is available at http://www.atmforum.com.

Attenuation

As signals are transmitted through lossy media, they are attenuated or reduced in power and strength. Attenuation is the reduction in signal strength from the time it is initially transmitted into a medium such as optical cable to the time it is received.

AUI - Attachment Unit Interface

IEEE specification for a node or repeater connection interface to an external Medium Attachment Unit (MAU). The AUI cable between the DTE/repeater and the MAU may be up to 50 m in length. In systems where the MAU is embedded into the DTE or repeater (such as 10BASE-T or 10BASE2) a physical implementation of the AUI may not be present. Defined in Section 7 of ISO/IEC 8802-3 : 1996 (ANSI/IEEE Std 802.3). See also "PLS."

Auto-Negotiation

An algorithm that allows two devices at either end of a 10 Mb/s, 100 Mb/s or 1000 Mb/s link advertise and negotiate enhanced modes of operation such as the speed of the link and whether or not the link is to run at half or full duplex. Auto-Negotiation is defined in Clause 28 of IEEE Std 802.3u-1995 and Clause 37 of IEEE Std 802.3z.

Base Page

The first Link Code Word transmitted within an FLP burst during Auto-Negotiation that conveys the device type and technologies supported by the transmitting node. The Base Page is transmitted during renegotiation, reset or power-on.

Baud Rate

The baud rate is a signaling speed term, defined as the number of times per second that the electrical or optical transmission medium can change state. This may be identical, greater or less than the data rate, dependent of the efficiency of the coding scheme employed.

BGP

BGP is a routing protocol that supports classless inter-domain routing and is the standard for routing between internet domains. RFC 1771 details BGP.

BFOC - Bayonet Fiber Optic Connector

The plug and socket connector used for fiber optic cables employed in 10BASE-FL, 10BASE-FB and 10BASE-FP network installations.

Blinding Time

The blinding time is the period that an Ethernet device does not monitor receive carrier activity from the network. For instance, a 10 Mb/s Ethernet DTE is permitted a blinding time after transmission of each frame, in order to ignore activity caused by the normal SQE Test burst returned by a transceiver to indicate the collision-detection process and AUI cable are operational and intact. In general, repeaters are not permitted to implement any blinding time to network activity.

Block Code

In a block code, the data stream is divided into a fixed number of bits in a block, each of which is translated into a block of data symbols. The data symbols used for Ethernet encoding schemes are based on either binary level (such as 4B/5B and 8B/10B) or ternary level (such as 8B/6T) signals. Symbols from the encoded alphabet can be chosen such that they exhibit properties that assist the robustness of the transmission scheme, such as:

- Maintaining DC balance on copper media, to avoid excessive positive or negative disparity symbols changing the line.

- Providing sufficient transition density by preventing the possibility of transmitting for long periods with no timing energy, to allow the receiver to decode symbols easily.

- Error checking for robustness by maintaining coding rules based on the state of previous symbols transmitted or received; a following symbol may be determined to be invalid based on these rules.

BNC - Bayonet Neill Concelman

The connector type for RG58 coaxial cable used in 10BASE2 (Cheapernet) network installations.

Broadcast Domain

A VLAN network in which traffic sent to the broadcast address (the DA field is all 1s) in a bridge interconnected network, is only forwarded to other ports on that bridge which have members of that particular VLAN attached. In contrast, a bridge that was not VLAN aware, would forward broadcast traffic received on one port, to all of its other ports (or at least, to those ports permitted by the Spanning Tree protocol).

Bridge

Bridges are devices that operate at the MAC sublayer level, above the PHY layer at which a repeater device operates. Bridge operation is defined by the IEEE 802.1D standard and connects IEEE 802 MAC technologies together. A bridge uses MAC-level information in order to make forwarding and filtering decisions.

Burst Length

The Burst Length is the length of the actual burst transmission by a DTE.

Burst Timer

The Burst Timer is used to time 1000 Mb/s half-duplex transmissions. A DTE can transmit frames until the burst timer expires, at which point it must relinquish the medium. The Burst Timer is started once transmission begins and expires after 65536 bit times.

Capture Effect

Capture Effect is a phenomenon in which a DTE that transmits successfully after a collision has a higher chance of transmitting new frames than a DTE which has lost the collision resolution. In a busy network, this results in a DTE having a long period of transmission while other DTEs are unable to transmit. Capture Effect makes the network throughput appear more efficient but introduces unfairness that increases latencies for many DTEs.

Category 3/5

Category 3 (Cat 3) and Category 5 (Cat 5) unshielded twisted pair (UTP), are the most common cable types used for LAN installations. The "category" rating refers to the electrical performance of the cable. Cat 5 is better quality cable than Cat 3, having less high frequency attenuation, lower susceptibility to external electromagnetic interference (EMI) and radio frequency interference (RFI), and reduced self emission of EMI/RFI. The performance requirements and recommended use of such cables are defined in two key documents. EIA/TIA 568-A (1995) is the applicable reference for North America. ISO/IEC 11801 incorporates cabling specifications with additional international considerations.

CDDI - Copper Distributed Data Interface

CDDI is a term trademarked by Crescendo Communications that refers to an FDDI network that operates over copper media; i.e., Copper Distributed Data Interface.

Chip (Integrated Circuit)

Chip is sometimes used as a contraction for microchip or Integrated Circuit.

CI - Control In

AUI differential pair circuit, operating at pseudo ECL levels. The MAU drives a 10 MHz signal on the CI circuit to indicate to the DTE or repeater that a collision has been detected on the network, that the MAU is the jabber state, or that an SQE Test from the MAU to the DTE is in progress. See also "Jabber" and "SQE Test."

Circuit Switching

A technique for switching cells or frames based upon time or space division multiplexing. Overall bandwidth is usually dedicated for the connection.

CMIP - Common Management Information Protocol

The ISO defined transport protocol to move management information through the network. Defined by ISO/IEC 9595/6, Information Processing Systems—Open Systems Interconnection—Common Management Information Protocol Specification.

CMOS

CMOS is the semiconductor technology used in the transistors that comprise most semiconductor devices. Semiconductors are made of silicon and germanium, materials which conduct electricity, but not enthusiastically. Areas of silicon and germanium materials are "doped" by adding impurities and become better conductors of either extra electrons with a negative charge (N-type transistors) or of positive charge carriers (P-type transistors). In CMOS technology, both kinds of transistors are used in complementary ways to form a current gate that forms an effective means of electrical control.

Collision

Collision is a term used to describe the condition when two or more Ethernet stations attempt to transmit data simultaneously. (Strictly speaking, they are transmitting data within the same slot time). All Ethernet networks use the CSMA/CD protocol which relies on each and every station detecting collisions and then backing off for a random period of time prior to retransmission. Collisions are normal in a properly functioning Ethernet network.

Collision Domain

A single CSMA/CD network comprised of Ethernet nodes connected by repeater(s). In 1000BASE-T networks, only a single repeater is permitted in a collision domain. In a single collision domain, only a single Ethernet node may transmit at any given time. If multiple transmissions occur simultaneously, a collision occurs.

Collision Likelihood

Collision Likelihood is the probability of a given packet experiencing at least one collision and is usually calculated at a given offered load.

Comma

A comma is a specific bit pattern, used in the 1000BASE-X (and Fibre Channel) 8B/10B encoding scheme, that allows synchronization of a receiver to the serial bit stream. In the absence of transmission errors, a comma cannot appear within a transmitted 10B code group and cannot occur across the boundaries of two adjacent 10B code groups. The comma is used to find transmission code group boundaries and ordered-set boundaries in the received bit stream. A comma is either the sequence 0011111 (comma+) or 1100000 (comma–). The 1000BASE-X coding scheme defines the /K28.5/ code group as the only comma character for normal operation.

Concentrator

A general term frequently used instead of repeater. Typically, a concentrator supports more than one network protocol, such as 802.3/Ethernet as well as 802.5/Token Ring. The terms "hub," "concentrator," and "intelligent hub" are frequently used inter-changeably to reference a multiport, multiprotocol device capable of statistics gathering, fault monitoring, and/or network management activities.

Conditioned Launch

Conditioned Launch is a technique of launching laser light that spreads the laser light source output so that it appears as an LED source for which the fiber optic cable was originally designed. By spreading the laser light across a greater power spectrum, DMD is minimized.

Conformance Test

A Conformance Test is a test performed on equipment in order to verify the equipment's compliance with a specification.

Congestion

A condition where the total network resources are exceeded by the total network demand.

CRC - Cyclic Redundancy

CRC is calculated by the MAC transmit process and checked by the MAC receive process of a station (DTE) to ensure integrity of the frame contents. The mathematical CRC is computed on the Destination Address, Source Address, Length/Type, and Data/Pad fields (all the frame except the Preamble, SFD, and FCS fields). The computed 32-bit CRC is appended as the last 4-bytes of every frame. See also "FCS."

CRC Error

A CRC Error is detected if the 4-byte field appended to the end of each 802.3/Ethernet frame does not match that at the receiver, where a 32-bit CRC is mathematically computed on the Destination Address, Source Address, Length/Type, and Data/Pad fields (the entire frame except the Preamble, SFD, and FCS fields) of the receive frame. The CRC is appended by the MAC transmit process and checked by the MAC receive process, and is used to verify the integrity of the frame contents. See also "FCS."

Crossover

Crossover refers to the fact that certain twisted-pair cable between Ethernet nodes need to switch or crossover the transmit and receive lines in order that the transmitter is connected to the receiver and vice versa. In Ethernet networks, Ethernet nodes are connected to switches and repeaters using straight-through cable and repeaters and switches are connected to each other using crossover cables.

CSMA/CD - Carrier Sense Multiple Access/Collision Detect.

The Media Access Control (MAC) protocol used in Ethernet and 802.3 networks, which determines the transmit and receive characteristics of each station. Defined in Section 4 of ISO/IEC 8802-3 :1996 (ANSI/IEEE Std 802.3). See also "MAC."

Cut-Through Switching

A technique of switching in which the incoming packets are forwarded prior to their complete arrival. Cut-Through Switching allows packets to be transmitted on their output ports immediately after the data link (MAC) and possibly network layer header lookups are complete. Cut-Through Switching reduces the total latency in a switch. Since Cut-Through Switching begins to transmit the packet prior to it being completely received, frame fragments may be forwarded by the switch in error. See "Fragment-Filtered Switching."

DA - Destination Address

The 48-bit field within the 802.3/Ethernet packet format which identifies the physical address of the intended recipient. The field immediately follows the Preamble/Start Frame Delimiter and precedes the Destination Address (DA) field. The 802.3 protocol supports individual, multicast, and broadcast addressing. See "Source Address."

Deference

Deference is the act of deferring or not transmitting due to the detection of packet transmission on a CSMA/CD LAN. An Ethernet node defers when it senses carrier on the network.

DI - Data In

AUI differential pair circuit, operating at pseudo ECL levels. Data received by the MAU from either the media or the DO circuit (or its logical equivalent), is driven onto the DI circuit for use by the DTE or repeater.

Differential Skew

Differential Skew is the skew, or offset in time, between two differential signals. Differential signals are two signals of opposite polarity that together constitute a pair of signals. Differential signals are used because of their immunity to noise events that affect both pairs of signals.

Dispersion

Dispersion is a phenomenon in which the velocity of propagation of an electromagnetic wave, such as light traveling through a fiber optic cable, is wavelength dependent. In an optical fiber, there are several significant dispersion effects, such as material dispersion, profile dispersion, and waveguide dispersion, that degrade the signal. Dispersion affects the ability of a signal to be recovered at the far end.

DMD - Differential Mode Delay

Differential Mode delay is the variation in propagation delay in light transmissions through a fiber caused by differences in group velocity among modes of an optical fiber. DMD is sometimes also called multimode group delay.

DO - Data Out

AUI differential pair circuit, operating at pseudo ECL levels. The DTE or repeater drives Manchester encoded data out on the DO circuit (or its logical equivalent), which is transmitted by the MAU over the physical media and the DI circuit.

DTE - Data Terminal Equipment

Communication station (or node) capable of reception and/or transmission of data. Generally includes the MAC and PLS sublayer functions, but may also include an embedded MAU.

ENDEC - Encoder/Decoder

The Manchester encoder/decoder, effectively the physical implementation of the 802.3 PLS sublayer. NRZ data output by the MAC is passed to the PLS function, Manchester encoded, and sent over the AUI DO circuit (or its logical equivalent) to the MAU. Manchester encoded data from the network (from other MAC devices) received on the AUI DI circuit is passed to the PLS function and decoded to extract clock and NRZ data, as well as the indication of receive carrier, which are returned to the MAC.

Excessive Defer

Excessive Defer is a condition in which the transmitting node has deferred transmission for a time that is twice as long as the maximum-size packet. Once an Ethernet station has begun deferring, it should generally sense carrier deassertion within 1518 byte times. If this does not occur, and the station is still deferring after two maximum-size packet times, excessive defer is indicated to management.

Exposed AUI

The AUI carries encoded control and data signals between a MAU and DTE. An exposed AUI is exposed to the user for connections to external MAUs. An exposed AUI uses a 15-pin connector. External MAUs may be placed up to 50 m away from the DTE.

Exposed MII

An exposed MII is an Media Independent Interface that is exposed to the user. Exposed MIIs are used to connect the MAC/RS sublayers to physical layers of different media types using external PHYs over a cable. An exposed MII in 100 Mb/s Ethernet uses a 40-pin connector.

Extinction Ratio

Extinction Ratio is the ratio of the low optical power level to the high optical power level on an optical segment. The Extinction Ratio of optical transmitters is usually measured in decibels (dB).

Fast Ethernet

Fast Ethernet is the colloquial name given to the IEEE 802.3u 100 Mb/s Ethernet standard.

FCS - Frame Check Sequence

A 4-byte field appended to the end of each 802.3/Ethernet frame. The field contains a 32-bit CRC, mathematically computed on the Destination Address, Source Address, Length/Type, and Data/Pad fields (the entire frame except the Preamble, SFD, and FCS fields). The CRC is appended by the MAC transmit process, checked by the MAC receive process, and is used to verify the integrity of the frame contents. See also "CRC."

Fiber Distributed Data Interface (FDDI)

An ANSI-defined 100 Mb/s network that uses a timed-token passing access protocol.

Fiber Optics

Fiber optics is a technology that uses glass or plastic fibers to transmit information. A fiber optic cable consists of a bundle of glass fibers, each of which is capable of transmitting messages at close to the speed of light. Generally, fiber optic cables have a much greater bandwidth than UTP or coaxial cables and are far less susceptible to external noise and interference. Due to its ability to carry large amounts of information, fiber optics is a popular technology for Ethernet LANs. All three Ethernet standards, 10 Mb/s, 100 Mb/s, and 1000 Mb/s have specified fiber optic cabling as one of their physical media.

Fibre Channel

Fibre Channel is a data-transfer architecture developed by a consortium of computer and mass storage device manufacturers that was standardized by the ANSI committee. The most prominent Fibre Channel standard is Fibre Channel-Arbitrated Loop (FC-AL). FC-AL was designed for mass storage devices that require very high bandwidth. Using optical fiber to connect devices, FC-AL supports full-duplex data-transfer rates of 100 MB/s. FC-AL serves as the basis for the physical layer specification of Gigabit Ethernet.

Flow

A flow is a sequence of messages that have the same source, destination (one or more), and quality-of service requirements. Applications that generate real-time traffic have very specific quality-of-service requirements, which are communicated to the network through a flow specification RFC 1363 defines a flowspec as "a data structure used by internetwork hosts to request special services of the internetwork, often guarantees about how the internetwork will handle some of the hosts' traffic."

FOIRL - Fiber Optic Inter Repeater Link

IEEE specification for inter repeater communications link, primarily aimed at significantly increasing the distance capabilities of an 802.3/Ethernet network. Defined in Section 9.9 of ISO/IEC 8802-3 :1996 (ANSI/IEEE Std 802.3).

Fragment-Filtered Switching

A technique of switching in which the incoming packets are forwarded after the first 64 bytes have completely been received. Since the IEEE 802.3/Ethernet minimum packet size is 64 bytes, the reception of 64 complete bytes guarantees that the incoming packet is not a frame fragment or collision remnant.

Frame

The portion of the 802.3 (or Ethernet) packet following the SFD (or Synch), which includes the Destination Address, Source Address, Length (or Type), LLC Data/Pad, and FCS fields, but excludes the preamble sequence. See also "Packet."

F-SMA -

The connector type employed in FOIRL network installations.

Full Duplex

Full-duplex data transmission means that data can be transmitted in both directions over a physical medium simultaneously. Full-duplex data transmission doubles the effect total bandwidth capability of any given node and is supported only over point-to-point links. Full-duplex transmission for Ethernet networks is defined by IEEE Std 802.3x-1997.

Full-Duplex Repeater

A repeater that supports full-duplex connections on all its ports, instead of the half-duplex connections supported by ordinary repeaters. Also referred to as a "Buffered Repeater."

GMII - Gigabit Media-Independent Interface

A logical signal interface that is the 1000 Mb/s equivalent to the 100 Mb/s MII. The GMII attaches to the Reconciliation Sublayer and PCS Layers, allowing multiple media types to be connected to the 1000 Mb/s MAC sublayer. The Gigabit Media-Independent Interface is generally not used for connection to most fiber and short-haul copper media since these media use the same encoding scheme. However, for connection to 1000BASE-T networks using Category 5 cable, the GMII is required.

Half Duplex

Half-duplex data transmission means that data can be transmitted in only one direction over a physical medium. Half-duplex transmission is used by traditional Ethernet networks running the CSMA/CD protocol.

Hub

A general term frequently used instead of repeater. See also "Concentrator" and "Repeater."

IAB - Internet Advisory Board

The group within the Internet community responsible for the administration of protocol standards.

IETF - Internet Engineering Task Force

The group within the Internet community responsible for the development of protocol standards.

IP Address

The IP Address is a 32-bit quantity used to identify a node that is using the Internet Protocol (IP). It is usually represented in decimal notation separated into four 8-bit values delimited by periods. For example, 192.168.1.1. The IP Address is also known as an Internet Address.

IPG - Inter Packet Gap

The minimum time permitted between back-to-back packets on the 802.3 network, specified as 96 bits. Note that aphenomenon known as IPG shrinkage can cause the IPG to be reduced below 96 bits.)

IP Switching

A form of Layer 3 switching developed by Ipsilon that specifically utilizes IP layer information to switch packets from source to destination. IP switching uses the concepts of flows to decide between switching and routing packets.

Isochronous

Isochronous is derived from Greek (equal + time) and pertains to networks and applications that require fixed timing, such as voice and digital video transmission. Isochronous data transfer ensures that data flows continuously and at a steady rate in close synchronization. FireWire, the IEEE 1394 High Performance Serial Bus, uses an isochronous interface.

Jabber

In 10 Mb/s networks, a MAU is required to interrupt a station which is transmitting for an excessive period of time, to prevent the network from disruption. The MAU is required to enter the jabber state if it detects continuous DO circuit (or its logical equivalent) activity for 20–150 ms. During the jabber state, transmission to the network is disabled and collision is returned to the DTE via the CI circuit (or its logical equivalent). The MAU will remain in this state until DO circuit activity stops for a period of 0.25–0.75s. In 100 Mb/s networks, repeaters prevent jabbering DTEs by terminating their transmissions after 40,000 bit times. 100Mb/s and 1Gb/s versions perform the jabber function in the repeater, not the PMY

Jam

A DTE that detects a collision is required to complete the Preamble/SFD sequence (if it has not already done so) and subsequently continue to transmit for an additional 32 bit times. The Jam sequence can be any arbitrary pattern, providing it is not the calculated CRC. In a repeater, if a receive collision is detected, it will ensure that at least 96 bits are sent to all ports except the receiving (colliding) port, if necessary by appending an additional Jam sequence to the frame. When a repeater detects entry into the transmit collision state, a new 96-bit Jam sequence will be transmitted to all ports. In this case, the Jam sequence must start with the first bit as a one and continue with 62-bits of alternating "1, 0,1, 0…," with the remainder being an arbitrary pattern.

Jitter

In a digital signal, jitter is the variability of signals due to timing errors built up while transmitting over cables.

LANE

The LANE protocol emulates a Local Area Network running over an ATM network. Specifically, the LANE protocol defines mechanisms for emulating either an IEEE 802.3 Ethernet or an 802.5 Token Ring LAN.

Late Collision

A collision occurring after the "slot time" (512 bit times) has elapsed. A DTE that detects a collision outside the slot time (after 512 bits have been transmitted, starting with the first bit of preamble) will not retry the packet transmission, passing this requirement back to upper layer protocols. Late Collisions are an indicate that the network span is over sized or that a physical equipment problem exists. See also "Slot Time."

Latency

Latency, when used in the context of networking, is the amount of time it takes a packet to travel from source to destination. Together, latency and bandwidth define the speed and capacity of a network. An example of the use of latency is the amount of time it takes for a packet to enter a switch and then exit the switch. This time is generally referred to as the switching latency of the switch.

L2 (Layer 2) Switch

The term "Layer 2 switch" is commonly applied to packet forwarding based on the OSI/ISO Layer 2 (e.g., MAC header addresses) information, to switch packets from source to destination. The definition of an L2 switch has become synonymous with the traditional definition of a bridge. A multiport bridge/L2 switch forwards traffic based solely on the information contained in the Layer 2 or data-link layer information, and possibly some VLAN information (in newer implementations). Data-link-layer information consists of the IEEE 802 destination MAC and source MAC addresses. The IEEE 802.1D definition implies that the L2 switch implements forward, filtering, and learning processes, and the device implements the Spanning Tree protocol.

L3 (Layer 3) Switch

L3 switch generally describes a multiport bridge/router that forwards traffic based on the information contained in the Layer 3 or network layer information (the traditional definition of a router), as well as the Layer 2 or data-link-layer information (the traditional definition for a bridge), and possibly some VLAN information. Data-link-layer information consists of the IEEE 802 destination MAC and source MAC addresses. Network-layer information typically consists of the network layer's protocol header, such as the IP header or IPX header (addresses as well as other information fields). Layer 3 switching generally implies that the forwarding function is performed at wire-speed for multiple ports, and therefore that the bridging/routing functions are performed largely in hardware.

Length

The 2-byte field in the 802.3 frame immediately following the Source Address field and preceding the Data field that defines the total number of data bytes contained in the frame. The valid range is 46–1500 bytes. For values less than 46 bytes, Pad characters are added to the Data field of the transmit frame to ensure that the minimum size frame is observed (64 bytes); these are removed at the receiving station. The field is transmitted with the high-order byte first, in LSB to MSB order. See also "Type."

LCW - Link Code Word

The Link Code Word is the 16 bits of data encoded in an Fast Link Pulse (FLP) Burst. The Base Page and Next Page are Link Code Words.

Link Fail

Link Fail is the state entered at the conclusion of an unsuccessful Link Test or Auto-Negotiation sequence. Link Fail can occur due to incompatible capabilities at the devices at the end of the link, a bropken physical link, or equipment powered-off, faulty, or missing.

Link Pass

Link Pass is the state entered at the conclusion of a successful Auto-Negotiation sequence. Link Pass is an indication that Auto-Negotiation has completed successfully and the link is ready for the transmission of data-link layer frames.

MAC - Media Access Control

The MAC sublayer defines the medium independent capability for frame transmission and reception using the CSMA/CD access method. Defined in Section 4 of ISO/IEC 8802-3Ê:1996 (ANSI/IEEE Std 802.3).

MAC Control Frame

A specific type of MAC frame that has special properties. A MAC Control frame conveys special information to the MAC itself (rather than just being passed transparently to the upper layers. An example of a MAC Control frame is the PAUSE frame. This frame is used to turn off the transmitter of a remote DTE. A MAC Control frame is a normal minimum size (64 bytes excluding preamble/SFD) 802.3/Ethernet frame.

MAC Control Sublayer

The MAC Control Sublayer that sits between the MAC Sublayer and the MAC Client Sublayer. This is the entity that detects special MAC Control frames, and reacts to them.

Manchester Encoding

Manchester encoded data is used for data transmission across the AUI (and across all of the common media currently defined for 802.3 networks at data rates of 10 Mb/s). Each bit of information is converted into a "bit-symbol," which in turn is divided into two halves. During the first half of the bit-symbol, the representation is the complement of the data bit being encoded, and during the second half of the bit-symbol, the representation is identical to the data bit value. In this way, a transition is guaranteed in the center of every bit-symbol, hence clock and data information are encoded into a single serial representation. Manchester encoding/decoding is performed in the PLS sublayer. See also "ENDEC" and "PLS."

MAU - Medium Attachment Unit

The physical and electrical interface between a DTE or repeater and the actual medium. The MAU is connected to the DTE by an AUI, although this may not be visible if the MAU is embedded within the DTE or repeater. A different MAU is required to support each different type of medium (cable type).

MDI-X - Media Dependent Interface Crossover

MDI-X refers to the crossover function being performed at the Media Dependent Interface or MDI. MDI is the standards term used for connectors, such as the RJ-45.

Message Page

A Message Page is a Next Page sent during Auto-Negotiation that contains a formatted or predefined 12-bit message field.

MIB - Management Information Base

Network devices which can be managed embed a MIB. The MIB is effectively an internally located table of variables which an external device can access. Several published MIB standards exist for various network devices. The work to create a MIB for 802.3 repeaters is defined in IEEE 802.3 Section 19, Layer Management for 10 Mb/s Baseband Repeaters. This information was also used as the basis of the definition for the "Repeater MIB" in RFC 1368, which defines the SNMP encoding for an 802.3/Ethernet repeater. In addition, many vendors publish their own MIBs and/or extensions to existing MIBs.

MIB-I - Management Information Base 1

Defines the core set of managed objects for the Internet suite of protocols. Primarily focused on monitoring network interfaces and the protocol stack. Defined in RFC 1156. See also "MIB," "MIB-II," and "RMON MIB."

MIB-II - Management Information Base 2

Defines extended capabilities over MIB-I, primarily focused on monitoring the network interfaces and the protocol stack (including SNMP). Defined in RFC 1213. See also "MIB," "MIB-I," and "RMON MIB."

MII - Medium Independent Interface

A logical signal interface that is the 100 Mb/s equivalent to the 10 Mb/s AUI. The MII attaches to the Reconciliation Sublayer and PCS Layers, allowing multiple media types to be connected to the MAC sublayer. See also "RMII."

MJLP - MAU Jabber Lockup Protection

MJLP is used to interrupt a 10Mb/s repeater's transmission if it has transmitted continuously for longer than 5 ms or 50,000 bit times. The repeater will then, re-enable transmission after 96 bit times. MJLP is not implemented on 10 Mb/s or 100 Mb/s repeaters.

MLT-3

MLT-3 is an encoding scheme used by 100BASE-T. MLT-3 encodes a bit as presence or lack of transition, exactly as in NRZI. What makes MLT-3 different is that the base waveform is a 3-state alternating wave. Rather than alternating between 0 and 1 as a binary encoding scheme such as Manchester encoding, MLT-3 alternates from -1 to 0 to $+1$, back to 0, then back to -1, repeating indefinitely. A zero is encoded as a halt in the back-and-forth progression. Using MLT-3, it is possible to represent four or more bits with every complete waveform at 0, $+1$, 0, and -1.

Modal Bandwidth

Modal Bandwidth refers to the total number of light pulses that can be transmitted over a fiber and still be extracted at the destination as individual pulses. Modal Bandwidth is usually expressed in MHz-km. In a multimode fiber, individual light rays travel different distances, and take different amounts of time to transit the length of a fiber. This being the case, if a short pulse of light is injected into fiber, the various rays emanating from that pulse will arrive at the other end of the fiber at different times, and output pulse will be of longer duration than the input pulse. Modal dispersion or pulse spreading limits the number of pulses per second that can be transmitted down a fiber and still be recognizable as separate pulses at the other end. This, therefore, limits the bit rate or bandwidth of a multimode fiber.

MPOA - Multiple Protocols Over ATM

MPOA is an extension of LANE that allows the use of multiple protocols over ATM-based networks using NHRP.

Multimode Fiber

All fibers consist of a number of substructures including a core, which carries most of the light, surrounded by a cladding, which bends the light and confines it to the core, surrounded by a substrate layer (in some fibers) of glass which does not carry light, surrounded by buffer layers that are used for protection. In multimode fiber, the core diameter is relatively large compared to the wavelength of light. Core diameters range from 50 μm to 1,000 μm, compared to the wavelength of light of about 1 μm. This allows light to propagate through the fiber over several different paths, or modes, hence the name multimode fiber.

Next Page

Subsequent Link Code Words transmitted within an FLP burst during Auto-Negotiation that convey additional information not contained in the Base Page. Next Pages are only transmitted if both devices are capable of supported Next Pages, as determined by the Next Page Able bit in the Base Page.

NHRP

NHRP provides cut-through routing extensions to the Classical IP over ATM routing model.

Octet

Terminology used within various standards including Ethernet and 802.3 to denote 8 bits (1 byte) of information.

Offered Load

Offered Load is usually measured as a percentage of total available network bandwidth that is offered (or introduced) in a network. For example, if 500 Mb/s of data are being transmitted on a 1 Gb/s network, the Offered Load is 50%.

OID - Organizationally Unique Identifier

The OID is a 3-byte (24-bit) value assigned by the IEEE that uniquely identifies a vendor. It is generally used as the first 24 bits of the IEEE MAC address.

One Port Left

One Port Left is a state entered in all repeaters in which all attached ports except one have stopped transmitting. The repeater waits in the One Port Left state, transmitting a Jam indication to all ports until either the last port becomes quiescent or additional ports are detected transmitting.

Ordered Set

An ordered set is either a single special code-group or a sequence of code groups consisting of an initial special code group, followed by additional special or data code-groups. Ordered sets are always 1, 2, or 4 code groups in length. Ordered sets are used to transmit control or delimiting information across a link.

Packet

An 802.3/Ethernet packet is defined as the entire transmitted bit sequence as viewed on the network medium, from the first bit of the preamble sequence to the last bit of the FCS field. See also "Frame."

Parallel Detection

Parallel Detection is a term used in Auto-Negotiation that specifies the ability to detect 100BASE-TX and 100BASE-T4 specific link signaling, as well as NLP and FLP sequences.

Partition

A repeater may auto-partition a port based on excessive duration of collision or consecutive number of collisions. When in the partitioned state, the repeater continues to transmit to the port, but reception from the port is monitored but not repeated by the repeater (including collisions) to the rest of the network.. The repeater can "unpartition" the port if it transmits to the port in the normal course of retransmission, and detects no collision indication for a specified time period. Partition is often used in the network industry to merely indicate a port on a repeater or hub has been disabled.

Pause Frame

A MAC control frame that is used to stop a MAC from transmitting frames for the amount of time specified by the PAUSE timer. The PAUSE frame is used by full-duplex stations to control the number of inbound packets in order to relieve congestion.

Pause Timer

A specific MAC Control Parameter that is contained in a PAUSE frame. The Pause Timer is a 2-byte value that is transmitted most significant byte, LSB, first. The Pause Timer specifies the amount of time that a given MAC should stop all transmissions.

PCS - Physical Coding Sublayer

A sublayer used in 1000BASE-T to couple the GMII and the PMA. The PCS contains the functions to encode 8 data bits into 10 bit codes using 8B/10B coding to transmit over the physical media. Defined in Clause 36 of the IEEE 802.3z specification. Other PCS encoding fuctions are used for 100BASE-T devices.

PLS - Physical Layer Signaling

IEEE specification which defines the signaling scheme between the MAC sublayer, through to the AUI, which provides the interface for a medium attachment unit (MAU). Defined in Section 7 of ISO/IEC 8802-3 : 1990 (ANSI/IEEE Std 802.3). The PLS sublayer is physically implemented by the Manchester encoder/decoder function. NRZ data output by the MAC is passed to the PLS function, Manchester encoded, and sent over the AUI DO circuit (or its logical equivalent) to the MAU. Manchester encoded data from the network (from other MAC devices), received on the AUI DI circuit (or its logical equivalent), is passed to the PLS function, and decoded to extract clock and NRZ data, as well as the indication of receive carrier and collision, which are returned to the MAC sublayer. See also "AUI" and "ENDEC."

PMA - Physical Medium Attachment

The portion of the MAU that contains the active circuitry responsible for the interface of the AUI circuits to the specific network medium.

PMD - Physical Medium Dependent

The portion of the PHY or physical layer responsible for interfacing to the physical media. For 1 Gb/s operation, the PMD defines 1.25 Gb/s, full-duplex signaling systems that accommodate multiple media. The PMD is based upon the Fibre Channel PMD. Defined in Clause 23 of IEEE Std 802.3u-1995 and Clauses 38 and 39 of the IEEE 802.3z specification.

Preamble

An alternating "1, 0, 1, 0....." sequence at the start of each frame transmission. The preamble for 802.3 networks is defined as 7 bytes long, followed by a 1-byte SFD; whereas the preamble for Ethernet networks is defined as 62 bits long, with a 2-bit "Synch" character (hence both have an overall preamble/start delimiter length of 64-bits). When Manchester encoded, the preamble sequence produces a 5 MHz frequency at the start of each frame, which is used by a receiving station or repeater as a reference to decode the receive clock and data.

Punch-Down Block

A term used commonly in the telecommunications industry. A Punch-Down Block is usually located in a wiring closet and is used to terminate and connect cabling from different sources. Basically it's a terminal strip, where large numbers of cables can be connected. Used in the networking industry as the interconnection point between the cabling from high port count internetworking devices (such as repeaters, switches or routers), and the cable run to each user desktop (often referred to as the "home-run"). Frequently used where 25-pair cables (capable of carrying 12 10BASE-T connections) are broken out to the individual 2- or 4-pair cable runs to the desktops.

PVC - Permanent Virtual Connection

A PVC is a connection set up by network management, in which a set of switches between an ATM source and destination ATM system are programmed with the appropriate VPI/VCI values.

QoS - Quality of Service

QoS is a term used to define the specific parameters required for a user application. The service parameters may be defined in terms of bandwidth required, jitter, latency, and delay. ATM supports QoS guarantees by providing support for CBR, ABR, and UBR traffic.

QTP - QTag Prefix

The QTag Prefix is the 4-byte header inserted in VLAN Tagged packets. The QTag Prefix is inserted in a normal Ethernet/802.3 packet, between the Source Address field and the Type/Length field. The QTag Prefix contains the Tag Protocol Identifier (TPID) in the first 2 bytes, and the Tag Control Information in the second 2 bytes.

Repeater

An 802.3/Ethernet repeater in its most generic form is an "n" port device, which supports the 802.3 protocol only. A repeater is used to extend the physical topology of the network, allowing two or more cable segments to be coupled together. When data is received on a single port, the repeater retransmits the incoming bit stream to all other ports, performing signal retiming and amplitude restoration. When data appears simultaneously on more than one port, the repeater transmits a collision to all ports, including the receiving ports. In addition, the repeater can isolate a port if it detects faults, such as excessive number or duration of collisions, to prevent disruption of the rest of the network. In a 10BASE-T,

100BASE-T, and Gigabit Ethernet networks, repeaters provide central points of connectivity, ideally suited to the incorporation of statistics gathering and network-administration functions. Initially defined in IEEE Std. 802.3k-1992 (Supplement to ISO/IEC 8802-3:1992 [ANSI/IEEE Std. 802.3, 1992 Edition]), later subsumed by Clause 30 in 802.3u, and most recently modified by 802.3z and 802.3 ac.

Repeater Management

The generic term used to describe the 802.3 Supplements "Layer Management for 10 and 100 Mb/s Baseband Repeaters" (Section 19 and Section 30). The Repeater Management Standard defines the MIB variables for an 802.3 repeater. Defined in IEEE Std 802.3k-1992 (Supplement to ISO/IEC 8803-3 :1992 [ANSI/IEEE Std 802.3, 1992 Edition]). See also "Repeater MIB."

Repeater MIB

The generic term used to describe RFC 1368, which defines the MIB variables and their encoding for use by SNMP. See also "Repeater Management."

RFC - Request For Comment

A specification administered and developed by the Internet community (IAB/IETF). The specifications are public domain, and detail the TCP/IP Internet protocol suite.

RIN - Relative Intensity Noise

A laser is a very highly tuned quantum effect oscillator. When a laser source is used to transmit light through fiber, a certain amount of optical power is reflected back into the laser device due to connectors and optical lens interfaces. This reflected optical power disturbs the purity of oscillation in the laser, and this appears as optical noise. This is called as Relative Intensity Noise and is measured in dB/Hz since it has characteristics similar to thermal noise in resistors.

Rise Time/Fall Time

In the context of optics, Rise Time is defined as the time it takes for the output power of a transmitter to rise from 20% to 80% of its final value when the input is a unit step current. A perfect transmitter would have rise time of zero. The Fall Time is the inverse of Rise Time, the amount of time it takes for a transmitter to fall from 80% to 20% of its final value.

RMON MIB - Remote Network Monitoring Management Information Base

Defines the MIB attributes for a network monitoring device, with detailed statistic, fault diagnostic, performance monitoring and historical trending capabilities. Defined in RFC 1271. See also "MIB-I" and "MIB-II."

RMII - Reduced Medium Independent Interface

The RMII is an MII-like electrical signal interface that reduces the number of signals connecting the RS and PCS layers. The RMII allows multiport physical layer devices to be constructed by reducing the total implementation "tax" assessed on multiport devices. See also "MII" and "Exposed MII."

Router

Routers are devices that operate at the network-layer level, above the MAC layer at which a bridge or L2 switch device operates. A router uses network-layer information in order to make forwarding and filtering decisions. Routers are sometimes referred to as Gateways. The distinction between Layer 3 switches and routers has blurred, since both make decisions based upon network-layer data.

RS - Reconciliation Sublayer

The RS or Reconciliation Sublayer is a 100 Mb/s sublayer defined to be beneath the MAC sublayer and above the PCS sublayer. The RS essentially maps the behavior of the MAC to the electrical signals of the MII interface. The RS was required to map the operation of a multiple bit width MII's to the bit-wide MAC sublayers.

Running Disparity

The disparity of a code group is determined by counting the number of 1s and 0s in the code group. Disparity neutral groups have the same number of 1s as 0s. Positive disparity code groups have more 1s than 0s, while negative disparity code groups have more 0s than 1s. Running disparity is calculated by using the disparity of any given code group and the value of the disparity of the previous code group and adding them. Running Disparity is used as an error check at the receiver.

Runt Packet

A runt packet is any IEEE 802.3/Ethernet packet that is less than 64 bytes. The minimum packet size on an Ethernet is 64 bytes and therefore, any packet fragments found on the network that are less than 64 bytes are considered runts and are invalid.

RSVP

A protocol designed to enable senders, network nodes and receivers to communicate information required to guarantee a Quality of Service (QoS) in the network. RSVP is a control protocol, much like ICMP, that is used by applications within IP end-systems to indicate to nodes transmitting to them the nature of the packet streams that they wish to receive.

SA - Source Address

The 48-bit field within the 802.3/Ethernet packet format which identifies the senders unique physical address. The field immediately follows the Destination Address (DA) field. See also "Destination Address."

SFD - Start of Frame Delimiter

The SFD immediately follows the alternating "1, 0, 1, 0....." preamble sequence. The SFD for 802.3 networks is defined as a 1-byte field consisting of the pattern "1', 0, 1, 0, 1, 0, 1, 1;" whereas for Ethernet networks a 2-bit pattern of "1, 1" at the end of preamble signifies the "Synch" character (although the byte containing the SFD/Synch character is identical in both cases). The first bit of the 802.3 frame (the Destination Address field) immediately follows the SFD. See also "Preamble" and "Synch."

Single-Mode Fiber

All fibers consist of a number of substructures, including a core, which carries most of the light, surrounded by a cladding, which bends the light and confines it to the core, surrounded by a substrate layer (in some fibers) of glass which does not carry light, surrounded by buffer layers that are used for protection. In single-mode fiber, the core diameter (usually around 9 μm) is much closer in size to the wavelength of light, about 1.2 μm. This limits the light transmission to a single path, or mode, down the core of the fiber.

Slot Time

The round trip propagation delay of the network, defined as to be 512 bit times. Effectively the time taken for a node which starts transmitting at one end of the network, to recognize a collision caused by another node which is located at the furthest point away on the network and which commenced its transmission at the same point in time. A DTE should always detect a collision within the slot time in a normally configured and operating network. A collision outside the slot time (after 512 bits have been transmitted, starting with the first bit of preamble) is referred to as a late collision. See also "Late Collision."

Smart Squelch

A capability incorporated in the twisted pair receiver of most 10BASE-T MAUs. Noise "hits" from coresident services, such as analog telephone ringer circuits, can exhibit amplitudes which exceed the receive "squelch" thresholds in a 10BASE-T MAU receiver for a few bit times. To prevent such a spurious noise event from generating an illegally short fragment (which would be extended to 96 bits at the repeater) or causing a potential collision at a transmitting DTE (which may be a late collision), most 10BASE-T MAUs, implement a "Smart Squelch" feature. This feature uses knowledge of the expected receive Manchester characteristics to place additional qualification requirements on the receive waveform. This requires (in the case of the previously listed devices) that correct amplitude, pulse width, and pulse sequence/ordering is observed before the receiver effectively "unsquelches" to allow the incoming pulse train to be regarded as valid Manchester data.

SNMP - Simple Network Management Protocol

The Internet-specified protocol for the movement of management data in a heterogeneous network environment. Defined in RFC 1157.

Spanning Tree

A technique that detects loops in a network and logically blocks any redundant paths, ensuring that only one route exists between any two nodes. The Spanning Tree Protocol is used in an IEEE 802.1D bridged network and most bridges, and switches implement Spanning Tree.

Spectral Width

Spectral Width is the range of wavelengths that transmitters emit. A perfect transmitter emitting light at a single wavelength is said to have zero spectral width. For a laser diode, Spectral Width is typically 1 to 5 nm, whereas LEDs have Spectral Widths of 20 to 100 nm.

SQE - Signal Quality Error

A 10 Mb/s pulse train passed from the MAU (using the CI circuit) to a DTE or repeater to indicate an error condition on the network, such as collision or excessive transmit duration (jabber).

SQE Test - Signal Quality Error Test

Frequently referred to as "Heartbeat." An 802.3 MAU, when connected to a station (DTE), is required to send a brief collision indication back to the DTE after the end of each transmission. When the transmission from the DTE completes on the DO circuit, within 0.6–1.6 μs the MAU should start to return a collision indication to the DTE using the CI circuit, of duration 10±5 bit times. The test is intended to notify the DTE that the MAU collision circuitry is operational and that the AUI cable is intact. Note that the SQE Test function must be disabled when a MAU is connected to a repeater.

Store-and-Forward Switching

A technique of switching in which the incoming packets are forwarded only after they have been completely received and checked for errors. Store-and-Forward switching guarantees that no errored packets are forwarded since the incoming packet is completely checked prior to retransmission. Store-and-Forward switching is useful when bridging between to dissimilar networks or networks of different speeds.

SVC

An SVC is a connection that is set up automatically through a signaling protocol such as Q.2931. SVCs do not require the manual interaction needed to set up PVCs.

Synch - Synchronization

The "Synch" immediately follows the alternating "1, 0, 1, 0....." preamble sequence in an Ethernet frame, and indicates that the first bit of the frame (the Destination Address field) will immediately follow. The Synch for Ethernet networks is a 2-bit pattern of "1, 1" at the conclusion of the preamble. For 802.3 networks, a 1-byte SFD field is defined, consisting of the pattern "1, 0, 1, 0, 1, 0, 1, 1" (hence the byte containing the Synch/SFD character is identical in both cases). See also "Preamble" and "SFD."

Tag Switching

A form of switching originated by Cisco Systems that relies on tags prepended to packets on which switching decisions are made.

TBEB - Truncated Binary Exponential Backoff

TBEB is the backoff algorithm used by IEEE 802.3/Ethernet CSMA/CD compliant nodes. Once an Ethernet node experiences a collision, it backs off prior to attempting to retransmit in a binary exponential (i.e., {0,1}, followed by {0,1,2}, followed by {0,1,2,3}, etc.) slot times. It does this until a truncation value of 15 is reached. After 15 consecutive collisions, the colliding node will truncate the exponential backoff and drop the frame.

TCP/IP - Transmission Control Protocol/Internet Protocol

The Internet protocol suite, which defines a wide range of network services, to allow heterogeneous network system operation. The suite is a layered set of protocols, and covers all aspects of network service and communication. Primarily defined in RFC 791 and RFC 793., although many other related RFCs are applicable to the protocol suite.

Throughput

Throughput is the total amount of data transferred from one place to another or processed in a specified amount of time. Data transfer rates for LANs, such as Ethernet, are measured in terms of throughput. Throughputs for Ethernet networks are measured in Megabits per second or Mb/s. For example, Gigabit Ethernet has a maximum theoretical throughput of 1000 Mb/s.

Transceiver

Frequently interchangeable with MAU. The strict definition is that an Ethernet/802.3 transceiver is a circuit (typically a VLSI implementation) that converts the electrical signals of the AUI to those associated with the appropriate transmission medium. Typically the transceiver required additional components such as transformers, filters, electro-optical converters, connectors, etc., to provide complete MAU functionality. See also "MAU."

TTL - Transistor-Transistor Logic

A common type of digital circuit in which the output is derived from two transistors. The first semiconductors using TTL were developed by Texas Instruments in 1965.

Type

The 2-byte field in the Ethernet frame, immediately following the Source Address field, and preceding the Data field, which defines the protocol type of the frame. The Type specification has no meaning at the MAC level and is passed to higher level protocols. In the 802.3 frame, this field defines the length of the data portion of the frame. Note that Ethernet Type identifiers fall outside the range for valid 802.3 packet Length values. The field is transmitted with the high order byte first, in LSB to MSB order. See also "Length."

Unformatted Page

An Unformatted Page is a Next Page sent during Auto-Negotiation that contains an unformatted 12 bit message field. The use of this field is defined through Message Codes and information contained in the Unformatted Page.

UTP - Unshielded Twisted Pair

Unshielded Twisted Pair is a popular type of copper cable that consists of two unshielded wires twisted around each other. UTP cabling is used extensively for local-area networks (LANs) and telephone connections. UTP cabling does not offer as good protection from interference as coaxial or fiber optic cables, but is far less expensive and is the bulk of the wiring on which 10 Mb/s and 100 Mb/s Ethernet networks operate. See Cat 3/5 UTP.

VCI - Virtual Channel Identifier

A field within the 53-byte ATM cell which is used to hold the virtual channel number.

VID - VLAN Identifier

A 12-bit field containing the identity of the VLAN to which a packet is associated. The VLAN identifier is contained in the Tag Control Information field of the QTag Prefix.

Virtual Circuit

A virtual connection established through the network from source to destination. Packets or cells are routed from source to destination over the same path for the duration of the connection.

VLAN - Virtual LAN

The technical definition for a VLAN is that it is a logical broadcast domain, or a Virtual LAN. A VLAN is a logical broadcast domain overlaid on a physical network. The logical VLANs are specified and differentiated through the use of a VLAN Tag. The concept of a Virtual LAN (VLAN) is to allow network operators to configure and administrate a corporate network, while providing users the connectivity and privacy they expect from having multiple separate networks.

VLAN Tag

The VLAN Tag, defined in IEEE 802.3ac and 802.1Q, is a 4 byte field, inserted between the original Ethernet frame's Source Address field and Type/Length field. The VLAN Tag is used to differentiate logical VLANs.

VLSI - Very Large Scale Integration

The current level of computer semiconductor miniaturization, referring to microchips containing in the hundreds of thousands of transistors. LSI or Large Scale integration means semiconductors containing thousands of transistors. MSI or Medium Scale Integration means semiconductors containing hundreds of transistors, and SSI or Small Scale Integration means semiconductors containing tens of transistors.

VPI - Virtual Path Identifier

A field within the 53-byte ATM cell that is used to hold the virtual path number. This is defined as a group of virtual channels.

Window

The total number of frames, packets or cells that are unacknowledged (outstanding) at a given time. No more data may be transmitted when the window is full. Windowing protocols include TCP, LAP, and X.25.

Index

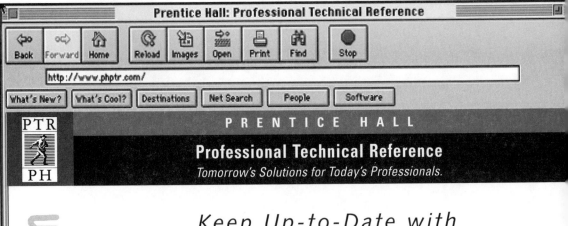
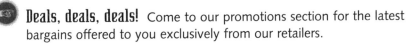